Studies in Medieval and Renaissance Music

10

JUAN ESQUIVEL

A Master of Sacred Music during the Spanish Golden Age

Juan Esquivel was a cathedral choirmaster and composer, active between *c.*1580 and *c.*1623, a Golden Age in Spain during which all aspects of the arts flourished. He was one of the few peninsular composers of his generation to see his works published; he is known to have produced three large volumes of sacred polyphony – masses, motets, hymns, psalms, Magnificats, and Marian antiphons – under the titles *Liber primus missarum*, *Motecta festorum* (both published 1608) and *Tomus secundus, psalmorum, hymnorum . . . et missarum* (published 1613); they reveal him to be a highly skilled craftsman.

This first full-length study of his life and works presents a critical assessment of the man and his music, setting him within the social and religious context of the so-called Counter-Reformation. Beginning by outlining the facts of his life, the book goes on to offer an analysis and assessment of his output.

CLIVE WALKLEY was until his retirement a part-time lecturer in music and music education at Lancaster University.

Studies in Medieval and Renaissance Music
ISSN 1479-9294

General Editor
Tess Knighton

This series aims to provide a forum for the best scholarship in early music; deliberately broad in scope, it welcomes proposals on any aspect of music, musical life, and composers during the period up to 1600, and particularly encourages work that places music in an historical and social context. Both new research and major re-assessments of central topics are encouraged.

Proposals or enquiries may be sent directly to the editor or the publisher at the UK addresses given below; all submissions will receive careful, informed consideration.

Dr Tess Knighton, Clare College, Cambridge CB2 1TL
Boydell & Brewer, PO Box 9, Woodbridge, Suffolk IP12 3DF

Juan Esquivel

A Master of Sacred Music
during the Spanish Golden Age

Clive Walkley

THE BOYDELL PRESS

First published 2010
The Boydell Press, Woodbridge
ISBN 978-1-84383-587-5
The Boydell Press is an imprint of Boydell & Brewer Ltd
PO Box 9, Woodbridge, Suffolk IP12 3DF, UK
and of Boydell & Brewer Inc.
668 Mt Hope Avenue, Rochester, NY 14620, USA
website: www.boydellandbrewer.com

A CIP catalogue record for this title is available
from the British Library

The publisher has no responsibility for the continued existence or accuracy of URLs for external or
third-party internet websites referred to in this book, and does not guarantee that any content on
such websites is, or will remain, accurate or appropriate.

Papers used by Boydell & Brewer are natural, recyclable products
made from wood grown in sustainable forests

MIX
Paper from
responsible sources
FSC® C013604

Typeset in Adobe Jenson by
Word and Page, Chester

Printed in Great Britain by
CPI Antony Rowe, Chippenham and Eastbourne

CONTENTS

ILLUSTRATIONS

TABLES

MUSICAL EXAMPLES

ACKNOWLEDGEMENTS

THE WRITING OF THIS BOOK has been a journey of discovery. Until my forties I had not encountered music of the Spanish 'Golden Age'. As a music student in the late 1950s, I encountered the name of Victoria in an examination paper ('add two additional parts to treble in the style of . . .') but knew nothing of the music of Morales, Guerrero, Lobo, Vivanco and, of course, Esquivel until I gained acquaintance with this wonderful music through the publications of Mapa Mundi; these led me to make contact with Bruno Turner.

It is Bruno I must thank above everyone else for setting me off on this journey of discovery, for the generous loan of microfilms, for sharing with me his infinite knowledge of and enthusiasm for Spanish sacred music of the Golden Age, and for his constant advice and support. But there are, of course, many others who have helped me along my way. Robert Stevenson's *Spanish Cathedral Music in the Golden Age* has been my 'bible' throughout this study; I have found myself referring to it many times and it still proves stimulating reading. Many years ago, the late Professor Robert Snow kindly lent me his microfilm of Esquivel's *Tomus secundus* (1613), and his own work on this comprehensive volume has laid the foundation of my Chapter 6. Michael O'Connor, a former recipient of a Fullbright Scholarship, pointed me in the direction of information and source material I had missed during my first visits to Spain prior to his research. I owe a deep debt of gratitude to Michael for sending me his transcripts of the Oviedo chapter acts and for allowing me to read sections of his Ph.D. thesis during the draft stage.

Access to information locked away in Spanish archives is not always easy to obtain and I want to thank in particular my Spanish friends – members of the Garcia family from Mostoles, Madrid – who made it possible for me to gain access to material previously unavailable; their friendship and support has been invaluable. Matilda Olarte (Universidad de Salamanca) also was immensely helpful in enabling me to negotiate my way through what, to an outsider, appeared to be a confusing and frustrating system. The custodians and archivists attached to the cathedrals of Badajoz, Calahorra, Ciudad Rodrigo and Coria, and the librarians of Salamanca University, all deserve to be mentioned; all were immensely helpful when approached to make documentation available for study.

Many English friends have given positive support to this project. I want to thank in particular Dr Lucy Crispin, formerly a lecturer in English at St Martin's College, for her skill as a proofreader; her eagle eye averted many linguistic infelicities. Ann Bond, formerly a lecturer in music at Manchester University, drew on her extensive knowledge of Renaissance music as she made many helpful comments on early drafts of several chapters. Hugh Keyte spent many hours working on the canon which opens Esquivel's motet volume of 1608, suggesting lines of inquiry concerning the symbolism of this piece. Helen Rawlings, Senior Lecturer in Spanish at the University of Leicester, was helpful in suggesting relevant source material relating to the Church, religion and society.

Several friends, all member of the North West Early Music Forum (NWEMF), deserve special thanks. Gill Mitchell and Philip Gruar advised on Latin translations of motet and hymn texts; the translation of the Dedicatory Letter to Don Pedro Ponce de León is all Gill's work. Clive Tolley provided helpful advice on the preparation of my draft for publication. Many members of NWEMF sang through various performing editions of Esquivel's works in workshops and at the Forum's annual Summer School; to them and also to members of my chamber choir, The Pro Nobis Singers, I must express my thanks for their willingness to share my enthusiasm.

Over the years, professional colleagues from the departments of music and Spanish at the University of Lancaster have made helpful suggestions; I must also thank many members of the library staff for their cooperation in ordering secondary source material.

I owe special thanks to Tess Knighton for her encouragement and enthusiasm for this project; without this support, I should have given up years ago. My thanks must also go to Caroline Palmer and the editorial staff of Boydell and Brewer who have been helpful and patient during the final stages of the book's preparation.

Finally, I want to thank my long-suffering wife for her patience during the many Spanish 'holidays' undertaken in pursuit of information in dusty archives. Holidays they were, yes; but always engineered to take in places with an Esquivel connection – in particular Ciudad Rodrigo, a town both of us have grown to love.

PREFACE

To call any historical period a 'Golden Age' is an extravagant claim to make. And yet, when the huge outpouring of cathedral music by the vast number of composers active in Spain during the sixteenth and early seventeenth centuries is examined, the sheer quality of it can make such a term justified. Even if not all the music of this epoch has the quality of gold, a significant amount earned the admiration of contemporary musicians, and it continues to evoke admiration today. No student of Renaissance music can afford to ignore this rich body of evidence for a once-thriving living tradition, and no general historian can ignore the fact that the music of the Church in Spain in the sixteenth and early seventeenth centuries was a powerful expression of Spanish Counter-Reformation culture.

A complete history of the Golden Age of Spanish Church music has yet to be written, but a significant inroad was made almost fifty years ago when the American author Robert Stevenson produced his ground-breaking publication *Spanish Cathedral Music in the Golden Age*. It was Stevenson who set out the chronological limits of this Golden Age as he saw it (1530–1611, the year 1611 marking the death of one of the supreme masters of the age, Tomás Luis de Victoria), although, of course, such a period cannot have a precise beginning and end. Since the publication of that pioneering work in 1961, much further work has been done in the English-speaking world and in Spain on this fascinating and – until recently – much neglected area of musicological and historical research. Stevenson himself has since published revisions to some of the information found in his original study and other writers have added extensively to the field. Hitherto undocumented archival sources have revealed much information about individual musicians and their position in the Church hierarchy. Much more is known about performance practice than was known in 1961 and, of course, much more of the music has been transcribed and made available in modern performing editions; one has only to consult the catalogues of specialist music publishers to see the advances that have been made in this respect.

Stevenson's approach was to highlight the life and work of three masters from his chosen period: Cristobal Morales, Francisco Guerrero and Tomás Luis de Victoria. But in order to paint a more complete picture, in part 2 of his monumental book (subtitled 'Other Church Masters'), he gives the names of a further thirty-five Church composers all active in Spain during the reign of Philip II (1555–98), adding that this list is by no means complete. Then follows a detailed study of four of these thirty-five: Juan Navarro, Alonso Lobo, Sebastián de Vivanco and Juan Esquivel.

All four men, in their own individual way, made a contribution to the spread of Franco-Flemish polyphony throughout the Spanish peninsula, and all four have been the recipients of further biographical and musicological study since 1961. But each one merits a lengthier study than has been attempted in the various dissertations and monographs that have appeared in recent years. This study concentrates on one of the four, Juan Esquivel. Its purpose is to provide up-to-date biographical information and analytical commentary on a composer who may be less well-known than some of his contemporaries, but who nevertheless made a significant contribution to Spanish cathedral music in his time.

Again, to say that a composer has made a 'significant contribution' to the music of any period is a bold claim to make, but one which I believe is justified, and for which there is evidence in Esquivel's case, as I demonstrate throughout this book. Yet Esquivel, along with so many composers of his generation, still remains an obscure figure: little of his music is published; little of it has been recorded; in spite of extensive research, he remains for most students of Renaissance music a name in a history book. The reasons for his neglect are, I believe, partly historical and partly historiographical.

It is, of course, inevitable that in the course of time the achievements of some composers will go unrecognised. Precious volumes of music can go uncatalogued and neglected for years; war, pestilence, fire, flood, vandalism and so forth can result in the destruction of valuable historical evidence. This is certainly true in Esquivel's case: at least one collection of his music has been lost to us; surviving copies of another published volume are all mutilated in some way; another (a unique exemplar) was only rescued from invading troops in the Spanish Civil War through the foresight of a young altar boy. At a time when little sacred music was published in Spain, it is perhaps amazing that any of Esquivel's music survived the ravages of time to reach the point of publication.

But Esquivel's neglect cannot be explained purely on historical grounds alone; the works of many composers have suffered a similar fate. Another factor is our interpretation of history which can often lead us to false conclusions.

We live today in a museum culture when we revere and wish to preserve our cultural heritage. Historiographically, there is a tendency to view the past through the works of the 'great' composers: we first decide who the giants of an age are, and then we see them as that age's representatives. As part of this process, we have established a canon of acceptable works, made familiar through performances and recordings. But we are selective in what we preserve. In choosing items for our museum of musical works, we accept what we regard as the best while rejecting or ignoring others, often through ignorance rather than through close examination and thorough evaluation.

Whilst it may be true that some composers are of such exceptional quality that they deserve the epithet 'great', and whilst it may be true that every age has its Bach or Beethoven, such an approach to the history of an art form gives us a distorted view of music's development and the characteristic achievements of an age. For alongside the universally acknowledged great composers worked men of lesser stature, conscientious, highly trained musicians, whose music must be taken into account if we wish to arrive at a more balanced understanding of the music produced at a certain point in time. The work of the 'lesser men', as some historians have described Esquivel and other Spanish cathedral composers of his generation, may be more typical of the kind of music produced than those who reach the very highest pinnacle of achievement. As the distinguished musicologist the late Howard Mayer Brown recognised in his *Music in the Renaissance* (London, 1954), the history of music is shaped by the accomplishment of individuals. All individual composers, great and small, contribute to a nation's musical achievement, and to neglect the lesser-known names, like Esquivel, is to do a disservice to our writing and understanding of the historical process. We must leave ourselves open to revisiting the canon; we must open the museum doors and be ready to admit the newly discovered, or relatively unknown. As we revisit our Golden Age of Spanish cathedral music, our ears need to be opened to the sounds of Esquivel and the music of a large number of other hitherto unknown composers as their music is brought to our attention. We must place their music alongside those Spanish masters who have already achieved recognition; unless we undertake this re-evaluation, our understanding of the cultural life of this remarkable period in music's history cannot be anything but inaccurate and false. We may be surprised by what we hear!

Esquivel is known to us through three extant publications only: *Liber primus missarum* (1608), *Motecta festorum* (1608) and *Tomus secundus, psalmorum, hymnorum . . . et missarum* (1613). He was an upholder of a certain tradition rather than an innovator and, although his output cannot rival in size that of many composers of his age, these three large publications certainly contain enough music to mark him out as a skilled craftsman who deserves attention, and whose work embodies the spirit, and enshrines so typically the values, of Spanish Counter-Reformation religious life.

The chapters which follow survey Esquivel's three published collections of music in detail. The first chapter re-examines the labels 'Golden Age' and 'Counter-Reformation', and sets Esquivel in the religious and social context of his day. It provides background information on the three centres where the composer worked, and sets out a brief introduction to the musical organisation within the Spanish cathedral system during the sixteenth century.

An attempt is made to establish a chronology for the main events in the composer's life, drawing together what little documentary evidence remains. Following a description of the sources, the remaining chapters offer an analytical discussion of the music, comparing Esquivel's works with those of his contemporaries. Since few of Esquivel's works are in print, many musical examples illustrate the text. Finally, the music of this composer is re-evaluated and a more balanced assessment of his achievements than is presented in earlier literature is offered.

SIGLA FOR THE POLYPHONIC MANUSCRIPTS

ÁvilaA 9	Ávila. Convento de Santa Ana. MS 9
ÁvilaC 1	Ávila. Archivo de la Catedral. MS 1
GranCR 3	Granada. Capilla Real, Archivo de Música. MS 3
GranCR 7	Granada. Capilla Real, Archivo de Música. MS 7
LedesmaC s.s.	Ledesma. Archivo de la Catedral. Manuscript without number
LonBLR 8 G.vii	London. British Library, Reference Division. Department of Manuscripts. MS Royal 8 G.vii
MálaC 4	Málaga. Archivo Capitular de la Catedral. MS 4
MontsM 1085	Montserrat. Biblioteca del Monestir. MS 1085
PlasC 4	Plascencia. Archivo de Música de la Catedral. MS 4
SegC 3	Segovia. Archivo Capitular de la Catedral. MS 3
SevBC 1	Seville. Catedral Metropolitana, Biblioteca del Coro. MS 1
SilosA 21	Santo Domingo de Silos. Abadía Benedictino, Archivo. MS 21
TaraC 2/3	Tarazona. Archivo Capitular de la Catedral. MS 2/3
TaraC 5	Tarazona. Archivo Capitular de la Catedral. MS 5
ToleBC 7	Toledo. Biblioteca Capitular de la Catedral Metropolitana MS B.7
ValenC 2	Valencia. Archivo de la Catedral. MS 2
VallaC 5	Valladolid. Catedral metropolitana, Archivo de Música. MS 5
VallaC s.s.	Valladolid. Catedral Metropolitana, Archivo de Música. Manuscript without number
VallaP s.s.	Valladolid. Parroquia de Santiago. Manuscript without number

I

RELIGIOUS LIFE AND CATHEDRAL MUSIC IN SPAIN IN THE TIME OF THE COUNTER-REFORMATION

COUNTER-REFORMATION OR CATHOLIC REFORMATION?

B Y THE TIME Esquivel announced his publications to the world in 1608, the roots of the Counter-Reformation had been firmly established for over a century. A Spain united by Ferdinand and Isabella had championed the cause of a militant Catholicism which, largely through Spain's isolation from the rest of Europe and the establishing of the Inquisition in 1478, set itself on a collision course with the Protestant challenge which emerged during the course of the early sixteenth century. Charles V and his son, Philip II, sought to build on the achievements of their predecessors, further consolidating the monarchy's power base and control of national institutions, and rooting out heresy in face of the Protestant threat. By the end of the sixteenth century the Church in Spain was an institution effectively under the control of the monarchy: it was a Church with a mission and a strong power base; a Church firm in its doctrines.

Esquivel was born towards the end of the sixteenth century – towards the end of a period that saw an extraordinary burst of creative energy resulting in an abundance of religious works of art, architecture, music, philosophy, poetry and prose writings. Yet the same age produced appalling acts of violence, cruelty and oppression, all in the name of religion. How can these apparent contradictions be reconciled? An answer to this question is beyond the scope of this study, but what we can say is that without the intensity of religious belief found in the Spanish Church in the sixteenth century, and the need to give it expression in art, music and literature, our world would be greatly impoverished. Such was the power and magnitude of the artistic achievements of Spain in its Golden Age – the age of the Counter-Reformation.

Before delving further into events which formed the backdrop to Esquivel's work as a cathedral musician, we need to examine this term, Counter-Reformation, which has long been a cause of hot dispute amongst historians. Used as a convenient means of indicating a distinctive historical period, it has been described as a 'Johnny-come-lately' in the lexicon of European periodisation since the term was not invented until the 1770s; and not until the 1860s was it accepted universally to signify a single phenomenon with global significance.[1] But is the term adequate for use as a label to

1 David M. Luebke, ed., *The Counter-Reformation: The Essential Readings* (Oxford, 1999),

embrace the whole cultural, religious and social life of an age?

The old reactionary view of a Counter-Reformation as a political reaction to Protestantism has increasingly been challenged by modern historians, who are anxious to stress the pro-active and spiritual dimension of the age: a reformation based on faith and commitment shared in all sections of society; a rejuvenation from within.

The argument for a rethink of the Counter-Reformation label was presented in a classic essay written in 1946 by the catholic historian, Hubert Jedin.[2] In Jedin's view, there were in fact two separate movements often mistakenly lumped together under the 'Counter-Reformation' label: 'Counter-Reformation', as a term which, used correctly, describes the Catholic Church's reaction to religious schism and its attempts to restore the one true faith; and 'Catholic Reformation', a reformation of the Catholic Church from within, which commenced some time before Martin Luther posed his challenge to Catholicism in 1517.[3] In Jedin's view, both terms are needed in order fully to comprehend the changes that were taking place within the Church during the sixteenth century. As he saw it, '*The Catholic Reform was the church's reorientation toward Catholic ideals of living through an internal process of renewal, while Counter-Reformation was the self-assertion of the church in the struggle against Protestantism*' (author's italics).[4]

Other writers are equally unhappy with the term 'Counter-Reformation' but for different reasons. H. Outram Evennett, for example, argues that the term does not reflect the new kind of spirituality that was sweeping the Catholic Church during the sixteenth century, a spirituality epitomised, for example, in Ignatius Loyola's *Spiritual Exercises* (1541). Evennett saw the Counter-Reformation as 'first and foremost a powerful religious movement'.[5] Although at the official level it reached its climax with the doctrinal tracts of the Council of Trent – the historic gathering of influential, high-ranking, power-wielding churchmen, cardinals and theologians,

pp. 4–5. Albert Elkan, 'Entstehung und Entwicklung des Begriffs "Gegenreformation"', *Historische Zeitschrift* 112 (1914), pp. 473–93.

    2 Hubert Jedin, 'Catholic Reformation or Counter-Reformation?', trans. David M. Luebke, in Luebke, *The Counter-Reformation*, pp. 21–45. The essay originally appeared as 'Katholische Reformation oder Gegenreformation?', in Hubert Jedin, *Katholische Reformation oder Gegenreformation? Ein Versuch zur Klärung der Begriffe nebst einer Jubiläumsbetrachtung über das Trienter Kanzil* (Luzern, 1946), pp. 7–38.

    3 On 31 October in that year, Martin Luther, then professor of theology at the University of Wittenberg in Saxony, posted his famous ninety-five theses, *Disputation for the Clarification of the Power of Indulgences*, to the church door of the city's castle church. The notion of indulgences – in effect paying for the privilege of pardon for sin – was anathema to what became the Protestant movement.

    4 Jedin, 'Catholic Reformation', p. 45.

    5 H. Outram Evennett, 'Counter-Reformation Spirituality', in John Bossy, ed., *Spirit of the Counter-Reformation* (Notre Dame, 1970), pp. 23–42, quoted in Luebke, *The Counter-Reformation*, p. 49. This view is reiterated by H. Daniel-Rops, who sees the Counter-Reformation in terms of 'an immense and prodigious movement of fervour, which uplifted the Christian soul almost everywhere (more especially in Italy and Spain), a kind of spiritual sublimation operated by the saints'. For Daniel-Rops, the Counter-Reformation was not a reaction to Lutheranism, nor was it essentially different from other reforms in the history of the Church, which occurred for similar reasons – a desire to remain faithful to the unalterable tradition of the Church. See H. Daniel-Rops, *The Catholic Reformation*, trans. John Warrington (New York and London, 1962), pp. 1–4.

which put the stamp of approval on the official teachings of the Catholic Church in the tempestuous years of the mid-sixteenth century – its roots were in the fifteenth century, or even earlier. Inevitably influenced by outward circumstances – the challenge of Protestantism – in essence it represented a departure from the contemplative mysticism of the Middle Ages; it was a turn towards more vigorous and self-disciplined meditation and prayer; it emphasised zealous, worldly activism in the form of charity and labour for personal sanctification; and it saw a revival of the sacraments, especially Confession and Communion, at least on behalf of the reformed monastic clergy if not of the laity.

Yet another label is provided by John O'Malley in his discussion of Ignatius Loyola and the Jesuit movement.[6] O'Malley rejects the terms 'Counter-Reformation' and 'Catholic Reformation' and instead recommends using the term 'Early Modern Catholicism' – a term he sees as being less judgemental. It suggests change and continuity, leaves the question of chronology open, and includes both Counter-Reformation, Catholic Reformation and even Catholic Restoration as terms of analysis, but, further, 'it suggests that important influences on religious institutions and "mentalities" were at work in "early modern society" that had little to do with religion or "reform" as such.'[7]

The French writer, Jean Delumeau, reads the Counter-Reformation differently.[8] He accepts that the Catholic Reformation was of significant importance during the sixteenth century, but argues that it was at its height much later in the late seventeenth and early eighteenth centuries. Delumeau saw the rejuvenation of the Catholic Church and the development of its spirituality in two distinct periods: the pre-Reformation, and the Council of Trent (1545–63) with its aftermath.[9] In his view, the Council of Trent, which most historians see as the climax of the Church's period of reform, created a rupture in the history of the Catholic faith by breaking it into two periods, the second of which lasted right up to Vatican II.[10]

Why then continue to use what some see as an incomplete, or even misleading, label to describe the world into which Esquivel and his many colleagues entered? Quite simply, it is still the most widely recognisable designation.[11] As an indicator of historical periodisation which coincides with so much music to which we ascribe the label 'Renaissance', it is a convenient term to use; it coincides also with our use of the term 'Spanish Golden Age' in relation to Church music; but it also embraces the historiographical concepts of reform, and spiritual renewal within the Catholic Church. It is, therefore, the term adopted throughout this book.

Esquivel was a priest, a member of a religious community and subject to the rules of that community and its constraints (and one might add its stresses and

---

6 John W. O'Malley, SJ, 'Was Ignatius Loyola a Church Reformer? How to Look at Early Modern Catholicism', *Catholic Historical Review* 77 (1991) pp. 177–93.

7 John O' Malley in Luebke, *The Counter-Reformation*, p. 81.

8 Jean Delumeau, *Catholicism between Luther and Voltaire: A New View of the Counter Reformation* (London, 1977).

9 Ibid., p. 1.

10 Ibid., p. 4.

11 Luebke, *The Counter-Reformation*, p. 3.

frustrations, as later chapters will show). He received his musical training as a member of a historic Church that was experiencing a period of spiritual regeneration; a historic Church that, for the first time in its history, was faced with doctrinal challenges, when suspicion, distrust and heresy within a community was rife (or imagined to be so), and prescription and proscription in religious matters abounded. His understanding of Christian doctrine would have been informed by Counter-Reformation teaching, for he began his professional life shortly after the last session of the Council of Trent. If one wishes to understand why Esquivel's music – or indeed the music of any composer of his generation – is as it is, it is not enough to study musical texts in isolation. Technical analysis will take us so far, but for a deeper understanding we must relate his music to its social and religious background. We need to look at the job of a *maestro de capilla*, post-Council of Trent; we need to look at the institutions in which he worked; and we need to examine the role of music, and its organisation within the Church. But first we need to remind ourselves of the religious turmoils that beset Spain in the sixteenth century because they form the backdrop to the musical life of the Church in Esquivel's time. However, unravelling the nature of Catholicism in sixteenth-century Spain is not an easy task: there is a strong strand of spirituality – deep personal yearning for closeness to God – linking Christianity with Judaism and Islam which bore fruit in the religious mysticism of figures like Teresa of Ávila and John of the Cross later in the century; there is also a reformist strain – a desire, official and unofficial, to remove corruption from the Church's institutions. Throughout, there is a paranoid suspicion among churchmen of any rival culture, a suspicion supported by secular authorities.[12] The word 'militant', therefore, seems to be an appropriate term to describe the state of the Church at this time.

THE CHURCH MILITANT

BY THE END OF THE SIXTEENTH CENTURY, the Spanish Church was deeply embedded in the whole fabric of everyday life; it was an ideological, political, economic and cultural force within society. Many theologians and members of religious orders played a role in government, and at the local level parish priests often carried out non-religious duties such as collecting tithes and acting as notaries. The Church was a major landowner and the provider of education and charity.[13] Much of the groundwork for these achievements had been laid in the fifteenth century through the policies of Ferdinand and Isabella (*los reyes catolicos*). Backed up by the power of the Inquisition established by Ferdinand and Isabella in 1478 and under their control, the newly established monarchy sought to root out apostasy and heresy, first against the Jews, forcing them to convert to Christianity or face

12 Diarmaid MacCulloch, *Reformation: Europe's House Divided 1490–1700* (London, 2004), p. 64.
13 Helen Rawlings, *Church, Religion and Society in Early Modern Spain* (Basingstoke, 2002), p. xiv.

expulsion, and next against the Moslems. To begin with, the process of persecution was limited to the areas of Castile and Aragon but then later extended to the whole of Spain. The process of enforced conversion took many years to bring about. But Spanish society was never completely purged of Jewish and Moslem influence; nor was anti-Jewish and Moslem sentiment as widespread as was once thought. Converted Jews (*conversos*) and converted Moslems (*moriscos*) – the New Christians – made valuable contributions to society, as modern research has shown, and even some churchmen opposed the violent persecutions that took place throughout the age of the Counter-Reformation. But sadly, through persecution of these minority groups, the face of Spain was irrevocably changed: those purges on minority members of Spanish society brought to an end the centuries-long cohabitation (*convivencia*) of these diverse ethnic and social groups; it also established a climate of fear within the country.

Although, as modern historians have argued, the religious persecution of Jews and Moslems owed more to cultural, racial and socio-economic differences than religious differences, the Church in Spain was wary of any challenge to its authority, so that when the spectre of Lutheranism first appeared in the 1520s, it immediately aroused opposition. The powers of the Inquisition were unleashed on any showing signs of dissent in their beliefs and practices in order that the Church's power base should remain firm.

After the accession of Charles V to the throne of Spain in 1516, mistrust first fell on the *alumbrados* or Illuminists of New Castile. They were not in a formal sense a sect but a protest movement. Within the groups were Franciscans of *converso* origin, and *beatas* (groups of pious women), and lay members. What united them was their interest in devotional literature – works like St Thomas à Kempis's *Imitation of Christ* – and their advocacy of private, meditative prayer over formal ceremony as a means of communion with God. There were those known as *recogidas*, who practised a disciplined form of meditation, and the *dexados* who 'abandoned' themselves to the love of God. It was the latter group which came under suspicion. Many prominent members were arrested, accused of being tainted by Lutheranism and disseminating a deviant form of spirituality. Charges were hard to prove, however, and those arrested did not suffer the same horrific fate as so-called heretics before them had done.

One of those imprisoned in 1532, suspected of being an *alumbrado*, was the reformer and writer Juan de Ávila (*c*.1499–1569). Despite his name, Juan de Ávila was from La Mancha in southern Spain. His major contribution to reform was in the area of religious education, particularly among the poor; in his writings he was critical of the existing social order with its emphasis on wealth and privilege. He believed that priests should pray and intercede for all mankind, not just the rich and powerful; he condemned the process by which young men with no genuine calling could enter the priesthood 'by virtue of the chaplaincies of their lineages'.[14] His theology was built on the foundations of mental prayer and mediation; he emphasised faith over liturgy. He was a strong influence on Teresa of Ávila, who

14 Jodi Bilinkoff, *The Avila of Saint Teresa* (Ithaca and London, 1989), p. 82.

described him as 'a man deeply versed in everything relating to prayer'.[15] Teresa, of course, embarked on her own spiritual journey carried along by ecstatic visions – her heart pierced by an angel with a burning arrow, as famously depicted in Bernini's Baroque sculpture – which resulted in the founding of the Discalced Carmelite Order, based not on wealth and privilege as a means of access, but on the principles of poverty, humility, piety and obedience. St Ignatius Loyola (1491–1556), founder of the Society of Jesus, was another major religious reformer influenced by Juan de Ávila. The Jesuit movement became an international cornerstone of the Counter-Reformation's educational mission; Loyola himself was arrested in 1526 as an alleged *alumbrado* and after his release left Spain in 1527 never to return, leaving his movement to be continually harassed by the more conservative Dominicans, who suspected the Jesuits of giving allegiance to the papacy before the crown.

Given his strongly expressed views it is not surprising that those in authority, who came from the privileged classes, should seek to silence Juan de Ávila's voice; moreover, he was of *converso* origin. But Juan was shortly cleared of all the flimsy charges against him and resumed his preaching activities. His proposals for clerical reform were to bear fruit later at the Council of Trent.

Another group to meet with hostility were the Erasmians, followers of the Dutch reformer, Erasmus (*c.*1466–1536). Erasmus's teachings and scurrilous attacks on theologians and the lax disciplines of mendicants made him many enemies, and when one reads the following from his satirical work *Praise of Folly* (1509), it is not hard to see why:

> The happiness of these people [the theologians] is most nearly approached by those who are popularly called 'Religious' or 'Monks'. Both names are false, since most of them are a long way removed from religion . . . . I don't believe any life would be more wretched than theirs . . . . The whole tribe is so universally loathed that even a chance meeting is thought to be ill-omened – and yet they are gloriously self-satisfied. In the first place, they believe it's the highest form of piety to be so uneducated that they can't even read. Then, when they bray like donkeys in church, repeating by rote the psalms they haven't understood, they imagine they are charming the ears of their heavenly audience with infinite delight.[16]

Although no doubt slightly exaggerated for the sake of effect – a characteristic of Erasmus' writings – there is, no doubt, a good deal of truth in his claims. Erasmus' more serious work, in which he outlined his brand of Christian humanism, was his *Enchiridion militis Christiani* (*Handbook of a Christian Soldier*) of 1503, a book which attracted much attention. In it he criticised paganism, superstition and immorality, and he promoted his vision of a Christ-centred faith and downplayed outward ceremony and ritual in favour of quiet, austere devotion springing from

15 Cited by E. Allison Peers, *A Handbook to the Life and Times of Saint Teresa and Saint John of the Cross* (London, 1954), p. 123.

16 Erasmus, *Praise of Folly*, ed. Betty Radice (Harmondsworth, 1971), p. 164. As A. H. T. Levi points out in his footnote to this edition, by the time Erasmus came to write his satire serious attempts at monastic reform were being made, but some orders – the Franciscans in particular – were very distrustful of learning which they regarded as leading to heresy.

inward contemplation. His influential Greek New Testament of 1516 was a major piece of biblical scholarship, and was produced at the same time as Spanish scholars and others were working on the polyglot Bible at Alcalá University. Cardinal Jiménez Cisneros (archbishop of Toledo, 1495–1517) had founded this institution in 1508. Situated outside Madrid with the *colegio mayor* of San Ildefonso as its centrepiece, it soon became a thriving focus for humanist culture in Spain. It was Cisneros who initiated the Complutensian Polyglot – *Complutum* being the Latin name for Alcalá – finally published in 1522 as a six-volume edition, in which the Latin Vulgate was accompanied by two parallel columns in Hebrew and Greek with a critical commentary. Other publications followed, including a Castilian version of Erasmus' *Enchiridion* in 1526.

Erasmus was well aware that he was admired by kings and courtiers, as he makes clear in *Praise of Folly*. Charles V certainly held him in high esteem, and although his departure from Spain with many Erasmians at court in 1529 reduced the numbers of those in high places who supported him, he still had the support of the two most senior clerics in Spain, Alonso Manrique de Lara, archbishop of Seville and Inquisitor General (1523–38), and Alonso de Fonseca (archbishop of Toledo 1523–34). Another supporter was Juan de Vergara (1492–1557), a prominent humanist scholar at Charles's court, secretary to Cisneros, a professor at Alcalá, canon of Toledo and a personal friend of Erasmus. His case is typical of those Erasmians who aroused the suspicion of the Inquisition.

In 1533, Vergara was arrested, accused of being a Lutheran, Illuminist and Erasmian, causing Rodrigo Manrique, son of the Inquisitor General, to write from Paris to the prominent Spanish philosopher Juan Luis Vives in the following terms:

> You are right. Our country is a land of pride and envy; you may add, of barbarism. For now it is clear that down there one cannot possess any culture without being suspected of heresy, error and Judaism. Thus silence has been imposed on the learned. As for those who have resorted to erudition, they have been filled, as you say, with great terror. At Alcalá they are trying to uproot the study of Greek completely.[17]

Two years later in an *auto de fe* held publicly, as all such trials were, Vergara was acquitted of any charges of heresy but obliged to abjure his errors, and was confined to monastic seclusion for one year. On his release in 1537 he resumed his post as canon of Toledo, and although his health had been affected by his trial, he lived until 1557.

Vergara was not a subversive as the more conservative members of the Inquisition thought: he was a scholar whose mind was genuinely stimulated by the new ideas emerging in northern Europe. But this case illustrates the fear which any challenge to the status quo in matters of religious thought could generate in the minds of those in power. As Henry Kamen has pointed out, the illuminist and mystical traditions were never explicitly concerned with points of doctrine, and moved subtly to Lutheran positions – such as a belief in justification by faith alone – without ever formally rejecting Catholic dogma. There was no indigenous

17 Cited in Henry Kamen, *Spain 1469–1714: A Society of Conflict* (3rd edn, London, 2005), p. 123.

Lutheran movement in Spain, no native heresy on which to build.[18] There was widespread interest in Luther's views, but an effective ban on the import of certain books prevented diffusion.

But as England, France and Germany experienced the full force of the Protestant challenge, the Spanish authorities continued to be vigilant following Charles V's abdication in 1556 and the period of the regency which followed. The appointment of the ruthless and ambitious Fernando de Valdés as Inquisitor General in 1557 resulted in a new wave of investigations into alleged Protestant cells in the cathedral chapters of Valladolid, where the royal court was in residence, and Seville where Valdés was an absentee archbishop.[19]

The origins of the Sevilian Protestant movement, in the very heart of the cathedral chapter, had already been uncovered in the early 1550s. Many humanist scholars from Alcalá had been appointed as cathedral canons during the time that the Erasmian sympathiser, Alonso Manrique, was archbishop there. The magisterial canon, Juan Egidio, and his successor Constantino Ponce de la Fuente – both humanist scholars and the latter of New Christian origin – were accused of unorthodox teachings by the Inquisition. In 1552, Egidio was made to retract ten propositions and was sentenced to a year of seclusion: he subsequently died in peace in 1556. Ponce de la Fuente was less fortunate: he was arrested in 1558, branded a heretic, and died in custody two years later.

A turning point in the history of the Inquisition came in 1558 when Valdés obtained powers from Pope Paul IV which allowed him to extend the Inquisition's field of investigation beyond the secular reaches of society into the higher echelons of the Church.[20] A year later, following the discovery of heresy among members of the Sevillian chapter, Bartolomé de Carranza, the Dominican friar and archbishop of Toledo and the most senior figure in the Church, was arrested. Although he was eventually released after a trial and a period of imprisonment (he died in May 1576 within less than one month of being released), his trial illustrates the hysteria that was sweeping certain sections of Spanish society, spreading fear in its wake.

Another of Valdés's repressive acts was the introduction throughout Castile of the first native Index of forbidden works. Although control of licences and printing was vested in the council of Castile, the Inquisition was permitted to operate a parallel system of censorship.[21] This Index resulted in the banning of works by Protestant reformers and the searching of bookshops for forbidden material; books

18 Kamen, *Spain 1469–1714*, p. 124.

19 Valdés, as an absentee archbishop, governed his see via 'vicars general'. He was in residence from 1549 to 1550. He remained Inquisitor General until 1565, when he fell out of favour at court and was replaced in this role by Diego de Espinosa.

20 Letter of Valdés to Paul IV, 9 September 1558, printed in Henry Charles Lea, *A History of the Inquisition in Spain*, III, p. 556, cited by Rawlings, *Church, Religion and Society*, p. 39.

21 Kamen, *Spain 1469–1714*, p. 126. The Index of 1559 was followed by a much more comprehensive one covering a wider range of material in 1583, although only about two dozen of the hundreds of items mentioned were Castilian literary works. The Index was not such an obstacle to culture as is sometimes supposed; it did not interrupt the import and sale of non-controversial material and booksellers in Barcelona were able to import foreign books without any problem (see Kamen, *Spain 1469–1714*, p. 198.)

were expurgated, offending passages cut out; some books were publicly burnt; vernacular translations of the Bible were forbidden and seminal publications like St Ignatius' Loyola's *Spiritual Exercises* fell victim to censorship – perhaps surprising in the latter case since they embodied the essential elements of doctrine accepted by the Council of Trent. Publications of music did not escape scrutiny, not, of course, on the grounds of possible subversive influence, but on their need to conform to liturgical requirements. As we shall see in Chapter 3, Esquivel's published music was scrutinised for its 'fitness for purpose' as well as its technical merits by those appointed to license its contents and ensure such conformity.

When Philip II returned to Spain from Flanders in 1559 following the abdication of his father, Charles V, he soon established his power base: the crown made all major ecclesiastical appointments, papal bulls needed royal approval before they could be published, the Inquisition was under the monarch's control (a power originally granted to Philip's predecessors, Ferdinand and Isabella, by the pope) and continued to attempt to keep heresy at bay by the public spectacle of the *auto de fe*, the trial of those who had 'confessed' to their misdemeanors.

Much has been written on the Inquisition and its powers. Sometimes these accounts have been exaggerated and sensationalised, for, after all, repressive measures were common in other European countries during the sixteenth century. Although Spain at this time was the only European country to have a national institution dedicated to eliminating heresy, the Inquisition's activities were not primarily directed against formal heresy. Execution rates between 1540 and 1700 were actually lower than virtually any contemporary secular court of justice in Iberia or elsewhere;[22] torture was the exception rather than the rule and the death penalty was used in few cases after the early sixteenth century as the Inquisition evolved from being an instrument of repression into one of persuasion.[23] The Inquisition became a means by which the Counter-Reformation Church could hold ordinary Catholics to the faith, a means of guarding against blasphemy and the sacrilegious, and of protecting the sanctity of marriage and guarding against sexual immorality. Any brought forward for examination were tested on their doctrinal knowledge. Inquisitor General Valdés described the process in his *Instructions* of 1561:

> After the interrogation concerning identity, the prisoner must declare his genealogy, as far back as possible . . . . Then he must be asked where he grew up, with whom, if he has ever studied in a school, whether he has ever left the country, and if so, with whom . . . . And he must be questioned about prayers and Christian doctrine, where and when he confessed, and with which confessors.[24]

Esquivel could not have been unaware of the powers and influence of the Inquisition because his birthplace, Ciudad Rodrigo, was one of the towns visited.

22 MacCulloch, *Reformation: Europe's House Divided*, p. 421.
23 Kamen, *Spain 1469–1714*, p. 197.
24 Miguel Jiménez Monteserín, *Introducción a la inquisición española* (Madrid, 1981), pp. 205–6, cited in Anne J. Cruz and Mary E. Perry, eds., *Culture and Control in Counter-Reformation Spain* (Minneapolis, 1992), p. 11.

The Inquisitor of Llerena, Licenciado don Simón de Gaztelu, arrived in the city in 1603, and it must have been soon after his arrival that members of the cathedral chapter were embroiled in a scandal. Five members and other priests denounced the bishop, Don Martin de Salvatierra, to the Inquisition. Although the accusations were probably unfounded – symptomatic, no doubt, of the hysteria that could engulf a community under stress – the event must have shocked the community. The bishop died in December 1604 before charges could be laid against him. Had he lived on, it is likely that he would have survived since, unlike the Inquisitions of Seville, Valencia, Barcelona, Zaragoza, Cuenca and Toledo, which had a reputation for being particularly repressive, that of Llerena could be considered the most indulgent and tolerant. However, the Inquisition was soon called to act again: in September 1610, in accordance with royal decree, nearly ninety-five Moslems were expelled from the city when the *moriscos* were finally banished from Spanish soil.[25]

COUNTER-REFORMATION SPIRITUALITY AT THE LOCAL LEVEL

THE CHURCH MILITANT was the outward manifestation of inner struggles and intense feeling, strongly held convictions and firmly established practices; in addition, it manifested bigotry, jealousy and hatred, and it was driven by religious professionals. But, as the historian William Christian reminds us, in Philip II's Spain there were two levels of Catholicism: on one level, the official beliefs and practices of the institutional Church; on the other, those of the lay people, whose religion was prompted more by superstition than informed belief in the official doctrines of the Church, and who placed their reliance on particular sacred places, images, relics, local saints and idiosyncratic ceremonies. Nor was there any distinction, in this respect, between towns and cities; both shared the same emphasis on local beliefs, customs and practices.[26]

Nowhere is the intensity of devotion to religious belief and practice at a local level more clearly demonstrated than in Toledo – the city immortalised in art by El Greco. Toledo was the capital of the largest and wealthiest diocese in the peninsula, the location of the archdiocesan appeals court, and headquarters of the Spanish Inquisition. Its archbishop was primate of Spain.[27]

Between 1575 and 1580, Philip II sent his chroniclers into the towns and villages of New Castile with a printed questionnaire which delved into the religious belief

---

25 Feliciono Sierro Malmierca, *Judiós, moriscos e inquisición en Ciudad Rodrigo* (Salamanca, 1990), pp. 17, 20, 65. A formal decision to expel the *moriscos* was made by the Council of State on 4 April 1609. Between 1609 and 1611, a total of over 300,000 were forced to leave Spain, the result of long-standing animosity on the part of Christians and Moslems. See Helen Rawlings, *Church, Religion and Society*, pp. 22–5.

26 William A. Christian, *Local Religion in Sixteenth-Century Spain* (Princeton, 1981), p. 3.

27 Toledo was the largest archdiocese in Europe and the richest after Rome. See Rawlings, *Church, Religion and Society*, p. 59, for a short summary of the territorial divisions of the Spanish Church in the sixteenth century.

and customs of local people. Toledo, at that time, was a city of 11,000 households, 1,240 of whom lived in caves or cellars supported by religious brotherhoods.[28] The priest who answered Philip's request for information responded with pride, as the following quotation demonstrates:

> Toledo is not agricultural, but rather industrial and commercial; indeed, as a measure of its nobility and urbanity, it can be said that no plough or pair of yoked mules will be seen within its gates or on its bridges.[29]

Toledo attracted the 'professional' religious. A tax survey carried out in 1591 revealed that, in a city of approximately 50,000 inhabitants, over 2,000 – about 5% of the population – were priests. There were 26 churches, 36 monasteries and convents, 18 shrines (each devoted to a different saint), 12 oratories and 4 religious colleges; as the city's population dwindled in the following years, 9 more religious houses were added.[30]

In terms of individual numbers, Toledo had 1,000 nuns and *beatas* (women who made a vow of chastity, wore a habit and chose to follow a religious rule of some kind; devout single or widowed women) compared with only 400 male religious.[31]

Over the region of New Castile as a whole, in the 530 places of Philip's survey, there were at least 61 monasteries, convents and *beaterías* of female religious; within these lived over 1,500 male religious and 1,900 nuns and *beatas*. Franciscans dominated, with only a small number of Augustinian, Dominican, Hieronymite and new Discalced Carmelites represented outside major centres.[32]

These statistics provide concrete evidence of the climate of religiosity which permeated all levels of society and which had a long history stretching back through centuries. Three manifestations of this climate were the prevalence of vows, the number of chapels and shrines built, and the emphasis on relics.

---

28 Christian, *Local Religion in Sixteenth-Century Spain*, pp. 9–13. Christian points out that Madrid at this time was still only half the size of Toledo, with about 6,000 households, but at a time of rising prosperity in New Castile there was a rapid rise in population levels and also in religious establishments. Toledo had a large population of artisans because it was a textile city specialising in weaving of silk; it was also home to a colony of *moriscos* plus immigrants from Galicia and Asturias, and it attracted many rural poor. Much of Christian's information throughout his study is drawn from Carmelo Viñas y Mey and Ramón Paz, *Relaciones histórico-geográfico-estadísticas de los pueblos de España hechas por iniciativa de Felipe II* (Reino de Toledo, pt. 1, 1951; pt. 2, 1963).

29 Christian, *Local Religion in Sixteenth-Century Spain*, p. 8, based on Carmelo Viñas y Mey and Ramón Paz, *Relaciones*, III, p. 506.

30 Allan W. Atlas, *Renaissance Music: Music in Western Europe, 1400–1600* (New York and London, 1998), p. 612. In his *Historia Civitatense* – a history of Ciudad Rodrigo – the historian Antonio Sánchez Cabañas speaks of thirty churches in Esquivel's home town, Ciudad Rodrigo, although by his day (the early seventeenth century) some of them were in ruins, others had become convents and not all were within the walled city itself. In addition, there were nine convents and twelve hermitages. See Antonio Sánchez Cabañas, *Historia Civitatense*, modern edition ed. Ángel Barrios García and Iñaki Martín Viso (Salamanca, 2001), pp. 157–9.

31 Christian, *Local Religion in Sixteenth-Century Spain* p. 16.

32 Ibid., pp. 15–16.

Vows – deliberate promises made to God for some greater good – were made sometimes by a whole village, including the clergy, for deliverance from pestilence, natural disasters and adverse weather conditions; there were vows of chastity, vows to fast or visit a shrine, and so on. The vow promised the observance of certain stated acts of devotion in exchange for a saint's intercession with God. Observance of vowed days and participation in its rituals such as processions and attendance at a votive mass, held in honour of a local saint, were enforced in many places by specific rules and fines. Canonically speaking, vows had to be fulfilled under penalty of falling into mortal sin, although commutation – a change or exchange – of vows was big business in the sixteenth century.[33]

A renewed use of images in the eleventh and twelfth centuries led to a localisation and spread of shrines and chapels with their associated relics. Chapels were built, and images erected in greater and greater numbers, to which votive offerings were made; Marian shrines were particularly favoured. The only difference between town and countryside in this respect was in the placing of shrines: in Toledo, for example, sacred places were in the city; miraculous images, powerful relics and sites of apparitions were in the parish churches, convents and the cathedral, while in agricultural towns most sites were outside in the country. There were many con artists making their living from shrines and pilgrim routes by faking miracles. Shrine histories-cum-miracle books were published, so many in fact that the Council of Trent questioned and set up norms for the declaration of miracles and apparitions, which henceforth needed the approval of a bishop.[34]

From the monarch downwards, there was a huge interest in the collection of relics – a cult which pre-dated the devotion to images. Philip II assembled a collection of over 7,000 relics at the Escorial from all over Europe using his ambassadors and royal relatives as intermediaries.[35]

Although Philip's survey did not question whole communities on their attitude to the afterlife – it could not do so because its concern was the corporate religious life – we know that it was a constant preoccupation with people from all walks of life. We hardly need reminding that life expectancy in the violent period of the sixteenth century was short, and one index of concern for life beyond the grave is the pious works set up in wills. In theory, all Christians were obliged to make a will; it was a way of placing one's soul *en carrera de salvación* – on the road to salvation,[36] for a monetary gift to some religious institution enabled individual Christians to request prayers for their passage to the life hereafter. Chaplaincies, monasteries and hospitals included in their foundation prayers for the intentions of their founders. As we shall see in Chapter 2, Esquivel and his parents were themselves beneficiaries of this system.

The brotherhoods, or *cofradías*, which developed during the Middle Ages as charitable bodies, and whose members joined together for devotional purposes,

33 Ibid., pp. 31–3.
    34 Ibid., pp. 103–4. In practice, as Christian points out, the Council was merely continuing a practice of questioning the veracity of such phenomena already in place by the mid-fifteenth century.
    35 Ibid., p. 135.
    36 Carlos M. N. Eire, *From Madrid to Purgatory: The Art and Craft of Dying in Sixteenth-Century Spain* (Cambridge, 1995), pp. 22–3

continued to grow in number during the sixteenth century. Fear of dying alone was a frightening prospect and many of the brotherhoods were concerned with the act of dying and acted like salvation cooperatives – or 'burial clubs' of sorts – praying for the souls of the dead and taking part in funeral corteges.[37] Virtually every parish in the city of Toledo had a brotherhood devoted to souls in Purgatory;[38] in all, the city had 143 brotherhoods in 1576, serving a population of some 60,000, equivalent to one per 84 households.[39] Since Toledo was socially mixed, many were based on trades – blacksmiths, clothiers, labourers and so forth; each had its own saint to whom the members directed their prayers. In addition to providing burials, masses and vigils for the dead, the confraternities dispensed charity, supported hospitals and encouraged pious devotions; some attracted an elite membership of distinguished nobles, canons and intellectuals. But charges of corruption were made against them. Juan de Ávila, for example, in his first memorandum to Trent, complained of 'great larceny and wrongdoing' within the confraternities; many were abolished in the 1580s under royal decree and with papal blessing.[40]

There were often conflicts of interest between the clergy on the one hand and the laity on the other. Parishioners sometimes objected when priests reproved them and imposed penances on them for not attending mass, or for violating holy days. It seems that interruptions in the middle of mass were not uncommon; the following comment from the *Constituciones sinodales* of Burgos (1575) may not be untypical of what was happening elsewhere:

> Sometimes it has happened that when priests or preachers are rebuking ills or vices or sins of the people, the person referred to, or those that claim authority in the town, stand up and reply to him, and at times speak words that are rude, indecent, and unworthy of such a place.[41]

But, as we shall see, it was not just the laity who were guilty of impropriety during mass: priests and musicians (many of whom were also priests) exchanged insults and even came to blows.

Votive and rogation processions to out-of-town shrines were another source of friction between clergy and laity. They often resulted in sexual immorality and drunkenness, so that a number of bishops (including those from Sigüencia and Toledo) sought to ban processions beyond a certain distance, usually a league. The archdiocese of Toledo, however, was one of the most tolerant, and as late as 1601 continued to allow vigils in town churches so long as they were adequately supervised.[42]

Holy days, too, were responsible for breaches of discipline. The winter cycle of festivals culminated in the processions of Lent and Holy Week; in the summer months came the feasts of the Ascension, Corpus Christi and Assumption; added

37 Ibid., p. 134.
38 Christian, *Local Religion in Sixteenth-Century Spain*, pp. 142–3.
39 Cited in Rawlings, *Church, Religion and Society*, p. 96.
40 Christian, *Local Religion in Sixteenth-Century Spain*, pp. 167–8.
41 Ibid., p. 167.
42 Ibid., p. 164.

to these were days set aside for the beatification and canonisation of saints. The sheer number of holy days to be observed interfered with the normal work pattern of the laity, who, in addition, sometimes ignored the official holy days sanctioned by the Church, preferring to create their own according to local custom.

Again, the *Constituciones sinodales* of Toledo (1582) offer an indication of the scale of the problem: in addition to about 52 Sundays and holy days that always fell on a Sunday, the Church observed 40 additional holy days; of these, by chance, about five would fall on a Sunday. This meant that, in theory, people in this and other dioceses with a similar burden of feast days, would be unable to work about 85 days of the year.[43]

Perhaps more than any other festive occasion, the feast of Corpus Christi offered the most potential for a breakdown of law and order.[44] This popular feast, celebrated in summer on the Thursday after Trinity Sunday, was one which caused controversy in the post-Tridentine period. Instituted in honour of the Blessed Sacrament by papal bull in 1264, it had become by the mid-sixteenth century a mixture of sacred and secular elements, theatrical performances, floats, dance and music – a mixture which Church authorities were anxious to control. The popular custom of including giants – large figures made out of wood and paper and painted to represent saints and historic heroes – in particular incurred the wrath of Church authorities, especially when attempts were made to bring them into church for mass, the climax of the celebrations.[45]

Similar tensions arose in relation to dance: from the Middle Ages these were an integral part of festive occasions, sacred and secular, and an accepted part of Corpus Christi celebrations, when dances were enacted before the high altar in the presence of the holy sacrament. It is difficult for us to know how widespread was opposition to dancing in church; but evidence suggests that the new reforming spirit disapproved of mingling sacred and secular dances in church buildings, and, of course, dancing which brought men and women into bodily contact. There were denunciations of dancing clergy – a not uncommon practice on ordination – but not all such denunciations may have been as extreme as that published by the Franciscan Juan de Dueñas at Toledo in 1583:

> those who are dedicated to God should not be present at the vain spectacles of this world. What can we say of some priests and religious who when they sing their first mass perform great dances and games in the churches and monasteries; who also dress in strange clothes, wear masks, and go to jousts and other inappropriate games, for which some dress themselves as women, others as shepherds, others as

43 Ibid., p. 175.
44 The feast of Corpus Christi has been well documented. See Ricardo Arias, *The Spanish Sacramental Plays* (Boston, 1980), and Francis G. Very, *The Spanish Corpus Christi Procession* (Valencia, 1962), cited in Henry Kamen, *The Phoenix and the Flame: Catalonia and the Counter-Reformation* (New Haven and London, 1993). For a description of the Corpus Christi tradition in Burgo de Osma see José Ignacio Palacios Sanz, 'Música y tradición en la fiesta del Corpus, en la catedral de El Burgo de Osma (Soria)', *Anuario musical* 49 (1994), pp. 179–210.
45 Kamen, *The Phoenix and the Flame*, p. 185.

nobles? And what is worst of all is that he who is most dissolute and profane in these activities thinks he is the most successful. They also perform profane farces, sing lewd songs, alien to all decency and purity, all of which is banned and prohibited and most specially condemned in ecclesiastical persons.[46]

Even before this, the provincial councils of Tarragona and Valencia in 1565 had forbidden the custom of dancing before the sacrament at Corpus Christi, or before church altars; but evidence suggests that the tradition of dancing in church survived long after the Council of Trent, so much so that a royal order was issued in 1777 forbidding this ancient practice.[47]

Another modification to Corpus Christi traditions, post-Trent, was the transformation of the *autos*, the plays which were performed as part of the celebration. These were transformed into *autos sacramentales*, sacred dramas performed in the presence of the blessed sacrament, which the Church saw as a medium for religious instruction. The transformation from sacred to secular took some time to bring about; as late as 1625 the cathedral chapter in Burgo de Osma prohibited plays in front of or behind the *coro* unless they were sacred in nature because 'they offered too many improprieties and indecencies'.[48]

CHURCH REFORM AND THE COUNCIL OF TRENT

IF THE CHURCH was to succeed in imposing its will on the ordinary people, it also had to put its own house in order, for according to official reports of Church councils and synods, it was riddled with secularism, absenteeism, ignorance, and low levels of morality and discipline.[49]

The process of internal reform was long and hard. The foundations for long-term ecclesiastical reform in the Spanish Church were first established by Ferdinand and Isabella towards the end of the fifteenth century and continued throughout the reigns of Charles V and Philip II.

Partly in a bid to extend their control over the Spanish Church, the catholic monarchs endorsed a number of reforming measures put forward by two important assemblies of clergy convened in Castile: the Toledan Provincial Council held in 1473 (the first since 1429) and a Congregation of Castilian clergy, held in Seville in 1478.[50]

46 Juan de Dueñas, *Quarta, quinta y sexta parte del espejo de consolacion de tristes* (Toledo, 1591), cited in Kamen, *The Phoenix and the Flame*, p. 191.

47 Palacios Sanz, 'Música y tradición'. See Kamen, *The Phoenix and the Flame*, pp. 189–92, for a full discussion on the topic of dancing.

48 'Libro de actas capitulares', vol. IX, fols. 684–5, cited in Palacios Sanz, 'Música y tradición'.

49 Rawlings, *Church, Religion and Society*, p. 50. Rawlings cites the following sources relating to this topic: José Sánchez Herrero, *Concilios provincales y sínodos toledanos de los siglos xiv y xv* (La Laguna, 1976); Antonio García y García (ed.), *Synodicon Hispanum*, vols. I–VII (Madrid, 1987–97); Fidel Fita, 'Concilios españoles inéditos', *Boletín de la Real academia de la historia*, 22 (1893), pp. 209–57; Christian Hermann, 'L'église selon les Cortes de Castille, 1476–1598', *Hispania sacra* 27 (1974), pp. 201–35.

50 Rawlings, *Church, Religion and Society*, p. 51.

The issues raised by these councils included some of those which would be discussed by the more influential Council of Trent at its final session some seventy years later. The central issues were the need to provide adequate training for the clergy, and to eradicate ill-discipline within the clerical estate and the establishing of the important principle of residence. Such reforms in these areas were long overdue, but difficult to put into practice since there was a long history of corruption and ill-discipline within the Church at every level, from the papacy downwards.

The case of Pope Paul III (1534–49) is a good example of the attitude which prevailed at the very top of the Catholic Church in the sixteenth century. Sympathetic to reform within the Church, he was the man under whose influence the Council of Trent was called. He was made a bishop at the age of 20 and elected cardinal at the age of 24 in spite of not being interested in religion – a not unusual phenomenon, given the history of such elections. Only later in life, in his fifties and after a spiritual awakening, was he ordained a priest. He was elected pope at the age of 66, but in spite of his dedication to reform he immediately created two of his 15-year-old grandsons cardinals.[51]

The two Castilian assemblies put forward various badly needed measures for the reform of the clergy: a knowledge of Latin to be obligatory, three years training in theology, canon law or the liberal arts, compulsory residence in all Church offices, those in holy orders to demonstrate good conduct. In practice, they had little effect: they were regional in their impact and required the backing of a much more influential gathering of churchmen in order to have an influence throughout the Spanish Church.

Following these attempts at reform, there were no significant new initiatives until the Council of Trent's first meeting in 1545. Charles V spent twenty-four of his forty years as king (1516–56) out of the country. Although he was known to be sympathetic towards the idea of a general Church council, seeing it as one of the solutions to the Lutheran problem, he was absorbed with political problems for much of this time: the Protestant threat, the Turkish advance in the Mediterranean, rivalry with the Francis I of France. For their part, successive popes were unwilling to consider such a council, aware that it could prove a serious challenge to their authority and expose the fragility of their power base; there was certainly enough evidence of corruption to justify deposition and replacement.

It is important for us to remember at this point that, apart from the matter of clerical reform, there were two other critical issues that Europe's political and spiritual leaders needed to settle to ensure political and religious stability throughout central Europe. One was the question of where supreme authority in the Church lay: was it with the papacy, as popes over many centuries had maintained, or with individual rulers? If the latter, they had as much right as the pope to exercise both political and financial control of the Church within their own territories. The other critical issue was the challenge presented to the Catholic Church by Protestantism. In Charles V's Spain, 'counter reform was prioritised over Catholic reform';[52] and it was counter reform which was to take priority.

51 Keith Randel, *The Catholic and Counter Reformations* (London, 1990), p. 25.
52 Rawlings, *Church, Religion and Society*, p. 53.

All parties eventually agreed to the calling of a General Church Council. The independent bishopric of Trent was the place selected. Although now part of modern-day Italy, in the mid-sixteenth century it was recognised as being within the Empire and yet close to the northern boundary of the Papal States.

The council met in December 1545 for the first of what were to be three sessions, spread over the period 1545–63.[53] Thirty-one bishops attended, three quarters of whom were Italians. This was less than 5% of those eligible to attend; Spain was represented, but Francis I of France forbade his bishops to attend. The council had two overriding concerns: the need to reaffirm traditional Catholic teaching in response to the challenges presented by Lutheranism, and the need to eradicate corruption and ill-discipline in the Church's professional body. Reform of Church music was an issue not discussed until the council's third session in 1563, but in order to get the flavour of the state of the Counter-Reformation Church in the mid-sixteenth century, we must briefly examine these two key issues of Church doctrine and discipline on which delegates to the council focused their attention.

The first two sessions affirmed the importance of the bible *and* tradition in the life of the Catholic Church – in opposition to Protestant belief which stressed the centrality of the Scriptures: in Luther's view, *scriptura sola* was the sole source of truth. The authority of the Vulgate (the Latin version of the scriptures produced by St Jerome in the fourth century) was accepted in spite of its known errors of translation; contemporary scholarship by humanists like Erasmus was rejected. The following extract from the *Dogmatic Canons and Decrees* gives a flavour of the repressive nature of the council's deliberations on this matter:

> the same sacred and holy synod…ordains and declares that the said old and Vulgate edition, which, by the lengthened usage of so many ages, has been approved by the Church, be, in public lectures, disputations, sermons and expositions, held as authentic….
>
> And wishing, as is just, to impose a restraint in this matter also on printers, who now without restraint … print without the license of ecclesiastical superiors the said books of sacred Scripture and the notes and comments upon them of all persons indifferently, and with the press ofttimes unnamed, often even fictitious, and what is more grievous still, without the author's name, … (this synod) ordains and decrees that henceforth the sacred Scripture, and especially the said old and Vulgate edition, be printed in the most correct manner possible; and that it shall not be lawful for anyone to print or cause to be printed any books whatever on sacred matters without the name of the author; nor to sell them in future or even to keep them unless they shall have been first examined and approved of by the ordinary; under pain of the anathema and fine imposed in a canon of the last council of the Lateran [1512–17]: and, if they be regulars, besides this examination and approval they shall be bound to obtain a license also from their own superiors, who shall have examined the books according to the form of their own statutes.[54]

53 Council meetings were sporadic affairs. Meetings were held in twenty-five sessions of varying length. The first session lasted technically from December 1545 to September 1549, the second from May 1551 to April 1552 and the third from January 1562 to December 1563. See Keith Randel, *The Catholic and Counter Reformations*, pp. 48–9.

54 H. J. Schroeder, *Canons and Decrees of the Council of Trent* (Rockford, Illinois, 1978). As

The council acknowledged the importance of 'good works' – again in contrast with the Protestant approach: *sola fide*, faith alone, in Luther's view was enough for salvation. The central place of all seven sacraments (baptism, confirmation, matrimony, extreme unction, penance, ordination and the eucharist) was reaffirmed: in Luther's view only two, baptism and the eucharist, had validity; also affirmed was the Catholic belief in transubstantiation (the belief that the defining essence – the *substantia* – of the bread and wine of the eucharist become the actual body and blood of Jesus), a doctrine that was anathema to Protestants.

At the third and most important session, convened by Pope Pius IV (1559–65), two hundred and fifty fathers gave assent to doctrinal decisions taken earlier by previous delegates.[55] Overall numbers of those in attendance had grown over the years: Italians again greatly outnumbered delegates from other countries, but this time a French contingent was present.

Disciplinary issues were addressed at this final session. There was a considerable body of opinion in favour of strengthening the spiritual and political power of bishops – a view which had permeated all three sessions of the council and which now became the dominant issue, with the Spanish representatives strongly in favour of reform. Many bishops of a more worldly disposition were reluctant to give up their freedoms; there were those whose 'sole occupation in life is wandering idly form court to court, or abandoning their flock and neglecting the care of their sheep in the flurry of worldly affairs'.[56] After much acrimonious discussion, it was finally agreed that bishops should reside in their benefices, a decision which met the demands of the Spanish bishops, whose view was that residence was demanded by God's law: they maintained that all bishops were directly ordained by God, not the pope.[57] Bishops were to be true spiritual leaders, visiting parishes in their dioceses once a year; they were required to regulate admissions to holy orders and watch over religious communities; they were to attend a provincial synod every three years; to hold diocesan synods every year.

Reforms were initiated in the middle ranks of the Church. Four professional canonries were to be created in each cathedral and collegiate church: a canon lector, a canon magister, a canon penitentiary and a canon theologian. In addition,

Jean Delumeau has pointed out, there was no prohibition on translating or reading the Bible in the vernacular; private use of translations was permitted. It was the Index (list of banned material) of 1559 and 1564 which banned all reading of the Bible in vernacular translation. See Delumeau, *Catholicism between Luther and Voltaire*, p. 9.

55 Jean Delumeau points out that most important decisions on tradition, original sin, justification, the Eucharist and the other sacraments were taken in assemblies which never numbered more than seventy-two voters. Larger numbers of voters had been present at previous Church Councils – three hundred bishops at Lateran III and four hundred at Lateran IV – but at Trent here were never more than 237 voters although there were some fifty theologians who had no vote. See Delumeau, *Catholicism between Luther and Voltaire*, p. 7.

56 Council of Trent, Sixth Session, quoted in Delumeau, *Catholicism between Luther and Voltaire*, p. 17.

57 MacCulloch, *Reformation: Europe's House Divided*, p. 304. The argument here is a theological one: is the pope merely *primus inter pares* – the first among equals – or is he God's representative who rules by divine right?

graduate status was required for senior capitular officeholders.[58]

Parish priests were to be better instructed: a knowledge of Latin was to be required before a candidate could begin minor orders; candidates for the subdiaconate would be have to be at least twenty-one years of age and twenty-two for the diaconate; ordination was to be preceded by a comprehensive examination of both conduct and religious knowledge.[59] Seminaries were to be set up in every diocese to improve the quality of training. No candidate should be admitted 'who is not at least twelve years old, born of a legitimate marriage, who cannot adequately read or write, and whose natural goodness of disposition and strength of will do not offer the hope that they will undertake the permanent ecclesiastical ministry'.[60] Priests were expected to be of good conduct, 'serious, modest and devout' in dress, attitude, manner and speech; clergymen not wearing clerical dress were to be suspended, or even deposed and deprived of their benefice;[61] they were to preach every Sunday and provide Christian education for the laity; they were to keep records of baptisms, marriages and deaths. Regular clergy were to adhere rigorously to the rule of their order, maintaining the traditional vows of poverty, chastity and obedience.[62]

Following pontifical approval of the council's decisions on 26 January 1564, the confirmatory bull *Benedictus Deo* was issued publicly in June. This was followed two years later by the parish catechism – the *Catechismus ex decreto concilii Tridentini ad parochos* – for which Pius IV's nephew, the young, energetic Cardinal Borromeo, was largely responsible; the revised Breviary and Missal appeared in 1568 and 1570 respectively.[63] It is the revision of the latter, of course, which had most practical significance for composers of Esquivel's generation: a change in text meant revisions to music already in use, an issue which will be touched upon later.

The debate at Trent had been deeply divisive, with the pope's authority seriously challenged; but as the pope still had the ultimate right to appoint bishops, the papacy remained strong – perhaps even stronger than it had been in 1545. However, as might be expected, the practical implementation of the council's proposals proved difficult: vested interests in the status quo were, after all, long established, and lethargy and laxity difficult to eradicate.

Spain was the first European country to give complete and unequivocal acceptance to Trent's proposals. Philip, who had inherited the throne from his father in 1559, quickly signified his approval in a royal *cédula* (decree) on 12 July 1564. But his acceptance was on his own terms: he refused to acknowledge the pope as 'bishop of the universal Church' and his acceptance was tempered by the clause 'my royal rights being in no way infringed'.[64] In other words, he saw himself as head of the Church in Spain and its territories.

In Spain, the traditional method of introducing change in the Church had been

58 Rawlings, *Church, Religion and Society*, p. 55.
59 Ibid., p. 55.
60 Delumeau, *Catholicism between Luther and Voltaire*, p. 21.
61 Ibid., p. 191.
62 Rawlings, *Church, Religion and Society*, p. 55.
63 Delumeau, *Catholicism between Luther and Voltaire*, p. 24.
64 Ibid., pp. 24–5.

through the medium of the provincial councils – councils which covered a specific ecclesiastical province. These passed decrees which were then passed down to
diocesan synods for implementation. But in the eighty years preceding the closure
of Trent the number of such synods had been remarkably low, about one every
thirty years. This number was derisory given Trent's decision that synods should
be annual events. Ciudad Rodrigo – Esquivel's birth place – for example appears
to have had only one synod in one and a half centuries from 1400 to 1565. In April
1565 Philip sent out instructions to his archbishops ordering the summoning of
provincial councils which were tightly controlled by the Royal Council: no council
was allowed to meet unless with official permission and with a royal representative
present; all decisions had to be submitted to the Royal Council for approval.[65]

Although the councils met with a considerable amount of opposition from
clergy and debates were very lively affairs, they were of supreme importance: 'the
central episode of the Spanish Counter-Reformation, fulfillment of the aspirations
of a generation of reformers, and a historic step in the evolution of the peninsular
Church'.[66] The issues discussed were wide-ranging, as the following examples show.

The Toledan council, which met between September 1565 and March 1566, limited the food menu of prelates, ordered synods to be held annually, laid down rules
on preaching and instruction, and ordered that 'music in divine praise should not
imitate the profane sound of the theatre, nor the strains of shameless love or of war'
– an echo, perhaps, of the discussion that had already taken place on the nature of
Church music at Trent. The council of Valencia had controls on school books and
banned the works of Ovid and Martial; churches were to be closed at night ('since
at night many bad things tend to be done'); dancing was banned 'that the images of
saints be painted and carved with decency'.[67]

Many of the areas put forward for reform had, of course, been aired earlier
(e.g. at the Toledan provincial council of 1473 and the congregation of Castilian
clergy, held in Seville in 1478), and many met with a lukewarm response from
local clergy. Cathedral clergy, who still formed semi-autonomous power bases
within many diocesan churches, and whose independence was threatened by
reform proposals, were in some cases openly hostile; parish clergy objected among
other things to the high cost of annual synods and demands for residence. The
setting up of seminaries also had mixed results. Some twenty were established in
the period 1564–1600, but cathedral chapters were reluctant to provide the necessary funding and the traditional universities feared the loss of their status.[68] Many
failed to provide adequate training: the level of literacy was so variable that parish
clergy in the remote parts of the Spanish peninsula were barely literate, and in the

---

65 Kamen, *The Phoenix and the Flame*, pp. 56–60. When the councils of 1565 met, there had
been no provincial assemblies anywhere in Spain (apart from Catalonia) for forty-three years: see
Kamen, p. 58.

66 Ibid., p. 61.

67 Ibid., pp. 63–4. The issue of clerical misbehaviour and moral laxity in general makes
fascinating reading. See *The Phoenix and the Flame*, chapter 7, for many amusing and informative
examples.

68 Rawlings, *Church, Religion and Society*, p. 71.

1580s the bishop of Oviedo claimed that half his clergy did not understand the Latin Gospels in the mass, nor did they have the basic knowledge to enable them to administer confession.[69]

The reorganisation of religious houses, another of Philip's objectives, was undertaken with some rigour; it was another means of extending his control over the religious life of the country. Smaller orders were abolished and smaller monasteries handed over to larger bodies; all religious houses were made to conform to the original rule of their foundation; all female convents were made to practise the strict cloister. Again, there was opposition and sometimes incumbents had to be driven out by armed troops; some female religious refused to accept strict enclosure. However, new foundations were created and, as is well known, made a considerable impact on the religious life of the times: the Jesuit Order (the Society of Jesus) and Teresa of Ávila's Discalced Carmelite Order – given recognition in 1593 – are just two notable examples.

As we have already seen, the *cofradías* came in for criticism at the Council of Trent, and at the succeeding provincial councils. Their numbers had grown greatly throughout the century and many had amassed funds under false pretences; moreover, in their persistence in administering the sacraments and arranging local forms of worship, they offered a serious challenge to the clergy. Council decrees reined in their powers. The Toledan provincial council of 1582–3, for example, sought to limit the size of the *cofradías* 'since they have grown to such an extent that they are capable of great harm'.[70] The influence and practical assistance given to local people continued, however, in spite of the restrictions laid down by Trent and the provincial councils, particularly in connection with burial rites. In Madrid, to quote just one example, the number of requests for confraternities to be present at funerals actually went up in the 1560s and remained high for several years to come.[71]

In the aftermath of Trent, Philip was able to achieve 'the unique distinction of presiding over a wholly autonomous Church, in which not only the nomination of all bishops and prelates but of all heads of religious orders passed under the survey and control of the crown'.[72] Yet, in practice, the pace of change was slow: the Church had to break through the barrier of popular ignorance and custom and the results of so much discussion and legislation met with only partial success. Spain's vast territory meant that some rural areas were little influenced by change: moral laxity, indifference to change among the clergy, and the simplistic faith of the people continued; episcopal visits were few, and synods were rarely convened. Vested interests in such powerful bodies as the cathedral chapters and mendicant orders hindered the reform programme, and as far as the common people were concerned, things probably appeared to change very little: they were probably put off religion by the Church's ineffectual attempts to make the spiritual dimension of life meaningful to them.

---

69 Kamen, *The Phoenix and the Flame*, p. 343.

70 *Constitutiones sinodales* (Toledo, 1583), fol. 49v, cited in Rawlings, *Church, Religion and Society*, pp. 98–9.

71 Eire, *From Madrid to Purgatory*, pp. 135–6.

72 Kamen, *The Phoenix and the Flame*, p. 76.

The celebration of mass is a case in point. Even after the imposition of the new Roman rite in 1569, services were conducted in Latin by priests at the high altar, far away from the laity; in cathedrals, the *coro* (enclosed choir area) formed a barrier (as it can do now in English cathedrals) between the scene of the action and the general populace. Thus, services would be largely unintelligible, and it is not surprising that comings and goings during the ceremony, conversations and other signs of disrespect were common. Sometimes only the women and children went into the building, leaving the men chatting and playing dice at the church door within earshot of the priest's voice, an acceptable practice in the eyes of the clergy; or the men whiled away their time during mass in the tavern. Particularly in the minds of those from rural communities, the church as a building was associated with commercial and social affairs as well as religious activities, so that attendance at mass was a social occasion. After Trent, the numbers attending mass weekly were supposed to be recorded by the priest in a book, and although there is evidence to suggest that attendance and the observance of the Sabbath and holy days improved after Trent, active participation was minimal.[73]

Another issue opened up to examination by the council was the matter of frequency of communion and confession by lay persons, an issue on which there seemed to be great disagreement. The Jesuits insisted that both communion and confession should be used as frequently as possible, while others spoke out strongly against this:

> In some parts the devotion to communion has grown so much that many lay-people, men and women, married and unmarried, go to communion so often that they receive the Blessed Sacrament every day. This seems to be excessive frequency, and it should be considered whether at this time the people should be encouraged to receive the Blessed sacrament more than once a year.[74]

In contrast, a well-known confessor's manual laid down: 'men of honour [laymen] should go to communion at least four times' in the year, and as for the religious 'the Council of Trent has now ordered that all nuns confess and go to communion at least once a month'.[75] This quotation reminds us of the importance attached to confession by the Counter-Reformation Church. Manuals seeking to abolish irregularities practised by some clergy appeared, and new regulations were laid down on the importance of making confession before a licensed priest, and in a specially constructed confessional box offering anonymity to the penitent; parish clergy were expected to keep registers of confession. Helen Rawlings has neatly summed up the expectations of a 'good Catholic' after the Council of Trent:

---

73 A seventy-five per cent minimum compliance was recorded in Cuenca during the period 1564–80, rising to eighty-five per cent in the period 1581–1600. Sarah T. Nalle, *God in La Mancha: Religious Reform and the People of Cuenca, 1500–1650* (Baltimore, 1992), p. 131.

74 List of reforms demanded by the bishops of Castile in the 1550s and recorded in Juan Tejada y Ramiro, *Colección de canones y de todos los concilios*, 6 vols. (Madrid, 1859), in Kamen, *The Phoenix and the Flame*, pp. 121–2.

75 Martín de Axpilcueta Navarro, *Manual de confessores* (Barcelona, 1576), in Kamen, *The Phoenix and the Flame*, p. 122.

A 'good Catholic' was characterised by his knowledge of the four essential prayers of the Church (the Lord's Prayer, the Apostles' Creed, the *Ave María* and the *Salve Regina*) and the Ten Commandments; his abstention from labour on Sundays and attendance at mass; his participation in Holy Communion and his confession of his sins at least once per year during the season of Lent; his observance of the traditional feast days of the religious calendar; his receipt of the sacraments of baptism and marriage at the hands of the local priest; his recourse to the sacrament of extreme unction on the point of death; and his ordering of masses for the delivery of his soul.[76]

Trent and its aftermath, then, marked an important stage in the history of the Counter-Reformation. Firmly enshrined in a set of doctrines, conservative in nature, it ensured the continuity of the Catholic faith in the face of the challenge from Protestantism; and its influence on Church music was far-reaching and long-lasting.

In matters of faith, the Church's very conservatism ensured the survival of a liturgy and patterns of worship that provided Church musicians with a model which changed little, particularly in Spain and its New World territories. Unlike the new Protestant faith, which required new genres, such as the anthem and service settings for example, and which put the emphasis on the vernacular, Catholic composers in Spain had a received body of tradition. The texts of the Latin mass and the Offices continued to provide a rich source of material; and perhaps the unchanging nature of the centuries-old ritual was one reason for the preservation of an essentially conservative musical tradition which went on into the next century when, outside Spain, musical styles were changing. It is true that new techniques such as the *basso continuo* were introduced in Spain around the turn of the century, and polychoral music also made its appearance (in Victoria's masses of 1600, for example, which were published with an organ part duplicating choir one). But there was no sudden stylistic upheaval causing a rupture with the established tradition of liturgically ordered and essentially polyphonic Church music, written according to a late Renaissance aesthetic; old choir books were preserved and mended, and continued to be used at the *facistol*. Moreover, sacred music by Renaissance masters went on being copied into the eighteenth century, and there is a very strong reason for this – the power of the *cabildos* (the cathedral chapters), which had no wish to make changes to the established order.[77] In an authoritarian and stratified society,

76 Rawlings, *Church, Religion and Society*, p. 79.

77 The transition to the Baroque is outlined by José López-Calo in his study *Historia de la música española 3. Siglo XVII* (Madrid, 1983). See also Louise Stein's chapter 'Spain', in Curtis Price, ed., *The Early Baroque Era from the Late Sixteenth Century to the 1660s* (Basingstoke and London, 1993), where the transition to the seventeenth century in Spain is discussed with admirable clarity. Among factors impacting on the history of Spanish Church music in the seventeenth century, Stein lists the paucity of music publications (when compared with the large number of literary text demanded by a growing readership); the shift in population away from the countryside to urban centres; the attraction of Madrid a the seat of royal power – with its obvious appeal to musicians, painters and writers; and a gradual lessening of demand for religious art in favour of the secular, in response to social and economic changes. As Stein makes clear, the *villancico* – subject, as it was, to secular influences – became a widely cultivated and popular genre in seventeenth-century Spain; it

and at a local level where any real changes were implemented, the *cabildos* were a powerful and conservative force; they ensured continuity and conformity with the demands of Trent for a long to come.

The Council of Trent and music

THE COUNCIL did examine music and its role in the Church but not until its third and final session in 1562–3. Indeed, music, as it is now recognised, played a relatively minor role in the Council's deliberations. There were, after all, much more urgent issues demanding attention – other (non-musical) abuses of the mass, the question of episcopal residency, clerical education and conduct, to name but three. And yet it is obvious that musical practices were a concern to several reform-minded participants at Trent, and much preliminary committee time was spent preparing material for presentation to the full Council to be enshrined in a formal decree. The following outline of the Council's deliberations on music relies heavily on Craig Monson's 2002 study 'The Council of Trent Revisited'.[78]

A multinational committee appointed in July 1562, which included representatives from Italy, Spain, France and Austro-Hungary under the chairmanship of the humanist Ludovico Beccadelli, collected submissions on reform of abuses of the mass; these included suggested reforms of musical practices. After much discussion, a draft proposal was presented for consideration in the general congregation on 10 September 1562; it included the following pronouncement on music:

> Canon 8. All things should indeed be so ordered that the masses, whether they be celebrated with or without singing, may reach tranquilly into the ears and hearts of those who hear them, when everything is executed clearly and at the right speed. In the case of those masses which are celebrated with singing and with organ, let nothing profane be intermingled, but only hymns and divine praises. The whole plan of singing in musical modes should be constituted not to give empty pleasure to the ear, but in such a way that the words may be clearly understood by all, and thus the hearts of the listeners be drawn to the desire of heavenly harmonies, in the contemplation of the joys of the blessed.[79]

Although its intentions are clear, the proposal was never accepted in this form; all that remained after discussion in the general congregation was a short statement on music as part of a single decree 'concerning the things to be observed and avoided in the celebration of the mass': 'They shall banish from church all music that contains, whether in the singing or in the organ playing, things that are lascivious or impure'.[80] This statement was published in the canons and decrees of the twenty-

---

could absorb new techniques, and adapt itself to local traditions, tastes and circumstances in a way in which High Renaissance polyphony could not.

    78 Craig A. Monson. 'The Council of Trent Revisited', *Journal of the American Musicological Society* 55 no. 1 (2002), pp. 1–37.

    79 Translation cited in Reese, *Music in the Renaissance*, p. 449.

    80 Ibid. As Craig Monson has pointed out ('The Council of Trent Revisited', p. 11), Reese created

second session of the Council on 17 September 1562.

This was not the end of the matter, however; music again occupied the attention of the delegates at the twenty-fourth session in 1563. From an exchange of correspondence between Emperor Ferdinand I and his emissaries at Trent in August of that year, it is clear that one of the subjects raised in preliminary committee meetings was that of polyphony. The newly appointed and influential papal legate, Giovanni Morone, had actually banned polyphony in Modena for a brief period in 1537 and it seems likely that a possible ban on polyphony was one of the subjects discussed in these meetings. However, no such ban found its way into the proposals finally put before the congregation between 11 September and 2 October; nor was the issue of textual intelligibility specifically enshrined in any final decree. Order and decorum were the major concerns, as the following extract from Canon 12 demonstrates:

> With regard to the proper direction of the divine offices, concerning the proper manner of singing or playing therein, the precise regulation for assembling and remaining in choir, together with everything necessary for the ministers of the church, and suchlike: the provincial synod shall prescribe an established form for the benefit of, and in accordance with the customs of, each province.[81]

An attempt was made to ban polyphony as a part of the discussions on the reform of female religious orders which took place at the twenty-fifth session of the Council in 1563, but all references to nuns' music were dropped from the decrees of the final session, 3–4 December, which brought the Council to a close.[82]

After the Council, the question of textual clarity, which had sparked so many lively debates in preliminary gatherings leading up to the full meetings in congregation, was raised once again. Gabriele Paleotti, future archbishop of Bologna and the figure who had played such an important role in drafting canons on abuses, pointed out in his manuscript 'Acts' of the Council 1562–3 that this issue had all along been a concern of delegates. In his final redrafting of his 'Acts' – initially sketched during the Council and redrafted several times in subsequent years, but never published until the nineteenth century – Paleotti provided the following statement:

> In the deliberations regarding music in divine service, although some rather condemned [than approved] it in churches, the rest, however, and especially the Spanish, gave their vote that it should by all means be retained in accordance with the most ancient usage of the Catholic Church to arouse the faithful to love of God, provided that it should be free of lasciviousness and wantonness, and provided that, so far as possible, the words of the singers should be comprehensible to the hearers.[83]

---

a misleading impression of the Council's legislation on music by stringing together the preliminary eighth canon, which had not been approved, and this final published version – a procedure followed by many other musicologists since. Interestingly, as Monson reports, the Spanish delegates were staunch advocates for the retention of music.

81　Translation in Monson, 'The Council of Trent Revisited', p. 18.

82　Ibid., p. 22.

83　Translation in ibid., p. 23.

This abiding concern for textual intelligibility is reflected in the actions of Cardinal Carlo Borromeo in 1565. Borromeo and fellow cardinal, Vitellozzo Vitelli, both influential members of the commission established by Pius IV the previous year to carry out Tridentine reforms in Rome as part of the emphasis on reform at a local level, were given the task of examining masses written in a reformed manner. In his role as archbishop of Milan, Borromeo commissioned a mass from his chapel master, Vincenzo Ruffo (c.1508–87), in a style which was in accordance with his views on the need for intelligibility in Church music.

Borromeo's influence on Ruffo's compositional style has been well document-ed.[84] But although his views on Church music may have had a direct impact on the general style of the music he favoured in his own diocese, in practice they had little immediate impact in the wider world. Moreover, the general recommendations made by delegates to Trent merely reflect views expressed earlier in the century by Protestant reformers like Calvin, and churchmen of a humanist disposition like the Roman bishop Cirillo Franco (c.1500–75), whose earlier call for reform in Church music was made out of the need, as he saw it, to get back to the ancients, for whom the text was of paramount importance. Glorifying the achievements of classical antiquity was, after all, a typical Renaissance viewpoint and one not just restricted to Church music. But however much the ancient world may have provided a justi-fication and inspiration of sorts for the new emphasis on textual clarity, in practice, the Renaissance world had little real knowledge of classical procedures; those who advocated this new approach were driven more by contemporary philosophy than a genuine desire to imitate the ancients.

Borromeo's attempt to regulate Church music was, of course, motivated by the desire for general conformity and uniformity within the Church: standardisation in such matters as clerical dress, vestments and ritual was seen as important in an attempt to establish universal discipline. But the task of reforming the liturgy was ultimately the task of churchmen and composers at the local level, as the extract from Canon 12 above, with its mention of provincial synods, demonstrates; however, in practice, the imposition of the new Tridentine rite took a long time to achieve – at least a generation as a minimum, and in some cases more than half a century.[85]

Part of the problem was the difficulty in obtaining or even affording new books; another issue was clerical obstinacy and perhaps the conservative desire to stick to the old ways. In the more remote areas of Spain – some areas of Catalonia for example – this was a particular problem. In Barcelona, the parish church of Santa Maria del Pi appointed a music teacher who 'must teach all the priests, both ben-eficed and chaplains ... and also the students, plainsong and organ song, and how to say the masses on Sundays and feast-days';[86] the canons complained that the chant was alien and difficult to learn, a view repeated elsewhere.

---

84 See Lewis Lockwood, *The Counter-Reformation and the Masses of Vincenzo Ruffo* (Venice, 1970).

85 Kamen, *The Phoenix and the Flame*, p. 101.

86 Arxiu Parroquial, Santa Maria del Pi, Barcelona, Comunidad: Determinacions, lletra C 1575–1606, fol. 43*v*, cited in Kamen, *The Phoenix and the Flame*, p. 101.

The new Roman Breviary, issued by Rome in July 1568, and the new Roman Missal which followed in February 1569, were authorised by Trent as a means of controlling Church discipline and were supposed to supersede all rites currently in use, except for churches which could prove that their rite was more than two centuries old – like the ancient Mozarabic rite practised in Toledo. But again there were difficulties in gaining acceptance of the new rites. Philip II attempted to impose a monopoly by setting up a distribution centre for the new materials – printed by the Antwerp firm of Plantin – in the Jeronimite monastery at Escorial, forbidding importation from Italy. This practice was soon undermined, but there is every reason to think that the new books may have posed a financial problem. They had to have a special type-face, not only for the words, but also for the music and accompanying illustrations; moreover, they were traditionally done not on paper but on parchment, which added greatly to the cost.[87]

Given these issues, it is not surprising that many dioceses and religious houses adhered to local custom. Although by Esquivel's time many would have conformed in matters of textual assignment, rubrics, calendar and so forth, as far as music was concerned, choice of melodies for use with antiphon and hymn texts, as well as tones used by the celebrant at mass, may have corresponded to local tradition rather than Roman practice.[88] Moreover, further reforms were yet to come: another revised Breviary was issued by Pope Clement VIII in 1602 and Esquivel and other composers of his generation had then to conform.

THE ORGANISATION OF SPANISH CATHEDRAL MUSIC IN THE SIXTEENTH CENTURY

B EFORE LOOKING IN DETAIL at the organisation of music within the cathedral structure it is worth remembering that the institutions served by Esquivel and his fellow musicians were established long before the Counter-Reformation, not as power bases for a militant Church, but as centres of prayer and worship, with a liturgy that had evolved over a period of many centuries. The many artistic products we admire today, masses, motets, Magnificats etc., were written to further this spirit of devotion, and each genre had its own special place and function within the liturgy.

There are many scattered sources of information concerning the organisation of music within the cathedral system in Spain during the sixteenth century in Spanish, but few English-language accounts; consequently, it would be useful to outline the role played by musicians in the Church during the Golden Age. The following is a brief account of the system which prevailed throughout Spain during the sixteenth century.

87 Kamen, *The Phoenix and the Flame*, pp. 95–6. The whole process of production and distribution of the new rite (*nuevo rezado*) is documented in detail by Vicente Bécares, *Aspectos de la producción y distribución del nuevo rezado*, in Ian Fenlon and Tess Knighton, eds., *Early Music Printing and Publishing in the Iberian World* (Kassel, 2006), pp. 1–22. Bécares includes examples of legal contracts showing the huge costs of printing the newly required missals and breviaries.

88 See Robert J. Snow, *The 1613 Print of Juan Esquivel Barahona*, Detroit Monographs in Musicology 7 (Detroit, 1978), pp. 18–19.

The role of the *maestro de capilla*

Each Spanish cathedral had a group of musicians, singers and instrumentalists, known collectively as the *capilla de música*, whose sole *raison d'être* was the provision of music to enhance the splendour of the liturgy. The exact number of musicians depended, of course, on economic circumstances – on the wealth of each individual institution – and to a certain extent on the supply of musicians available for employment.

At the head of the musical establishment was the *maestro de capilla* appointed by the cathedral chapter (the *cabildo*) headed by the dean. The position of *maestro de capilla* was key to the smooth running of the musical life of the cathedral. In the sixteenth century the obligations of the *maestro* were enshrined in cathedral *estatutos* (statutes) or *reglamentos* (regulations), which probably reflected earlier unwritten traditions. The post was a highly desirable one: it offered some security in return for faithful service to the religious community, although it entailed hard work and long hours. It certainly resulted in many frustrations.

In general terms, the demands of the job varied little from cathedral to cathedral so that we can summarise the responsibilities of a typical *maestro* as follows: he was expected to take charge and regulate the singing of *canto llano* (plainsong) and *canto de órgano* (mensural music, that is polyphony) at all the main services of the cathedral community – mass and the offices – throughout the Church year; he was expected to rehearse the choir and hold classes in the cathedral every day, teaching the choir boys all the music necessary and giving lessons in plainsong, polyphony, counterpoint and composition to any cathedral dignitaries and canons who wanted to learn; he was expected to find replacements for choir boys who could no longer be of service when their voices broke; in most cathedrals he was expected to house, clothe and feed the boys, teach them the basic skills of literacy and act *in loco parentis* in disciplinary matters; in addition to ensuring the provision of Latin-texted polyphonic music throughout the year, he was expected to compose music in the vernacular (the *villancicos*) for the feasts of Christmas and Corpus Christi.

The statutes of some cathedrals go into considerable detail, spelling out the exact times when the *maestro* was to be 'on the job'. The statutes of León cathedral, for example, specifically state for the morning: 'from the hour of prime [sung at around six or seven in the morning] until the hour after the conclusion of the lesser hours'; in the afternoon, 'from one o'clock until one hour after Vespers' during the months from October to May, and from two o'clock during the rest of the year.[89] *Maestros* who failed to meet the requirements were subject to severe disciplinary measures: they could be fined, or even put under house arrest. Petty quarrels arose frequently over such matters as the *maestro's* prebend (salary), his seat in the *coro* (the choir enclosure), or, if he was a priest, his altar duties. Esquivel's teacher, Juan Navarro, had to fight for his privileges when he left Ciudad Rodrigo for Palencia in 1574; clearly he was of a volatile disposition, and was disciplined for striking the

89 Samuel Rubio, *Historia de la música española 2. Desde el 'ars nova' hasta 1600* (Madrid, 1983), p. 19.

Precentor across the face during Vespers.[90] Sometimes these disputes resulted in lawsuits, as we shall see in Esquivel's case.

Chapelmasters were usually appointed after a rigorous public examination to test their musicianship: they had to demonstrate their competence in counterpoint by completing set exercises, they had to show their ability to direct singers at the *facistol* (the lectern), and they were given twenty-four hours in which to compose a motet and a *villancico*. Finally, having completed all the musical tests they had to prove their *limpieza de sangre* (purity of blood) to indicate their freedom from Jewish and Moorish racial origin, a condition of membership required by cathedrals and other institutions.[91]

If a vacancy had to be filled quickly, one or two canons might be given the job of finding some suitable candidate. Sometimes a chapter would offer a high salary in an attempt to lure a likely candidate away from his existing post, as happened in 1564 when Rodrigo Ordóñez in Burgos reported to the cathedral chapter that he had been offered a higher salary (*ración*) elsewhere.[92]

The organist

Every cathedral had an organist, sometimes two, as for example in Burgos, where, in 1492, the names of two men are recorded in the chapter acts: Juan de Burgos, who played on principal feasts, and Juan Martínez, who played on the rest of the days of the year.[93] Next to the *maestro de capilla* organists were key figures in the cathedral musical establishment, and the post was demanding. Everyday duties required routine accompanying skills, such as accompanying the psalms, and improvising short passages to fill gaps in a service (as organists do today); but on other occasions, the musical demands were clearly greater.

Taking the order and statutes of León as an example, the organist was expected to alternate with the singers, adding *fabordones* (improvised harmonisations of a given chant) during the first and last psalm of Vespers; in addition, on major feast days and patronal festivals he had to play for Compline and Matins, and he was expected to improvise embellishments (*glosas*) to motets played as solos when the occasion demanded. Interestingly, the role of the organist at mass is not specified in these statutes.[94]

The chapter acts of Malaga make it clear that another function of the organist was to play the portative organ – an instrument which almost all cathedrals

---

90 Ibid., p. 22.

91 Ibid., p. 27. The chapter acts for Seville record that on 1 September 1573, Geronimo de Peraça was installed as organist, 'proofs of the purity of his lineage having been adduced'. See Robert Stevenson, *Spanish Cathedral Music in the Golden Age* (Berkeley, 1961), p. 159.

92 Rubio, *Historia de la música española*, p. 18. For a more extended discussion on the duties of a *maestro de capilla* in sixteenth-century Spain, see Jane Morlet Hardie, '"Wanted, One Maestro de Capilla:" A Sixteenth-Century Job Description', in David Crawford and G. Grayson Wagstaff, eds., *Encomium Musicae: Essays in Memory of Robert J. Snow* (Hillsdale, NY, 2002), pp. 269–84.

93 Rubio, *Historia de la música española*, p. 39.

94 Ibid., p. 40.

possessed – during the annual Corpus Christi procession. Competitions for organists' posts were demanding, requiring competitors to demonstrate, in a liturgical context over a period of several days, their powers of improvisation as well as accompanying skills.

The singers

Every cathedral had a group of singers (*los cantores*) trained to sing polyphony. The adult singers were designated according to their voice range as *tiple, contralto* (male alto), *tenor, contrabajo*, corresponding to our modern-day SATB choir. The soprano line was sung by male falsettists, who were sometimes joined by castrati. This seems to have been the case in Burgos when, in 1547, a singer by the name of Juan Garcia was dispatched to Valladolid in search of a castrato singer there, and again in 1550 when it was proposed that the sub-precentor be given the job of finding 'a *caponcillo* with a good voice'.[95]

The singers could be married or unmarried laymen, or ordained clergymen. As a general rule, all singers were salaried, their salaries consisting of a *media ración* (a half-prebend) paid in cash and occasionally supplemented by payment in kind – bread or a chicken; sometimes they were given help with the purchase of clothing. Salary disputes were common as the cathedrals vied with one another in attracting the best singers.

The number of adult singers varied greatly from place to place. A relatively wealthy establishment like Burgos, for example, had ten adult singers in 1538, whose names and salaries are specified in the capitular acts, and whose salaries ranged from between 70,000 and 20,000 *maravedís* per year, depending on length of service.[96] This contrasts with Coria, the diocese adjacent to Ciudad Rodrigo where Esquivel was born, where the cathedral's capitular acts of 1590 record the names and salaries of only seven singers in total whose salaries range from 30,000 *maravedís* down to 15,000.[97] Coria may be described as a middle-income diocese, so that an even less wealthy diocese like Ciudad Rodrigo may have had still fewer singers with even smaller salaries.[98] What is interesting about the example of Coria, however, is the disposition of the voices: two *tiples*, three *contraltos*, one *tenor* and one *contrabajo*. For the next twenty-five years or so there were never more than two soprano voices, two counter tenors, three tenors and three basses at any one time; in this period, the total number of adult singers in post for any one year seems not

---

95 Ibid., p. 30.

96 Ibid., p. 30.

97 Maria del Pilar Barrios Manzano, 'La música en la catedral de Coria (Cáceres) (1590–1755)' (Ph.D. dissertation, University of Extremadura, 1993), p. 359.

98 See Rawlings, *Church, Religion and Society*, pp. 63–4. Rawlings lists the scale of Spanish bishoprics (in ducats), c.1570. Bishoprics are divided into high-, middle- and low-status dioceses with Ciudad Rodrigo appearing in the lowest group (income below 15,000 ducats). Top of the list comes the archbishop of Toledo with an income of 220,000. Salamanca and Coria, the two neighbouring dioceses north and south of Ciudad Rodrigo respectively, appear in the middle-status group, where the incomes of the incumbents are both given as 26,400 ducats.

to have exceeded nine, which would probably have been enough to cover the music in the cathedral's normal repertoire, though this number might have been amplified on special occasions when music of greater splendour could be called for.[99] Given the method of singing polyphony, the singers grouped around the *facistol* on which was situated a single choirbook, the small number of singers should not surprise us.

To the adult singers were added boys' voices, variously referred to in the capitular acts as the *seises* or sometimes *mozos de coro*. The choir boys remained distinct and separate from the altar boys: the former were trained in counterpoint and polyphony, whereas the altar boys learned to sing plainsong and assist at the altar.

The singers of polyphony were complemented by members of the cathedral clergy, like the choir chaplains (*capellanes*), and about a score of clerics whose principal function was the execution of the plainchant which formed the musical core of the cathedral's worship – a service for which they were paid. Any canon with a suitable voice and relevant knowledge could take part; if he needed help, the *maestro de capilla* held daily classes which he could attend.

The *ministriles*

The *capilla de música* also included instrumentalists, mostly players of wind instruments referred to in cathedral documents as *ministriles*. In the late Middle Ages and early Renaissance, their role seems to have been a ceremonial one, accompanying processions like the annual Corpus Christi parade, but instruments seem to have found their way into church during the mid-fifteenth century.

One example is found in the Castilian chronicle *Hechos del condestable don Miguel Lucas de Iranzo* of the 1460s and 1470s, where it is recorded that in the cathedral at Jaén on Christmas morning trumpets and drums played at various times during mass.[100] They may have played on other feast days too during the year, but there is no documentation to suggest that such appearances were anything other than sporadic; nor is there any mention of instruments accompanying singers.

The situation changed during the course of the sixteenth century as more and more churches employed instrumentalists. Shawms (*chirimías*) and trombones (*sacabuches*) are mentioned with more and more frequency and to these instruments were added *flautas* (recorders) and the *bajón* (dulcian) – the instrument which doubled the bass line with the singers in polyphony; at the beginning of the seventeenth century these instruments were joined by the harp.

The cathedral chapter of Seville voted to form a wind band made up of five players (three shawms and two trombones) in 1526 to use on feast days to accompany processions; other cathedral chapters soon followed.[101] During the course of the

---

99 See Maria del Pilar Barrios Manzano, 'La música en la catedral de Coria', pp. 211–21, for full discussion of the role of singers in Coria.

100 Kenneth Kreitner, 'Minstrels in Spanish Churches, 1400–1600', *Early Music* 20 (1992), p. 534.

101 Kreitner, 'Minstrels in Spanish Churches', p. 537. Kreitner gives a chronological list of cathedral bands established during the sixteenth century. From this table we can see that sixteen

century the role of the wind band seems to have changed: from having a separate function, playing ceremonial fanfares, processional music and incidental music to cover movement during the ceremony, the band began to play a more integral part in the liturgy, alternating with the voices in some liturgical items. Calendars of the feasts of the liturgical year survive for a number of cathedrals from mid-sixteenth to mid-seventeenth century and these provide invaluable musical details. One striking example is the case of León cathedral, an institution for which ample documentation survives.

The *Constituciones* of around 1550 outlines the minstrels' function in some detail. Thus, on the eighteen most important feasts of the Church year, they were expected to play a motet before First Vespers began; afterwards they were to alternate with the organ and singers in the first and last psalms; they were also to play the first and last verses of the hymns and those of some of the Magnificat and the *Deo gratias*; further, they were expected to play processional music at the entry and exit of the choir. In mass of these solemn feasts, they were to play the first and last Kyries, at the Offertory at the raising of the host, and at the *Deo gratias*.[102] To this list might be added a further thirty-five lesser feasts in which the minstrels were expected play a significant, albeit more modest, role. What is significant, however, about the duties specified in the León *Constituciones* is that there are few occasions when the minstrels double the choir. All the liturgical items specified – hymn, Magnificat, psalms, litanies, seasonal Marian antiphons and the Kyrie of the mass – seem to have been played *alternatim*. But we must not be too dogmatic on this issue: it is very difficult for us to know how much doubling of voices and instruments occurred in Church services in the sixteenth century; local practices probably varied according to circumstances.[103]

other cathedrals followed Seville's lead. A separate column records the first mention of the *bajón*; interestingly, only six cathedrals are listed as having *bajón* players between 1530 and 1598. See also Juan Ruiz Jiménez, 'Ministriles y extravagantes en la celebración religiosa', in John Griffiths and Javier Suárez-Pajares, eds., *Políticas y prácticas musicales en el mundo de Felipe II: estudios sobre la música en España, sus instituciones y sus territorios en la segunda mitad del siglo XVI*, Coleccion Música Hispana. Textos. Estudios 8 (Madrid, 2004). An outline map of Spain on p. 202 shows the geographical and chronological spread of minstrel groups during the century; the geographical coverage is greater then the information given by Kreitner.

102 Kreitner, 'Minstrels in Spanish Churches', pp. 541–2. The solemn feasts mentioned are Circumcision, Epiphany, Purification, Annunciation, Holy Saturday, Easter, Ascension, Pentecost, Trinity, Corpus Christi and its octave, Transfiguration, Assumption, Nativity of the Virgin, the feasts of the cathedral's patron St Froilán, All Saints, the Immaculate Conception and Christmas. See also Rubio, *Historia de la música española*, pp. 46–7; Douglas Kirk, 'Churching the Shawms in Renaissance Spain: Lerma, Archivo de San Pedro Ms. Mus.1' (Ph.D dissertation, McGill University, 1993), pp. 163–5 (where, on p. 163, Kirk suggests the date of 1544 for the León constitutions); Douglas Kirk, 'Instrumental Music in Lerma, c.1608', *Early Music* 23 (1995), p. 404.

103 Kirk, 'Instrumental Music in Lerma', p. 408. The role of instruments is still a hugely contentious issue. Kreitner, for example, has now revised his 2003 interpretation of the León regulations, rejecting a literal translation of the Spanish 'En la misa tañan el primero y postrero chirie; a la ofrenda; y al alçenar; y al deo graçias'. He does not now believe the instrumentalists accompanied the singers *colla parte* in polyphony: 'Passages like "they play the first and last Kyrie" actually mean . . . that the band was supposed to play a little something between the introit and Kyrie,

What music did the minstrels play during the entrances and exits, during procession, as 'incidental' music at specified points in the ceremonies? Drawing on parallels with the situation in late-sixteenth-century Italian churches, where during mass and Vespers instrumentalists might play a *canzona francese*, Spanish musicians probably played virtually any kind of music – motets, chansons or madrigals – when 'free' music (music not specific to the day) was required; texture, mood and sonority were probably more important than genre in deciding what was appropriate at a particular moment.[104]

All three institutions in which Esquivel worked were known to have employed minstrels in addition to the vocal members of the *capilla*; their presence raises specific performance issues, as we shall see in later chapters.

THE INSTITUTIONS IN WHICH ESQUIVEL SERVED

W E NOW LOOK in more detail at the institutions in which Esquivel worked, beginning with the cathedral in his home town, Ciudad Rodrigo.[105]

and then another little something between Kyrie and Gloria'. See *Early Music* 37 (2009), p. 267. This is strongly rejected by Juan Ruiz Jiménez, who, on the basis of surviving documentary evidence (minstrel books and music for organ), argues for an *alternatim* practice in the mass that concurs with the documents. Moreover, he does not accept Kreitner's belief that *alternatim* practice was limited in the Office to psalms and not used in hymns and the Magnificat; documentary evidence in his view suggests the contrary. Thus, on the basis of all available evidence, he concludes that the issue of simultaneous performance of minstrels and singers must be left wide open; practices probably varied at different times, in different places and in different ceremonies. See Juan Ruiz Jiménez, in *Early Music* 38 (2010), pp. 169–70.

104 Kirk, 'Instrumental Music in Lerma', pp. 404–6. Kirk illustrates his argument with extended reference to repertoire, *c.*1608, associated with San Pedro, the collegiate church and ducal chapel of the duke of Lerma. In a manuscript referred as DK 2, Kirk itemises nearly a hundred pieces of sacred and secular music – all arranged in groups by mode final or by voice range (indicated by clef combination) which, he suggests, provide ideal repertoire for instrumentalists required to play continuously for a period of time. See Kirk, 'Churching the Shawms in Renaissance Spain', pp. 200–5, for a full discussion. Other evidence suggests that music was often bought for the use of the minstrels and not the choir. For example, the chapter acts of Seville cathedral record that on April 1572 Canon Alonso Mudarra was commissioned to buy a book of Guerrero's masses 'which is needed by the instrumentalists', and 'to oversee the repair of the book out of which they play Venites at Matins', cited in Stevenson, *Spanish Cathedral Music*, p. 158. Yet another more recently discovered example may be cited: MS 975 in the Archive of Manuel de Falla, which contains over a hundred sacred and secular works – psalms, hymns, motets, masses (including Rodrigo de Ceballos's *Missa tertii toni*), madrigals and chansons. Texts are added partially, to some voices only in some of the pieces, and sometimes by two different hands in the same piece. This suggests that this manuscript – of vocal music – was for minstrel use. See M. Christoforidis and J. Ruiz Jiménez, 'Manuscrito 975 de la Biblioteca de Manuel de Falla: una nueva fuente polifónica de siglo XVI', *Revista de musicología* 17 (1994), pp. 205–36.

105 The account of developments at Ciudad Rodrigo and Calahorra draws heavily on the articles by José López-Calo in the *Diccionario de la música española e hispanoamericana*, *s.v.* 'Ciudad Rodrigo', III, pp. 722–7. The translations are the author's own.

Ciudad Rodrigo

The diocese of Ciudad Rodrigo is an ancient foundation. The cathedral chapter was instituted in 1161 and construction of the present-day cathedral commenced in 1170; considerable remodelling and architectural change took place in the sixteenth century and beyond. In addition to its musical heritage, one of the great artistic treasures of the cathedral is its fifteenth-century *coro* with its elaborately carved misericords and fine plateresque carvings designed by Rodrigo Alemán.

The diocese and the cathedral have suffered many setbacks in the course of their history. In the first place, proximity to Salamanca was a cause of friction. Almost from the beginning the cathedral chapter in Salamanca fought against the project and later made life as difficult as possible for the chapter in Ciudad Rodrigo, seeking to annex the territory for itself.

Secondly, the position of the town itself, almost on the border with Portugal, made it subject to frequent attacks in wars between Castile and Portugal in the fourteenth and fifteenth centuries. A period of relative calm in the sixteenth century was marked by the reconstruction of churches in the diocese before again the territory was plunged into chaos in the War of Portuguese Independence (1640–68). The town and its frontier villages were sacked and the cathedral lost almost all its possessions. But worse was to come: many archival documents were forcibly destroyed during the nineteenth century, and then in the middle of the last century, during a heavy storm, part of the cathedral roof collapsed; many volumes of chapter acts and other documents suffered water damage or were completely destroyed.

The capitular acts commenced in 1443. The records of the musical life of the institution which survive, prior to Esquivel's time, make frequent reference to the appointment of chapelmasters, precentors, organists, priests and choir boys, and it is clear that, like every other cathedral, the chapter spent considerable sums of money to attract good candidates. The first *maestro de capilla* was appointed in 1494, Giraldin Bucher (*alias* Buxer, Buxel, Bujel). He was succeeded by his son, Diego, in 1522; following this appointment there was a steady stream of *maestros* – Juan Cepa, Cuñeda, and Juan Navarro (Esquivel's teacher) – before Esquivel's succession to the post in 1591.

It seems that *ministriles* were received at a very early stage in Ciudad Rodrigo, in contrast to practice in other cathedrals. An act of 1544 makes reference to trumpeters; they are ordered to play on all *fiestas*; they were to play as a group of four, otherwise the chapter would not pay the salary. Starting from 1565, a year in which some new instrumentalists were received, the acts always refer to *ministriles*, four or five in number at first, but then five seems to have been the norm. On 21 October of that year the town hall made an agreement to help pay for alto minstrels through an annual payment of 2,000 *maravedís* and, in 1567, a canon was charged with the task of bringing from England 'diferencias de instrumentos de menestriles, flautas [probably recorders] y orlos [wind instruments, possibly crumhorns] y otros instrumentos para servir la iglesia'. There are further references in the capitular acts to the purchase of shawms, mute cornets and sackbuts. It is interesting to note that one of the minstrels serving the Church in 1567 was Milanese; others were Spaniards.

Chanzonetas de Navidad are first mentioned in 1560, and it is clear that their performance involved acting or the uses of stage machinery.[106] Throughout the seventeenth century, there are various notices that record the *maestro de capilla* setting aside various days before the feasts of Christmas and Corpus Christi to compose the required *villancicos*; the singers and instrumentalists, too, had days set aside to learn and rehearse the new music in the *coro*. In 1687, the cathedral still had a collection of *libros de canto* composed by Esquivel, and mention is made of the instruments played there around this time: sackbuts, shawms of various sizes, cornets, small *bajones*, harp and organ.

A useful document for filling in details of the cathedral establishment at Ciudad Rodrigo in Esquivel's day is the *Historia Civitatense* by the seventeenth-century historian Antonio Sánchez Cabañas. The original manuscript of this work is in the library of Salamanca University,[107] and a complete modern edition is now available, replacing an older abbreviated version.[108] Sánchez Cabañas was a native of Cáceres and came to Ciudad Rodrigo cathedral as a choir chaplain (*capellán de coro*) and prebendary with the post of cantor.[109] In chapter one of the second part of his lengthy work, he records in minute detail the staffing structure of this ancient cathedral establishment, useful information which enables us to see how a relatively small cathedral functioned in the late sixteenth and early seventeenth centuries.

According to Cabañas, in ancient times the cathedral was a Benedictine establishment with no more than twelve canons, who lived in community with their bishop. In Cabañas's time there were eighteen canons, eleven *raçioneros* (prebendaries), twenty-two *capellanes* (choir chaplains), two priests, six sacristans and a head sacristan. Seven senior posts are named: the first to be named is the dean; below the dean is the *chantre* (precentor), a position which carries a prebend, but the post holder is not a canon and therefore does not have voting rights; next come the archdeacons of Sabugal (now in Portugal) and Camaces; the fifth post is that of schoolmaster, who is the richest of the dignitaries named because he receives two prebends – one by virtue of his office and another because he is a canon; next comes the post of treasurer; finally, the archdeacon of Ciudad Rodrigo, the last of the senior prebendary positions to be added to the list.

There were also four other prebendary *ex officio* canons: a doctoral canon who was a lawyer and given the responsibility of looking after the cathedral's legal affairs; a magisterial canon who had preaching responsibilities; a lectural canon who had

---

106 *Chanzonettas* were similar in style to the *villancicos*: songs with refrain, usually sacred, and related in form to the sixteenth-century Italian *canzonetta*.

107 Biblioteca Universidad de Salamanca, MS 1708–10, 3 vols.

108 Antonio Sánchez Cabañas, *Historia Civitatense. Estudio introductorio y edición*, ed. Ángel Barrios García and Iñaki Martín Viso (Ciudad Rogdrigo, Salamanca, 2001).

109 M. Hernández Vegas, *Ciudad Rodrigo: la catedral y la ciudád*, 2 vols. (2nd edn, Salamanca, 1982), II, p. 176.

the job of expounding scripture; lastly, a canon penitentiary who heard confession. With reference to this last, it is interesting that Cabañas adds that this was a post demanded by the Council of Trent. Clearly, he was up to date in his knowledge of what was expected by the reformed Catholic Church; indeed, before beginning his outline of senior posts he had already mentioned a canon from chapter twelve of the Council's twenty-fourth session.

Cabañas implies that eight of the eleven prebendary post-holders receive only a half-prebend; among these are the *maestro de capilla*, organist and singers, of whom the latter, it seems, received only a quarter of a prebend. Of the twenty-two choir chaplains listed, twelve had ascended from the ranks of *mozos de coro*; they received only an eighth of a prebend.[110] Thus, Ciudad Rodrigo had a highly structured cathedral establishment typical of that found in many cathedral institutions in the late sixteenth century. Although the cathedral may not have ranked as one of the foremost musical establishments of the time, for a relatively small and low-income diocese (see footnote 98) the number of officials is impressive and indicates a highly organised ecclesiastical structure fully capable of attracting and supporting musicians of the first rank. According to Cabañas, the cathedral had a capitular income of 30,000 ducats and another 3,000 from the fabric; added to this was a sacristy rich in ornaments, vestments and other objects associated with Church ritual.

Piecing together all these diverse fragments of knowledge from different sources, one builds up a picture of a cathedral with a vigorous musical life, a situation which would present a challenge to Esquivel in his role as *maestro de capilla*.

Calahorra

The diocese of Calahorra in the province of Rioja is one of the most ancient in Spain; in the Middle Ages it became one of the most extensive, holding more than a thousand parishes. After a legal dispute in 1221, regarding the seat of the bishopric, Calahorra became the place where the bishop resided.

Little evidence is available regarding the status of music prior to the sixteenth century, but from the beginning of the century the capitular acts make frequent reference to the appointments of *maestro* (not yet called *maestro de capilla*), organists and other musicians. In comparison with many other cathedral establishments, the records in Calahorra are remarkably well preserved. Having said that, the cathedral has in fact lost what must have been a large body of music composed in the sixteenth and seventeenth centuries.

The capitular acts commence in 1451, at which time it seems polyphony was not sung in the cathedral. The *mozos de coro*, at that time in the charge of the archdeacon, numbered only two, but by 1470 there were four of them and polyphony was sung. A chapter statute for that year describes a situation that was common elsewhere: the *maestro* had to teach 'canto de organo and counterpoint to the choir boys and sing it in all official ceremonies'; moreover, 'the *maestro* and choir boys and contrapuntists must attend solemn mass'. By this time the cathedral had an

110 Sánchez Cabañas, *Historia Civitatense*, pp. 147–57.

organ and an organist. It is strange, therefore, that an inventory of *libros de coro* (choir books) of 1490 lists only *libros de canto llano* (plainchant books); there is no mention of polyphony.

By 1515, there were four professional singers in the choir, a number that in the following years augmented progressively. The first *maestro de capilla* to be mentioned by name was Juan Gómez de Quintanar, who by virtue of his office as singer and *maestro* was expected to sing *canto de órgano* on all feast days of duplex rank; 'he should teach the choir boys, beneficed clergy and priests of the choir who want to learn'.

The first mention of *ministriles* is in 1534, when it was agreed to employ them for the feasts of Ss Emeterio and Celedonio, Calahorra's patron saints. But there is no further mention of minstrels until 1571, after which time they are mentioned regularly. Clearly, the cathedral amassed quite a large collection of instruments. A highly detailed document of 1593 gives an interesting account of the number and types of instrument the cathedral possessed: two sackbuts, two *bajones* – 'one large and the other small' – six shawms, four tenor and two soprano, seventeen *flautas* (recorders), three small flutes, three black cornetts, three cornamuse, a chest of fifes 'with fine pieces', one dulcian 'with its box', the dulcian itself decorated with silver, 'three very old dulcians of little value', four *vihuelas de arco* (bowed vihuelas) with three *arquillas* (bows) decorated with silver, apart from the double bass which lacked the tip and four other bows without decoration. This is an impressive list by the standards of the day.

From 1545, the number of rehearsals for the singers is codified. At that time, there had to be twice-weekly rehearsals, but later they were to be daily except on the days when they would have *canto de órgano*. *Castrati* are mentioned for the first time in 1551. In 1552 five books of motets by Guerrero were bought, to be followed in 1593 by a book of music by Victoria, for which the chapter paid six ducats.

1567 is the first mention of the feast of Corpus Christi, when the *maestro de capilla*, Francisco Velasco, requested some money and a lamb for the feast. In 1572, there is an agreement by which the *maestro de capilla* and the singers should be given a fortnight's licence in order to prepare the *villancicos* and *chanzonetas* that they had to sing in the Christmas feast. 1574 is the first agreement which mentions that a bonus of two ducats should be paid to the *maestro de capilla* for the Christmas festivities; these included scenic representations.

During the ultimate decades of the sixteenth century, instruments already performed an essential role in the cathedral's services, but the minstrels performed under their own director and not under the directorship of the *maestro de capilla*. Clearly this situation had changed by 1635, for an agreement of that year gives the *maestro de capilla* authority to order the minstrels to 'play different songs, and not the same ones in all feasts'.

The musical life of the cathedral continued with vigour into the seventeenth century, and to the normal body of wind instruments were added stringed instruments. In 1601, a Venetian named 'Gabriel', a player of the *vihuela*, was employed to teach this instrument; other stringed instruments mentioned around this time are the *violones*, and *vihuelas de arco*.

The Christmas *villancicos* are specifically mentioned in chapter acts of 1603 and 1604. By then it had become standard practice for two canons to examine the *villancicos* with a view to censoring their words and music and, if thought necessary, to request changes. The seriousness in which composition of these pieces was taken is encapsulated in a later act of 1627: if the music did not conform to the appropriate degree of gravity and authority which such a day required, 'the *maestro* must put it into such a form that it is the best it can be'.

Oviedo

The diocese of Oviedo is even older than the dioceses of Ciudad Rodrigo and Calahorra. It can be traced back to the reign of Alfonso II in the ninth century. The original cathedral building was erected by Alfonso's father; Alfonso II built a new cathedral on the ruins of this structure, which was in turn replaced by the present-day cathedral of San Salvador, work on which was begun at the end of the fourteenth century but not completed until 1556.

The independent region of Asturias, with Oviedo as its capital, was an important centre of Visigothic culture, and the cathedral practised the ancient Mozarabic rite. However, little is known of the musical life of the cathedral prior to the sixteenth century: the fourteenth-century *Libro de las constituciones* of Bishop Gutierre de Toledo (bishop of Oviedo 1377–89) speaks only of a precentor and sub-precentor without giving details of their musical obligations; and the *libros de cantorales* (books of plainsong) preserved today date from after the seventeenth century. Already in the fourteenth century the church is known to have possessed an organ, or possibly two organs,[111] but not until the publication of the cathedral's statutes in 1558 do we have detailed information on how music in the cathedral was organised.

The capitular acts commenced in 1508, and shortly afterwards the cathedral's first *maestro de capilla* was appointed, probably as a singer – a *primus inter pares* – rather than a musician given an obligation to compose.[112] Thus a succession of chapel masters preceded Esquivel's appearance in this role in 1581, by which time, as the 1558 *Estatutos de la santa iglesia catedral de Oviedo* of D. Diego Aponte de Quiños make clear, polyphony was sung at First and Second Vespers, at solemn mass on double feasts, at the principal mass on Sundays, on feast days commemorating the dead, at the principal feasts of the Virgin and at Matins of each of these. The duties of those responsible for the musical life of the cathedral – *maestro de capilla*, *chantre* (precentor), *sochantre* (sub-precentor), *contrabajo* (bass singer), *capellanes de coro* (choir chaplains), *mozos de coro* (boy choristers) and organist – are outlined in detail, together with other (non-musical) posts. There is mention of *ministriles* in the *Estatutos*, but the capitular acts of 1595 make reference to four named individuals. The only instruments cited are the *bajon*, and the flute which one player later requested.[113]

111 Emilio Casares Rodicio, *La música en la catedral de Oviedo* (Oviedo, 1980), p. 16–17.
112 Ibid., p. 71.
113 Ibid., p. 110.

With the exception of the *ministriles*, the salaries paid to these musicians are recorded and give a good indication of the importance attached to the various duties. The *maestro*, organist and *contrabajo* each received a whole prebend; three prebends, divided into six semi-prebends, were allotted to six *capellanes*, who in return were expected to sing *canto de organo* (polyphony). Folio 36 of the Oviedo statutes lays out the duties of the unspecified number of boy choristers who were expected to assist both the *maestro* and sub-precentor; a half-prebend was distributed among all of them – a small amount of money, given what would be expected of them in the year-by-year servicing of the cathedral's music.[114]

There were frequent acquisitions of polyphonic choir books during the sixteenth century. Music by Guerrero and Victoria was once part of the cathedral's library, and some of the music which Esquivel included in his 1608 publications may well have been performed in Oviedo. The cathedral seems to have had a taste for dramatic para-liturgical forms on festive occasions. In addition to the celebrations of Christmas, Corpus Christi and the feasts of Oviedo's patronal saint, Eulalia, the chapter acts make reference to the *sibila*, *auto* (religious play) and *entremés* (interludes). The *sibila*, a dramatic form of Mozarabic origin and a mixture of sacred and secular elements, was performed on Christmas night: alongside the traditional figures associated with the Nativity, there appeared various legendary figures, among whom was the celebrated sibyl of Cumae, whose prophecy was concerned with the transience of life and the final judgement after death. By the sixteenth century, the *sibilas* were polyphonic compositions sung in the vernacular and the chapter acts make clear that it was the chapelmaster's responsibility to compose new settings each year.[115] None of this music survives, so that our picture of the musical life of Oviedo in the time of Esquivel is sadly incomplete. But sufficient documentation survives to create a picture of a rich musical environment in that city. Here, as elsewhere, the life of a *maestro de capilla* would have been a very busy one.

114 Ibid., p. 88.
115 Ibid., pp. 101–4.

Plate 1. Esquivel in full clerical dress, as reproduced by Albert Geiger

2

BIOGRAPHICAL DETAILS

THE KNOWN FACTS OF ESQUIVEL'S LIFE ARE FEW: we do not even know the date of his birth. The amount of contemporary documentary evidence available to us is slender and sometimes conflicting, and has led to much speculation on the part of later scholars. In an attempt to unravel the facts of Esquivel's life we shall first examine the documentary evidence that does remain and then study the contributions of recent scholars who have attempted to shed further light on the composer's life and work.

During the sixteenth century, detailed records were kept of cathedral chapter meetings. The minutiae of day-to-day decisions made by the chapter on such matters as the fabric of the building, the employment of musicians and so forth were recorded in the capitular acts (*actas capitulares*); these make fascinating reading as well being a valuable source of information for later historians. Thus it is to the *actas capitulares* of the cathedral of Ciudad Rodrigo, Esquivel's birthplace, that we turn for the first piece of documentary evidence.

There, in an isolated reference for 22 October 1568, it is recorded that Juan de Esquivel is received as a *mozo de coro*.[1] The term *mozo de coro* was usually applied to the altar boys as distinct from *seises* – members of the choir who were trained in polyphony – although, as Samuel Rubio has noted, not all capitular acts make a clear distinction between the two groups; sometimes the term *mozo de coro* is applied indiscriminately to both groups.[2] In the absence of any clear interpretation of this terminology we cannot be sure to which group Esquivel belonged. This is unfortunate since it would help to shed some light on his age when admitted to the service of the cathedral.

The *seises* were young boys, frequently six in number, hence their name. They were chosen by the *maestro de capilla* and admitted to cathedral service by the chapter by virtue of their vocal ability. Having been admitted, they usually lived with the *maestro* who had the additional task of providing for their physical needs as well as being responsible for their musical training. The *mozos de coro*, on the other hand, were older boys admitted only on examination by a sub-committee appointed for the purpose by the cathedral chapter. This sub-committee consisted of the sub-precentor, the chapelmaster and another canon. The Malaga acts specify

1 Ciudad Rodrigo, 'Actas capitulares', VII, fol. 174r.
2 Rubio, *Historia de la música española*, p. 34.

the material for the examination: Christian doctrine, reading, writing and helping at mass.[3] It is obvious that the content of this examination is more appropriate for older rather than younger children. Thus, if Esquivel was admitted as a *seisé* – that is as a choir boy – he may well have been as young as eight or nine; if he was admitted as a *mozo de coro*, he may well have been slightly older, perhaps a young teenager around thirteen or fourteen. All that we can say for certain, therefore, regarding his date of birth is that he was born around or just before 1560, depending on how we interpret the information given in the capitular acts.

Whichever group Esquivel belonged to, the influence of the Church on his upbringing was clearly profound. As an altar boy, he would have built up an enormous knowledge of chant and an understanding of liturgy that could not have failed to influence his musical thinking; as a choirboy, of course, his musical training would have been far more comprehensive, giving him a detailed knowledge of the art of counterpoint as well as enabling him to function effectively as a singer.

Unfortunately, there are no further references to Esquivel in those sections of the capitular acts of Ciudad Rodrigo cathedral which have survived. The last reference is for 17 October 1572 on folio 227*v*. After that the volume skips to folio 240, which is blank, as are the following folios until 244. Those following until the end of the volumes have suffered gravely from damp in such a way that for the most part they are illegible. In effect, then, we are deprived of any useful information until March 1642, the next legible entry, which is long past the time when the archives could have been of use to us in investigating the musical life of the cathedral in the time of Esquivel.

It is again to the seventeenth-century historian Antonio Sánchez Cabañas that we must turn for more details. His *Historia Civitatense* gives us valuable if only brief information on Esquivel's career and his music, although, as we shall see, some of the writer's facts are inaccurate. Cabañas writes concisely, recording facts as he remembers them without much elaboration. He names Esquivel's predecessors in the post of *maestro de capilla* in Ciudad Rodrigo; he states that Esquivel was a native of the city, a choir boy at the cathedral there, and a pupil of Juan Navarro. He then lists the churches Esquivel went on to serve: Oviedo, where he was a canon,[4] Calahorra and Ávila before he returned to Ciudad Rodrigo. According to Cabañas, Esquivel had a strong attachment to the cathedral for 'no a querido dexarla por otra ninguna yglesia por que el amor de su patria le fuerca no salir del la' ('he did not want to vacate it for any other church because love of his native land was too strong to enable him to leave it').[5]

Then follows reference to three printed works: a book of masses and another of motets for all the year; and another large volume which contains three books, the

---

3 Ibid., p. 35.

4 Sánchez Cabañas, *Historia Civitatense*, p. 154. It is unlikely that Esquivel was a canon since his name is not recorded in the cathedral's 'Libros de límpia de sangre' for the 1580s. These books indicate 'purity of blood', i.e. freedom from Jewish or Moorish racial origin, proof of which would have been a requirement for the position of a cathedral canon at that time. I am grateful to Michael O'Connor for drawing my attention to Oviedo's 'Libros de límpia de sangre'.

5 Ibid.

first of *fabordones*, the second of hymns, and the third of Magnificats and masses. Of the last he tells us:

> This volume is all of three hundred leaves and is valued by those of the Royal Council at thirty ducats. It is a book of great importance and useful for all the churches of Spain and no-one should have to be without it because his music is skilful and very sonorous to the ear.[6]

These three volumes can be identified as the *Liber primus missarum* (1608), *Motecta festorum et dominicarum cum communi sanctorum* (1608) and *Tomus secundus, psalmorum, hymnorum . . . et missarum* (1613).

But perhaps the most interesting piece of information of all is a reference to another book of music. In the second part of his *Historia Civitatense*, on folio 19*v*, we find scribbled in the margin the following:

> In 1623 another book was printed in Salamanca of songs for instrumentalists and *fabordones*, hymns and motets. It is a curious book and for study.[7]

As far as I am aware, there is no extant copy of this book and it is not clear what Cabañas means when he uses the phrase 'de estudio'. But the reference implies that Esquivel was probably still alive in 1623, several years after the publication of what has hitherto been assumed to be his last publication of 1613.[8]

Given Cabañas's eulogy, his reference to the composer is tantalisingly brief. No evidence is given to support his assertion that Navarro was Esquivel's teacher, although, given that the older master was chapelmaster in Ciudad Rodrigo in the time of Esquivel's youth, this is quite likely.[9] Nor is there any documentary evidence to support the Ávila connection. Andrés Sánchez Sánchez's recent account of music in Ávila cathedral during the sixteenth century lists every *maestro de capilla* since the inception of the post in 1526 up until 1594;[10] Esquivel's name does not appear on this list, although he did visit the city in 1589 in search of an organist for Calahorra, and it may be this visit that Cabañas was referring to when he stated – albeit

6 Ibid. 'es todo este bolumen de trecientas hoxas y esta tasado por los del Real Consezo en treinta ducados es libro de mucha consideracion y provecho para todas las yglesias despaña y ninguna abria destar sin el porque su musica es artificiosa y muy sonora al oydo.'

7 Ibid., p. 154, n. 61. 'el año de 1623 saco otro libro a luz inpresso en Salamanca de canciones para ministriles y favordones himnos y motetes. Es libro curiosso y de estudio.'

8 An inventory for the year 1627 at Zamora cathedral ('Libro de visitas pastorales del fondo documental de la catedral de Zamora', libro II, fols. 118*v*–119*r*) records: 'quatro libros de Esquibel de canto de hórgano grandes' ('four large books of polyphony by Esquivel'). Maybe, given the date, this is the missing book of 1623 referred to by Cabañas. See Alejandro Luis Iglesias, 'El maestro de capilla Diego de Bruceña (1567/71–1623 y el impreso perdido de su *Libro de misas, magnificats y motetes* (Salamanca: Susan Muñoz, 1620)', in Crawford and Wagstaff, *Encomium Musicae*, p. 459.

9 Navarro was chapelmaster at Ciudad Rodrigo from 1574 until 1587, following his dismissal from Salamanca on disciplinary grounds. See Stevenson, *Spanish Cathedral Music*, p. 246.

10 A. Sánchez Sánchez, 'La música en la catedral de Ávila hasta finales del siglo XVI', in *De música hispana et aliis: miscelánea en honour al Prof. Dr. José López-Calo, S.J., en su 65° cumpleaños*, I (Santiago, 1990), pp. 363–85.

incorrectly – that Esquivel served there. The Oviedo and Calahorra connections, however, can be verified with reference to the capitular acts of the respective cathedrals where Esquivel's name does appear.

The post of *maestro de capilla* in Oviedo became vacant in 1581. Esquivel's appointment came as a result of a protracted legal battle – no doubt typical of many – made necessary by the cathedral authority's mishandling of the appointments process.[11] The chapter acts record the affair in some detail.

On 18 March, the chapter received a letter from Alonso Puro, chapelmaster in Zamora, expressing his interest in the post.[12] The chapter, however, had already sent an emissary, one Gonzalo de Solis, to look for a suitable replacement for the vacant prebend. As recorded in the chapter meeting of 27 March, Solis sent a letter saying that he has made contact with Esquivel, who was willing to come to Oviedo and demonstrate his suitability for the post.[13]

On 6 April, the chapter agreed to invite Alonso Puro to demonstrate his abilities in front of two named individuals and all the musicians the next day.[14] This he clearly did, for two days later the chapter agreed to lend him 100 *reales*,[15] presumably to cover his expenses, and he was given the option of staying in Oviedo or leaving until the time came for a contest.

On 5 May the chapter voted to examine Esquivel's abilities along with those of Alonso Puro.[16] But the following day, Esquivel appeared in person and presented a petition, in effect demanding the post promised to him.[17] He followed this up with another petition on 10 May, further reiterating his claim.[18]

The chapter was in a state of disarray, and the matter of two rival candidates clearly took up much time at chapter meetings, as the acts from May to September make evident. After what seems to have been an acrimonious debate on 11 May, a vote was taken in favour of Alonso Puro.[19] More petitions from the two rival candidates followed and the matter was finally taken to the chancery court of Valladolid, where, after much legal wrangling, Esquivel was declared the holder of the post on 15 November:

> This day a notary read an order from Prior Bandera, provisor of León, as apostolic judge, in favour of Juan Esquivel . . . and an edict and order in favour of the said Juan de Esquivel and, following the reading by the said notary, it was ordered that

11 A full account of this protracted dispute, based on a study of the chapter records, may be found in R. Arias del Valle, 'El magisterio de capilla de la catedral de Oviedo en el siglo XVI (1508–1597)', *Studium Ovetense* 6–7 (1978–80), pp. 128–32.

12 Oviedo cathedral, 'Actas capitulares' 1581–4, XVII, fol. 203*v*.

13 Ibid., fol. 205.

14 Ibid., fol. 207.

15 In Esquivel's time, in Castile, the main gold coin was the *ducado* or ducat, although this was gradually replaced by the *escudo*; the main silver coin was the *real*, while the coin of lesser value – for everyday use – was the *maravedí*. A ducat was worth 375 *maravedís* and 11 *reales*; one *real* was worth 34 *maravedís*. Accounts were kept in ducats even after the introduction of the *escudo*.

16 Ibid., fol. 216.

17 Ibid., fol. 216*v*.

18 Ibid., fol. 217*v*.

19 Ibid., fol. 218.

he should be given possession of the prebend of *maestro de capilla* within three days upon pain of excommunication.[20]

On 18 November Esquivel was officially installed as *maestro*.[21] Although we cannot be certain of his precise age when he took up this appointment, this small piece of legal history helps us to build up a more complete profile of the composer. If the conjectural date of his birth (around 1560) is correct, he must have been in his early twenties by the time he succeeded to this chapelmastership. It is unlikely that he would have been appointed to such a responsible post in his late teens, although it is just possible given that his more senior contemporary, Guerrero, took up his first chapelmastership at Jaen in 1546 when only eighteen.[22]

The tests for competitors for the post of *maestro de capilla* in Oviedo were as demanding as elsewhere. Candidates were asked to compose a motet in three, four or more parts based on a given plainsong, and set a psalm or antiphon text as proof of their compositional ability; further, at Oviedo, they were asked to compose a *villancico* on a text in Castilian.[23]

The cathedral's *Libro de estatutos y constituciones* lays out the duties of the chapel-master.[24] He was expected to teach singing 'to the people of the church' (i.e. anyone who wished to learn); this, of course, included the choir chaplains and boy choristers. Times for the lessons were specified. He was to provide music for double feasts of four copes, First and Second Vespers and High Mass; High Mass on every Sunday of the year; All Souls' day and specified Church anniversaries; Saturdays in Paschal time; the Marian feasts of the Assumption, Purification, Annunciation and Christmas, and at other times as directed by the president of the *coro*.[25] As elsewhere in Spain, he was also responsible for the examination of choir boys, but not responsible for their board and lodging, a situation which must have released him from some of the pressures felt by some of his distinguished contemporaries, including Guerrero, who did not find this task easy.[26]

20 'Leyo un notario este dia un mandamiento del prior bandera probisor de leon como juez apostolico en favor de Juan esquibel ... y un auto y orden en favor del dicho Juan esquibel y despues de leydo por el dicho notario parece manda se le de posesion dentro de tres dias de la prebenda de maestro de capilla sopena de excomunion.' Oviedo cathedral, 'Actas capitulares' 1581–4, XVII, fol. 267.

21 Oviedo cathedral, 'Actas capitulares' 1581–4, XVII, fol. 269.

22 Stevenson, *Spanish Cathedral Music*, p. 139.

23 Casares Rodicio, *La música en la catedral de Oviedo*, p. 85. Generically, the term *villancico* denotes learned songs composed by professional musicians in the vernacular, performed in a sacred context. For an introduction and summary of modern research into this characteristically Spanish genre, see Tess Knighton and Álvaro Torrente, eds., *Devotional Music in the Iberian World, 1450–1800: The Villancico and Related Genres* (Aldershot, 2007), pp. 1–14.

24 *Libro de los estatutos y constituciones de la Santa Iglesia Catedral de Oviedo, con el Ceremonial y Kalendario de sus fiestas antiguas, Ordenado por don Diego Aponte de Quiñones Obispo de la dicha iglesia, conde de Norveña y del consejo del Rey nuestro Señor, Juntamente con el Dean y Cabildo de su Santa Iglesia* (Salamanca: Juan Fernandez, 1558).

25 *Estatutos de la Santa Iglesia de Oviedo*, fols. 14–16, cited in Casares Rodicio, *La música en la catedral de Oviedo*, p. 84.

26 Guerrero was admonished at least twice in his career for his failure to give adequate attention to his choir boys. See Stevenson, *Spanish Cathedral Music*, pp. 160 and 170.

In addition to this formidable list of obligations must be added the composition of *villancicos* and music for the *autos* (religious plays) as required, especially at Christmas and Corpus Christi. The chapter acts make clear that Esquivel was paid extra for these and it is surprising that, given the number of references to them, none of this music seems to have survived.

The composition of *villancicos* must have been a formidable task for composers of Esquivel's generation – and indeed for composers of future generations throughout the seventeenth and eighteenth centuries. New *villancicos* were expected at the major festivals of Christmas, Epiphany and Corpus Christi – the Christmas season in particular imposing a heavy burden. We have no knowledge of the numerical requirements made of Esquivel in his three posts as *maestro de capilla*, but we do have numerical data for some cathedrals. For example, Toledo cathedral in 1604 required fourteen *villancicos*: ten for Christmas – eight at Matins and two at mass; and one for the feasts of St Stephen, St John the Evangelist, Circumcision and Epiphany. This number was probably exceeded in other establishments and gradually increased during the seventeenth century, making necessary some recycling of previously composed pieces for lesser liturgical occasions, since it would have been impossible for composers to find time to write the huge number of new compositions of this type required every year. The occasional nature of this repertoire was probably the main reason why we no longer have examples of Esquivel's contribution to this fascinating genre.[27]

It is clear from the chapter acts that Esquivel met with mixed fortune during his tenure in Oviedo and some clashes with the chapter are reported. One such clash occurred as a result of the practice of the musicians, including the *maestro de capilla*, of hiring themselves out to other parishes, presumably to enhance their incomes. On 25 March 1582 the chapter ordered this practice to cease.[28] Following this, the acts of 20 April make reference to 'many errors made by the singers in the *coro*'.[29]

The following year, again on 20 April, Esquivel brought to the chapter's attention the fact that the cost of providing music for the forthcoming *autos* of Corpus Christi would be more expensive.[30] He mentioned that in León there was a man who could do this and he was asked to arrange this.

In July, 1583, he requested and was granted permission to visit his home area to sing a new mass.[31] This request probably arose out of his desire to sing his first mass as a priest in his home town, although there is no actual record of his ordination. It may also explain why he felt it necessary to ask someone else to compose music for the Corpus Christi celebrations.

27 See Knighton and Torrente, *Devotional Music in the Iberian World*, pp. 99–148, for numerical data and for an in-depth exploration of performance practice, ceremonial context and function in relation to the *villancico*. Although Torrente's discussion is centred on the Book of Ceremonies of Salamanca cathedral compiled at a later date (*c*.1700), his chapter contains much useful information that is relevant to an earlier period.

28 Oviedo cathedral, 'Actas capitulares' 1581–4, XVII, fol. 314.

29 Ibid., fol. 319*v*.

30 Ibid., fol. 400*v*.

31 Ibid., fols. 414 and 415*v*.

In spite of extra payments for the composition of *villancicos* Esquivel seems not to have managed his finances well. By 3 August 1584 he was much in debt ('esta muy endeudado') and unable to pay off his loans;[32] the following year, a minute of 16 September implies that he and another chapter member (Pedro Ruiz) were both bankrupt, and it was agreed to discuss the matter at the first chapter meeting in October.[33] Finally, on 4 November, he abandoned his post, perhaps seeking a way out of his financial difficulties.[34] Following his sudden departure, the chapter agreed on 12 November to ask one Melchior de Arguelles to compose the Christmas *villancicos* since Esquivel had not done so before he left.[35]

As Cabañas's account implies, Esquivel's next move was to the cathedral of Calahorra in the Rioja region, where the post of *maestro* became vacant in 1585 following the death in April of the previous incumbent, Francisco de Belasco.[36] The appointment process, recorded in detail in the chapter acts, was a protracted affair and offers further insight into the complex and cumbersome administrative procedures that must have been replicated throughout Spain during the sixteenth and seventeenth centuries when vacancies for Church musicians arose.

Although Belasco died in April, it was not until 25 May that the chapter agreed to put in motion a procedure to find a successor.[37] On 26 September, further discussion took place: the organist, Domingo Garro, had at first signified his intention to stand for the post but had then withdrawn. It seems that there were no other suitable local candidates, but there were good musicians from Medinaceli, Oviedo, Burgos, Bilbao, Santo Domingo and from other places who were interested in the post. However, it was decided to extend the period when applications could be made until St Martin's day, 11 November, presumably in order to widen the field.[38]

On Tuesday, 12 November, the order went out that the notice for the vacant prebend, previously fixed to the doors of the cathedral, should be removed and four candidates were to be examined, the chapelmasters from Pamplona and Oviedo (Esquivel), Bilbao and Logroño. These gentlemen were to present themselves before a senior canon, Sebastián Fernandez, and Domingo Garro was ordered to be present.[39]

The examination took place the following day, and the applicants were given three tests: each was expected to demonstrate his ability directing the choir at the *atril* (lectern) in the performance of Josquin's *Missa fa re mi re*;[40] they were set the task of devising soprano and bass voice parts for the 'Et incarnatus' of the Credo from the same mass; lastly, they were given the plainsong antiphon *Gaude Sion filia*

---

32 Oviedo cathedral, 'Actas capitulares' 1584–6, XVIII, fol. 39.

33 Ibid., fol. 136.

34 Ibid., fol. 146.

35 Ibid., fol. 153.

36 His death is recorded in Calahorra cathedral, 'Actas capitulares' 1585–7, CXVII, fol. 154*v*.

37 Ibid., fol. 160*v*.

38 Ibid., fol. 176*v*.

39 Ibid., fols. 184*v*–185*r*.

40 Ibid., fols. 186*v*–187*r*. Actually *Missa Faisant regretz*, in which Josquin makes extensive use of the *fa re mi re* motive from Alexander Agricola's chanson *Tout a par moy*. In Agricola's chanson, the motive is attached to the phrase *Faisant regretz* in line four and appears throughout the second half of the chanson as a *cantus firmus*.

qui celebras beati Dominici hodie annua solemnia and asked to write a polyphonic setting in five parts with two soprano parts, setting the antiphon as a *cantus firmus* in breves. All candidates were ordered to appear at the chapter meeting the next day[41] – presumably to hear who was to be appointed. Esquivel was the successful candidate and his presence at a chapter meeting is recorded in the minutes for 23 and 29 November, where he is listed as a *medio racionero*.[42]

As *maestro*, his duties were very similar to those he performed in Oviedo: he was expected to teach singing and counterpoint not only to choir boys and adult singers, but to any prebendary who wished to learn both plainsong and polyphonic settings of psalm verses, antiphons and other items for the celebration of Vespers; he was expected to prepare music for the mass and Holy Office, and officiate over the singers at all daily masses, the Mass for the Trinity on Wednesdays, and the Saturday votive Mass for the Virgin; he was also required to provide the customary *villancicos* and music for the feasts of Christmas, Easter, Pentecost and Corpus Christi.[43]

Several references to the *maestro de capilla* in the chapter acts are of little significance; they deal with the day-to-day minutiae of cathedral administration, such as making corrections to books in the cathedral's library, admitting new choirboys and so forth. However, other entries suggest that, as at Oviedo, Esquivel's time in Calahorra was not entirely trouble-free.

On 13 August 1588, it is recorded that he and a licentiate by the name of Manzanedo were confined to their respective houses day and night under threat of a hefty fine of fifty ducats.[44] On 5 September, the sentence was lifted but the chapter reserved the right to renew it if necessary.[45] On 3 October 1588, he was again subject to disciplinary proceedings for falsely stating that a choirboy was ill when this was not so, but excused the fine of the day for this minor misdemeanour.[46]

A journey to Ávila in search of a new organist must have had significance for Esquivel. Protracted correspondence between the cathedral chapter and Alonso Gómez, an organist at Ávila cathedral, is recorded in the acts and reveals the delicate negotiations which often took place between cathedral chapters and their prospective employees in the late sixteenth century.

Gómez had come to the notice of the Church authorities in Calahorra as a suitable candidate to fill the vacant organist's post there, and on 19 May 1588 it was agreed to offer him a half-prebend.[47] But nearly one month later the members of the chapter were clearly divided on the procedure to follow; the vote was split between those who were happy to accept Gómez by virtue of his reputation, and those who thought it necessary to go to Ávila to hear him play. It was finally resolved to send

41 Calahorra cathedral, 'Actas capitulares' 1585, CXVII, fol. 187r.
42 Ibid.
43 These duties are set out in the 'Estatutos y Ordenanzas de esta Sancta Iglesia Cathedral de Calahorra que hizo el Htmo S.or Obispado Don Pedro Manso con asistencia de los Comisarios de dho Cavildo en la dha Ciudád a 11, dias del mes de Abril de 1595', fol. 213.
44 Calahorra cathedral, 'Actas capitulares' 1588, CXVIII, fol. 24v.
45 Ibid., fol. 75r.
46 Ibid., fol. 84r.
47 Calahorra cathedral, 'Actas capitulares' 1588, CXVII, fols. 57r and 57v.

one Damien Torres to perform this duty.[48] However, over one year later, Gómez had still not taken possession of the post. A chapter act of 13 October 1589 suggests some impatience on behalf of the dean, who pointed out that the post had been vacant for such a long time, and it was finally agreed to offer the candidate the job.[49] Esquivel was dispatched to Ávila in search of Gómez, who appeared before the chapter on 11 November to express his thanks to the chapter, as was the custom.[50]

While in Ávila, Esquivel would probably have made contact with Sebastián de Vivanco: both men were to become near neighbours, Vivanco in Ávila and Esquivel in Ciudad Rodrigo; moreover, their respective works were published by the same publisher in Salamanca, Artus Taberniel.[51]

During Esquivel's tenure, there are references to breaches of discipline on the part of the choir. Ordered worship was a particular concern of the post-Council of Trent reformers who wished to encourage the imposition and invention of silence.[52] Pre-Tridentine worship could be noisy, with a celebration of mass profaned by the sound of chatter from the laity who attended. Cut off from the centre of activity in the *coro*, it is not perhaps surprising that the laity reacted in this way, but the conduct of the clergy was in some instances little better. Cathedral canons were notorious for their persistent chatter, quarrelling in the aisles, and shouting across the building.[53] To find references to the need to be silent in public worship therefore is no surprise. Thus, a chapter minute of 4 June 1590 reminds the chapter that silence in the *coro* is expected.[54] Twelve days later the same subject came up for discussion again.[55] This minute of 16 June suggests that orderly discussion was lacking at times in chapter meetings as well as in the *coro* and expresses the resolve of the members of the chapter to deal with the problem.

Several times in the acts, there are hints at some of the tedium that must have attached itself to the post of *maestro de capilla*. Clearly, choir discipline was an issue for Esquivel. Almost two years after his appointment he was still seeking instruction in what he must do in the service of the cathedral. A chapter act records that 'the musicians should obey the master and always when they come to sing at the school';[56] shortly after, we are told 'the choirboys should obey the *maestro de capilla* and enter and leave the *coro* with reverence'.[57] There are references to the revelries on the day of the Holy Innocents (28 December), an old ritual in the Church calendar (it can be documented back to the twelfth century), when here, as well as elsewhere in Spain, roles where reversed and a boy bishop ruled for the day. In 1587 there must

48 Calahorra cathedral, 'Actas capitulares' 1588, CXVIII, fol. 62*v*.

49 Ibid., fol. 174*r*.

50 Ibid., fol. 186*r*.

51 Francisco Rodilla León, 'Nuevos datos sobre la capilla musical de la catedral de Calahorra a finales del siglo xvi. El magisterio de Juan Esquivel de barahona (1585–1891)', *Nassarre-Zaragoza* (2004), p. 405.

52 Kamen, *The Phoenix and the Flame*, p. 129.

53 Ibid., p. 129.

54 Calahorra cathedral, 'Actas capitulares' 1590, CXVIII, fol. 248*r*.

55 Ibid., fol. 257*v*.

56 Calahorra cathedral, 'Actas capitulares' 1587, CXVII, fols. 362*r* and 362*v*.

57 Ibid., fol. 394*v*.

have been some trouble at this annual event because a chapter act of 24 December that year forbids the choirboys to make a boy bishop for the forthcoming feast.[58]

In passing, it is worth noting that not all choristers described as *mozos de coro* were young boys. This is clear from the acts which refer to 'capons' (*castrati*). Thus, for example, Juan Buatista from Nájera was received as a *mozo de coro* on 2 June 1590 with the privilege of having his own room – an indication, perhaps, that he was not accommodated with the younger choristers in the house of the choirmaster, as was common practice.[59]

Ensuring a regular supply of choristers must have been a major concern for Esquivel and the cathedral chapter, and several chapter acts record evidence of what must have been delicate financial negotiations with the adult singers, not all of whom were ordained clergy or members of the religious community. Early in Esquivel's tenure (3 November 1587),[60] the chapter had voted to increase the number of *mozos de coro* to eight, but we are not informed why this was thought to be necessary.

The instrumentalists (*ministriles*), too, gave trouble. On 15 June 1587, one Sebastián Pérez was dismissed from his post, 'por justa causas'.[61] Six days later, as ordered by the dean and chapter, he gave an account on the state of the cathedral's instruments.[62] He was soon replaced by one Damián de Torres.[63]

Esquivel left Calahorra in 1591, but the exact reason for his departure is not clear. On 20 April, he had been granted leave of absence, but there is no mention of his whereabouts in the minutes of the chapter meeting for that day.[64] He may have gone 'home' to Ciudad Rodrigo since the post of *maestro* had been vacant there since February, when Alonso de Tejeda, the previous incumbent, moved on to León.[65] Perhaps his failure to be given a full prebend was a constant cause of dispute with the cathedral authorities; or perhaps it was love of his home area, as Cabañas implies, that drew him back. In a letter from Ciudad Rodrigo received by the cathedral chapter on 1 June (sadly now lost), he stated his reasons for leaving Calahorra, whatever they were, and agreed that his half-prebend should be declared vacant.[66] The chapter accepted his resignation and on 13 July agreed to pay the portion of the meat ration owing to him.[67]

In 1601 Esquivel appears to have rejected a post at Burgos cathedral. The chapter acts for 13 July record the chapter's agreement to invite Esquivel 'hacer demostración de su habilidad' ('to demonstrate his proficiency').[68] He may also have turned down an appointment at Salamanca cathedral for, on Wednesday, 7 August 1602, there was a debate in the cathedral chapter concerning the appointment of a new chapelmaster

58 Ibid., fol. 403r.
59 Calahorra cathedral, 'Actas capitulares' 1590, CXVIII, fol. 247v.
60 Calahorra cathedral, 'Actas capitulares' 1587, CXVII, fol. 379r.
61 Ibid., fol. 362r.
62 Ibid., fol. 362v.
63 Ibid., fol. 369v.
64 Calahorra cathedral, 'Actas capitulares' 1591, CXVIII, fol. 287r.
65 Alonso de Tejeda, *Obras completas*, ed. D. Preciado, I (Madrid, 1974), p. 22.
66 Calahorra cathedral, 'Actas capitulares' 1591, CXVIII, fol. 294r.
67 Ibid., fol. 298r.
68 J. López-Calo, *La música en la catedral de Burgos*, IV: *Documentario musical, Actas capitulares*, II (1601–28) (Burgos, 1996), p. 19.

to fill the post vacated previously by Alonso de Tejeda; the organist, Barnardo Clavijo del Castillo, and a prebendary named Zarate, recommended Esquivel, and it was agreed that he should be approached in Ciudad Rodrigo.[69] If an offer was made, Esquivel declined the post, for it is recorded that Sebastián de Vivanco appeared before the chapter to express his thanks for the benefit bestowed upon him.[70]

After this point information on Esquivel is sparse because, as we have seen, the chapter acts covering the years after which he took up his post in Ciudad Rodrigo no longer exist. However, we know that he was there in 1608 because the title page of his mass publication of that year bears the description *Missarum Ioannis Esquivelis*[71] *in alma ecclesia Civitatensi portionarii, et cantorum praefecti . . .*[72] This confirms his position as a prebendary and chapelmaster. Moreover, an engraving shows Esquivel in clerical dress (see Plate 1). That he was still at the cathedral in 1613 we know from the title page of his *Tomus secundus* of that year where he is again described as a *civitatensis* and a *portionarius* (see Plate 2), and the approbation and licence to print refer to him as *maestro de capilla*. From the dedicatory letter to this publication we know that Pedro Ponce de León, a former bishop of Ciudad Rodrigo, was his benefactor (see Chapter 3 for more details).

This account of Esquivel's life leaves many questions unanswered. All that we know may be summarised in a few words: he was probably born in the small town of Ciudad Rodrigo, fifty miles south-west of Salamanca, around 1560 and received his early musical training in that city; he moved to the position of chapelmaster at Oviedo in 1581 and Calahorra in 1585 before returning to his home town, Ciudad Rodrigo, in 1591, where he stayed until he died some time after 1623.

But there is one more interesting piece of information given to us by Antonio Cabañas which reveals something of the esteem in which Esquivel was held in his native city. In one of his descriptions of the cathedral of Ciudad Rodrigo found in his *Historia Civitatense*, Cabañas says:

69 'el señor racionero Zárate dio relación de la suficiencia de Esquivel, maestro de capilla de Ciudad Rodrigo, y el maestro Clavijo a quien se remitió entró en el cabildo e hizo relación de su suficiencia. Y, oídos ambos, el cabildo acordó que el dicho maestro de capilla le traiga consigo el dicho señor racionero Zárate que dijo iba a Ciudad Rodrigo, para que sea visto y examinado y se trate de recibirlo.' Salamanca cathedral, 'Actas capitulares' XXXIIII (1600–16), fol. 18r–v, in Tejeda, *Obras completas*, I, pp. 41–2, 46.

70 'Este día [miércoles, 2 de octubre de 1602] y cabildo entró en él maestro Vivanco, maestro de capilla, y depués de haber dado gracias de la mercad que se le había hecho en su provisión, y ofrecido sevirla en general y particular y dado cuenta de otras cosas.' Salamanca cathedral, 'Actas capitulares' XXXIIII, fol. 123, in Tejeda, *Obras completas*, I, p. 46.

71 There has been some confusion over Esquivel's name. 'Ioannis Esquivel' appears on the title page of his printed music in 1608 and 1613, but in the approbation by the poet-musician Vicente Espinel, and the printing licence issued by Martin de Córdoba, his name is shown as 'Juan' and 'Ioan de Esquivel Barahona' respectively. There are other variants, but it seems likely that 'Juan Esquivel Barahona' is his correct full name. Since Spaniards retain the name of both parents, it is possible that 'Esquivel' is the family name of his father and 'Barahona' that of his mother. See Snow, *The 1613 Print*, p. 9.

72 This is the title given by Albert Geiger in his article 'Juan Esquivel: ein unbekannter spanischer Meister des 16. Jahrhunderts', *Festschrift zum 50. Geburtstag Adolf Sandberger* (Munich, 1918), pp. 138–69.

this sacred temple has twenty-eight altars, and one of these privileged, which is that
dedicated to San Ildefonso, on which is said requiem mass for the repose of souls in
purgatory by applying to the dead the indulgence *per modum suffragi*. On this altar
is said every Monday of the year a Requiem Mass for the *maestro de capilla*, Juan de
Esquivel, and for the souls of his parents.[73]

This was common practice in the Catholic Church throughout Europe, when
Christians sought release from purgatory – believed to be a temporary abode to
which the soul went immediately after death – by setting aside money to pay for
masses to be said on their behalf for the repose of their souls. This often resulted in
large sums of money being paid to priests to perform this ritual, and an obsession
with the number of masses said and the number of candles burnt. The Council
of Trent, concerned with what it regarded as 'suspicious' liturgies, put an end to
this practice by making the following pronouncement in its 'Decree concerning the
things to be observed and avoided in the celebration of the mass':

> They [the local ordinaries] shall completely banish from the Church the practice of
> any fixed number of masses and candles, which has its origins in superstitious wor-
> ship rather than in true religion.[74]

'Superstitious' masses disappeared but were soon replaced with a specially
approved liturgy, the *Missa del anima*, which could be said to gain release from purgatory at specific, indulgenced altars.[75] Clearly, it is this devotion to which Cabañas's
text refers. Who paid for this mass bequest is not clear. Esquivel's wealthy patron,
Don Pedro Ponce de León, died in 1615; he may have provided for the repose of
the souls of Esquivel and his family in this way; or perhaps a member of the family, or even Esquivel himself, willed money for this purpose. But in an age when
concern for the afterlife was a major preoccupation of everyone, whatever his or
her status in society, Cabañas's mention of this practice in relation to Esquivel must
be interpreted as a mark of respect for the composer; he was a figure to be revered
even after death.

Sadly, we have no other documentation to help us fill out this scant outline of
his life, and unless and until further documentary evidence does become available,
we are unlikely to extend our biographical knowledge further than what has been
established above; for the moment, Esquivel must remain a shadowy figure.

73 Sánchez Cabañas, *Historia Civitatense*, p. 156.
74 Schroeder, *Canons and Decrees of the Council of Trent*, Session 22, chap. 9, p. 151.
75 See Eire, *From Madrid to Purgatory*, chapter 4, 'Planning the Soul's Journey', where there is a
full discussion of the topic of pious requests based on examination of the wills of Madrileños before
and after the Tridentine reforms.

3

SOURCE MATERIALS

A S WE HAVE ALREADY SEEN, our knowledge of Esquivel the composer comes to us through three publications only. These are the *Liber primus missarum* (1608), *Motecta festorum* (1608) and *Tomus secundus, psalmorum, hymnorum . . . et missarum* (1613). In addition to the missing volume of 1623, he may well have written other works; given the importance of Corpus Christi processions in sixteenth- and seventeenth-century Spain, it would be surprising if he had not produced works for these ceremonies. The capitular acts of Oviedo mention records of payment to Esquivel for the composition of *villancicos* and music for the *autos de corpus*, but none of this music seems to have survived.

It was a remarkable achievement that Esquivel was able to see all three of his volumes through Spanish printing presses when so few of his fellow countrymen succeeded in this respect. The huge expense involved and the paucity of printers no doubt explains the scarcity of printed polyphonic music at this time. Although over fifty books containing vocal polyphony and/or instrumental polyphonic music were published in Spain and Portugal in the period 1535–1648, the total number of music books does not begin to compare with those for the major centres of music publishing in Italy, France or the Low Countries.[1] And as Anglés pointed out many years ago, in the regions of Castile, Aragon and Navarre in the period 1598 to 1628, the number of published volumes of sacred polyphony did not exceed twelve.[2] In addition to the three volumes of music by Esquivel the principal publications were: Philippus Rogier, *Missae sex* (Madrid, 1598); Tomás Luis de Victoria, *Missae, Magnificat . . .* (Madrid, 1600); Alfonso Lobo, *Liber primus missarum* (Madrid, 1602); Victoria, *Officium defunctorum* (Madrid, 1605); Sebastián de Vivanco, *Liber magnificarum* (Salamanca, 1607) and *Motetes* (Salamanca, 1610); Miguel el Navarro, *Liber magnificarum* (Pampeluna, 1614); Sebastián Aguilera de Heredia, *Liber canticorum Magnificat* (Zaragoza, 1618); Stefano Limido, *Armonia espiritual* (Madrid, 1624); Sebastián López de Velasco, *Libro de misas* (Madrid, 1628). That Esquivel was successful was probably due to the generosity of Don Pedro Ponce de León, bishop of Ciudad Rodrigo from 1605 until 1609. The Latin dedication to the *Tomus secundus* (to be examined later) implies that Don Pedro underwrote the cost of

1 Fenlon and Knighton, *Early Music Printing*, p. ix.
2 Higinio Anglés, *La música española desde la edad media hasta nuestros días* (Barcelona, 1941), p. 55.

this publication, and he may well have done so for the two 1608 volumes.[3] Without financial support, and the relatively close proximity of Salamanca, a centre for the book trade, it is difficult to see how a chapelmaster of Esquivel's stature, employed by one of the least wealthy cathedral establishments in northern Spain, could have met the considerable costs of publication of two large volumes of music.

Printing came late to Salamanca by comparison with other urban centres. It increased in pace during the sixteenth century in an attempt to satisfy the demands for academic and religious texts, particularly after the Council of Trent.[4] Esquivel's publisher was Artus Taberniel. Having arrived from Antwerp – an important centre of book publishing – around 1588 during a period of economic uncertainty, he established a reputation for publications of high quality, publishing scientific book engravings as well as books of polyphony.[5] On his arrival in the city, he seems to have earned his living as a typecaster, but he soon opened a bookshop, distributing texts published by the highly respected Antwerp printer, Plantin. His work as a printer began in 1598, and it was he who introduced into the city the type necessary for printing the large books of music which were placed on the *facistol* (lectern).[6]

Without any previous experience of music printing, Taberniel turned his attention to the production of the choirbooks by Vivanco and Esquivel, producing first Vivanco's *Liber magnificarum*, soon to be followed by Esquivel's volumes. His model, in terms of layout, design and general appearance, seems to have been Andreo Antico's *Liber quindecim missarum*, printed in Rome in 1516 by the woodcut method. The title page shows a kneeling figure – presumably the printer himself – with open music book in hand before the figure of Pope Leo X. The book shows a simple canon to the words 'Vivat Leo Decimus, Pontifex Maximus'.[7] The same iconography of a kneeling figure is adopted by Taberniel for the title pages of Vivanco's *Liber magnificarum* and Esquivel's *Liber primus missarum*, although, in each of these cases, the dedicatee is not the pope; as we shall see shortly, the evidence suggests that Esquivel's work was dedicated to the Virgin.

Another more immediate model is the series of choirbooks produced by Juan de Flandres that began with the printing of Rogier's *Missae sex*. These books may

3 There is some doubt about this, however, depending on how we interpret Esquivel's remarks in his dedication of the *Tomus secundus* to Don Pedro. He says: 'I chose you to be . . . my patron and Maecenas in all things'. But in the next sentence he says: 'This particular moment [1613] fulfils a long-held desire to offer some vigorous token of my respect and gratitude'. This suggests that this was the first time he had dedicated a work to the prelate. Perhaps the bishop was not the actual dedicatee of the earlier volumes, but he may have assisted in providing funds to make publication possible.

4 See Ian Fenlon, 'Artus Taberniel: Music Printing and the Book Trade in Renaissance Salamanca', in Fenlon and Knighton, *Early Music Printing*, pp. 117–45.

5 Alvaro Torrente, *Diccionario de la música española e hispanoamericana, s.v.* 'Taberniel', X, p. 109. Taberniel published volumes of polyphony from 1602 until his death in 1610, when his business was continued by his widow, Susana Muñoz, and subsequently by his son.

6 Susana Muñoz, *Viuda de arte Taberner*. See Alejandro Luis Iglesias, 'El maestro de capilla Diego de Bruceña (1567/71–1623) y el impreso perdido de su *Libro de misas, magnificats y motetes* (Salamanca: Susana Muñoz, 1620)', in Crawford and Wagstaff, *Encomium Musicae*, p. 460 n. 123.

7 Fenlon, 'Artus Taberniel', p. 138. Fenlon describes this publication as the 'ur-model' for all future printed choirbooks.

be seen as an attempt to produce a Spanish equivalent to the Italian and Flemish choirbooks which had been circulating in Spain for decades; the fonts in Taberniel's work stem from the same source.[8]

Robert Stevenson has already commented on the magnificence of Taberniel's production of Vivanco's *Liber magnificarum*, describing it as 'a choirbook that by virtue of its luxury and accuracy rivals the best Plantin publications'.[9] Esquivel's 1608 books of printed polyphony do not quite rival the splendour of Vivanco's *Liber magnificarum*, but they are substantial publications, printed to high standards – though not entirely error-free, as we shall see – and therefore expensive.

Having succeeded in getting his music published, Esquivel was clearly anxious to ensure its dissemination and to recover his costs. He began – immediately it seems – to circulate copies round a number of cathedral establishments. An examination of archival material reveals some interesting details.

Hardly was the ink dry on the page of his *Liber primus missarum* when he made contact with Burgos cathedral. The capitular acts record that on 16 June 1608 there was discussion in the chapter meeting on the contents of a letter from Esquivel in which he suggested that the chapter might like to consider purchase of his book of masses. The chapter entrusted Damián Bueno to examine the book and report back.[10] The canon's report was obviously favourable because on 7 July the chapter agreed they would send Esquivel 12 ducats for the volume.[11] The following year Esquivel made contact again, this time informing the chapter of his new publication of motets. At their meeting on 9 October the chapter asked the *maestro de capilla* (Bernardo de Peralta) to consider the book and report back.[12] Three days later he reported his approval and the chapter agreed that the *maestro de capilla* should pay 12 ducats for it.[13]

Similar discussions took place elsewhere. Thus, in the capitular archives of Badajoz cathedral for 11 September 1609, we find it recorded that 'J(uan) de Esquivel, *maestro de capilla* of Ciudad Rodrigo, should be given 400 *reales* in return for the two books of music which he sent to [the cathedral] on his own account'.[14] This entry must refer to the *Liber primus missarum* and *Motecta festorum* and may account for the presence of both volumes in the cathedral library there today. It is, moreover, clear from the capitular acts that the composer also sent a copy of his *Tomus secundus* of 1613 to the cathedral but, for whatever reason, the chapter returned it to him.[15]

8 Ibid., p. 137.

9 Stevenson, *Spanish Cathedral Music*, p. 278.

10 'Actas capitulares' 1608, fol. 480, in López-Calo, *La música en la catedral de Burgos*, IV, p. 130.

11 'Actas capitulares' 1608, fol. 492 in López-Calo, *La música en la catedral de Burgos*, IV, p. 132.

12 'Actas capitulares' 1609, fol. 47*v* in López-Calo, *La música en la catedral de Burgos*, IV, p. 148.

13 'Actas capitulares' 1609, fol. 48 in López-Calo, *La música en la catedral de Burgos*, IV, p. 148.

14 '11 de septiembre de 1609: A J(uan) de Esquivel, maestro de capilla en Ciudad Rodrigo, se le den 400 Reales en recompensa de dos libros de música que imbió a la fábrica por su cuenta.' Badajoz cathedral, 'Actas capitulares' (1609) fol. 260, in S. Kastner, 'Música en la catedral de Badajoz (años. 1601–1700)', *Anuario musical* 15 (1960), p. 80.

15 Badajoz cathedral, 'Actas capitulares', 1610–16, fol. 193. See Solis Rodriguez, 'El archivo musical de la catedral de Badajoz', in María García Alonso, ed., *El patrimonio musical de Extramadura:*

Perhaps it was at the suggestion of Taberniel that the composer sent a copy of the *Liber primus* to Seville cathedral; a copy was received at almost the same time as Sebastián de Vivanco sent his *Liber magnificarum*. Both books appear listed in the inventory of 1618 but had disappeared by the time of the next inventory in 1644.[16]

In 1613 the composer sent *un libro de canto* to Coria cathedral.[17] The chapter secretary was instructed to reply, saying that, for the moment, the cathedral did not require any more books of polyphony. However, the chapter's final decision must have been reversed since two books of Esquivel's music survive there.

The capitular acts of Oviedo cathedral for 1615 record that in that year Esquivel was paid 100 *reales* by the cathedral chapter for 'The book of masses, hymns and motets' ordered by the *maestro*, Villa Corta.[18] This must refer to the composer's *Tomus secundus* of 1613. If so, in comparison with the sum paid by the Church authorities in Badajoz, the recorded payment for this is rather paltry; the one surviving copy of the *Tomus secundus*, in the church of Santa María de Encarnación in Ronda, is a large volume of nearly 600 pages – over twice as large as the two 1608 volumes put together.

The circulation and dissemination of polyphony was, of course, normal procedure – at least from the time of Morales. Cathedrals needed musical materials to fulfill the requirements of the liturgy and so were potential customers for 'new' music. In Zaragoza, for example, – a city that was well-placed to receive new material, situated as it was on a major trade route for books[19] – an inventory of 1546 records the presence of books of polyphony in manuscript and printed form by local composers and those of international standing. The inventory includes Morales's *Missarum liber primus* (Rome, 1544; Lyon, 1545). Morales, seemingly, bought sufficient paper for the printing of 500 copies, 300 of which were for distribution in Italy, and the rest sent to Spain.[20] Esquivel, then, in inviting purchase of his music, was following in the footsteps of his forebears.

---

cuaderno de trabajo no. 1 (Trujillo, Caceres, 1991), p. 26, n. 23.

16 Juan Ruiz Jimenéz, *La librería de canto de órgano: creación y pervivencia del repertorio del renacimiento en la actividad musical de la catedral de Sevilla* (Seville, 2007), pp. 168 and 234.

17 'Actas capitulares' 1613: *Documentario musical* 876 in Pilar Barrios Manzano, 'La música en la catedral de Coria', p. 253.

18 Oviedo cathedral, 'Actas capitulares' 1615, 20 March, XXII.

19 See Tess Knighton, '*Libros de Canto*: The Ownership of Music Books in Zaragoza in the Early Sixteenth Century', in Fenlon and Knighton, *Early Music Printing*, p. 216. Zaragoza was the archiepiscopal see of the kingdom of Aragon as well as the political, juridical and administrative capital. In the sixteenth century, it was an important centre for printing and had close links with Barcelona and thus the Mediterranean; geographically, it was situated between Lyons in France and Medina del Campo in Castile, both towns which regularly held international book fairs.

20 Tess Knighton, ' La circulación de la polifonía europea en el medio urbano: libros impresos de música en la Zaragoza de mediados del siglo XVI', in Andrea Bombi, Juan José Carreras and Miguel Ángel Marín, eds., *Música y cultura urbana en la edad moderna* (Valencia, 2005), pp. 337–49. In the second half of the sixteenth century, Toledo cathedral acquired a significantly large collection of polyphonic books produced outside the town. These included presentation manuscripts from Guerrero and Ceballos, and printed books from Morales, Victoria and Vivanco. See Michael Noone, 'Printed Polyphony Acquired by Toledo Cathedral, 1532–1669', in Fenlon and Knighton, *Early Music Printing*, pp. 241–74, for a full account of recent research undertaken in the archive of Toledo cathedral.

All three of his publications are in choirbook format. They are all modest in dimensions (less than 60 x 40 cm) compared with many manuscript choirbooks of the period, a fact which suggests they may have been intended as presentation or library copies unless, of course, Esquivel worked with very small forces; for everyday use his choristers may have worked from manuscript copies.

LIBER PRIMUS MISSARUM (1608)

THE *LIBER PRIMUS* is the first of the two publications of 1608 and Badajoz cathedral appears to hold the only extant copy, although items from the print are found elsewhere.[21] The volume runs to 253 numbered pages. The full title, which can only be supplied with help from Albert Geiger,[22] is as follows: *Missarum Ioannis Esquivelis in alma ecclesia civitatensi portionarii, et cantorum praefecti, liber primus.* At the bottom of the title page appear the words: *Superiorum permissu, Salmanticae ex officina typographica Arti Taberniel Antwerpiani, anno a Christo nato M.DC.VIII.* The Badajoz copy, cited in RISM A/1/2 as item E 825, however, is defective and lacks not only its title page and other prefatory information but also pages 1–2, 55–90 and 237–44. The final numbered page (verso) contains the colophon: *Salmanticae excudebat Artus Tabernelius Antwerpianus XVI kalendas Marcias M.DC. IIX.* The IIX here means '8'; Taberniel died in 1610.

Since the Badajoz copy tells us so little, we are reliant on Albert Geiger for further information. He discovered what was apparently a complete copy of the work in the bookshop of a Munich antiquarian, Ludwig Rosenthal, where it was listed as item 807 in Rosenthal's catalogue 153.[23] From this copy Geiger was able to supply the missing title and furnish us with further details. According to Geiger the work bore no dedication, but the Munich copy included a copper engraving (by Estorga, an unknown Spanish master) of Esquivel kneeling before an altar over which hangs a painting of the Virgin with the Infant Jesus, a reproduction of which he included in his article (see Plate 1).

In the opinion of Robert Snow, the absence of an earthly patron suggests that the volume may have been dedicated to the Virgin;[24] and the wording on the engraving 'Sancta et Immaculata virginitas, quibus te laudibus eferam nescio' ('O holy and immacualate virginity, I know not with what praise to exalt thee') certainly reinforces this view, as does the number of Marian motets included.

As we have seen, the engraver is clearly repeating the idea he had observed elsewhere of a kneeling figure paying homage. The title page of Vivanco's sumptuous

---

21 The antiphon, *Asperges me*, is included in the *Tomus secundus* and the funeral motet, *In paradisum*, appears as the final item in the *Motecta festorum*. A copy of the *Missa Ductus est Jesus* found its way to America. It was acquired from the native population in 1931, appearing on folios 27v–36r in a manuscript source owned by Octaviano Valdés, a canon of Mexico City cathedral. See R. Stevenson, *Renaissance and Baroque Musical Sources in the Americas* (Washington, 1970), pp. 131–3.

22 Geiger, 'Juan Esquivel'.

23 Snow, *The 1613 Print*, p. 93.

24 Ibid.

Liber magnificarum shows the composer kneeling before a crucifixus; no human figure other than the composer is present, suggesting dedication to the Deity, a view reinforced by the lettering on the book being offered up to the crucifix: 'DONUM DE DONIS TUIS'.[25] However, such a dedication would not be unusual: seven of the eight masses of Guerrero's *Missarum liber secundus* (Rome, 1582) are dedicated to the Blessed Virgin;[26] Victoria's motet collections of 1583 and 1589 both bear the same dedication.[27] It appears from the evidence that Spanish composers frequently dedicated their works to the Blessed Virgin, to the Blessed Trinity, or to Christ Himself.

The volume opens with the antiphon *Asperges me (à4)*; then follows the *Missa Ave Virgo sanctissima (à5)*, *Missa Batalla (à6)*, *Missa Ut, re, mi, fa, sol, la (à8)*, *Missa Ductus est Jesus (à4)*, *Missa Gloriose confessor Domini (à4)*; finally the *Missa pro defunctis (à5)*, and the funeral motet *In paradisum (à6)*.

The Badajoz copy lacks its title page, other prefatory information and pages 55–90, 237–44. This results in the loss of the *Asperges me*, *Missa Batalla* (lacking part of the Kyrie, the whole of the Gloria and part of the Credo) and parts of the *Missa pro defunctis* (the Sanctus and communion antiphon are incomplete; the Agnus Dei is missing entirely). Partial reconstructions of missing sections of the *Missa Batalla* can be attempted since Geiger printed transcriptions of some extracts in his article.

It is tempting to speculate on Esquivel's motives for putting together this heterogeneous collection of works. Practical, perhaps even commercial, considerations may have influenced his compilation, which offers a potential customer a polyphonic setting of the antiphon preceding mass, five mass ordinaries (two large-scale and three smaller-scale works) and music for the dead. The antiphon and *missa pro defunctis* both incorporate into the polyphony chants traditionally associated with the Spanish rite; three of the mass ordinaries are parody works, modest in dimension, based on motets by Guerrero; another is a battle mass based, not on themes from a Spanish war *villancico*, as Geiger supposed, but on Janequin's chanson *La guerre* (1529), and perhaps intended as a thanksgiving offering after a time of war; yet another is an even larger-scale work, scored SSSAATTB, based on the hexachord and perhaps intended for a festive occasion. Clearly, this is a retrospective collection and Esquivel may have compiled it with the intention of including all the works he had composed up to that time which he thought worthy of publication.

MOTECTA FESTORUM (1608)

THERE APPEAR TO BE only four surviving copies of the *Motecta festorum*: one is owned by The Hispanic Society of America in New York City; another is housed in the cathedral library of Badajoz cathedral; a third copy is in the possession of the cathedral at Burgo de Osma; the fourth copy (recently restored)

---

25 A reproduction of the title page appears in Fenlon, 'Artus Taberniel', p. 135.
26 Stevenson, *Spanish Cathedral Music*, p. 182.
27 Ibid., p. 185.

came to light in 1995 during the recataloguing of the extensive cathedral archive in Coria (Cáceres).[28] All four copies are incomplete, lacking pages of musical text plus prefatory pages of text (dedication, approbation and licence and so forth) which might have yielded interesting and valuable historical information. However, by studying all four copies, it is possible to piece together a complete picture of the work's contents and to attempt a musical reconstruction.

The Badajoz copy, listed in RISM A/1/2 as item 826, lacks its title page, all preliminary textual material, and pages 1–2 and 269–71. The copy owned by the Hispanic Society of America is also damaged; everything before page 11 is missing, as are pages 107–10, 225–8, 255–6 and 263–6. The badly damaged final page, 271, does show the colophon except for a few letters on the reverse side. It reads: *[Sal]manticae excudebat [A]rtus Tabernelius [A]ntwerpianus quinto [k]alendarum Iulii [M].DC.IIX.* This copy was acquired from the Leipzig antiquarian Karl W. Hiersemann, who offered it for sale as item 251 in his catalogue *Musik und Liturgie* of 1911.[29] Hiersemann printed the title of the publication as it may have been. Thus it reads: *Esquivel, Juan, motecta festorum et dominicarum cum communi sanctorum, IV, V, VI, et VIII vocilus* [sic] *concinnanda*. It is probable that Hiersemann borrowed this title from the book's previous owner, the Spanish musician and bibliophile, Federico Olmeda, who may himself have given the book this title, perhaps having seen at some time another complete copy elsewhere.[30]

Hiersemann's catalogue entry continues as follows: *Impreso en-fol. mayor (58 x 38 cm). Salmanticae excudebat Artus Tabernelius Antwerpianus quinto calendarum Julii M.DC.IXX. (1608). Encuadernacion original de piel roja ornament. de hierros a frio, sobre madera.*[31] Thus we see that the book was bound in red leather ornamented with metal on wood. It is, as already noted, modest in dimensions by the standards of many Spanish manuscript choirbooks of the period.[32]

The Burgo de Osma copy of the *Motecta festorum*[33] was first described by the Spanish musicologist Higinio Anglés, who discovered it there in 1928.[34] The copy, bound in black leather on wood, is in a poor state of preservation, lacking its title

---

28 For information on the recataloguing in 1994, see Antonio Ezquerro Estebán, 'Memoria de actividades de RISM-España/1995', *Anuario musical* 51 (1996), pp. 247–69.

29 Snow, *The 1613 Print*, p. 94.

30 Ibid.

31 Ibid.

32 Many manuscript collections of Spanish polyphony dating from the mid- to late sixteenth century were of huge dimensions. For example, Toledo, Archivo y Biblioteca Capitulares de la Catedral Metropolitana, 17.99, a manuscript collection of motets by Morales, Josquin and others, measures 72 x 50 cm. Many manuscripts preserved at the Escorial are even larger. Slightly later, San Lorenzo de El Escorial, Real Biblioteca del Monasterio, 2, measures 82.8 x 56.8 cm. Copied in 1604 and containing masses and motets by, among others, Palestrina, Rogier and Lobo, it is probably the largest known choirbook from the Renaissance period. See Jerry Call, 'Spanish and Portuguese Cathedral Manuscripts', *The New Grove Dictionary of Music and Musicians* (London, 2001), XXIII, pp. 927–9, for further details.

33 Libro de atril no 2: Archivo musical de la catedral de El Burgo de Osma (Soria).

34 See Higinio Anglés, *Diccionario de la música labor* (Barcelona, 1954), p. 843, where Anglés describes the volume. Also, *Die Musik in Geschichte und Gegenwart*, III (Kassell und Basel, 1954), p. 1540.

page and all preliminary textual material. The last page of music is 268 and the following pages are missing: 3, 7, 8, 51, 52, 245–8.

The copy in the musical archive of Coria cathedral in Cáceres Province (*Libro de facistol* no. 64) has recently been restored and is now in a relatively good state of preservation. It has been rebound and now measures 56 x 39 cm. Although the initial pages are missing, the colophon appears on the final page: *Salmanticae excudebat Artus Tabernelius Antwerpianus quinto kalendarum M.DC.IIX.* This publication enables us to see all the motets Esquivel clearly intended for this volume.

From the title, supplied somewhat hypothetically by Hiersemann, and a study of the contents, we see that Esquivel's intention was to provide material for: 1. specific feasts throughout the Church year arranged in chronological sequence; 2. commons of saints; 3. Sundays in the penitential seasons. There are two additional motets for Holy Week and the collection ends with a motet 'for any necessity' and two for the burial service.

The inclusion of material following the chronological sequence of the liturgical year was the customary procedure at this time.[35] In addition to Esquivel's, two other Spanish examples may be cited, Vivanco's *Liber motectorum* (Salamanca, 1610) and Guerrero's *Motteta Francisci Guerreri...* (Venice, 1570). Unfortunately, the Vivanco volume is severely damaged; only thirty motets are complete, but this is sufficient to indicate the composer's intentions. He begins his series with a motet for the first Sunday in Advent, interrupts the chronological flow with a series of motets for the commons of saints, and resumes it again with motets that continue through Lent to Ascensiontide.

Guerrero's plan differs from that of Vivanco: after an introductory motet, another set of works covers the period from Advent to Easter; a group of motets honouring non-scriptural saints and five for various commons follow; the volume closes with a group of motets for general occasions. Like many composers of the period he groups his works according to the number of voices employed, beginning à4 followed by motets for five, six and eight voices respectively.

Esquivel chooses not to adopt this method of organisation for the contents of his volume, but the chronological pattern is similar. The complete list of motets is set out in Table 1 (with the title supplied editorially). All the other works are completely preserved in one or other of the surviving sources.

TABLE 1. The Contents of *Motecta festorum* (1608)

Title	Feast	No. of voices	Pages
Ave Maria		7	1
Salva nos	In Dominicis	5	2–5
Peccavi super numerum	In Dominicis	4	6–9
Surrexit Dominus	In Die Resurrectionis	5	10–13
Filiae Hierusalem	In Festo Sancti Marci	4	14–15
Tanto tempore	In Festo Sanctorum Philippi et Iacobi	5	16–17

35 Stevenson, *Spanish Cathedral Music*, p. 286.

Vox clamantis	Dominica Tertia Adventus	4	192–5
Canite tuba	Dominica Quarta Adventus	4	196–7
Simile est regnum	Dominica in Septuagesima	4	198–203
Cum turba plurima	Dominica in Sexagesima	4	204–9
Ecce ascendimus	Dominica in Quinquagesima	4	210–15
Emendemus in melius	Post Cinerum	4	216–19
Ductus est Jesus	Dominica Prima in Quadragesima	4	220–7
Assumpsit Jesus	Dominica Secunda in Quadragesima	4	228–33
Erat Jesus	Dominica Tertia in Quadragesima	4	234–23
De quinque panibus	Dominica Quarta in Quadragesima	4	240–3
In illo tempore	Dominica in Passione	5	244–9
O vos omnes	Feria Sexta in Palmis	4	250–3
Christus factus est	In Coena Domini	4	254–5
Pater misercordiae	Pro quicumque necessitate	4	256–61
Delicta iuventutis meae	Pro Defunctis	4	262–5
In paradisum	Pro Defunctis	6	266–71

Ten motets from this publication are preserved in an eighteenth-century choirbook in Oviedo cathedral library (Libro de atril no. 4).[36] This manuscript, of a hundred folios, contains several anonymous works (two masses, a *Te Deum laudamus* and funeral invitatory), four motets by Juan Paez and the ten motets by Esquivel beginning on folio 69*v*. Esquivel's works are preceded (folios 68–9) by the Latin inscription: 'Incipium motetes quatuor et quinque voces ab Dominica Prima Adventus usque ad dominicam terciam quadragesime inclusive, Mter. Ioannes Esquivel'. Then follow the ten motets indicated by the Latin title. The motet *O vos omnes* is copied into Libro de atril no. 3, folios 14–15. This same motet also found its way to Portugal, where it is preserved in the library of the ducal palace in Vila Viçosa (Livro de música, no. 12, folios 18*v*–19).[37]

All these works must have been composed after Esquivel's brief stay in Oviedo otherwise their entry would have been recorded by the capitular acts, which are most meticulous in reporting the admission of new works.[38] When the cathedral acquired Esquivel's 1613 collection this was duly recorded in the acts.[39]

An even larger eighteenth-century collection of motets from the *Motecta festorum* is to be found in a choirbook in the archives of Plasencia cathedral, catalogued as MS 1. This volume contains sixty-two motets, which the eminent musicologist Samuel Rubio has examined in some detail.[40] That works by Esquivel were still copied and considered to be worthy of use in the eighteenth century is evidence of the regard in which he must have been held long after his death. This should not entirely surprise us, however, since we know from an examination of many Spanish cathedral archives

---

36 These are listed in Casares Rodicio, *La música en la catedral de Oviedo*, p. 214. There is an error in this list: the motet *Cum turba plurima* is listed twice.

37 I am indebted to Michael O'Connor for this information.

38 Casares Rodicio, *La música en la catedral de Oviedo*, p. 22.

39 Ibid.

40 Samuel Rubio, 'El archivo de música de la catedral de Plasencia', *Anuario musical* 5 (1950), pp. 147–68.

that much sixteenth-century polyphony was not simply preserved for historical reasons alone: the worn state of many items suggests that they were frequently used and part of a living tradition – a matter already touched on briefly in Chapter 1.

The presence of such stylistically out-of-date material can be taken as evidence of the conservative nature of Church music in Spain – a fact that has been commented on by many historians of Spanish music – but it also serves to remind us that tradition and innovation existed side by side in the repertory of Spanish cathedrals in the seventeenth and eighteenth centuries. Two styles were recognised: the *prima prattica* of the sixteenth century and the *seconda prattica* gradually introduced in the years following. Many works by composers of previous generations, highly esteemed in their day, achieved canonic status; so, for example, in Seville cathedral we find listed in 1644 masses, motets, hymns, lamentations and so forth, preserved in parchment by Morales, Guerrero and Lobo, and evidently still in use. In the course of time, some of these 'classical' works may have been moved from their former designations to occupy a place in feasts of lesser rank; those which remained in feasts of greater importance, on occasions, must have been adapted to the new aesthetic requirements (changes in vocal forces, use of instruments, for example) in order to keep their place.[41]

Tomus secundus, psalmorum, hymnorum . . . et missarum (1613)

IN 1973, the late Professor Robert Snow discovered a copy of this extensive volume in the church of Santa María de la Encarnación in Ronda, where the work is preserved today. The full account of his amazing find, together with a detailed description of contents, commentary and musical examples, is to be found in his monograph *The 1613 Print of Juan Esquivel Barahona*.[42] What follows is a summary description of essential information; readers requiring more detail are directed to Professor Snow's work.

The volume contains 593 numbered pages plus four initial pages unnumbered bearing title, approbation, printing licence and dedication; a final unnumbered page contains the colophon. The book, bound in leather-covered boards, now measures 51 x 37 cm, the pages at some stage having been trimmed. The title page (see Plate 2) may be translated: *The Second Volume of Psalms, Hymns, Magnificats and the four seasonal Marian Antiphons, and also Masses by Juan Esquivel, a native of Ciudad Rodrigo and Prebendary of the Cathedral of the same city.* The colophon, page 593v, reads: *Salmanticae excudebat Franciscus de Cea Tesa Cordubensis, quint kalendas Marias anni M.DC.Xiii.*

At the time of the volume's publication in 1613, the publication of music for the mass and the Office together in one single volume was unusual, and it is possible

---

41 The process of creating a musical canon is discussed by Juan Ruiz Jiménez in *La librería de canto de órgano*, pp. 229 ff. His reference is to the repertory of Seville cathedral and is based on close examination of the archival evidence remaining there.

42 Snow, *The 1613 Print*, pp. 10–17.

IOANNIS, ESQVIVEL, CIVITATENSIS,

ET EIVSDEM SANCTAE ECCLESIAE PORTIONARII,
PSALMORVM, HYMNORVM, MAGNIFICARVM, ET B.
MARIÆ QVATVOR ANTIPHONARVM DE
TEMPORE, NECNON ET MISSARVM

TOMVS SECVNDVS.

Omnia ad vſum Breuiarij Romani per Clementem Pontificem
Maximum reformati.

AD PRAESTANTISSIMVM, ET REVERENDISSIMVM
DOMINVM FRATREM D. PETRVM PONTIVM DE LEON
CAMORENSEM EPISCOPVM, REGIVMQVE
CONSILIARIVM.

SVPERIORVM PERMISSV.

SALMANTICÆ

Excudebat Franciscvs de Cea Tesa Cordubenſis
Anno M. DC. XIII.

Plate 2. Title page of the *Tomus secundus* of 1613

that the music may originally have been assembled in three separate collections. This is suggested by the approbation, printing licence and index. Vicente Espinel in his approbation speaks of the 'tres cuerpos de Música' and Martin de Cordova, *comissario general*, who granted the licence on behalf of one Alonso Ruyz, whose name appears at the foot of the page (seen in Plate 3 as partly torn away), speaks of 'tres libros que [Juan de Esquivel Barahona] ha compuesto de música, uno de Missas, otro de Magnificas, y otro de Hymnos, y Salmos'. The use of the word 'Index' three times on the index page to separate out the various sections also suggests this (see Plate 4). Perhaps Esquivel put the three, originally separate, collections together to make his music more saleable once he had found a sponsor who would underwrite the cost of printing. The process of binding several volumes together would reduce the cost to book dealers and owners and was not an unusual sixteenth-century practice.[43]

The title page and Espinel's approbation both imply that the contents conform with the requirements of the newly reformed Roman Breviary of Pope Clement VIII, issued in 1602. Without this conformity a licence would not have been granted. But, in addition, the quality of the music and its suitability for liturgical use were also considered.

From the approbation we can see that Espinel, one of the most highly regarded poets and novelists of his day and himself a consummate musician,[44] admired Esquivel's music for its qualities of 'gentle harmony' ('apacible consonancia'), its 'elegant craftsmanship' ('gentil artificio'), its technical merits ('es música buena casta, assi en lo practio, como en lo teorico') as well as its use in the service of the Church. A similar opinion was expressed by the prior and members of the convent of San Lorenzo El Escorial, whose opinions were also sought before the licence to print was given.

Esquivel's chosen printer was Francisco de Cea Tesa, a native of Córdoba, who probably set up his business in Salamanca because of the presence of a prestigious university in that city. From the licence we can see that some form of primitive copyright was practised in Spain at this time since, a publisher having been chosen, anyone else caught reproducing any part of the publication within a ten-year period was subject to excommunication and a hefty fine of 500 ducats ('Y mandamos so pena de excommunion mayor, y de quinientos ducados, que ninguna otra persona sino el dicho Jua[n] de Esquivel Barahona, pueda imprimir alguno de los dichos libros'). Further, from the licence we can see that Esquivel for his part was ordered to give a free copy of his publication to the monastery of San Lorenzo as a gesture of thanks. No copy of this work is to be found there today, however.

The dedicatory letter in Latin which follows the licence is addressed to Don Pedro Ponce de León, whose coat of arms appears on the title page. He came from a very distinguished family; many of his ancestors were *conquistadores* and the family tree can be traced back many centuries. His father, Cristóbal Ponce

43 Soterraña Aguirre Rincón, 'The Formation of an Exceptional Library: Early Printed Music Books at Valladolid Cathedral', *Early Music* 37 (2009), p. 385.
44 Stevenson, *Spanish Cathedral Music*, p. 295.

APROBACION DEL MAESTRO ESPINEL.

POR mandado del Señor don Martin de Cordoua, Presidente del Consejo de la santa Cruzada, vi tres cuerpos de Musica compuestos por Iuan de Esquiuel Barahona, Racionero, y Maestro de Capilla de la Catedral de Ciudad-Rodrigo. Los quales son de Missas, Magnificas, Hymnos, Salmos, y Motetes, y otras cosas tocátes al culto diuino, todo conforme al rezo nueuo. Tienen muy apacible consonancia, y gentil tissico, es musica de muy buena casta, assi en lo pratico, como en lo teorico, sera del seruicio de Dios, y de la Iglesia imprimirlos. En Madrid a siete de Diciembre de 1611.

                 Vicente Espinel.

LICENCIA DEL COMISSARIO GENERAL.

NOS el Licenciado don Martin de Cordoua, del Consejo de su Magestad, Prior y Señor de la Villa de Iunquera, de Ambia, y su tierra, Comissario General de la santa Cruzada, y otro si juez Apostolico, y Real para lo tocáte a los libros del nueuo rezado, &c. Por la presente damos licencia a Ioan de Esquiuel Barahona, Racionero, y Maestro de Capilla de la santa Iglesia de Ciudad-Rodrigo, para que pueda hazer imprimir tres libros que ha compuesto de musica, vno de Missas, otro de Magnificas, y otro de Hymnos, y Salmos, en qualquiera emprenta de estos Reynos, sin que por ello incurra en pena ni censura alguna. La qual dicha licencia damos por quanto nos consta lo tiene por bien el padre Prior, y Conuento de S. Loréço el Real, y atento a que seran muy vtiles para el culto diuino de las Iglesias: y queremos que valga por tiempo de diez años que corran, y se quenten desde el dia de la fecha desta. Y mandamos sopena de excomunion mayor, y de quinientos ducados, que ninguna otra persona sino el dicho Ioã de Esquiuel Barahona, pueda imprimir alguno de los dichos libros, al qual assi mismo mandamos que despues de impressos los dichos libros dé vn par dellos al dicho Monasterio de S. Lorenço el Real en reconocimiéto desta gracia. Dada en Madrid a nueue dias del mes de Março de mil y seyscientos y doze años. Y mandamos se imprima al principio de los libros esta licencia.

                              El L.do Don Martin
                              de Cordoua.

                 Por mandado de su Señoria.

                          Alonso Ru

Plate 3. Approbation and Licence of the *Tomus secundus*

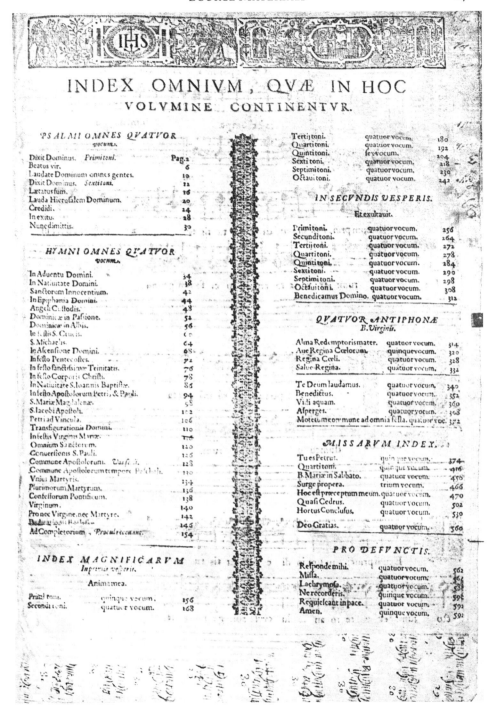

INDEX OMNIVM, QVÆ IN HOC
VOLVMINE CONTINENTVR.

Plate 4. Index page of the *Tomus secundus*

de León (1518–73), was the wealthy duke of Arcos, and Morales served as his chapelmaster in his private palace at Marchena, thirty miles east of Seville, from 1548 until 1551. Francisco Guerrero dedicated his first publication, *Sacrae cantiones* (1555), to this worthy gentleman, who was a humanist and a passionate lover of music.[45]

Don Pedro studied at Salamanca University, where he rose to the position of rector. He took the Dominican habit in the convent of San Esteban, a centre for theological studies, and was prior of the convents of Palencia and Buytrago (Buitrago del Lozoya north of Madrid) before becoming bishop of Ciudad Rodrigo in 1605. He remained in that diocese until 1609, when he was promoted to the see of Zamora. But the low temperature of Zamora was damaging to his health and he was eventually offered the bishopric of Badajoz; he died in 1615 without ever taking possession of this see.[46]

Don Pedro's arrival in Ciudad Rodrigo must have come as a breath of fresh air to the townsfolk in general, and to the ecclesiastical community in particular. His predecessor, Don Martín de Salvatierra, was of a terrible disposition, and had a great love of litigation. Throughout his time in the diocese, he had many struggles with the cathedral chapter. As we have seen in Chapter 1, these resulted in a denunciation to the Inquisition – a case without precedent in the diocese. Although the accusations against him were probably insignificant and not followed through (the Inquisition did not have jurisdiction over bishops), when he died in 1604 the chapter would not allow him to be buried in the cathedral. His body was interred instead in the hermitage of San Salvador.[47]

The adulatory and somewhat obsequious tone of the composer's dedication to Don Pedro appears to be modelled on Guerrero's 1555 dedication to Cristóbal Ponce de León; such adulatory dedications were conventional at this time. He addresses his patron with the customary formality and then suggests that he chose Don Pedro above all others because of his saintly qualities:[48]

The Dedication
To the most illustrious Lord, Brother Don Pedro Ponce de León,
Most Worthy Bishop of Zamora, Juan Esquivel, Citizen of Ciudad Rodrigo,
Prebendary of the Cathedral and Director of Music sends greetings in the Lord.

In past years, honoured Lord, when, by the operation of Divine Grace, you took upon you the governance of the Church, you bound the whole people to you by manifest and unmistakable proofs of your love. Above all, your gentleness and kindness of spirit won my heart so that I chose you to be, from that time forth, my patron and Maecenas in all things.

---

45 A paraphrased translation of this dedication is to be found in Stevenson, *Spanish Cathedral Music*, pp. 179–80.

46 Gil González Dávila, *Teatro ecclesiástico de las iglesias metropolitanas y catedrales de los reynos de las dos Castillas, vivad de sus arzobispos y obispos y cosas memorables de sus sedes*, 4 vols. (Madrid, 1645–1700), II, pp. 421–2, s.v. 'Don Fray Pedro Ponce de León'.

47 Sierro Malmierca, *Judios, moriscos e inquisición en Ciudad Rodrigo*, p. 17.

48 The full Latin text may be found in Appendix 1 in Snow, *The 1613 Print*, pp. 91–2.

This particular moment fulfils a long-held desire to offer some vigorous token of my respect and gratitude. It has not taken much deliberation for me to wish to set in print a certain collection of sacred songs, and to submit it to the judgement of a particular prince, according to the received custom; and many arguments presented themselves which drove me inevitably towards your patronage rather than that of any other.

Esquivel then goes on to praise his patron's ancestors for all their worthy deeds:

Let me consider the antiquity of your house. I call to mind your ancestors' virtuous endeavours over the last 600 years to spread the Christian faith. Histories clearly confirm the victories that were jubilantly reported from Granada and Morocco. Further, their sacred and religious monuments testify what estates and possessions enriched the many temples of their deities. All these things, as is common knowledge, have been restored to the service of the true God and to the pious employment of his kings. Subsequently, they proceeded to win – deservedly – not only the overlordship of Archbriga, Zara, Martia and Gades and of other towns,[49] but also to obtain legitimately by felicitous marriage alliance the additional patrimony of the counts of Toulouse and Narbonne and of the kings of Legio and of Aragon.

But, as these things may perhaps have faded from memory over such an interval of time, it is wonderful to relate how, in recent years, with what ardour of spirit and fortitude your brother, the most excellent Duke Roderigo, supported by a most brilliant band of subordinates, set about driving away from Cádiz the treacherous English – the rest of Andalucia's nobility quaking the while – and avenging the wrongs done to the sanctuaries and shrines of holy women. So it was that the mere rumour of his approach could propel from that quivering and plundered city those very enemies, awe-struck at his prowess.

Esquivel then praises Don Pedro's ascetic qualities; his rejection of the comfortable life style of a cardinal, with all its trappings of wealth, in favour of life as a humble Dominican:

In case any man should ignorantly suppose you to be inferior to your forebears in any respect, I believe you to have been prompted by the impulse of divine inspiration when, exchanging a soft and delicate tunic for a coarser garment – resisting the crude purple – you chose the more ascetic life and the plain habit of the Dominican family. Indeed, if they attained amid the clamour of trumpets, the clashing of arms and the roar of the canon a human and necessarily fickle and perishable fame by their spectacular aspiring to the power of the Spanish kings, you shone no less than they when, after your assiduous study of the Holy Scriptures, you girded yourself for the work, fortified with the armour of every virtue. Indeed, content with freely embraced poverty, amid continual mortification of the body, abstinence from food, unwearied vigils, suppression of your self-will, with public addresses to the populace and private counsels in confession did you regulate yourself and your Christian flock, so that no

---

49 Archbriga: today the town of Arcos de la Frontera, thirty-one miles north-east of Cádiz; Zara: a Croatian port on the Adriatic Sea seventy miles north-west of Split; Martia: possibly Martiago; Gades: Cádiz.

one could doubt you to have secured by your labours an ample glory in heaven and innumerable sons and daughters for Christ, the King of kings.

Esquivel suggests that Don Pedro was the inspiration for his own studies:

And, true as these things are, yet more aptly and justly should I acknowledge the fruits of my own lamplight studies, developed with greater zeal and diligence than before, in celebrating the Divine Office with much more solemnity, to have been attributable to you: for by your cherishing of the greater things and by your reverence for God, the Giver of all, we have understood that nothing has ever been more valuable or venerable than incontrovertible tradition; for you have always directed the whole course of your life and all your actions to promoting tirelessly the growth and spread of the true religion by the dedication of your faith.

Lastly, he asks Don Pedro to accept his 'modest' work as token of his respect:

Accept then, most admirable Prince, this modest volume of Psalms, Hymns, Magnificats and Masses, a little symbol signifying the slightness of its author which, should you deign to promote it under the generous protection of your name, I should consider that enough crowning recompense had been accorded my labours.

What remains, then, but that God, Greatest and Best, should sustain your tenure safely for many long years, to the glory of His name, and the lustre of His Church.

Turning now to the musical contents of the print, it can be seen that the heading *Psalmi omnes quatuor* on the index page is not quite correct as the *Nunc dimmittis* is a canticle sung at Compline. All the other items listed are Vesper psalms, with two settings of *Dixit Dominus*, one in tone 1 and one in tone 6 (see Table 2).

TABLE 2. Psalm Settings in the *Tomus secundus*

Psalm	Tone
1. Dixit Dominus (109)	1
2. Beatus vir (111)	4
3. Laudate Dominum (116)	8
4. Dixit Dominus (109)	6
5. Laetatus sum (121)	3
6. Lauda Jerusalem (147)	7
7. Credidi (115)	5
8. In exitu Israel (113)	Peregrinus

Moreover, some of the psalms have some verses scored for five voices while *Dixit Dominus* (second setting) has verse 8 scored for SAT.

As Robert Snow has pointed out, at first glance, the collection of Vespers psalms found here seems incomplete: only seven of the sixteen psalms used in First and Second Vespers on feasts of duplex rank in the *temporale* and *sanctorale* and in Sunday Vespers are included. However, the psalms selected for inclusion do form a coherent set, since they are all psalms sung at First Vespers on different occasions during the liturgical year, which suggests that the assembling of such material was the composer's intention; perhaps in Ciudad Rodrigo in Esquivel's time psalms at Second Vespers were sung monophonically or sung to simple *falsobordone* formulas.[50]

Thirty hymns for use at Vespers and one for Compline (*Te lucis ante terminum*) make up Esquivel's hymn cycle (see Table 3).

TABLE 3. Hymn Cycle in the *Tomus secundus*

Title	Feast	Verses set	Total no. of verses
Conditor alme siderum	In Adventu Domini	2, 4	6
Christe Redemptor omnium *Ex Patre*	In Nativitate Domini	2, 4 (SAT)	7
Salvete flores Martyrum	Sanctorum Innocentium	2	3
Hostis Herodes impie	In Epiphania Domini	2, 4	5
Custodes hominum	Angeli Custodis	2, 4	4
Vexilla Regis prodeunt	Dominicae in Passione	1, 6	7
Ad coenam Agni providi	Dominicae in Albis	2, 8	8
Vexilla Regis prodeunt	In festis S. Crucis	2, 6	7
Tibi Christe splendor Patris	S. Michaelis	2	4
Jesu nostra redemptio	In Ascensione Domini	2, 4	6
Veni Creator Spiritus	In festo Pentecostes	2, 4 (SST)	7
O lux beata Trinitas	In festo sanctissimae Trinitas	2	3
Pange lingua gloriose	In festo Corporis Christi	2, 5 (SSAT)	7
Ut queant laxis	In Nativitate S. Joannis Baptistae	2, 4	5
Aurea luce	In festo Apostolorum Petri et Pauli	2	4
Pater superni luminis	S. Mariae Magdalenae	2, 4	5
Defensor alme Hispaniae	S. Iacobi Apostoli	2, 4	7
Petrus beatus	Petri ad Vincula	2	2
Quicumque Christum	Transfigurationis Domini quaeritis	2, 4	5
Ave maris stella	In festis Virginis Mariae	2, 4	7
Christe Redemptor omnium *Conserva*	Omnium Sanctorum	2, 4	7
Doctor egregie Paule	Conversionis S. Pauli	2	2
Exultet caelum laudibus	Commune Apostolorum	2	6
Tristes erant Apostoli	Commune Apostolorum tempore Paschali	2, 6	6
Deus tuorum militum	Unius Martyris	2	5
Sanctorum meritis	Plurimorum Martyrum	2	6
Iste confessor	Confessorum Pontificum	2	5
Jesu corona virginum	Virginum	2	5
Fortem virili pectore	Pro nec Virgine nec Martyre	2, 4	5
Urbs beata Jerusalem	Dedicationis Ecclesiae	2, 4	5
Te lucis ante terminum	Ad Completorum	2	3

The cycle comprises hymns which are sung at Vespers on feasts in the Breviary of Clement VIII of duplex rank. A feature of the settings is Esquivel's adherence

50 Snow, *The 1613 Print*, p. 18.

to Spanish tradition: hymns are based on chant melodies of Spanish origin, or are variants of melodies known elsewhere. The texts of two hymns are peculiar to Spanish usage: St James – patron saint of Spain – and the hymn for the feast of guardian angels. Except in two instances – *Vexilla Regis* for Passion Sunday and Palm Sunday, and *Pange lingua* for Corpus Christi – Esquivel set either one or two even-numbered verses of each hymn. No canonic devices are employed in the hymn settings.

The sixteen Magnificat settings are in two cycles: one, settings of the odd-numbered verses for use at First Vespers; two, settings for even-numbered verses for use at Second Vespers – a service of a slightly lower rank than First Vespers. All eight tones are used in each cycle. Canon is employed extensively in the first cycle (see comments in chapter 6). Esquivel closes this group of Magnificat settings with a four-part setting of *Benedicamus Domino* for use at the conclusion of the Vespers service.

Next come the four seasonal Marian antiphons sung after certain office hours: *Alma Redemptoris mater (à4)*, *Ave Regina coelorum (à4)*, *Regina caeli (à4)* and *Salve Regina (à5)*. The chant melody traditionally associated with each antiphon is paraphrased in one of the four parts, and again the composer allies himself with Spanish practice, utilising chant peculiar to the Spanish tradition for *Ave Regina* and *Regina caeli*.

All the five miscellaneous items are chant-based. Of these five, two are for use in Office hours: an *alternatim* setting of *Te Deum laudamus*, sung at Matins on principal feasts, and *Benedictus*, sung daily at Lauds. *Vidi aquam*, *Asperges me* and the item described as *Motetum commune ad omnia festa* all have their place within the context of the mass. *Asperges me* is a duplication of the motet appearing in the 1608 collection, while the short *Motetum commune ad omnia festa (à4)* is clearly included for its practical usefulness – a multi-purpose motet in which it was possible to insert into the text the name of whichever saint was being remembered: 'O sancte N—, lumen aureum, Domini gratia servorum gemitus solita suscipe clementia'.

Finally, we come to the masses: six ordinaries with a setting *à5* of the *Deo gratis*, and the *Missa pro defunctis (à4)* together with items from the office for the dead: *Respond midi (à4)*, a lesson from Matins; *Ne recorderis (à5)*, a responsory from Matins and settings *à4* and *à5* respectively of the vesicle *Requiescant in pace* and the *Amen* response.

Of the mass ordinaries in this collection, the first four are based on chant material; only *Quasi cedrus* and *Hortus conclusus* borrow pre-existing polyphonic material, unlike the mass ordinaries of the 1608 collection, in which four of the five fall into this category.

Another significant feature of the 1613 masses is the omission of sections of the Sanctus. The four sections of the full text ('Sanctus', 'Pleni', 'Hosanna', 'Benedictus') are found in three of the five mass ordinaries in the 1608 masses – *Ave Virgo sanctissima* omits the 'Pleni'; the Hexachord Mass omits the 'Hosanna' – but in the 1613 collection the full Sanctus text is set in only one mass, *Hortus conclusus*. This omission of part of the Sanctus text is a typical feature of nearly all Spanish masses after the first decade of the seventeenth century, a practice which became standardised about 1620, when only two or three sections were set in one continuous unit.[51]

What prompted the curtailment of the Sanctus and, later in the seventeenth century, a shortening of the long tripartite Agnus Dei? Most probably it was the desire to shorten the liturgy, or to make way for the singing of a motet after the Sanctus. Moreover, given the importance of improvisation in the Renaissance, when a mass was based on chant material such an omission would provide the organist with an opportunity to demonstrate his improvisatory skills by providing a paraphrase of the missing portion.

The Ronda copy of the *Tomus secundus* is the only copy to survive intact, but during the previously mentioned RISM-sponsored recataloguing of the rich musical archive of Coria cathedral, another partially preserved copy was found.[52] Having undergone restoration, it is now catalogued as *Libro de atril* no. 53. Sadly, only pages 34–156, 256–99 and 301–71 remain; thus the psalm settings are missing, as are the Magnificats for First Vespers and the seven masses.

The presence of this mutilated document, and the copy of the *Motecta festorum* to be found there, may be accounted for by the close proximity of Coria, in neighbouring Cáceres province, to Ciudad Rodrigo. Interchanges of musicians and resources between Ciudad Rodrigo, Plasencia, Salamanca and other regional centres in nearby Portugal were common over a long period in the history of music in this region.[53] Moreover, the market for Esquivel's books would most certainly have included the New World, given the demand for polyphonic works by the newly established churches there. The trade in liturgical books is well-documented and many manuscript and printed sources by Esquivel's contemporaries are known to have been bought by the major church centres.[54]

In conclusion, one can only speculate that Esquivel would have disseminated his three published books more widely geographically than the centres in which exemplars are found today. Given the effort involved in overcoming all the obstacles to publication, it is likely that more copies would have been produced and offered to the larger cathedrals where polyphony was practised – Ávila, Burgos, Salamanca to name but three – in addition to the cathedrals with which he had been connected during his professional life and, of course, the Escorial. Sadly, time has obliterated any record of negotiations that might have shed light on a wider dissemination process, and we must be thankful that at least what remains enables us to form a clear if incomplete impression of this composer's achievements.

---

51 Ibid., p. 24.

52 See Antonio Ezquerro Esteban, 'Memoria de actividades de RISM-España/1995', *Anuario musical* 51 (1996), p. 264, where all the items preserved are listed.

53 See Pilar Barrios, *Diccionario de la música española e hispanoamericana, s.v.*'Coria', IV, pp. 3–4.

54 See María Gembero Ustárroz, 'Circulación de libros de música entre España y América (1492–1650): notas para su estudio', in Fenlon and Knighton, *Early Music Printing*, pp. 147–77. The author discusses the trade in music books between Spain and America in detail. There is no mention of Esquivel's works in the author's 'list of printed books of music conserved in Iberoamerican archives and libraries before 1650' in the appendix to her article.

4

THE MASSES OF 1608

Missa Ave Virgo sanctissima

E SQUIVEL OPENS HIS FIRST BOOK OF MASSES with a polyphonic setting of the antiphon *Asperges me*. Liturgically, this antiphon precedes the Kyrie of the Ordinary; by printing a polyphonic setting of this item at the head of his volume the composer is emphasising the completeness of his publication. Perhaps he had seen a copy of Morales's volume of masses published by Moderne at Lyons in 1551, or Nicolas du Chemin's miscellaneous collection *Missarum musicalium* (Paris, 1568), both of which open with a polyphonic setting of the same antiphon.[1]

The setting is a paraphrase of the ancient mixolydian chant melody, itself a Spanish variant of the *Asperges* chant found on page 11 of the *Liber usualis*.[2] The chant appears in the *superius* with the accompanying voices imitating it frequently in the conventional manner. The setting is competent and unremarkable; only one particular feature deserves comment.

At the setting of the phrase 'misericordiam tuam', just before the final chord at the end of the second section, Esquivel approaches the cadence with part-writing that, when analysed vertically, produces a 6/4–5/3 chord progression, as Ex. 4.1 *a* demonstrates.

Ex. 4.1. Chord progressions approaching a cadence

---

1 Stevenson, *Spanish Cathedral Music*, p. 289.
2 According to Geiger, the chant quoted by Esquivel is from a Spanish mozarabic Ordinarium. See Geiger, 'Juan Esquivel', p. 140.

The progression arises naturally out of the contrapuntal movement of the part-writing, but it is not common in the works of Esquivel's contemporaries and could have been avoided by using one of the standard cadential cliches more typical of this period, as at Ex. 4.1*b* and *c*.

Other examples of the 6/4–5/3 progression are encountered elsewhere in Esquivel's work.

Although his style and technique are in general conservative, he seems aware of some of the new trends that would emerge more openly in the works of composers of the next generation. We shall encounter many examples in the following chapters. Here, we must note the number of obligatory accidentals that appear at the cadences. Stevenson draws attention to this when comparing Esquivel's *Asperges* setting with those of Morales and du Chemin.[3] The growing specification of accidentals at cadence points was, of course, a stylistic feature of music, sacred and secular, throughout the sixteenth century, and in suggesting the raised leading-note Esquivel is doing nothing that is unusual. However, the number of inflected leading-notes in his music is extensive; the sense of modality is weakened by the number of accidentals specified, or implied; in this respect he may be compared with Victoria, who seems to specify more accidentals than Guerrero, for example.[4]

Esquivel follows this *Asperges* setting with what is obviously a tribute to Guerrero. His first mass ordinary is a parody mass on that composer's celebrated five-part canonic motet *Ave Virgo sanctissima*, a work much admired in Guerrero's lifetime. It was first published in 1566 (Paris) and again in 1570 and 1597 (Venice). Francisco Pacheco, the future father-in-law of the painter Velazquez, admired the work for its beauty of sound and excellent construction and commented that, wherever it was performed in Spain, it 'brought any number of musicians fame and approbation'.[5]

Based on a Marian antiphon text in liturgical use in sixteenth-century Spain, the two soprano lines are in canon *ad unisonum* throughout. Certain musical motives have a fundamental structural likeness, as shown in the brackets in nos. 2, 5 and 9 of Ex. 4.2 below, imparting an element of compositional unity to the work: perhaps this is one of the reasons why it has gained so much admiration both now and in its own time.

The placing of a particular work at the head of a volume as a means of paying homage is not unusual:

> If position in a series means anything, then the facts that in their first books of masses (1544, 1566, 1576, 1602, 1608) Morales's first parody chose Gombert; Guerrero's first

---

3 Stevenson, *Spanish Cathedral Music*, p. 289.

4 Again, this is a matter commented on by Stevenson. When comparing Guerrero's *Missa Inter vestibulum* (1566) with Victoria's *Ascendens Christus* (1592), he writes: 'The ratio [of accidentals] is striking – almost five times as many obligatory accidentals per breve in the one [Victoria] as in the other composer. This phenomenon would not be so worthy of notice were it to be found only in isolated instances: it is important because the ratio will be found to differentiate Victoria's usage from Guerrero's in a general sense.' Stevenson, *Spanish Cathedral Music*, p. 403.

5 Ibid., p. 137.

parody chose Morales; and Victoria's, Lobo's, and Esquivel's chose Guerrero for their source; should prove how high was the esteem in which the seniors were held by the juniors.[6]

Esquivel is the last in a line of composers, all paying tribute to one another. Perhaps, also, he wanted to prove his worth as a composer, since the practice of reworking borrowed material was a recognised form of learning for Renaissance musicians.[7]

But there is another reason for the appearance of *Missa Ave Virgo sanctissima* at the head of the volume. If the *Liber primus* was dedicated to the Virgin, as was suggested in Chapter 3, the compositon of a mass drawing its material from a well-known Marian motet is the most obvious way to make this connection explicit.

The motet is rich in imagery: the Virgin is a 'maris stella clarissima' – a bright star of the sea; she is hailed ('salve') as a 'margarita pretiosa' – a precious pearl. It is also rich in symbolism, as Willem Elders has pointed out. There is, he argues, a visual symbolism in the number of times the four-note *salve* motive from the *Salve Regina* antiphon (no. 4 in Ex. 4.2) appears in visual form in the choirbook source (*superius II* as the *comes* is not notated): 'the twelve hails may therefore represent the pearls which are sometimes found in paintings of the Virgin's crown'.[8] But there is also audible symbolism at work here: the *salve* motive is actually *heard* fifteen times in all; this could be interpreted as a reference to the fifteen large pearls of the rosary – a symbol of the Virgin.[9]

These interpretations could be wide of the mark, of course; but it is interesting to observe that when we look at the construction of Esquivel's mass, which as we shall see is built on the melodic motives shown in Ex. 4.2, the number of appearances of motives one and four is twelve in each case (see Table 5).

6 Ibid., p. 290.

7 The practice has been likened by the late Howard Mayor Brown to the late-medieval and Renaissance literary concept of *imitatio*, one of the central concepts in the art of rhetoric, although, as Brown acknowledges, 'we shall never know whether such emulation or imitation was practised to compete with other composers – to demonstrate superior expertise using the same musical material – or to pay homage'. See Howard M. Brown, 'Emulation, Competition and Homage: Imitation and Theories of Imitation in the Renaissance', *Journal of the American Musicological Society* 25 (1982), pp. 1–48. This view of musical imitation as a form of rhetoric has been contested, however, by Rob C. Wegman, 'Another "Imitation" of Busnoy's *Missa L'homme arme* – and Some Observations on *Imitatio* in Renaissance Music', *Journal of the Royal Music Association* 114 (1989), pp. 89–202. Wegman accepts the principle that *imitatio* can be conceived as 'the practice of learning composition by studying and imitating the works of established masters' (p. 198), but argues that musical imitation for the Renaissance composer was not the musical equivalent of Renaissance literary imitation, which took as its model classical literature. This model of imitation was not adopted in music until the late-sixteenth-century attempts of the Camerata to imitate classical Greek music.

8 The number twelve was also associated with the Virgin after the 'apocalyptic woman' (Revelation 12: 1–2) had become a favourite theme in medieval art. In searching for further audible evidence to support this theory, Elders cites three works in which the incipit of the *Salve Regina* antiphon 'serves as a *soggetto ostinato*, which – as a hidden allusion to Mary – is restated twelve times'. These works are Josquin's five-part *Salve Regina*, copied between 1550 and 1554 into SevBC 1; an anonymous motet, *Tota pulchra es*, preserved in MS Royal 8 G.vii, and Guerrero's *Ave virgo sanctissima*. See Willem Elders, *Symbolic Scores: Studies in the Music of the Renaissance* (Leiden, 1994), pp. 68–9.

9 Ibid., p. 177.

Ex. 4.2. Melodic motives from Guerrero's motet *Ave Virgo sanctissima*

As Elders has reminded us elsewhere, 'quotations, borrowings and reworkings can be seen as a means of creating a symbolic connection between the text or textual connotation of the pre-existent material and the text of the new composition'.[10]

Given the close connection between Guerrero's motet and the mass, it seems probable that by placing the latter at the head of his volume Esquivel is seeking the Virgin's blessing on his work. Moreover, this argument is strengthened further when we examine the final Agnus Dei of the mass, in which Esquivel adopts a favourite device of Guerrero's, the melodic ostinato. The five-part texture is now increased to six and floating above the liturgical text in *superius I* is the head motive of Guerrero's motet with its accompanying text 'Ave Virgo sanctissima'. This is clearly a symbolic gesture of intercession, a prayer addressed to Mary the mother of the Lord himself.

Missa Ave Virgo sanctissima is a parody mass, and although the technique of parody writing is well documented,[11] before embarking on a detailed study of Esquivel's parody treatment of this celebrated model, some discussion of the relationship between Esquivel's approach to this technique and the generally accepted paradigm would be helpful.

Lewis Lockwood has outlined the essence of parody writing clearly: the composer seeks to elaborate – or re-elaborate – borrowed material, taking from his chosen model individual motives and phrases; sometimes the original complex is incorporated with minor modifications; at other times, new contrapuntal combinations are established.[12] Lockwood sees the motive as a unit of procedure: this, in

10 Willem Elders, *Studien zur Symbolik in der Musik der alten Niederlander*, Utrechtse bijdragen tot de muziekwetenschap (Utrecht, 1968), p. 40, in Wegman, 'Another "Imitation"', pp. 198–9.

11 See, for example, Lewis Lockwood, 'A View of the Early Sixteenth-Century Parody Mass', in Albert Mell, ed., *The Department of Music, Queens College of the City of New York Twenty-fifth Anniversary Festschrift* (New York, 1964), pp. 53–77; 'On "Parody" as a Term and Concept in Sixteenth-Century Music', in Jan LaRue, ed., *Aspects of Medieval and Renaissance Music: A Birthday Offering to Gustave Reese* (New York, 1966), pp. 560–75. Additional more recent studies include Quentin W. Quereau, 'Palestrina and the *Motteti del Fiore* of Jacques Moderne: A Study of Borrowing Procedures in Fourteen Parody Masses' (Ph.D. dissertation, Yale University, 1974); Harry E. Gudmundson, 'Parody and Symbolism in Three Battle Masses of the Sixteenth Century' (Ph.D. dissertation, University of Michigan, 1976); David J. Sibley, 'The Sixteenth-Century Parody Mass' (Ph.D. dissertation, University of Nottingham, 1989). Among older studies the following are relevant: Charles van den Borren, 'De quelques aspects de la parodie musicale', *Academie royale de Belgique. Bulletin de la classes des beaux-arts* 20 (1938), pp. 146–63; Walter H. Rubsamen, 'Some First Elaborations of Masses from Motets', *Bulletin of the American Musicological Society* 4 (1940); R. B. Lenaerts, 'The Sixteenth-Century Parody Mass in the Netherlands', *The Musical Quarterly* 36 (1950), pp. 410–21; Robert D. Wilder, 'The Masses of Orlando di Lasso with Emphasis on his Parody Technique' (Ph.D. dissertation, Harvard University, 1952); Johannes Klassen, 'Untersuchungen zur Parodiemesse Palestrinas', *Kirchenmusikalisches Jahrbuch* 37 (1953), p. 53–63; Johannes Klassen, 'Die Parodieverfahren in der Messe Palestrinas', *Kirchenmusikalisches Jahrbuch* 38 (1954), pp. 24–54; Johannes Klassen, 'Zur Modellbehandlung in Palestrinas Parodiemessas', *Kirchenmusikalisches Jahrbuch* 39 (1955), pp. 41–55; Helmuth Christian Wolf, 'Die aesthetische Augasung der Parodiemesse des 16. Jahrhunderts', in Miguel Querol et al., eds., *Miscelánea en homaje a Monseñor Higinio Anglés* (Barcelona, 1958–61), p. 1011.

12 Lockwood, 'A View of Parody Mass', p. 61. Compare with Reese: 'The distinctive feature of

his view, is the distinctive and essential feature of sixteenth-century 'parody' writing, the skill and art of which lay in the many transformations a composer could
wrest from previously formed motivic constructions.[13]

Not all writers agree with this emphasis on motivic borrowing, however.
Another more modern study by Veronica Francke has challenged Lockwood's view
that the melodic motive was the primary source of interest in the so-called 'parody'
mass.[14] Francke argues that motivic borrowing was only one of several methods
of recomposition open to the sixteenth-century composer, and she attacks what
she describes as 'a motive system of analysis': 'A motive system of analysis has limited value in conveying even an approximate picture of how a movement is formed
by borrowing and reworking methods. More significant is the manipulation and
refashioning of whole, integral textures derived from the model.'[15]

And the emphasis on elaboration of the whole polyphonic complex is a point
made by Michael Tilmouth in his *New Grove* entry on 'Parody'. Tilmouth sees the
essential feature of parody technique not in terms of a single part being appropri-
ated to form a *cantus firmus* in a derived work, but as the whole substance of a work's
course – its themes, rhythms, chords and chord progressions – being absorbed into
a new piece and subjected to free variation in such a way that it becomes a fusion of
old and new elements.[16]

This is the classical definition of parody technique, but it ignores the fact that
there were no universally agreed sets of procedures or rules for the recomposition
of material from a motet or madrigal in a mass. Cerone, an Italian writing for Spanish readers, discusses techniques to be followed in his *Melopeo y maestro* of 1613,
but his is a late attempt to set down certain procedures which were by this time
common practice.[17]

this type of Mass [i.e. "parody" mass] is that it is based, not on a single melody, like the normal cantus-
firmus and paraphrase types, but on the several voices of a polyphonic model, the simultaneous
appearance of all the voices, not least on one occasion, being characteristic though not indispensable'.
Reese, *Music in the Renaissance*, p. 202.

13 Lockwood, 'On "Parody" as a Term and Concept', p. 574. Lockwood (p. 569) dislikes the
terminology currently employed in musicological literature, pointing out that the term *parodia* was
unknown to Renaissance theorists, who devote little attention to the practice of polyphonic derivation
in their writings. The treatises of Vincentino (1555) and Zarlino (1558) give it scant attention; Pietro
Ponzio in 1588 and 1595 makes more extended reference to it, but only Pedro Cerone in his *El melopeo
y maestro* (Naples, 1613) discusses the concept in any detail. Lockwood prefers the term 'imitation' as
a more accurate description of much sixteenth-century compositional practice since the term *imitatio*
(meaning polyphonic borrowing) was one that was familiar to theorists and musicians.

14 Franke, 'Palestrina's Fifteen Five-Part Imitation Masses Modelled upon Motets: A Study of
Compositional Procedure' (D.Phil. dissertation, University of Oxford, 1990).

15 Ibid., p. 170. Franke's study adopts a method of analysis similar to that of Quentin Quereau as
described in his paper 'Sixteenth-Century Parody: An Approach to Analysis', *Journal of the American
Musicological Society* 31 (1978), pp. 407–41.

16 Michael Tilmouth, 'Parody', in *The New Grove Dictionary of Music and Musicians* (London,
2001), XIX, p. 145.

17 For example: 'in composing a mass, it is perforce necessary and obligatory that the inventions
at the beginnings of the first Kyrie, the Gloria, the Credo, the Sanctus and the Agnus Dei should be
one and the same'. Cerone, *El melopeo y maestro*, translated in Oliver Strunk, *Source Readings in Music*

Each composer developed his own methods of polyphonic elaboration and his procedures sometimes changed in the course of time. Thus, for example, Palestrina, in his later parody masses, moved away from his earlier tendency to concentrate on individual motives towards an interest in the borrowing and reincorporation of vertical structures and sonorities.[18] Other composers appear to follow the same procedures consistently throughout their creative lives. For example, Guerrero's main interest seems to have been in the motive; how one motive could be combined with another and in how many different ways. In speaking about Guerrero's *Missa Sancta et immaculata* (Paris, 1566), parodying Morales's motet, Robert Stevenson points out that the composer never quotes Morales's polyphonic *complex*; he takes Morales's motives, and uses them to devise new and unforeseen combinations. In Stevenson's view, such a mass as the *Sancta et immaculata* does not even exemplify the classic concept of parody because of this procedure.[19] Stevenson then coins the phrase 'permutation' mass for works exhibiting these features. Since Esquivel's *Ave Virgo sanctissima* mass falls into this category – as do the masses *Ductus est Jesus* and *Gloriose confessor Domini* to be discussed later – far from being limited in value, the motivic method of analysis will prove an appropriate and a useful tool.

Having discussed the symbolism inherent in this work and its place at the head of the volume, it is now time to examine its structure in some detail, considering first the Kyrie. In the following discussion all numerical references to motivic material refer to the musical examples shown in Ex. 4.2. Bar numbers correspond to those in the modern performing edition[20] although the musical examples shown below are at the original pitch of the source.

The Kyrie of this mass is the shortest of any mass ordinary in the volume (see Table 8 for a comparison). Each of the three sections is of equal length, twelve semibreves in transcription at halved note values.

Comparison with the source motet shows that the head motive (1) is drawn on by all five voices in the first Kyrie. But Esquivel does not merely replicate the texture of his model: he re-orders Guerrero's material so that in place of the original, T B Si Sii A, the order of entries is now A B T Si Sii. The Christe is devoted entirely to motive (6): the two canonic voices retain their original disposition in the model, but they are given an entirely new accompaniment. Kyrie II combines motive (2) with a new counter-subject.

From an analysis of this one short item, we get an insight into Esquivel's parody technique, an insight that is further confirmed when the lengthier movements of the mass are studied. Two features stand out: firstly, his interest in the manipulation of individual melodic motives from his source, as opposed to the borrowing and reincorporation of the original vertical structures of his model; secondly, his ability to devise new contrapuntal workings from borrowed material.

History (London, 1950), p. 265.

18 Franke, 'Palestrina's Imitation Masses', pp. 30 ff.

19 Stevenson, *Spanish Cathedral Music*, p. 199.

20 See Mapa Mundi, Spanish Church Music 155, transcr. and ed. Clive Walkley (London, 2003).

The following Gloria runs to 100 bars in transcription, divided into two almost equal sections, the second half beginning 'Qui tollis peccata mundi'. Of the four mass ordinaries in this collection from which comparisons can be made (the Gloria of the *Missa Batalla* is missing), the Gloria of this mass is the shortest in length owing to the fact that there is very little repetition of text and associated melodic material.

As the movement unfolds, we see that all motives from the source motet are drawn on during the course of the movement, but they are presented out of their original order. When the head motive is drawn upon, as it is twice in this movement, it is quoted in full and made the basis of imitation in four or five of the parts. The melodic shape of the motives undergoes very little modification: occasionally a motive is contracted, but it is usually quoted in full. The top two voices stick closely to material from the source while the lower voices frequently present new material. Seldom are two different motives from the source combined together: Esquivel either combines a motive with itself or with new material.

The Credo is the longest of Esquivel's four surviving settings of this text in the volume (the Credo of the *Missa Batalla* is missing). Its length is not due to extensive word repetition, but to the canonic form, which, of course, necessitates some word repetition in the canonic voice. The 194 bars of transcription are divided into four sections:

Section 1:   'Patrem omnipotentem' to 'descendit de coelis', 63 bars
Section 2:   'Et incarnatus est' to 'homo factus est', 17 bars
Section 3:   'Crucifixus' to 'non erit finis', 52 bars
Section 4:   'Et in spiritum' to 'Amen', 62 bars.

As commonly happens, the texture is reduced to three voices for the Crucifixus, where the canon is abandoned in favour of three independent voices (SAT). The Credo as a whole is saturated with quotations from the source motet and the various motives borrowed are quoted many times. As in the Gloria, the motives follow each other in an order determined by Esquivel and not that found in the source; there are more examples of different motives from the source being combined together in this movement than there are in the Gloria (see Ex. 4.3 for an example). Motives undergo little transformation, with the exception of the head motive, which appears in a contracted form. The top two parts nearly always draw

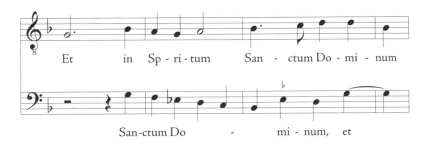

Ex. 4.3. Missa *Ave Virgo sanctissima*: combination of melodic motives in the Credo. *Tenor* and *bassus*, bars 133 ff.

Ex. 4.4. *Missa Ave Virgo sanctissima*: Sanctus, *tenor* and *bassus*, bars 1 ff.

on motives from the model, but, as in the first two movements, Esquivel never reproduces the whole polyphonic complex of the original.

Esquivel begins the Sanctus not with reference to Guerrero's head motive but with motives (3) and (4) combined (Ex. 4.4). Not only does this movement not begin with the head motive, it contains no reference to it in any of its three sections. Brevity is one of its chief characteristics: when transcribed into modern notation with note values halved, it measures only 16 bars in transcription.

This gives us a clue as to the occasion on which the mass was sung. Cerone suggests that when a mass is ferial – intended for week days – it suffices to use the motives of the imitation or invention of the subject in the Kyrie, Sanctus and Agnus Dei, 'two or three times at most'.[21] The Kyrie and Sanctus match Cerone's description, and it could be that Esquivel intended this mass as a votive mass to be offered to the Blessed Virgin Mary at a weekday ceremony.

The Osanna is in *tripla* mensuration; with note values quartered and with a time signature of 6/4 it measures only eight bars. The Benedictus, on the other hand, measures 23 bars. The brevity of the Sanctus arises out of Esquivel's condensed use of his motivic material, and the omission of the text 'pleni sunt coeli et terra gloria tua' – a section of text also omitted in three masses in the *Tomus secundus*; shortening a mass in this way is a not uncommon practice after the first decade of the seventeenth century.[22]

Esquivel's manner of setting the three sections of the Sanctus is close to Guerrero's, as demonstrated in his two masses *De Beata Virgine* and *Simile est regnum caelorum* from his *Liber secundus* (1582): the opening Sanctus section is followed by a *tripla* Osanna, succeeded by a Benedictus scored for three voices only (see Ex. 4.5). Esquivel's head motive for his Osanna even bears a passing resemblance to Guerrero's – a rising scale passage of three notes. However coincidental this may be, the fact that Esquivel treats his thematic material in a similar way is probably not. The similarity of treatment suggests that Esquivel was fully acquainted with Guerrero's masses as well as his motets; perhaps they were held up to him as models for study by his teacher, Navarro.

---

21 Cerone, *El melopeo y maestro*; translated in Strunk, *Source Readings*, p. 266–7.
22 Snow, *The 1613 Print*, p. 24. There was no consensus on which part of the text should be omitted; thus, only four of Esquivel's mass ordinaries in his two publications of 1608 and 1613 contain complete polyphonic settings of the whole of the Sanctus text. See Snow, pp. 24–6.

Esquivel

Guerrero

Ex. 4.5. A comparison of the opening of the Osanna from Esquivel's *Missa Ave Virgo sanctissima* with Guerrero's *Missa Simile est regnum*

Esquivel continues by making the gap between successive groups of entries closer than Guerrero, who allows his Osanna section to unfold over a longer time span. The rate of harmonic movement is rapid in both passages, and the stepwise movement of Esquivel's bass line shown in Ex. 4.6 results in a series of parallel triads disguised only by the contrapuntal movement of *altus* and *tenor* parts.

The Benedictus is beautifully written. The first phrase is based entirely on motive (6) with a fleeting reference to the head motive. The material for the 'in nomine' section is a subtle transformation of the tail-end of Guerrero's head motive (Ex. 4.6, Esquivel above, Guerrero below).

Ex. 4.6. Esquivel's transformation of Guerrero's head motive, *bassus*, bars 41 ff.

Only two invocations of the Agnus Dei are included in this mass. The first begins not with the head motive from the source, but with Guerrero's 'salve' motive, motive (4) in Ex. 4.2. Again, such an opening does not concur with Cerone's views on the appropriate way to begin a mass movement – further evidence that Cerone's ideas did not always accord with general practice. Again motives are presented in

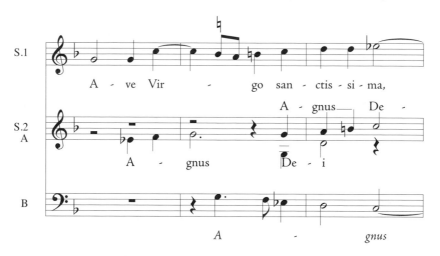

Ex. 4.7. *Missa Ave Virgo sanctissima*.
Motive permutations in the final Agnus Dei, bars 7–9

a different permutation from that of the model. The movement is a concise and skilful reworking of old ideas, and Esquivel displays the hand of a skilled craftsman using his technique to create a dignified musical setting of the poignant text.

In the second Agnus Dei, the five voices are expanded to six, as was the custom in continental mass settings. Canon is abandoned in favour of ostinato treatment of the head motive in *superius I*; four times it appears, each time separated by a breve rest (semibreve in modern transcription). There are new permutations of motives (1) and (6), the two motives which supply nearly all the thematic material for this movement, and references to motive (3) in bars 7–9 (see Ex. 4.7).

Esquivel's motivic borrowings from his model are summarised in Table 4. Table 5 shows the number of times each motive is selected for recomposition in the mass.

TABLE 4. Order of motives borrowed from the motet
Ave Virgo sanctissima as they appear in Esquivel's mass

Kyrie I	1
Christe	6
Kyrie II	2
Gloria	1, 5 combined with 7, 2, 3 (inverted), 6, 3, 4, 5, 7, 6, 2, 6, 1, 8, 4, 9
Credo	1, 4, 3, 4, 6, 9, 7, 4, 1 (incipit only), 4, 9 (incipit only), 4, 7, 1, 1, 3, 2, 6,// 3, 5, 6, 5, 2//4, 8, 9, 7, 3, 7, 3 (incipit only)//8, 6, 7, 4, 2, 9, 1, 7, 5, 6, 4, 3, 6, 3
Sanctus	3, 4
Osanna	3
Benedictus	6, 1 (fragment)
Agnus Dei I	4, 1, 9, 6, 3
Agnus Dei II	1, 6, 3

TABLE 5. Missa *Ave Virgo sanctissima*: frequency of motivic use

Motive from Source	1	2	3	4	5	6	7	8	9
Number of times used in the mass	12	6	13	12	5	13	8	3	6

The information gained from these tables is, of course, limited in scope. There are many different ways of approaching an investigation into the technique of parody writing, and the method of analysis used here is less sophisticated than Quentin Quereau's technique, which he calls 'motive entry relationship graphing';[23] but, nevertheless, it serves adequately to highlight important features of Esquivel's approach to parody composition as demonstrated in this work. The full extent of the composer's borrowing procedure is evident: no motive is left unused and several are used many times. A 'saturation principle' is at work: through his ability to integrate fully and convincingly all the principal motives from Guerrero's motet into a new work, and by a process of reordering and reworking the old and combining it with the new, Esquivel produces a composition that is worthy to be judged alongside those of his illustrious contemporaries. Judged on its merits, perhaps

---

23 Quereau, 'Sixteenth-Century Parody', p. 409. Quereau's system of analysis enables him to plot the contrapuntal relationships which exist between overlapping motive entries.

the mass would after all have earned the approval of Cerone, who writes: 'In the course of the mass, the more use one makes (whether with or without imitation) of motives from the middle or inside of the composition upon which the mass is written, the better and more praiseworthy the work will be'.[24] If we interpret the phrase 'motives from the middle or inside of the composition' to mean motives following the motet incipit, then Esquivel does just that.

Before we leave this mass, it is worth pointing out that Esquivel was not the only composer to set himself the task of writing a parody mass based on *Ave Virgo sanctissima*; there are at least three other examples. First to take up the challenge was the Flemish musician Géry de Ghersem. He was sent to Spain as a choirboy and became a pupil of Philippe Rogier. After Rogier's death in 1596 Ghersem prepared Rogier's *Missae sex* for publication and included his own *Missa Ave Virgo sanctissima à7* in the volume.[25] Although not as completely saturated with borrowed material as Esquivel's mass, it is another symbolic work. As a study in canon it goes far beyond Esquivel's mass in its display of canonic mastery. The canons begin with *cantus II* in Kyrie I marked 'Trinitatis in unitate', a reference to the Trinity, and all movements with the exception of the Crucifixus section of the Credo are in canon. In terms of technical brilliance, Esquivel's mass may not rival Géry de Ghersem's work, but it is a worthy tribute to his earthly and his heavenly patron. The two later parody compositions are by Pedro Rimonte (1604) and Juan del Vado (c.1670).[26]

MISSA BATALLA

ALBERT GEIGER first drew attention to Esquivel's *Missa Batalla* in 1918.[27] He described it as being in no way inferior to Victoria's *Missa pro victoria* (1600). Like Victoria, Esquivel based his mass on Clement Janequin's chanson *La bataille de Marignan*, also known as *La guerre* (1529) and not, as Geiger thought, on themes devised from a Spanish war *villancico*.

Although Geiger's attribution is incorrect, his article is valuable since it does contain extensive musical examples from Esquivel's mass, passages which we can no longer examine since the only complete movements remaining in the surviving exemplar are the Sanctus, Osanna, Benedictus, Agnus Dei I and II; only one page remains of the Kyrie, of the Credo only the final page. Geiger's article, therefore, is useful in helping us to piece together a more complete picture of this work; it also enables us to examine its relationship to its source more thoroughly and to compare it with other known works based on the Janequin model. In addition to Victoria's *Missa pro victoria* already mentioned, these include Janequin's own parody of his chanson, the *Missa La bataille* (1532), and Guerrero's *Missa De la batalla escoutez* (1582).

24 Cerone, *El melopeo y maestro*; translated in Strunk, *Source Readings*, p. 266.
25 See Géry de Ghersem, *Missa Ave Virgo sanctissima*, ed. Lavern I. Wagner, *Corpus mensurabilis musicae* 69 (Middleton, WI, 1974). Wagner describes this work as a 'contrapuntal tour de force'.
26 See Elders, *Symbolic Scores*, p. 176, n. 68.
27 Geiger, 'Juan Esquivel', pp. 48–160.

Morales also wrote a mass based on *La guerre* – now apparently lost; and the Biblioteca Medinaceli in Madrid is reported as having in its possession an anonymous *Batalla* mass (MS 607).[28] However, this too seems to have vanished: a request made some years ago to see the manuscript produced the response that it was not now listed in the library's catalogue.

Janequin's popular chanson seems to have inspired many composers to write instrumental battle pieces, and the vogue lasted well beyond the sixteenth century. In the field of sacred polyphony the composition of parody masses based on the chanson did not end with Victoria. Around 1648, the organist from Mexico City, Fabián Ximeno, wrote yet another mass based on *La guerre*.[29]

Why, we may ask, was *La guerre* such a popular choice of model for Renaissance composers? One explanation may be the multiplicity of musical motives employed in the chanson: potentially, these provide a rich store of materials for parody writing. *La guerre* is a relatively long piece and, in spite of much repetition of thematic material and the persistent use of one chord for long passages in part two, its ideas are clearly defined and full of character.

Another explanation for its popularity may be its subject matter. The text is rich in imagery: images of warfare are present throughout and it has been argued that composers may have used the chanson as a model because of the symbolic possibilities inherent in the text. Secular borrowings can be re-interpreted and given a theological significance; for example, the borrowing of a musical motive originally associated with the noise of the battlefield can be re-interpreted to symbolise a spiritual battle between the Church and the world.

Two interesting studies, which have included an examination of this question in relation to the three battle masses of Janequin, Guerrero and Victoria, are Luis Felix Merino's 'The Masses of Francisco Guerrero (1528–1599)' and Harry Edwin Gudmundson's 'Parody and Symbolism in Three Battle Masses of the Sixteenth Century'.[30]

Much of Merino's study is given over to an analysis of Guerrero's approach to parody writing in the eleven of his eighteen masses which use the technique. But in his study of the composer's *Missa De la batalla escoutez*, he seeks to illustrate in some detail what he considers to be the composer's borrowing of thematic material to suggest a hidden meaning.

Two examples will suffice to illustrate his case.

In the Credo, Guerrero employs the motive illustrated in Ex. 4.8 for the passage 'et expecto resurrectionem'.[31] This is derived from bars 29–33 of the model (Ex. 4.9).[32]

---

28 Stevenson, *Spanish Cathedral Music*, p. 235, n. 341.

29 Ibid., p. 235. A transcription of Ximeno's mass can be found in Alyson Roberts's study 'Parody Masses Based on Janequin's *La guerre*: A Critical Edition and Study' (MA dissertation, Queen's University, Belfast, 1977). The author also analyses battle masses by Giovanni Croce (1557–1609) and Francisco López (d. 1673). All these works are based, although somewhat loosely, on material from Janequin's chanson.

30 Ph.D. dissertations, respectively University of California, 1972, and University of Michigan, 1976.

31 Bar numbers refer throughout this chapter to the *Opera omnia* edition of Guerrero's *Missa De la batalla escoutez*. See *Opera omnia*, vol. IV, pp. 74–115.

32 Bar numbers refer to the Merritt and Lesure edition of Janequin's work unless otherwise

Et ex - spe - cto re - sur - re - cti - o - nem mor - tu - o - rum

Ex. 4.8.　Guerrero: *Missa De la batalla escoutez*, Credo, *cantus II*, bars 176 ff.

Phif - fres souf-flez, frap - pez tam-bours, frap - pez tam-bours

Ex. 4.9　Janequin: *La guerre, superius*, bars 29 ff.

Merino sees a symbolic connection here, presumably believing that Guerrero deliberately chose that particular motive, associated in the chanson with the noise and clamour of battle, because it seemed particularly appropriate to record the theme of rejoicing at the resurrection. Similarly, in the Sanctus, he draws a symbolic connection between the passages in Ex. 4.10 and 4.11.

Do - mi - nus De - us Sa - ba - oth

Ex. 4.10.　Guerrero: Sanctus, *cantus I*, bars 15–18

La vi - ctoi - re du no - ble roy, du no - ble roy Fran - coys -

Ex. 4.11.　Janequin: *La guerre, contratenor*, bars 9–13

This is interpreted as an expression of rejoicing in both chanson and motet: Janequin himself used his own chanson motive at this point in his *Missa La bataille*. Merino supports his interpretation by drawing attention to other studies by J. Klassen and W. Elders.[33]

Gudmundson's study is based on a close examination of *La guerre* and the three masses by Janequin, Guerrero and Victoria based on it. His central thesis is that the borrowing of thematic material found in these masses occurs for symbolic as

stated. See *Chansons polyphoniques*, I, ed. A. Tillman Merritt and François Lesure (Monaco, 1965), pp. 23–32. This edition gives only part I of the chanson but includes the *quinta pars* added by Verdelot. Another complete version of the chanson is given in vol. VII of *Les maitres musiciens de la renaissance française. Clement Janequin: Chanson (Attaignant, 1529)*, ed. Henry Expert (Paris, 1897).

33 Luis Felix Merino, 'The Masses of Francisco Guerrero (1528–99)' (Ph.D. dissertation, University of California, 1972), p. 77. The studies referred to are Johannes Klassen, 'Untersuchungen zur Parodiemesse Palestrinas', *Kirchenmusikalische Jahrbuch* 37 (1953), pp. 53–63: Willem Elders, 'Enkele aspecten van de parodie-techniek in de madrigaal missen van Philippus de Monte', *Tijdschrift van de verteniging voor Nederlandse muziekgeschedenis* 19, pp. 3–4 (1962–3), pp. 131–42.

well as compositional reasons. In this way, borrowed material, in its new context, is given an extra-musical significance. Thematic material is chosen to create textural parallels so that, for example, a phrase of the mass text is linked with a phrase of chanson text by being given the same musical idea in order to convey similar meaning. Techniques of word-painting are used, musical devices are manipulated to create descriptive interpretations of ideas contained in a word or a phrase, or groups of texts from different sections of the mass are shown to have common associations through the use of a unifying motive.

Throughout all three masses under discussion, Gudmundson is anxious to reveal examples of what he sees as Trinitarian symbolism, which he feels permeates these masses. He gives many examples, including the following:

1. Use of tripartite forms and selective use of triple meter (examples of the latter occur in Janequin's Gloria, Credo and Osanna; in Guerrero's Kyrie II and Osanna; in Victoria's Christe, Gloria, Credo, Sanctus and Osanna).

2. Use of triadic motives, e.g. the Credo of Janequin's mass (Ex. 4.12).

qui lo cu-tus est per pro phe - tas   et   u-namsanctam ca-tho - li-cam -

Ex. 4.12. Janequin's Credo, *superius*, bars 140–4

The bass line accompanying this triadic motive 'can symbolise the firm and unshakable faith upon which the church rests'.[34]

3. The reduction to three voices in Agnus Dei II of Janequin's parody.

The theme of Trinitarian symbolism is pursued at length, and in discussion of Guerrero's borrowed material, he is led to say: 'Guerrero's choice of these particular phrases, with their bellicose connotations, to express the unity of the Trinitarian Godhead, seems to reflect the military posture of the Church in Spain in the sixteenth century in its aggressive "missionary" activities in the New World, and in its defences against the influences of the Reformation'.[35] Although Gudmundson may appear to overstate his case, his discussion is penetrating and we shall return to the question of symbolism in relation to Esquivel's mass later in this chapter.

From Gudmundson's summary analysis of each work, and from observation of the score, we gain clear insight into each composer's working methods. Janequin sticks closely to his chanson when writing his mass. Each of the five major divisions begins with a reference to the opening motive of the model. He follows the original sequence of ideas, often borrowing the whole contrapuntal structure and adapting it to suit the new text. There is little transformation of thematic material, little attempt to present new juxtapositions of originally separate motives or to combine the old with the new. He makes limited use of new material and the only extensive original passage is the second Agnus Dei. He draws from both parts of his chanson but, not surprisingly, in view of the nature of the musical material in part two, quotes more extensively from part one.

34 Gudmundson, 'Parody and Symbolism', p. 125.
35 Ibid., p. 153.

Guerrero shows much more variety than Janequin in his compositional methods and much more imagination in using borrowed material. He too begins each major section of his mass with reference to the opening of the chanson, but no two beginnings are exactly alike. His techniques range from adding new counter-melodies to Janequin's ideas to paired entries in Agnus Dei II, and ostinato treatment in Agnus Dei I. Guerrero does not follow the original sequence of Janequin's thematic material but juxtaposes motives from different sections of the work, subtly transforming them by processes such as melodic inversion, compression or rhythmic alteration. His use of strictly new material is limited, and the extent of his compositional skill is thus revealed in his ability to reshape Janequin's ideas in ways which go much further than the French master. He employs much less motivic material than Janeqin, but uses it with far greater skill. His style, as always in his masses, is thoroughly contrapuntal.

Victoria's *Missa pro victoria* stands in contrast to both Janequin's and Guerrero's works. Written on a grander scale, it is a double-choir work and may have been written to please the light-minded and pleasure-loving young Philip III, whose musical tastes were very different from those of his serious-minded father.[36] Consequently, the work is much more harmonically conceived, with the tonic–dominant chord progressions – a strong feature of *La guerre* – given prominence. The secular derivation of this work is made abundantly clear in Victoria's choice of thematic material. Fanfare motives are used repeatedly and Victoria frequently quotes from part two of the chanson model, making much more use of this material than either Guerrero or Janequin himself in his own parody. Like Guerrero, he uses fewer points of imitation than Janequin. In the customary manner he begins each of the five movements of the mass with reference to the opening of *La guerre*, quoting the complete contrapuntal structure of bars 1–10, with minor modifications for the opening of the Kyrie I and the beginning of the Agnus Dei.

The secular element in Victoria's work is emphasised strongly in his use of repeated note figures derived from the model. Such secular elements appear in Guerrero's work only in two places: in the Credo, 'Et iterum venturus est', and 'Et unam sanctam catholicam', both derived from bars 20 ff. of the chanson (Ex. 4.13).

Et   or -   rez, si bien es-cou - tez

Ex. 4.13. Janequin: *La guerre, superius,* bars 20 ff.

Turning now to Esquivel's mass, or what remains of it, the evidence seems to suggest that his approach is much closer to that of Guerrero than to those of Janequin and Victoria, although Esquivel must have known Janequin's parody since he develops Janequin's head motive in Kyrie II.[37]

36 Stevenson, *Spanish Cathedral Music*, pp. 411–12.
37 Ibid., pp. 289–90.

Ex. 4-14.

Ex. 4-14 contd.

Esquivel: bars 10-11.   Janequin: bars 34-35.

Ex. 4.14. The relationship between Esquivel's themes and *La guerre*

The similarities between the two comparative passages are striking: both composers continue with the same thematic material (bars 29–35 of the chanson), drawing on the complete contrapuntal fabric in an almost identical manner. Generally, however, in later sections of the work, Esquivel adopts Guerrero's approach, saturating his own work with ideas from the source but compressing motives, working them together, adding new ideas or redistributing old ones without regard necessarily for the original order of material.

The musical examples above show the close thematic relationship that exists between Esquivel's mass and Janequin's chanson. The thematic extracts from the mass (Ex. 4.14) are taken from Geiger's article.

The beginning of the Sanctus shows the kind of contrapuntal ingenuity often found in Guerrero, where two or more contrasting motives are combined. The head motive of the chanson appears transposed in the bass and is combined with itself in retrograde form in *altus I* and with a triadic motive in the tenor. The whole idea is then repeated by *superius I* and *II*, and *altus II* (Ex. 4.15)

Ex. 4.15. Esquivel: Sanctus, bars 1–5

Esquivel adopts this method of construction again in both his Agnus movements, where the combination of three separate motives reveals a high level of contrapuntal dexterity.

Esquivel's Osanna is in *tripla* mensuration and is based on the same material as Guerrero's Osanna; but this time Esquivel does not attempt to combine his subject with a counter-subject as Guerrero does. His movement is more like Guerrero's second Kyrie, the only example of triple meter outside an Osanna in Guerrero's masses. Both composers use a single head motive in imitation as a means of construction.

Victoria uses triple mensuration frequently in his *Missa pro victoria*. It seems to hold a special significance for him in this work and is not confined solely to the more joyful sections of the text. However, comparisons between Esquivel's mass and Victoria's are difficult to make. Stylistically, the two works have little in common. The predominantly homophonic idiom of *Missa pro victoria*, and the emphasis on tonic/dominant and the antiphonal style of writing are not to be found in the remnants of Esquivel's work we have available to us, although Geiger drew attention to one particular homophonic passage from the beginning of Esquivel's Gloria, making stylistic comparisons with Palestrina (Ex. 4.16).[38]

Ex. 4.16. Esquivel: Gloria, bars 1–4

We cannot be sure, however, how much Esquivel employed this style in his *Missa Batalla*; on the evidence left to us, he seems to prefer to maintain contrapuntal interest throughout his works rather than write in a homophonic idiom.

Considerations of style raise the question of when and for what occasion the *Missa Batalla* was written. Battle music was often composed to celebrate a victory, but there were few outright victories to celebrate in Philip II's reign. As is well known, it was a turbulent time, marked, internally, by the Morisco problem and, externally, by the struggle in the Netherlands, the Turkish threat and wars with France and England. All these probably had little impact upon the daily life of the citizens of Ciudad Rodrigo; but they were directly affected by the War of Succession to the Portuguese throne in 1580 and 1581, although, according to Hernández Vegas, such skirmishes as took place were of a relatively minor order.[39] Although Esquivel was chapelmaster in Oviedo at this time, the *Missa Batalla* could have

38 Geiger, 'Juan Esquivel', p. 155.
39 Vegas, *Ciudad Rodrigo*, I, p. 308.

been presented to the citizens of Ciudad Rodrigo, Esquivel's birth place, as an act of thanksgiving for deliverance. Given that the style of the mass is nearer that of Guerrero's *Missa De la batalla escoutez* than Victoria's *Missa pro victoria*, it seems likely that the work dates from around the time of the publication of Guerrero's *Liber secundus* (1582) rather than after 1600.

In examining the remaining fragments of Esquivel's *Missa Batalla*, we find that, as with the *Missa Ave Virgo sanctissima*, Esquivel tends to compress his ideas into a short timescale. Table 6 below, comparing the relative lengths of seven of Esquivel's mass movements with the corresponding sections in the battle masses of Janequin, Guerrero and Victoria, clearly illustrates this. Brevity itself does not necessarily imply inferior quality, however, and as Table 6 demonstrates, Victoria contracts his material into an even shorter time span than Esquivel in some parts of his mass. Nevertheless, a closer examination of some of Esquivel's movements leads to the conclusion that his sense of design does not always match that of Guerrero.

TABLE 6. Relative length of individual movements in the battle masses of Esquivel, Janequin, Guerrero and Victoria

	Esquivel	Janequin	Guerrero	Victoria
Kyrie I	18	25	20	18
Kyrie II	15	24	32	8
Sanctus	21	51	43	21
Osanna	O 18	C 29	O¾ 29	3 13
Benedictus	20	29	38	12
Agnus Dei I	25	32	47	27
Agnus Dei II	24	33	52	–

Osanna II and Agnus Dei III have been omitted from this table as only Janequin sets these texts to new music

This is particularly obvious when the two masters' settings of the Benedictus are compared. The whole of Esquivel's Benedictus is shown in Ex. 4.17.

Guerrero's Benedictus has a firm sense of design. His movement is symmetrically balanced and at the mid-point he cadences on the dominant; each half of the movement develops separate ideas, thus reinforcing the binary design already established by the dominant cadence at the mid-point. Moreover, his ingeniously devised contrapuntal lines sound fluent and purposeful.

In contrast, Esquivel's setting is asymmetrical, and his writing is merely conventional. He begins with a typical Renaissance-style point not derived from the model, but the music appears to wander aimlessly, unsure of its tonal direction. While Guerrero uses accidentals sparingly, giving his passage a firm sense of tonal direction – moving from tonic to dominant and back again – Esquivel uses a surprising number of accidentals in such a short passage: an F♯ in bar 11, a C♯ in bar 12, to be followed by an F♯ again in bar 14 and a C♯ again in bar 18, hinting anachronistically at the key of D minor.

Interestingly, Guerrero concludes his Benedictus with the same cadential figure

Ex. 4.17. Esquivel: Benedictus

as Esquivel, but the harmonic treatment of the melodic formula is different (with an A replacing Esquivel's *altus* B♭, and a D minim in the bass replacing Esquivel's E–F progression). As can be seen, Esquivel sees no reason to avoid a diminished triad, unless, of course, he expected his singers to flatten the E in the tenor part. But, as Alan Atlas has pointed out, during the fifteenth and sixteenth centuries there were exceptions to the *mi contra fa* rule which prohibited the harmonic interval of the diminished fifth between two parts. Tinctoris, in the late fifteenth century, found diminished fifths in the works of 'many, many composers, even the most famous'.[40]

There are other passages, too, where Esquivel's contrapuntal ingenuity and sense of architectural design do not quite match those of Guerrero. One such example occurs in the Agnus Dei movements of each master, where, in spite of Esquivel's apparent dexterity in manipulating twelve vocal lines as he does in Agnus Dei II, the fertility of Guerrero's imagination and the superiority of his contrapuntal mastery exceeds that of the younger composer.

Ex. 4.18. Esquivel: Agnus Dei I, opening

Esquivel's first Agnus Dei setting works well. It begins (Ex. 4.18) with the head motive from the chanson, which is combined with an original counter-subject in *altus II* and the tenor motive used only once by Janequin in part two of the chanson for the phrase 'Pour secourir' (bars 50–1, ed. Henry Expert).

He continues to develop Janequin's material, skilfully borrowing and integrating the composer's 'Frere le le lan' motive from part two of the chanson (bars 20 ff.) for the phrase 'miserere nobis'.

In comparison, Guerrero gives his whole movement a sense of unity by employing a melodic ostinato. This is the head motive of the chanson in augmentation set as a *cantus firmus*. It is repeated throughout, at two bar intervals, and at two alternating pitches, six times in all. Against this, triadic motives – which are such a feature of the chanson – dominate the texture, further reinforcing the feeling of

---

40 Tinctoris, *The Art of Counterpoint*, trans. and ed. Albert Seay, Musicological Studies and Documents 5 (Middleton, WI, 1961). See Atlas, *Renaissance Music*, pp. 239–40. Atlas quotes Tinctoris's examples, which include works by Guillaume Fauges, Busnoys and Philippe Caron.

unity. Repetition appears again at at the end of the movement when the bass line intones the phrase 'misere nobis' six times, each time to the same melodic phrase.

The use of this motive in this way engenders a feeling of repose when the cadence is finally reached: words and music are beautifully matched and the skilful design of this movement displays a level of imagination and contrapuntal skill not reached by Esquivel. Moreover, this feeling is further reinforced when comparisons are made between the second of the two Agnus Dei settings.

Both movements are on a larger scale than the sections of the mass preceding them. Guerrero expands his five voices to eight (SSAATTBB) and Esquivel to twelve (SSSSAAATTTBB). This Agnus Dei setting is important because examples of Spanish Renaissance polyphony in twelve parts are rare and this movement is the largest in scale of any of Esquivel's works handed down to us. It is disappointing to find, therefore, that the movement is so short. The comparable section in Guerrero's mass is over twice the length (see Table 6). Why did Esquivel go to so much trouble for only 24 bars? Was he trying to prove he was the equal of his compatriots in his contrapuntal mastery? If this was the case, the movement is a disappointment because most of the time there are no more than eight voices sounding; only in the last four bars do all voices sound together.

Esquivel does not subdivide his forces into two six-part choirs as one might expect but attempts to maintain a contrapuntal texture throughout. He draws his thematic material almost exclusively from the triadic fanfare motives that dominate Janequin's chanson. There are so many of these that we cannot be quite sure which motives Esquivel had in mind when he borrowed from his source. His main imitative points are combined with short original motives; his individual lines are frequently broken up by rests. His total structure is divided into two overlapping sections: a cadence on C ending the phrase 'qui tollis peccata mundi' in bar 13 ends the first section as the bass heralds the beginning of the second section with a fanfare motive for 'dona nobis pacem'.

Perhaps the fragmentary texture and the use of many short motives was deliberate, an attempt to demonstrate that the work had a military flavour. If so, it is not entirely convincing, lacking cohesion, especially in its second section. It compares unfavourably with the masterly way in which Guerrero spreads his ideas over a much wider canvas.

Whereas Esquivel divides his movement into two subsections, Guerrero's Agnus Dei II can be subdivided into four; each section draws on different material from the model, beginning with paired entries of the head motive in section one and ending with a motive from the end of part two of the chanson at the close of the work. There is much ingenuity in his handling of borrowed material, and in the closing bars the head motive in retrograde is combined with material from the end of the chanson (Ex. 4.19).

Nothing as subtle as this occurs in Esquivel's handling of material. Guerrero's Agnus Dei setting is beautifully balanced and, along with the rest of the mass, is a fine example of his ability to build large-scale structures from borrowed material. But perhaps it is unfair to develop the comparisons further: only remnants of Esquivel's work survive and these do not allow us to see how he structured the larger movements of the mass. What remains has considerable merit and adds

Ex. 4.19.　Guerrero: the close of Agnus Dei II (*superius I* and *altus I*)

greatly to our knowledge of large-scale vocal polyphony and the sixteenth-century 'battle mass' in particular.

Earlier in this chapter reference was made to the symbolic interpretation given to the masses of Janequin, Guerrero and Victoria by Gudmundson. Had Gudmundson had access to Esquivel's *Missa Batalla* he may well have included this work in his study for, adopting his stance, it would not be difficult to put forward an argument seeking to prove that the composer chose certain motives because of their extra-musical connotations. It could be argued that, in his choice of his motivic borrowing, the composer was seeking to draw parallels between the spiritual realm and the natural world. Two examples will illustrate the point.

At the beginning of Agnus Dei I, Esquivel quotes fragments from the source that are associated with specific textual phrases: 'escoutez', 'Pour secourir', 'La victoire du noble roy, du roy Francoys'. Were these musical motives associated with these texts deliberately chosen to emphasise associations such as the following?

The Lamb of God comes to our aid just as the noble King Francis came to the aid of his people. Just as Francis, an earthly king won an earthly victory, so Christ as the heavenly King won a spiritual victory; he conquered sin, or in the words of the mass, 'he takes away the sins of the world'.

Similarly, in Agnus Dei II, Esquivel makes much use of the fanfare motives associated in the chanson with the noise of warfare. He concludes with the minor third interval, C-A, which Janequin sets to the word 'escoutez'. The Agnus Dei is a prayer of petition; perhaps by choosing warlike motives and attaching them to phrases like 'dona nobis pacem', the composer is seeking to emphasise that Christ has fought and won a battle but peace will only be given to those who really listen ('escoutez!').

This is conjectural, of course; nevertheless, the whole notion of symbolism in these battle masses cannot be dismissed out of hand, and there may be some truth in Gudmundson's notion that the bellicose connotations of the chanson are reflected in the military postures of the Counter-Reformation Church in Spain at the end of the sixteenth century. A militant Church was fighting for what it saw as truth. If, as the evidence seems to suggest, *La guerre* was so well known in Spain, perhaps it came to be used as a basis for parody not because it expressed 'the unity of the Trinitarian Godhead' (Gudmundson) but because it could be re-interpreted and seen as a symbol of spiritual warfare – truth against heresy. By identifying with the general theme of warfare, composers who used Janequin's chanson as a basis for their compositions were expressing their faith in a victorious Holy Catholic Church: Christ, the spiritual leader of his Church, is seen as replacing Francis, the temporal leader of his army; the Church's faith – the one true faith in the minds of the Counter-Reformation clergy – would be triumphant just as Francis's army was triumphant. This is again conjectural; but perhaps it does go some way to explain why Janequin's chanson was used by composers at different times and in different places during the late sixteenth century as the basis of composition for a mass.

MISSA UT RE ME FA SOL LA

ESQUIVEL'S NEXT MASS ORDINARY is again a large-scale setting, scored à8 for SSSAATTB. Such a vocal grouping might suggest the distribution of voices into two different choirs, but this was clearly not the composer's intention. As one might expect with an eight-part piece, there are contrasts in vocal groupings, but the mass can in no way be described as a polychoral piece.

The work is something of an enigma: given its overall length, and the omission of the first Osanna and a second Agnus Dei, it may be considered a *missa brevis*; but the grandeur of its structure suggests that it might have been written for some festal occasion. However, in the absence of documentary evidence, we can only speculate what this occasion might have been.

One clue may lie in the long association of the hexachord with the ancient Latin hymn, *Ut queant laxis*, a connection made by Lester Brothers in relation to an entirely different hexachord mass, that of the Tudor composer Avery Burton.[41] In seeking to identify Burton's *Missa Ut re me fa sol la* with a liturgical occasion, Brothers suggests that, as *Ut queant laxis* is proper to Second Vespers of the feast of St John the Baptist (June 24) Burton's mass may have been intended for this occasion.

The feast of St John the Baptist is a major feast in the Church's calendar and we know from the contents of the *Motecta festorum* that it was celebrated in Ciudad Rodrigo, since Esquivel included in his collection the motet *Descendit angelus Domini* for the feast. Thus, it is possible that Esquivel's Hexachord Mass may also have been written for the celebration of the feast of St John the Baptist. Hexachord masses bearing the title *Missa Ut queant laxis* continue to appear long after Avery Burton's setting (for example Carissimi, c.1650), lending further support to this theory.[42]

The hexachord was, of course, the common property of all Renaissance composers, and Esquivel's Hexachord Mass is only one of many based on this elemental material. In the course of his work on Avery Burton's mass, Brothers studied twenty-five extant hexachord masses, leading him to the conclusion that composers took up the scalar melody as a challenge to their ingenuity. No perfunctory exercises, these masses invariably show imagination and skill in fresh and distinctive

---

41 Lester C. Brothers, 'Avery Burton and his Hexachord Mass', *Musica disciplina* 28 (1974), pp. 153–76; 'New Light on an Early Tudor Mass: Avery Burton's *Missa Ut re mi fa sol la*', *Musica disciplina*, 32 (1978), pp. 111–26.
42 Brothers, 'New Light on an Early Tudor Mass', p. 121.

compositions, with, of course, varying results.'[43] This, then, provides another clue
to the enigma of the creation of Esquivel's mass: he may have wished to prove that
he was quite as capable as older and established masters in handling this basic
melodic material, the substance of countless counterpoint exercises throughout the
fifteenth and sixteenth centuries.

In passing, it is worth remembering that, although in numerical terms the
number of hexachord masses is relatively small – as compared, that is, with the
large numbers of works based on original material or written as parodies – the
vogue for using the hexachord covers a wide time span, from c.1500 to c.1740.[44]
In addition to Avery Burton's Hexachord Mass, other notable examples include:
Brumel's *Missa Ut re mi fa sol la*, published by Petrucci in Venice (1503), and probably the first to be written,[45] the hexachord masses by Morales and Palestrina,[46] and
Francisco Valls's *Missa Scala Aretina*, a splendid Baroque polychoral work written
around 1702 for performance in Barcelona cathedral.[47]

Esquivel's work invites comparison with the hexachordal masses of Morales and
Palestrina. The comparison is instructive, highlighting some resemblances, but also
some differences, in approach.

Given the esteem in which Morales was held,[48] and the fact that Esquivel's
teacher, Juan Navarro, was himself a pupil of the older master, it seems reasonable
to suppose that the young composer might have been made familiar with the works
of Morales. His music was disseminated widely inside and outside his native land,
and archival studies have revealed the extent to which his works formed part of the
repertory of many Spanish cathedrals well beyond their time of composition.

Although there is no direct evidence to link Esquivel with Palestrina, it is not
unlikely that he was familiar with the Italian master's works, which, given his reputation, may well have been held up as models of composition for young composers. Although contemporary documentation suggests that Palestrina's works were
not as widely disseminated in Spain as the works of native Spanish and Franco-
Flemish composers of an earlier generation, his music appears in choirbooks found

43 Ibid., p. 114.
44 Ibid., p. 114.
45 Antoine Brumel (c.1450–c.1520), *Opera omnia*, ed. Barton Hudson, Corpus mensurabilis
musicae 5, vols. I–VI (Middleton, WI, 1969–72), 'This Mass appears to be the earliest in which the
Guidonian hexachord serves as a cantus firmus; ... Brumel has exceeded his followers in the breadth
of his conception of the overall superstructure of the Mass'. *Opera omnia*, I, p. xvii.
46 Modern editions in Cristóbal de Morales, *Opera Omnia*, VII, ed. Higinio Anglés (Barcelona,
1964), pp. 36–57; *Le opere complete di Giovanni Pierluigi da Palestrina*, VI, ed. Raffaele Casimiri
(Rome, 1939), pp. 216–53.
47 Modern edition: Francisco Valls *Missa Scala Aretina*, ed. José López-Calo (London, 1978).
Other examples of masses based on the hexachord are mentioned by Cerone in his treatise *El
melopeo y maestro*: see Strunk, *Source Readings*, p. 268. Cerone mentions hexachordal masses by
Pietro Ponzio, Pietro Vinci and Josquin's *Missa La sol fa re mi*; Strunk in a footnote adds works by
de Kerle and Soriano.
48 Bermudo, the most knowledgeable Spanish theoretician of the age, described him as 'luz de
España en la música' ('the 'light of Spain in music'). See Juan Bermudo, *Declaración de instrumentos
musicales* (Osuna, 1555), fol. 84v.

in the library of the Escorial; moreover, the Hexachord Mass was copied into a large choirbook executed in Spain in the second half of the sixteenth century, now owned by the Hispanic Society of America.[49] It may well be that Esquivel gained a knowledge of Palestrina's mass from this manuscript. Two pieces of musical evidence may be brought forward in support of this.

Firstly, the *nota cambiata* figure, so much part of Palestrina's style, features very prominently in the first Kyrie (in *superius II*) and the Christe (again *superius II*) of Esquivel's Hexachord Mass. Although a common idiom in so much sixteenth-century polyphony, and not unique to Palestrina, it rarely appears in Esquivel's music in general; here, however, it is used boldly, almost self-consciously, as if to advertise its presence.

Secondly, is it purely co-incidental that the opening of Esquivel's Gloria begins with a chord progression similar to that of Palestrina (Ex. 4.20)?

Ex. 4.20.   Opening of the Gloria from the hexachord masses
of Esquivel (above)and Palestrina (below)

A homophonic opening like this is not a common feature of Esquivel's music, and stylistically it exhibits features not found in the other works in this volume. Technically, there are features that mark it out as old-fashioned. It seems to occupy a middle ground between, on the one hand, the essentially thoroughly contrapuntal style of Morales's Hexachord Mass and, on the other hand, the 'mixed' style of Palestrina's work, where passages of counterpoint and homophony appear juxtaposed. Although superficially grand in scale, it has structural weaknesses which become apparent on closer inspection and which create a sense of disappointment for the

49 See Stevenson, *Spanish Cathedral Music*, p. 126 n. 269. Stevenson gives few details beyond saying that the Hexachord Mass can be found at fols. 1v–33.

enquirer hoping to find a work to rival Palestrina's Hexachord Mass. Indeed, there are many aspects of the mass that tempt us into thinking that it may be an early work, dating perhaps from the composer's student days. Equally, however, there are other signs that suggest this was not so: the contrapuntal demands made by the manipulation of eight separate strands of melody are considerable and it is unlikely that a composer in the early stages of learning his craft would exhibit such skill in this respect as Esquivel does in this work.

Morales, Palestrina and Esquivel all make use of the hexachord in different ways, and although each composer works to a different ground plan, all three men have one feature in common: they limit their use of the hexachordal scale to its natural and so-called 'hard' form.

Morales begins each of his movements with a rising hexachord and uses this to generate many of his principal thematic ideas. He does not use the hexachord, as Palestrina does, as a *cantus firmus*; it generates ideas but at no point assumes a prominence above other melodic lines.

In commenting on Palestrina's mass, Gustav Reese has observed that:

> In the Hexachord Mass, Palestrina displays his great gift for building elaborate structures on the simplest material; superius II consists of only the ascending and descending *hexachordum durum* (absent from no section), which, in varying rhythmic forms, serves as *cantus firmus*. This hexachord and also the hexachordum naturale appear at times in the other voices, but the *hexachordum molle* is never present.[50]

Although there is no *cantus firmus* in Esquivel's mass, the hexachord features extensively throughout. In the Kyrie, for example, there are eighteen references to it: some are ascending, some descending; some are self-contained statements, others are part of a longer motive. However, there seems to be no overall plan which determines the use of the hexachord in this movement; rather it appears at random when and where it will fit. This impression is also gained from studying later movements; only occasionally does Esquivel use the hexachord to build an extensive section of imitation. Examples occur at the 'Domine Deus' section of the Gloria, the 'Amen' of the Gloria and the opening of the Credo. Although he achieves great variety in his use of the hexachord and displays considerable powers of imagination in his invention of melodic and rhythmic ideas derived from it, he does not match the richness of invention coupled to the essentially simple design of Palestrina's work.[51]

An interesting feature of Palestrina's mass is the use he makes of augmentation and diminution of note values in his presentation of the hexachord. A particularly fine example occurs in the second Kyrie, where each statement of the hexachord is progressively reduced from (in modern notation) semibreves to crotchets. There is nothing in Esquivel's mass to compare with this: thematic transformation in augmentation or diminution does not appear to interest him.

---

50 Reese, *Music in the Renaissance*, p. 473.

51 Henry Coates has pointed out that the Hexachord Mass was copied into the papal choirbooks in 1562 and was evidently composed before this date. See Henry Coates, *Palestrina* (London, 1938), p. 106.

A particularly interesting point of comparison between these three hexachord masses is the way in which cadences are formed at the end of a movement, or each main section of a movement. Palestrina always cadences on C or G; his *cantus firmus* always rises and descends to its starting point (C or G). Morales frequently ends with a rising hexachord which concludes its upward flight on A or E and which is harmonised either with a complete A major triad or an open fifth. Esquivel contrives to bring his sections to an end in a similar way, sometimes by way of using the rising hexachord but at other times not. A final cadence on A marks a sectional division nine times in the mass: an A major triad ends both Kyries; the second section of the Gloria ends with an open fifth on A at the phrase 'filius patris'; an A major triad again appears at the end of the first section of the Credo ('descendit de coelis'), and the second ('et homo factus est') and the final 'Amen'; another marks the end of the Sanctus ('gloria tua') and Benedictus; finally, the Agnus Dei concludes with yet another A major triad. It is difficult to understand in certain places why Esquivel chose to cadence on A; a reworking of his contrapuntal lines could have brought him back to his tonal starting point.

Ex. 4.21 shows the tonal transition from Kyrie I to the Christe, and from the Christe to Kyrie II. The tonal transition here within a single movement is an abrupt one and – as an examination of many masses of this period will confirm – is unusual. Generally, at a sectional division, the opening motive of a new section begins with a note which is a member of the final chord of the preceding section; or the opening chord of the new section will repeat the final chord. The Credo of Palestrina's six-voice *Missa De Beata Virgine* is one example: the prevailing tonality throughout the Crucifixus section may be described as C major, but the section ends with *cantus 1* ascending from G to E and Palestrina cadences on an E major triad; the following section then begins with the same chord. Sometimes when this procedure is adopted there is a change of modality; the major chord of the cadence will be made minor in the section which follows. In the case of the second Kyrie quoted above, one is left wondering how well Esquivel's singers would cope with such a transition!

In passing, it should be noted that the terms 'tonal transition' and 'tonality' are used here purely for convenience: no Renaissance theorist would recognise such terms; and yet the fact remains that much late-sixteenth-century music can be explained in tonal terms, as the late Howard Mayer Brown has pointed out.

In commenting on the Agnus Dei from Palestrina's *Missa Aeterna Christi munera*, Brown writes:

> Thus the overall plan, I–IV–I–V–I, is clearly organized and clearly tonal (though with a pattern different from later tonal schemes); even the vocabulary of chords, different as it is in many particulars from seventeenth- and eighteenth-century music, includes a surprisingly high percentage of progressions based on 'tonal' scale degrees – that is I, IV, and V in the tonic, subdominant and dominant 'keys'. For a presumably modal piece, this Mass section, like most of Palestrina's work, is remarkably susceptible to explanation in tonal terms.[52]

52 Howard M. Brown, *Music in the Renaissance* (Englewood Cliffs, 1976), p. 289. A similar view was expressed by Henry Coates and Gerald Abraham in 1968. In writing about the style of

Ex. 4.21. Hexachord Mass: sectional transitions in the Kyrie

Other writers deplore attempts to describe what they understand as modal music in tonal terms. Thus Bernhard Meier, a firm defender of the eight Church modes and their application in polyphony, argues that such a stance is contrary both to what can be observed in the music and to what contemporary theoreticians wrote about the nature of the modes in polyphony. He cites careful observance of the authentic and plagal modes, and the primacy of the tenor as being important compositional principles.[53] The tenor determines the mode – this is a point Meier

Palestrina's later masses, they say of the *Missa Aeterna Christi munera*: 'Based on a Matins hymn in Mode XI, identical with the modern major mode, it naturally manifests a leaning towards the diatonic'. See 'Latin Church Music on the Continent, 2: The Perfection of the *a capella* Style', in Gerald Abraham, ed., *The New Oxford History of Music*, IV (London, 1968), p. 322. Stevenson makes a similar point when discussing Victoria's masses. Taking as an example the *Missa quarti toni*, he says 'it cannot be gainsaid that a perfectly tidy (if anachronistic) harmonic analysis of the whole mass in A minor can be given'. Stevenson, *Spanish Cathedral Music*, p. 399.

53 Bernard Meier, *The Modes of Classical Polyphony*, trans. Ellen Beebe (New York, 1988), p. 56.

is careful to stress again and again. He draws on contemporary evidence to prove his point, quoting extensively from, among others, Cyriacus Schneegas,[54] an anonymous Italian author (Florence, Biblioteca nazionale centrale, MS Magl. XIX, 44: first half of the seventeenth century),[55] Praetorius,[56] Zarlino[57] and Aron.[58]

However, Meier draws his evidence exclusively from authors of the Italian and German schools. When reference is made to Spanish theory, a different picture emerges. Santa María, for example, advocates study of the upper voice part, not the tenor, since it is the highest part 'which so governs all the other voices that they do not stray outside the confines and limits of the mode'.[59] Moreover, supporters of the eight-mode system had to compete with Glarean's theories of twelve modes outlined in his *Dodecachordon* of 1547. Thus, we have conflicting evidence on the issue of modal attribution; it would seem that it was a subject much debated by sixteenth-century theorists and one on which there was no universal agreement.[60]

If we relate these arguments to the Agnus Dei passage from Palestrina's *Missa Aeterna Christe Munera* quoted by Brown above, we can hear and explain the passage in three different ways:

1. It can be attributed to the transposed Ionian mode – as Henry Washington does in the preface to his well-used edition;[61]

2. Based on Meier's arguments, it can be regarded as being in the Lydian mode since this mode could have a B♭ signature (*cantus mollis*). Thus, it can be seen that Palestrina preserves the authentic/plagal relationship of bass and tenor, alto and soprano;[62]

3. It can be heard tonally and be described, albeit anachronistically, as being in F major.

54 Meier, *The Modes of Classical Polyphony*, p. 56. Cyriacus Schneegas, *Isagoges libri duo* (Erfurt, 1591).

55 Meier, *The Modes of Classical Polyphony*, p. 57.

56 Meier, *The Modes of Classical Polyphony*, p. 62. Michael Praetorius, *Syntagma musicum*, III (Wolfenbuttel, 1619).

57 Meier, *The Modes of Classical Polyphony*, p. 63. Gioseffe Zarlino, *Le istituzioni armoniche* (Venice, 1558).

58 Meier, *The Modes of Classical Polyphony*, p. 70. Pietro Aron, *Trattato della natura et cognitione di tutti gli tuoni di canto figurato* (Venice, 1525).

59 Samuel Rubio, *Classical Polyphony*, trans. Thomas Rive (Oxford, 1972), p. 37. Santa Maria, *Arte de tañer fantasia* (Valladolid, 1565), fol. 63.

60 Meier's defence of and belief in the modal system as the governing principle of Renaissance polyphony has been subject to discussion by Harold Powers, who develops the concept of the 'tonal type' as a useful means categorising polyphony. See Harold S. Powers, 'Tonal Types and Modal Categories in Renaissance Polyphony', *Journal of the American Musicological Society* 34 (1981), p. 428–70; also, 'The Modality of "Vestiva i colli"', in Robert L. Marshall, ed., *Studies in Renaissance and Baroque Music in Honour of Arthus Mendel* (Kassel and Hachensack, 1974), pp. 31–46. Powers's views have been very influential in encouraging debate on this controversial issue of modal categorisation.

61 *Missa Aeterna Christi munera*, ed. Henry Washington (London, 1953).

62 If one wants to explain away Palestrina's compositions in modal terms, Glarean's twelve-mode theory provides a logical explanation, of course, but as Reese points out, in reality the 'new' modes already existed through the practice of flattening B within the Dorian and Lydian modes, so that in effect there were only five fundamental modes. Moreover, the distinction between an authentic mode and its plagal is, in polyphony, an academic one. See Reese, *Music in the Renaissance*, p. 186.

The aural evidence for this latter view is overwhelming and, as Brown has observed, a high percentage of chord progressions are based on primary triads, so that, to a listener in the twentieth century conditioned by post-Renaissance tradition, the music appears to have a key centre from which it may be heard to modulate frequently to the subdominant or dominant keys. To repeat: this concept of tonality would not, of course, be understood by musicians in the Renaissance, but for us in the twenty-first century it offers a workable alternative to the contentious efforts of contemporary theorists to account for a phenomenon for which they had no unequivocal explanation; it at least allows us to use a familiar conceptual framework to analyse what we see and hear. Thus, with reference to the hexachord masses of both Palestrina and Esquivel: instead of assigning them to the Mixolydian mode (because of the *ambitus* of the tenor), or to the Ionian mode (on the basis of Glarean's extension of the eight modes to twelve), we may follow Brown's approach and say that both works 'suggest' a C major tonality. This is beautifully illustrated by the opening of the Gloria of Esquivel's mass, where Ex. 4.20 is continued by the passage given in Ex. 4.22.

Ex. 4.22.   Esquivel: Gloria, *Missa Ut re me fa sol la*, bars 4–6

It is – using Brown's phraseology – 'remarkably susceptible to explanation in tonal terms'.[63] The opening phrase (Ex. 4.20) clearly outlines a diatonic C major chord progression, cadencing IIb[7]–V–I; its answering phrase outlines a diatonic progression cadencing IIb[7]–V–I on G, suggesting – albeit anachronistically, in post-Renaissance terms – a 'modulation' to G major. Symmetry of phrase structure, of course, is partly responsible for the effect of tonal shift and Esquivel employs the same principle again to close the first section of the Gloria (see Ex. 4.23). Here, the horizontal movement of his part-writing creates, vertically, an augmented triad (marked *) in bar 34, an interval which occurs frequently in his music.

63 References to what might be termed 'emerging tonality' in early music are highly contentious and a full discussion of this complex topic is beyond the scope of this book. Readers are referred to Cristle Collins Judd, *Tonal Structures in Early Music* (New York, 1998), where the different methodological approaches to the analysis of early music are discussed in great detail.

Setting aside the tonal implications of the chord progressions in the two hexa-chord masses by Palestrina and Esquivel, it is now necessary to examine the vertical disposition of the vocal lines in these works – and in Morales's Hexachord Mass – from a different standpoint.

It is obvious at a glance that Palestrina and Esquivel exploit both the horizontal and the vertical possibilities of their vocal lines, whereas Morales's primary concern is with the former. He achieves total equality between all four lines of his texture, drawing as we have seen already many of his principal motivic ideas from the hexa-chord itself. Except for one brief passage in the Credo ('Et incarnatus') his music is thoroughly contrapuntal throughout; Palestrina, in contrast, makes extensive use of homophony in the Gloria and Credo. There is, of course, nothing exceptional about this procedure in a late-sixteenth-century mass, although it is sometimes assumed that the appearance of chordal writing in Church music was the result of demands from the Council of Trent for textural clarity. But simple chordal-style masses were common in northern Italy in works which made no reference to Church reforms;[64] to infer that chordal writing is present in a work because of the deliberations of an ecclesiastical committee could well be wrong.

Such homophonic passages as that found at the beginning of the Gloria of Palestrina's mass are rare in Esquivel's music. More typical of his procedure is what may be described as a 'quasi-contrapuntal' style, as demonstrated, for example, in the first Kyrie (Ex. 4.24).

The whole of this passage is contrapuntal in the sense that every part, including the bass, is totally independent melodically and rhythmically; however, for the final few bars the *bassus* ceases to have contrapuntal equality with the upper voices. Its function is to provide a harmonic support for the contrapuntal movement above it. Palestrina's voice parts tend to move together at the rate of one chord per minim, or even at one chord per semibreve (in modern note values); Esquivel's voice parts pursue their rhythmic independence, changing chord more or less every crotchet. Two further examples should serve to make this point abundantly clear (Ex. 4.25 and 4.26).

It has been argued that homophonic writing is a characteristic of the Spanish school of polyphony, a view illustrated by the Spanish scholar, Dionisio Preciado, with reference to the motets of Alonso Tejeda. In his edition of the collected works of this contemporary of Esquivel, Preciado describes Tejada's style in the following terms:

> Two things show clearly this lack of polyphonic movement in the motets of Tejeda: the ease with which voices join, forming duos, trios and even block harmonies of four and more notes, and the independence of the lower part, which, many times, often goes off on its own in a form more harmonic than imitative. Parallel duos and trios abound on the basis of successive thirds and sixths. The formation of block harmony is obvious. The least polyphonic voice is the lowest, which many times marches along in leaps of the fourth and fifth without imitative pretensions.[65]

64 Lockwood, *The Counter-Reformation and the Masses of Vincenzo Ruffo*, p. 134.
65 Alonso de Tejeda, *Obras completas*, ed. Dionisio Preciado, 2 vols, I (Madrid, 1976), p. 138: 'Dos

Ex. 4.23.   Esquivel: Gloria, *Missa Ut re me fa sol la,* bars 28–35

Ex. 4.24. Esquivel: Kyrie I, *Missa Ut re me fa sol la*
(continued over three pages)

The parallel writing of Tejeda, as described by Preciado, is not a particular characteristic of Esquivel's style, however, and only the last sentence of this quotation has any relevance to his style of writing in the Hexachord Mass. Indeed, in the light of available evidence it is difficult to see why Preciado should infer that homophonic writing is a particularly Spanish characteristic. Vertical sonorities appear to be more prevalent in the late masses of Palestrina, where the composer displays his

cosas ponen de manifiesto principalmente esta falta de caminar polifónico en los motetes de Tejeda; la facilidad de unirse las voces, formando dúos, tríos y aún bloques armónicos de cuatro y más notas, y la independencia del bajo que, muchas veces, camina por su cuenta en forma más armónica que imitativa. Abundan los dúos y tríos paralelos a base de terceras y sextas sucesivas. La formación de bloques armónicos es notoria. La voz menos polifónica es el bajo, que muchas veces marcha en saltos de cuarta y quinta, sin pretensiones imitativas.'

predilection for homophony which is 'characterized by a richness of sound created by the scoring, severe part-writing, sensitive relationships between the voices and a splendid harmonic structure that can be identified as tonal'.[66]

Esquivel, then, is primarily a contrapuntist, preferring to maintain a contrapuntal texture even when working with a large number of voices. Although he does make use of contrasting vocal groups, the texture of his antiphonal groupings is nearly always 'quasi-contrapuntal' and not the block-harmony approach of Palestrina. Examples of antiphonal passages of this nature appear mostly, as we might expect, in the Gloria and Credo, where Renaissance composers frequently use contrasts of vocal texture as a means of highlighting the text and delineating textual divisions. Some examples will serve to illustrate Esquivel's procedure.

66 Franke, 'Palestrina's Imitation Masses', p. 179.

In the Gloria the acclamations 'Laudamus te' and 'gratias agimus tibi' are reserved for the full choir; 'Jesu Christe' receives the same treatment, while sub-clauses of the text are articulated by contrasting vocal sub-groups in a 'quasi-contrapuntal' manner. The sequence 'Domine Deus, Agnus Dei, Filius Patris' is scored contrapuntally for reduced voices so that the return of the full choir for 'Qui tollis peccata mundi' is particularly effective; likewise, the final contrapuntal 'Amen' for full choir works well.

In the Credo Esquivel separates out the various sections of the text in a similar manner with the same 'quasi-contrapuntal' approach as in the Gloria. Only once when using all eight voices does he adopt a block-harmony approach; this treatment is reserved for the section of the text 'genitum non factum, consubstantialem Patri, per quem omnia facta sunt'. Like Palestrina he reduces his voices to four for the Crucifixus, using the same vocal grouping (SSAA), and scores the following

Ex. 4.25.   Palestrina: Hexachord Mass, Credo, bars 1–9

section 'Et in Spiritum Sanctum, Dominum et vivificantem' for full choir. Full choir is used again for the final section, 'Confiteor' to the 'Amen'. The 'Amen' is again set contrapuntally with the rising quaver movement of the Gloria now reversed. A particularly effective voice reduction is the section beginning 'Et unam sanctam catholicam', where Esquivel reduces his voices to four, again employing block harmony. He writes symbolically in triple metre here to suggest the unity of the Church, a common practice that can be observed in other masses of the period. Other obvious examples of symbolism occur when the hexachord is employed pictorially in its descending and ascending forms to suggest the descent and ascent into heaven ('descendit de coelis'; 'et ascendit in coelum').

Another feature worthy of comment when comparing Esquivel's hexachord mass with those of Morales and Palestrina concerns the overall dimensions of the three masses. The relative proportions of the three works are revealed in Table 7. The figures given refer to the number of bars in each movement when each work is transcribed into modern notation.

Ex. 4.26. Esquivel: Hexachord Mass, Credo, bars 1–8

TABLE 7. Relative length of individual movements
in the hexachord masses of Morales, Palestrina and Esquivel

	Esquivel	Palestrina	Morales
Kyrie	17	26	11
Christe	30	28	12
Kyrie	9	30	13
Gloria	105	110	72
Credo	176	189	160
Sanctus	19	88	51
Osanna	–*	41	17
Benedictus	20	47	21
Osanna	–	(41)[†]	17
Agnus Dei I	22	66	24
Agnus Dei II	–	59	36
TOTAL NO. OF BARS	382	684	434

* There is no Osanna I. Esquivel goes straight on to the Benedictus after 'gloria tua'.
[†] As Osanna II is a repeat of Osanna I, its 41 bars have not been included in the total.

It can be seen that, in terms of length, Palestrina's mass was conceived on a grander scale than the comparable works of Morales and Esquivel: only in the Gloria does Esquivel approach Palestrina in the length of his writing. In building his elaborate musical structure Palestrina takes his time and allows for textual repetition: Esquivel, on the other hand, allows for little repetition of text or musical ideas and compresses many of his entries together into a short space. Ex. 4.27 illustrates this clearly.

Although we may admire the composer's economical use of thematic material and technical dexterity at this point, the texture is rather crowded; and the idea of the falling fifth used for the opening point soon gives way to a new one as the second phrase of the text is introduced. In the comparable passage of Palestrina's first Agnus Dei in his Hexachord Mass, three bars elapse before a third voice enters and the entries are spaced out over a longer period, allowing the music to unfold at a more leisurely rate.

Only one Agnus Dei appears in Esquivel's setting; Palestrina composes two, adding another canonic voice (*altus*) to augment his texture. Morales also adds a second evocation and expands his four voices to five in a similar manner to Palestrina. Interestingly, in this mass, Esquivel saw no reason to compose further music for a second Agnus Dei as he had done in the first two masses of this collection. Perhaps he considered that the structure he had created here could not be bettered by any further show of contrapuntal artifice.

Conciseness by itself, of course, is not necessarily a sign of poor-quality work, and there is a trend visible throughout the sixteenth century to shorten the mass setting as a whole.[67] However, when we compare Esquivel's ability to build large-

67 Lockwood, *The Counter-Reformation and the Masses of Vincenzo Ruffo*, p. 175.

Ex. 4.27. Esquivel: Hexachord Mass, Agnus Dei, bars 1–7

scale musical structures and his inventiveness in devising musical ideas with the same qualities in works by Palestrina, we are left with the impression that the Italian master is superior in both respects.

To quote just one example of Palestrina's powers of imagination and invention: nowhere in Esquivel's mass do we find such an interesting rhythmic motive as that from the Benedictus of Palestrina's Hexachord Mass (Ex. 4.28).

in no - mi - ne

Ex. 4.28. Palestrina: Hexachord Mass, Benedictus, bars 22–3

Although this is in essence simply a written-out decoration of the harmony note E, Palestrina makes it a characteristic feature throughout this section of his mass setting, using it to impart unity to his musical construction.

Esquivel never descends to the perfunctoriness demonstrated by Lassus in some of his masses;[68] but even so, however much one admires the contrapuntal skill undeniably exhibited in this work, the composer never matches the artful simplicity of Morales; nor does he display the fecundity of ideas and the architectural magnificence of Palestrina.

MISSA DUCTUS EST JESUS

THE NEXT MASS in the *Liber primus missarum* – and the least ambitious – is a parody mass based on Guerrero's motet *Ductus est Jesus*. The motet is headed 'Dominica prima Quadragesimae' indicating that it is intended for liturgical performance on the first Sunday in Lent. The text follows the first temptation of Jesus as recorded in St Matthew's Gospel 4: 1–4.

> Jesus was led by the Spirit into the desert to be tempted by the Devil. After he had fasted for forty days and nights, he was hungry and the Devil approached him saying, 'If you are the Son of God, command these stones to be made bread'. Jesus replied saying, 'Scripture says, "Man doth not live by bread alone but by every word that proceedeth out of the mouth of God".'

Guerrero produced two different settings of this text. The second version, the one used by Esquivel as a model for his mass, was published in his second book of motets in 1570 and reprinted in a valedictory collection in 1597. Another setting for five voices is to be found in his first book of motets published in Seville in 1555

68 'In his *chanson*-Masses he [Lassus] sometimes surpassed Gombert and the French composers in brevity, perfunctoriness, and failure to conceal secular models with highly unsuitable words', Coates and Abraham, *New Oxford History of Music*, IV, p. 335.

under the title *Sacrae cantiones*. The motet chosen by Esquivel is a fine construction, showing ingenuity in the manipulation of chosen motives, and Guerrero's mastery of small-scale form. He uses his material economically, setting out a series of distinct melodic motives which are well matched to the text. He makes sparing use of melismas: the first Sunday in Lent is not an occasion for exuberant music. But the motet does have its dramatic moments, as, for example, when Guerrero highlights Jesus's conversation with the devil. The chordal declamation, the contrasts of rhythm and texture employed to record this encounter, are highly effective. Guerrero's model provides Esquivel with a rich repository of building materials, clearly defined musical motives which can be accommodated to new words, and motives which lend themselves to juxtapositions, inversions and so forth.

Again, we can speculate why Esquivel chose to parody this particular motet. Was it for symbolic reasons, or was he attracted to the structure of Guerrero's motet? We must conclude, I think, that Esquivel chose the motet for its musical qualities rather than its subject matter; on the other hand, we cannot discount the possibility that he deliberately drew on the music of a Lenten motet for symbolic as well as musical reasons, intending the work for use in Lent, a penitential season. It is possible that the mass and motet were performed together on the same liturgical occasion (with the omission of the Gloria) thus creating a theological and musical unity between different parts of the service.[69]

The source motet's principal motives are shown in Ex. 4.29, and when they are isolated from the surrounding polyphony in this way, it can quickly be observed that they reveal a strong element of thematic unity. This tendency has been observed before in relation to Guerrero's celebrated *Ave Virgo sanctissima* motet, but the degree of thematic unity is even more marked here. Many motives are formed from a four-note melodic cell within the interval of a perfect fourth; the notes within that cell are then re-arranged to forge a new idea. Thus, with reference to Ex. 4.29, we can see that no. (5) is a reworking of no. (4); no. (14) is a reworking of no. (13); motive (1b) is, of course, an inversion of (1a); (3b) is a partial inversion of (3a). But beyond this cellular relationship, a further structural unity is observable in Guerrero's tendency to give prominence to certain intervals: thus, for example, the interval of the minor third (A-C) is prominent in nos. (4) and (5); similarly,

---

69 For a study arguing for the supremacy of motivic borrowings in the sixteenth-century parody mass, see Sibley, 'The Sixteenth-Century Parody Mass'. Sibley discounts any theory of symbolic borrowing. It is his contention that a composer's choice of material from a model was governed entirely by musical considerations, by the ability of motives, textures and so forth to generate satisfying musical structures. His work is impressive for the vast amount of technical data he assembles on a large number of pieces. He first summarises the writings of twentieth-century and Renaissance theorists on parody composition, concluding that no all-embracing theory of parody ever existed: there were some general guidelines but composers, then as now, had much freedom of choice and were expected to use their imaginations to develop their borrowed ideas in any way they felt satisfactory. He then proceeds to a detailed analysis of thirty-three sixteenth-century parody masses arranged in eight groups. He compares masses by different composers using the same model and also compares one group of masses with another. Tables and charts show the extent and ordering of borrowed material in each of the masses studied. The assembled data, expressed in percentage terms, is then rigorously analysed to support his thesis.

Ex. 4.29. The principal melodic motives from Guerrero's motet, *Ductus est Jesus*

the interval of the perfect fourth is a prominent feature in nos. (1a), (1b), (3a), (3b) and (14). The number of motives with intervals in common suggests that thematic connections of this kind are not merely coincidental, but are the result of deliberate decisions made by the composer to give his work structural unity.

The composer himself included a setting of this motet text in his *Motecta festorum*. The opening incipit (Ex. 4.30) shows some resemblance to Guerrero's, at least in its choice of note values.

Ex. 4.30. Esquivel's incipit for his motet *Ductus est Jesus*

There are further rhythmic similarities in the design of motives, but these may be coincidental, arising out of the need for rhythmic stress on important syllables. Unlike Guerrero, Esquivel made no obvious attempt in his motet setting to devise melodic material from a cell, nor does one melodic idea seem to grow organically out of another.

The *Missa Ductus est Jesus* is of modest dimensions, similar in length to *Missa Ave Virgo sanctissima*. In fact, all five mass ordinaries in this publication are of similar length, as Table 8 shows.

TABLE 8. Comparative length of the *Liber primus* (1608) masses in bars

	Ave Virgo	Batalla	Ductus	Gloriose	Hexachord
Kyrie	11	18	15	19	17
Christe	12	?	17	17	14
Kyrie	12	15	11	12	9
Gloria	100	?	114	112	105
Credo	194	?	175	191	177
Sanctus	16	21	26	25	19
Osanna*	15	18	17	18	12
Benedictus	23	20	19	20	20
Agnus Dei I	23	25	21	30	23
Agnus Dei II	31	24	28	30	–
TOTAL NO. OF BARS	437	?	443	474	396

* All five masses have only one Osanna.

Missa Batalla may have been somewhat longer since some of the remaining movements appear to have been conceived on a slightly larger scale, but given that we do not have the Gloria and Credo it is impossible to be certain of the dimensions of the whole. Numerical data alone, of course, tell us very little about the artistic merits of a particular composition, and nothing about the liturgical occasion for which it might have been intended, but numerical comparisons can be useful in revealing certain trends. For example, as we observed earlier, there is a general trend, 'visible throughout the [sixteenth] century towards shortening the mass setting as a whole'.[70] But how far does a statistical analysis confirm this, and how do Esquivel's masses conform to this view? A numerical comparison between the masses of Victoria, Guerrero and Palestrina, using the total number of bars as a statistical measure, leads to the following conclusions:

Victoria's masses are shorter than those of Guerrero and Palestrina. *Dum complerentur* (1576) is his longest mass, reaching 657 bars. This is closely followed by *Gaudeamus*, from the same book, 655 bars, and then *Surge propera* (1583). Twelve of his masses fail to reach 500 bars while only ten of Palestrina's forty-eight masses published before 1595 fall below 500 bars. Palestrina's forty-five masses published in 1554, 1567, 1570, 1582, 1590, 1593/4 and 1594 reach on average 612 bars; in comparison, Victoria's eighteen masses published in 1576, 1583, 1592 and 1600, extend to 464 bars only.[71]

Statistical comparison, movement by movement, sheds further light on the question of individual differences between composers, as Table 9, compiled by using Stevenson's information, shows.[72]

70 Lockwood, *The Counter-Reformation and the Masses of Vincenzo Ruffo*, p. 175.
71 Stevenson, *Spanish Cathedral Music*, p. 376.
72 Ibid., p. 376.

TABLE 9. Average length of mass movements by Victoria and Palestrina

	Victoria	Palestrina
Kyrie	50	71
Gloria	106	120
Credo	170	192
Sanctus	92	141
Agnus Dei	46	88
TOTAL NO. OF BARS	464	612

From this table we can see that both Victoria and Palestrina tend to exceed Esquivel in the length of their masses. Guerrero also writes at greater length: we cite as just one example his *Missa Simile est regnum* (1582), a parody mass on the motet of the same name by Morales. The number of bars of each movement is given in Table 10.[73]

TABLE 10. Guerrero's *Missa Simile est regnum*: number of bars in each movement

Kyrie I	15
Christe	18
Kyrie	26
Gloria	108
Credo	180
Sanctus	53
Osanna*	13
Benedictus	33
Agnus Dei I	34
Agnus Dei II	46
TOTAL NO. OF BARS	526

*triple time (O³⁄₂)

If we compare the parody masses of Palestrina and the above-quoted Spanish trio with the great Franco-Flemish master, Lassus, mere numerical comparisons become more difficult to assess as indications of typicality since his parody masses vary considerably in length (and also in quality!). Lassus's primary interest was the motet and not the mass.[74] Many of his masses are of the short 'missa brevis' species; short settings of the Ordinary (less than 300 bars in transcription) in which there is little text repetition and in which there are few melismas, works obviously written to fulfil a particular liturgical function and deliberately written in this simple style,

73 Bar numbers refer to the Mapa Mundi edition; Francisco Guerrero, *Missa Simile est regnum*, ed. Martyn Imrie, Spanish Church Music 53 (London, 1981). In this edition the note values of the Osanna are quartered and barred as 6/4, giving a total of thirteen bars compared with twenty-six bars in Francisco Guerrero: *Opera omnia* V, transcr. by Jose M. Llorens Cistero (Barcelona, 1986), where note values are halved.

74 Wilder, 'The Masses of Orlando di Lasso', p. 1.

perhaps for specific groups of performers. (As an example, Lassus's first mass in his 1560 publication, *Missa super 'Je ne menge poinct de porcq'*, has an opening Kyrie of six bars, a Christe of seven bars and a second Kyrie of ten bars.) These masses contrast with more musically developed forms such as, for example, the well-known *Susanne un jour*, a much more expanded work of 520 bars in length.

As far as the mass ordinaries in the *Liber primus missarum* are concerned, the above evidence seems to suggest that Esquivel follows the general sixteenth-century trend towards shorter masses. On average, Esquivel's 1608 masses appear to be shorter than the masses of his Spanish contemporaries, and certainly shorter than many of his non-Spanish contemporaries. Any comparisons with Lassus are difficult to make, however: in the first place Lassus's output is so much greater – thirty-eight out of a total of forty-one published masses are parodies;[75] secondly, Lassus's parody methods differ radically from those of Esquivel. Lassus gives more attention to the original polyphonic layout of the model than Esquivel does, and he reproduces the fabric of the original frequently; his parody methods are less uniform than Esquivel's and show signs of change and development throughout his working life.

All the parody masses in the *Liber primus missarum* show similar characteristics, and Esquivel's approach to parody writing in the *Missa Ductus est Jesus* is not unlike *Missa Ave Virgo sanctissima*, his first essay in this form. In reworking borrowed material, he employs the conventional techniques of his time: he uses the principal motivic material from his source to construct his points, and makes occasional reference, with some adjustments, to the model's polyphonic fabric. In Esquivel's parody writing, however, references to the complete polyphonic fabric of the model are not to be found as frequently as in the works of some of his contemporaries, and in this particular mass there is rarely an exact correspondence between the texture of the source and the composer's borrowings. Some examples will serve to illustrate his approach.

The first seven bars of the first Kyrie reproduce the texture of the source motet almost exactly; the order and layout of entries is preserved, and the original note values are accommodated to the new text.

In the Gloria, the music set for the phrase 'Filius Patris' reworks on a vertical plane Guerrero's phrase 'de ore Dei' from the *secunda pars* of his motet. Some symbolism may be intended here. This phrase closes the motet and the text is repeated extensively. In borrowing this material to close the first section of the Gloria, Esquivel may have wanted to give added meaning to his choice of material; to highlight the belief that Christ, the Son of the Father, is the living word who proceeds 'out of the mouth of God'. Guerrero's music for 'postea esuriit', also from the *secunda pars*, provides the basis for Esquivel's 'Tu solus Dominus'. The high tessitura of the *cantus* part at this point (a variant of motive 6 beginning on high G) may have been the reason why Esquivel chose this material to illustrate 'Thou alone art the most high'. Guerrero's three-part homophonic texture, which is used to set 'Qui respondens dixit', is borrowed by Esquivel for his setting of 'miserere nobis'.

75 Ibid., p. 53.

JUAN ESQUIVEL

Kyrie

Gloria

Credo

Sanctus

Ex. 4.31. Esquivel: opening section of the Kyrie, Gloria, Credo, Sanctus and Agnus Dei I from *Missa Ductus est Jesus*

In the Credo, the 'Crucifixus' borrows the homophonic phrase 'Si filius Dei es' from the beginning of the *secunda pars*. Again, Esquivel may have chosen to use this passage deliberately here to make a theological point. There is an element of uncertainty in the devil's taunt: 'If you are the Son of God . . .'; but according to Christian doctrine, Christ *is* the Son of God, and he demonstrated this by an act of obedience, dying on the Cross for all. All doubt is removed: the devil's music is now transformed into music of redemption.

But it is the principle of drawing on melodic cells from the source that is the foundation of Esquivel's parody technique, and this is fully demonstrated in this mass.

As we might expect, he draws on Guerrero's head motive to open each movement, with the exception of Agnus Dei II, and the transformations show resourcefulness, as Ex. 4.31 demonstrates.

In the Gloria and Credo, motives follow each other in quick succession. No attempt is made to combine motives that have appeared separately in the source as Guerrero frequently does, nor is there much use of original material.

The final Agnus Dei is underpinned by the melodic ostinato device, much used by Guerrero. The four-voice texture is now expanded to five, as was common practice for the second Agnus Dei, and motive (5) floats gently through the movement at two-bar intervals, sung by the added *superius* commencing first on C and then on G. There is no substantially new material in this movement, all three phrases of the text being based on motives from the source motet, nor does Esquivel indulge in any display of contrapuntal ingenuity of the kind frequently demonstrated by composers in their settings of the Agnus Dei text.[76]

Table 11 shows the order of motives borrowed from the model as they appear in the mass.

TABLE 11. Order of motives borrowed from Guerrero's motet *Ductus est Jesus* as they appear in Esquivel's mass.

Kyrie I	1a, 1b
Christe	2
Kyrie II	4
Gloria	1a, 1b, 3a, 12, 9, 5, 7, 14// 8,
	6, 11, 13, 10, 1b, 6, 3b, 14, 7 (inverted)
Credo	1a, 1b, 4, 9, 5, 3a, 10, 2, 12, 6// 1a, 1b, 4, 9// 8,
	7, 8, 4, 1a, 12, 14// 5, 3b, 3a, 4, 10, 3a (1b) Confiteor, 9, 11
Sanctus	1b, 4, 5, 14
Osanna	1a
Benedictus	7,4
Agnus Dei I	1a, 9
Agnus Dei II	5, 4, 13

Table 12 shows the frequency with which motives from the source appear in the mass.

TABLE 12. *Missa Ductus est Jesus*: frequency of motivic use

Motive from source	1a	1b	2	3a	3b	4	5	6	7	8	9	10	11	12	13	14
No. of times used	7	7	2	4	2	8	5	3	4	3	5	3	3	3	2	4

Again, these tables do not tell us anything about the artistic merit of this piece, but they do reveal interesting information on Esquivel's method of parody composition. The prominence given to the head motive in its two different forms has already been noted, but we can also see that Esquivel is concerned to use all the material from his source; in addition, motives do not follow the order they did in the source but are subject to new juxtapositions. If similar tables are drawn up for a work by Guerrero, the comparison is revealing. Tables 13 and 14 present the same data for Guerrero's *Missa Simile est regnum*.

From this data we can see that Guerrero is much more absorbed with the head motive in this mass than Esquivel is in *Ductus est Jesus*; he does not draw on all the thematic material available to him, preferring instead to devise new contrapuntal workings of familiar material ever more cunningly. Of course, one cannot draw general conclusions from a comparison of only two works, but on the evidence

---

76 The following are some notable examples: the second Agnus Dei of Victoria's *Ascendens Christus* mass (1592) where he writes a canon *trinitas in unitate*; Alonso Lobo's mass *O Rex gloriae* (1602) where we find *canon in unidecimam* between *cantus I* and *bassus* while *tenor I* declaims a *cantus firmus* to the words 'O Rex gloriae'; Guerrero's *Missa Simile est regnum*, a parody of his own motet, where he writes a canon *in diapason* between the *tenor* and *cantus II*. There are numerous other examples of this technique of enhancing the text at this the most sacred point of the mass.

of other works examined and in the light of observations made by Stevenson, we have some evidence to suggest that there is a distinct difference in each composer's approach to parody writing. Guerrero likes to extract the maximum potential from his head motive, combining it with other motives whenever possible; he is economical in his use of motives, using only one motive for a whole movement; he uses free material more often. He is a master of 'weaving loose threads drawn out of a source motet into a new, tightly meshed web'.[77]

TABLE 13. Guerrero's *Missa Simile est regnum*:
order of motives borrowed from source motet

Kyrie I	1
Christe	11
Kyrie II	18
Gloria	1, 2, 5, 6, 7, 9, 1, 4, 1, 10//11, 10,
	12 (quote from Stabat Mater), 1, 11, 1, 18
Credo	1, 2, 3, 1, 4, 2, 9, 1, 17, 18, 10// 1, 4, 8, 5, 4, 18// 11, 2, 1, 10,
	final stages of Credo appear to draw together fragments of
	many motives
Sanctus	19// 18, 1, 4, free?
Osanna	1
Benedictus	1, 15 for 'in nomine'
Agnus Dei I	1 as ostinato (augmentation) combined with new motive (18), 2
Agnus Dei II	1, 2, 17, 18, 3, 18, NB *à6*. Many different motives combined
	together in this movement plus other motives that cannot
	positively be identified as stemming from source.

TABLE 14. *Missa Simile est regnum*: frequency of motivic use

Motive from source	1	2	3	4	5	6	7	8	9	10	11	12	13	14	15	16	17	18
No. of times used	17	6	2	5	2	1	1	1	3	4	4	1	0	0	1	0	2	8

To sum up, the *Missa Ductus est Jesus* is soundly crafted and conventional in technique, but otherwise unremarkable. It was probably written for a choir of modest dimensions and for a liturgical occasion on which a demonstration of contrapuntal complexity was not expected, nor necessarily required. We know from other works that Esquivel was capable of more contrapuntal ingenuity than is demonstrated here, but in this work he saw no reason to show this ability. Although Guerrero, in his motet, highlights by textural contrasts and other means what dramatic content there is in the Temptation story, the subject matter is, after all, fairly 'emotionally neutral': it records the conversation between Jesus and the devil, and the event does not carry the emotional overtones of the Passion narrative, for example, which calls for a dramatic and expressive treatment of the text. This neutrality manifests itself musically in such features as choice of mode, or absence of exuberant melismas and

77 Stevenson, *Spanish Cathedral Music*, p. 195.

rich harmonies. In borrowing Guerrero's material, Esquivel does not attempt to do more with his thematic material than the material itself will allow; it is simply a resource and a stimulus for his own invention, and he succeeds in weaving his chosen material into a coherent musical whole, at the same time showing a solid level of craftsmanship.

MISSA GLORIOSE CONFESSOR DOMINI

FOR HIS LAST PARODY MASS in the *Liber primus missarum*, Esquivel again chose to quarry material from another work by Guerrero, his motet *Gloriose confessor Domini*. Like *Ductus est Jesus*, this motet appears in two different publications; it was included in the *Sacrae cantiones* of 1555 and re-issued as part of the *Motteta Francisci Guerreri* published by Antonio Gardano at Venice in 1570. In this version it bears the inscription 'de sancto Dominico'. The text is a prayer to St Dominic, the Castilian founder of the Dominican order:

> Gloriose confessor Domini, beate Pater Dominice, vitam angelicam gerens in terris, speculum bonorum factus es mundo. Et ideo cum Christo iam fine gaudes in caelis, Sancte Pater Dominice, ora pro nobis.

> Glorious Confessor of the Lord, Blessed Father Dominic who lead an angelic life on earth, you have become a mirror of good for the world. And, therefore, with Christ now without end, you rejoice in heaven. Holy Father Dominic, pray for us.

Because the subject matter of this motet is St Dominic, it is not without significance that Esquivel should choose to parody it, since, as we have seen, his patron Pedro Ponce de León was a Dominican. Esquivel may have written this mass during the time of Don Pedro's bishopric in Ciudad Rodrigo – perhaps for a celebration of the feast of St Dominic (which in the Roman calendar falls on 4 August) or even for the bishop's enthronement.

Geiger obviously thought highly of Esquivel's mass. He comments: 'The head motive is carried through all parts of the mass with great mastery. Neither Morales nor Victoria in any of their compositions more intimately penetrated the inner sanctum of Beauty than Esquivel'. Geiger illustrates with the opening of the 'splendid Osanna'.[78]

Guerrero's motet, scored for four voices set out in high clefs, is a fine construction, divided into two parts almost equal in length. The striking head motive set to the phrase 'Gloriose confessor Domini' soars symbolically and majestically upwards to reach the climax as the name of the subject is announced. The work is well proportioned, and fairly dense in texture; apart from one brief homophonic passage, suitably reserved for the phrase 'beate Pater Dominice', Guerrero weaves an endless thread of seemingly effortless counterpoint throughout. The motet's principal motives are shown in Ex. 4.32.

---

78   Geiger, 'Juan Esquivel', p. 164; trans. in Stevenson, *Spanish Cathedral Music*, p. 291.

Ex. 4.32. The principal motives from Guerrero's motet *Gloriose confessor Domini*

In this particular work, Esquivel comes nearer to Guerrero in his parody treatment than in any other parody mass from the *Liber primus*. In his parody masses, Guerrero is frequently more economical than Esquivel, making the maximum use of one idea from his source. In the *Missa Gloriose confessor Domini* Esquivel adopts a similar procedure, choosing to work with only the first four of the motives shown in Ex. 4.32, and paying particular attention to the head motive, as Tables 15 and 16 show.

TABLE 15. Order of motives borrowed from Guerrero's motet
Gloriose confessor Domini as they appear in Esquivel's mass

Kyrie	1
Christe	3a
Kyrie	1 (sung twice as a C F), 2, 3a
Gloria	1, 4, 3a, 3b, 4, 1, 4, 3a, 1
Credo	1, 4, 1, 3b, 1, 2, 4, 2, 4, 1, 3a, 4, 1, 3b, 3a, 4, 3a, 1, 3a, 4
Sanctus	1, 3b, 1 (sung four times as a C F)
Osanna	1
Benedictus	1, 3a
Agnus Dei	1, 4

TABLE 16. *Missa Gloriose confessor Domini*: frequency of motivic use

Motive from source	1	2	3a	3b	4	5	6	7	8
No. of times used	17	3	9	5	10	0	0	0	0

Instead of drawing on all Guerrero's motives he chooses to work only with four – 3b is, of course, a variant of 3a, and so for purposes of discussion these two may be regarded as one. Why is this?

Musical considerations, as always, must have determined his choice and treatment of material from his source, but it is also highly probable that his restricted borrowings occur for symbolic reasons. It is not without significance, I believe, that the four motives drawn from the source motet are the motives that Guerrero attaches to the text outlining the saintly qualities of St Dominic. The text describes the saint as 'glorious confessor of the Lord' ('Gloriose confessor Domini'); as one who leads 'an angelic life' ('vitam angeli'); as one who is a 'mirror of good' ('speculum bonorum'). In choosing to use this thematic material, Esquivel is attributing the same characteristics to his patron also; he too is 'a glorious confessor of the Lord', a blessed Father who leads an 'angelic life' and 'a good mirror' for the world. Thus, in quoting these themes so many times, Esquivel is making the bishop's goodness known to the world and, of course, pouring forth his own personal adulation – an adulation which he was to express verbally later in the dedication of the *Tomus secundus*.

Guerrero's head motive seems to become for Esquivel a 'motto theme', a kind of *idée fixe* for his patron. It dominates the opening Kyrie and appears twice as a *cantus firmus* in the *altus* of the second Kyrie. It features many times in the Gloria and Credo. In the Sanctus it appears yet again as an ostinato, floating serenely four times in the *superius*, beginning alternately on C and F in the manner of Guerrero and Morales before him. In the Osanna it is singled out for special treatment. *Superius* 1 and 11 are in canon; they state the head motive three times texted as in the motet.

The Osanna is a curious movement and quite unlike any other passage Esquivel ever wrote. The uniqueness of this passage lies not in the double canons that are a feature of the movement – a technique Esquivel repeated later in the *Tomus secundus* – but in its use of four different proportional signs in the four notated parts, and in the ungainly melodic shape of the *altus* with its awkward leaps in bars 9 to 10 and 14 to 15 (Ex. 4.33).

Ex. 4.33. *Missa Gloriose confessor Domini*, Osanna

There is some ambiguity in the choirbook instructions for the distribution of the vocal parts. The four notated parts, which appear on p. 212 of the choirbook, are designated as *Super I, Super II, Altus II* and *Bassus.* The other two parts are derived from the instructions *Superius II in subdiapente; Tenor suprabassum in diapente.* Thus, there is some confusion as to which voice sings the canonic part to be derived from *superius I.* Is this to be a treble voice, as the Latin canon implies, or is it an alto voice, since the instruction *altus II* appears clearly at the head of the notated *altus* part, which bears a C clef? In the transcript of this passage included in his article, Geiger printed this resolution of the canon as if sung by an alto voice, thus giving a vocal disposition of Soprano I and 2, Alto 1 and 2, Tenor (derived from the bass line) and Bass. In Ex. 4.33, the movement is transcribed in accordance with the printer's instructions, with the resolution sung by a soprano voice. The difference is an important one and is not merely a matter of deciding the correct choral layout on paper. In practice this mass would probably have been sung at a lower pitch than indicated since it is notated in high clefs. If this were the case, given Geiger's notation, the resolution of the canon would have been sung by a male voice in the tenor register. On the other hand, if sung by a treble voice, the pitch would be exactly the same, but, assuming the line was given to boy trebles (the *seises*), the vocal timbre would be entirely different.

Esquivel notates *superius I* with a C; *superius II* has a ₵; *altus II* has C with a dot and *bassus* O with a dot. The simultaneous appearance of four different proportional signs at this late date is surprising and seems a deliberate attempt on

Esquivel's part to give his music special emphasis; perhaps, even, to give a self-conscious display of his learning.[79] Such a demonstration of erudition at this, the most joyful point in the mass, may be another way of paying tribute to the Dominican order, for the Dominicans, like the Jesuits, put great emphasis on learning. Esquivel may have felt that, to gain the seal of approval for his compositions, he needed to put his learning on public display, like his contemporaries. The transformation of a learned device into a symbol is characteristic of Spanish *renacimiento* music in general – a fact to which Robert Stevenson has drawn attention.[80]

Two fine examples by Guerrero and Lobo might be cited. The first is to be found in Agnus I from Guerrero's *Simile est regnem coelorum* mass (Rome, 1582). The tenor voice sings G A B G c d e in semibreves, and then, after a breve's rest, the same figure is sung backwards. Above his *cancrizans initium* Guerreo inserts the instruction: *Vado et venio ad vos* ('I go away and I am coming to you') – Jesus's words at John 14: 28. Put in context the whole verse reads: 'Ye have heard how I said unto you, I go away, and come again unto you; if ye loved me, ye would rejoice because I said, I go unto the Father: for the Father is greater than I'.

Stevenson postulates that Guerrero may have intended his *cancrizans* to be an allusion to the Gospel for Whitsunday, and the mass for Pentecost.[81]

The second example is to be found in Osanna I of Lobo's *Prudentes virgines* mass where he inserts the rubric: *Cantus secundus vadit et venit, sed de minimis non curat. Idem Thenor in Octauam cancrizando.* This implies that *cantus II* is to sing only the semibreves of *cantus I* forwards and then to sing them in reverse order; after the completion of one complete cycle, *cantus II* must repeat the whole cycle again many times. Similarly, the tenor must imitate *cantus II* at the sub-octave, backwards. Following this, in Osanna II, we find the rubric: *Currebant duo simul. Sed Basis praecucurrit citius.* Both *tenor* and *bassus* are to sing from the same part, but each part has a different mensuration sign; the *bassus* has ⏀ while the tenor has O. Stevenson sees these canons as symbolic. The "wise virgins" were ready to shout

---

79 The most celebrated example of such erudition is, of course, Ockeghem's *Missa prolationum*, in which Ockeghem demonstrates his mastery of both canon and proportional notation. Another example of the simultaneous use of different proportional signs, closer to Esquivel's time, is to be found in Escobedo's Hexachord Mass, *Philippus rex Hispaniae,* written for the coronation of Philip II (modern edition ed. A. Fiumara with P. Raasveld, Mapa Mundi, 1997). See A. Fiumara, 'Escobedo's *Missa Philippus rex Hispaniae*: A Spanish Decendant of Josquin's *Hercules* Mass', *Early Music* 28 (2000), pp. 50–62). Also, one might add to this list Vivanco's *Missa Assumpsit Jesus*, published by Taberniel in 1608. In Osanna II, *superius II, altus* and *tenor* are in canon *trinitas in unitate*, and the proportional sign is used frequently at different times in the three inner voices against ₵ in the other parts. I am grateful to Bruno Turner for drawing this example to my attention and for his kindness in sending me a copy of his transcription. Thomas Morley gives two secular examples of different proportional signs in his *A Plain and Easy Introduction to Practical Music*, ed. Alec Harman (London, 1952), pp. 58–62: an extract from the madrigal *Diverse lingue* by Giulio Renaldi (c.1500–c.1570), *Madrigals and Neapolitans to Five Voices* (1576), in which each of the five voices is assigned a different proportional sign; the madrigal *All'acqua sagra* by Alessandro Striggio (c.1535–87), *Second Book of Madrigals* (1571), where Striggio has all six parts in different proportions in illustration of the text 'He [?] can change into a thousand strange forms'.

80 See Stevenson, *Spanish Cathedral Music*, p. 190.

81 Ibid.

Osannas when the Bridegroom arrived. Lobo symbolised their superior wisdom with exceptionally learned canons.'[82]

Would these, and similar examples of learning and symbolism, have been understood by contemporary Church congregations? Jeffrey Dean has questioned the notion that in the fifteenth and sixteenth centuries the aesthetic or technical characteristics of sacred polyphony performed in a liturgical context would be understood by all the members of a religious community present. He cites many examples of resistance to polyphony and believes that composers intended their work for the performers primarily and a few sympathetic outsiders.[83] If he is right, it is doubtful if those present when Esquivel's *Missa Gloriose confessor Domini* was sung, other than the singers themselves, would have been aware of the contrapuntal complexities implied by the then old-fashioned notation on the printed page, or have had the slightest notion of what Esquivel was seeking to convey in his music – not least the symbolism I am arguing for – beyond regarding the music as a means of carrying the liturgy forward. Apart from these singers, only those appointed to license and approve the book prior to publication would have had any idea of the compositional procedures, technical complexities or aesthetic merits of the music, and even they might not have been aware of all the symbolism contained within.

Although we do not have the Approbation and Licence to Print for either of the 1608 publications, we do know from the *Tomus secundus* how those charged with examining the book before publication regarded it. As we have seen, its elegant craftsmanship and technical merits were singled out for praise by Espinel in his approbation. I think we can assume, therefore, that a similar degree of scrutiny would have been applied to both 1608 publications; without an examination of the contents, the volumes would not have been sanctioned for use. I think we can also assume that both those volumes would have been given a similar rating for quality and artifice as well as liturgical suitability, and that Esquivel's cunning in this volume in particular would not have gone unnoticed. Whether all his hearers would have responded similarly is another matter, but one hopes that at least Don Pedro was aware of the tribute Esquivel was paying him. One would like to think that he smiled when he heard the *superius* ostinato floating serenely over the rest of the choir in the Sanctus and Osanna.

The ungainly melodic line of *altus II* has already been pointed out as being a feature of unusual interest in this movement. Esquivel clearly set out to differentiate this line from the surrounding texture – the syncopated semibreves (minims in transcription), annunciating the text in bell-like fashion – although it has some thematic relationship with the *bassus*, as Ex. 4.33 demonstrates. But beyond suggesting that its declamatory style is intended to highlight the text, and that the use of a fixed rhythmic scheme is intended as a further display of his technical skill, it is difficult to see why Esquivel wrote in this way. It would seem that there are no hidden devices at work here and that the disjunct intervals at certain points arise out of a need to make the line fit with the surrounding contrapuntal texture in order

---

82 Ibid., p. 267.
83 Jeffrey Dean, 'Listening to Sacred Polyphony c.1500', *Early Music* 25 (1997), pp. 611–36.

not to break the established rules of good counterpoint. Thus, for example, in Ex. 4.33, bars 8 and 9 are a thinly disguised attempt to avoid consecutive octaves with *superius II*; in bar 13, consecutive octaves with *superius II* are avoided by the upward leap of a sixth; similarly, in bar 15, the upward leap of a fourth is an attempt to avoid consecutive octaves with the *tenor* at this point. The notes the composer chooses are, in effect, the only ones open to him if he is to maintain his pre-ordained rhythmic scheme.

Following the Osanna, there are no more elaborate demonstrations of contrapuntal skill. The short three-part Benedictus is stylistically conventional; likewise, the single Agnus Dei, in which Esquivel expands his four voices to five. Presumably, this would have been sung three times with the singers adapting the underlay for the final invocation 'dona nobis pacem'.

But before we leave discussion of this mass, there is one further point of interest. The work ends with fanfare-like motives in all five voice parts as in Ex. 4.34. Where does this material come from? It is not found in the source motet.

Esquivel uses the same falling triad figure for the phrase 'descendit de coelis', with its plagal cadence and 4/3 suspension in the *superius*, in the Creed where the symbolism is

Ex. 4.34. *Missa Gloriose confessor Domini*, Agnus Dei closing passage

obvious: use of such a figure to illustrate descent is a familiar word-painting technique. It may well be that Esquivel repeated the idea in the Agnus Dei because the material fits the ending of the mass so well, not only musically, but emotionally.'Descendit de coelis' marks off a section of text and leads into the concept of the Virgin birth – an awesome concept, which singers need to take account of in performance. The end of the Agnus Dei is another 'special' moment when the worshipper, recognising the magnitude of Christ's sacrifice, humbly asks for forgiveness and peace – again an awesome moment to be sung with reverence in performance

But there is an alternative hypothesis: similar triadic fanfare-like motives are found in the Agnus Dei of Esquivel *Missa Batalla* – and, of course, Janequin's chanson, *La guerre*. This may be purely coincidental as fanfare-like motives are stock in trade for Renaissance composers; on the other hand, it is just possible that this choice of materials is deliberate. Fanfare motives recall the battlefield. Are these fanfares, then, intended to symbolise the battles fought by the Dominicans? Esquivel was certainly not the last composer to include war-like fanfares in setting the Agnus Dei; the seventeenth-century Cererols did the same thing in his *Missa Batalla*, and, of course, Haydn followed the same path in his *Paukenmesse*. The Dominicans were great teachers and defenders of the faith, like the Jesuits; in times past, they had been fighters against the Albigensian heresy. So perhaps we may read these fanfares as a reminder to his patron of his glorious past, and his present role as a defender of the faith.

The *Missa Gloriose confessor Domini* is Esquivel's last and, perhaps, most interesting parody mass in the *Liber primus*. Although modest in dimensions and conventional in style, it does seem to mark a step forward in the development of the composer's parody technique. Through a concentrated use of the head motive and the ingenious integration of Guerrero's material with material of his own, Esquivel succeeds in building a unified structure, sensitively responding to the text to create a work which is both a worthy tribute to his patron and a monument, albeit a modest one, to his own success as a composer of masses and as a servant of the Church. The masses of the *Liber primus missarum* are clearly the fruits of careful study of, and practice in, contrapuntal procedures over a period of many years. They show the extent to which Esquivel has absorbed the rich heritage of polyphonic tradition passed down to him by generation after generation of his fellow countrymen.

MISSA PRO DEFUNCTIS

By INCLUDING A SETTING of the *Missa pro defunctis* in the *Liber primus*, Esquivel assured himself a place in the history of liturgical music. Examples of the sixteenth- and early-seventeenth-century parody mass are numerous; examples of the sixteenth- and early-seventeenth-century Requiem Mass are not so numerous. The fact that the composer wrote not one but two settings – in 1608 and 1613 – makes it imperative that these works are included in any study of late Renaissance Spanish Church music, irrespective of the quality of the works in question.

In order to set Esquivel's contribution to this genre in context, we must outline briefly something of the historical development of Christian burial rites. A full study of this subject is beyond the scope of this book. The following brief account is based on the work of Richard Rutherford.[84]

Care for the deceased has always been a concern for the Christian Church, and after the birth of Christianity funeral formularies – guides to practice – soon began to appear. These went through a process of development over a long period of time, the eighth century being a significant period of growth. Extant sources from this time – in themselves an amalgamation of liturgical uses from different times and different places, and representing different stages of development – came to be widely disseminated throughout Europe. But some five centuries elapsed before these first early manuscripts, setting out a funeral liturgy, became crystallised into the Roman rite of burial in the thirteenth century.[85] The presence of the Requiem Mass as part of the funeral liturgy of the papal court put it in the mainstream of later Roman liturgical tradition, and its adoption by the Franciscans helped to establish the model for the future. After the introduction of the Roman Missal in 1570, the Requiem became the normative funeral mass for adults. But even after the Tridentine reforms, much of the ritual surrounding the day of death or burial was not codified until the *Rituale Romanum* initiated by Pope Paul V in 1614 – the first ever official document for the universal Catholic Church setting out in detail the ceremonial for burial.[86]

Socially, music played an important role in the process of honouring the dead, a fact which encouraged the development of polyphonic settings of music for both mass and Office for the Dead. Elaborate funeral rites – *exequias* or *honras fúnebres* – became a central element in Spanish life in the sixteenth and seventeenth centuries. Charles V's fondness for elaborate spectacle in relation to royal exequies as well as other court rituals set the tone for generations to come, and detailed accounts survive of the many royal exequies celebrated throughout Spain and the New World following the death of Philip II on 9 October 1598.[87] Although we have no record of the actual date of composition of Esquivel's *Missa pro defunctis*, nor any details of the occasion for which it was written, it is tempting to speculate that local exequies following Philip's death may have given birth to the work. It is in five parts, suggesting an occasion of some importance. However, there is no documentary evidence to support this; indeed, the presence in the print of the motet *In paradisum* – the

---

84 Richard Rutherford, *The Death of a Christian: The Rite of Funerals* (New York, 1980).

85 Ibid., pp. 37–8.

86 Ibid., pp. 69–78, provides a full account of the development of burial rites. A more summary account of developments during the same period may also be found in Geoffrey Rowell, *The Liturgy of Christian Burial: An Introductory Survey of the Historical Development of Christian Burial Rites* (London, 1977), pp. 57–73.

87 These are described in great detail in Eire, *From Madrid to Purgatory*, pp. 287–96. In churches where exequies were held, black draperies were hung throughout the entire church; the exterior entrance, the nave and transept were covered in sombre black and festooned with royal memorabilia. A huge catafalque lit with thousands of candles was erected; in the case of Seville cathedral, this was as high as the nave. Such a spectacle must have been awe-inspiring!

motet sung as a coffin is carried in procession for burial – suggests that the work was conceived for a funerary event, perhaps commissioned by a prominent citizen who wished to have his life commemorated in this way.

Turning now to the musical characteristics of polyphonic setting of the text of the *Missa pro defunctis*, we can see from the number of fifteenth- and sixteenth-century works which have survived that, unlike the Ordinary of the mass, which acquired a measure of uniformity in its external features early on in its history, the Requiem Mass enjoyed no such uniformity. The musical portions of the text as found in the *Liber usualis* – Introit, *Requiem aeternam*; Kyrie; Gradual, *Requiem aeternam*; Tract, *Absolve Domine*; Sequence, *Dies irae*; Offertory, *Domine Jesu Christe*; Sanctus; Agnus Dei; Communion, *Lux aeterna*; Postcommunion, *Requiescant in pace* – are unchanged from the missal of Pius V. However, at the end of the sixteenth century, few if any Requiems contained polyphonic settings of all these. The non-standardisation arose out of the practice of including additional items, such as funeral motets and other items not liturgically part of the *Missa pro defunctis*, and also from the varied treatment of the plainchant that, over a long period of time, had become associated with the Requiem Mass.

Following the process of absorbing the chant into the polyphonic texture – as happens in Ockeghem's Requiem, the earliest extant polyphonic Requiem possibly dating from sometime after 1470,[88] and the work which seems to have set a precedent for this procedure – there was no universal measure of agreement on which sections of the text should be chant-rendered and which should be set polyphonically. A cursory glance at the external features of just a small handful of works from the sixteenth century confirms this.

Morales's Requiem of 1544 (*Missarum liber secundus*) contains only those sections which belong properly to a mass for the dead. Plainsong intonations are used throughout, and his treatment of chant as a *cantus firmus* is strict. By comparison, Palestrina's setting of 1554 is liturgically incomplete; only the Kyrie, Offertory, Sanctus, Benedictus and Agnus Dei are set polyphonically. In style, the work is a paraphrase mass; the movements begin without the customary Gregorian intonations, but the chant is woven into the polyphonic texture.

Of Guerrero's two published settings, the first (1566) makes use of plainchant intonations and includes only those items proper to a *missa pro defunctis*, but in his second setting (1582), he inserts before the Agnus Dei the six-voice motet *Hei mihi Domine* – a responsory text from the second nocturn of Matins – and then concludes with a responsory and versicle from the burial service.

Victoria ended his first Requiem (1583) with the same burial service additions, but on republishing the work in 1592 he added two more responsories from the Office of Matins. By publishing his great Requiem of 1605 under the title *Officium defunctorum*, he thus indicated that it contained more than just the music of the mass itself.

---

88 Reese, *Music in the Renaissance*, pp. 76–7. Probably the first Requiem setting was Dufay's, since he ordered it to be sung on the day after his funeral in 1474. Sadly, the work is now lost. See Reese, *Music in the Renaissance*, p. 76.

Works by lesser-known composers reveal a similar diversity in the sections of the liturgical texts chosen for polyphonic setting and in the number of items from other services included. One notable example is Juan Vázquez's *Agenda defunctorum* (Seville, 1556), a monumental publication which included not just music for the Requiem Mass, but sixteen items from Matins and two from Lauds.[89] Likewise, Esquivel's two published Requiems contain additional items: the *Missa pro defunctis* of 1608 concludes with a setting of the ceremonial antiphon *In paradisum* from the Burial Service; the later Requiem of 1613 contains items from the Office of the Dead.

Earlier fifteenth-century Requiems show even more variety in their external features. Ockeghem's mass, for example, is a highly sectionalised structure with an Introit, a lengthy Kyrie (in seven contrasting sections), Graduale, Tract and Offertory only. Ockeghem's approach contrasts with that of Antoine de Fevin, whose work is the most nearly complete of all the earliest Requiems. Severe in style, with a predominance of long note values and an absence of rhythmic activity, it includes settings of all liturgical movements except the Sequence.

Further comparisons could be made, but the above is sufficient evidence to illustrate the absence of uniformity in the outward form of the Renaissance Requiem as it developed during the course of the fifteenth and sixteenth centuries. However, one overriding principle gave a measure of conformity to all known examples of works of this genre: the universal acceptance of the appropriate chant melodies as a basis for composition. There was considerable variation in the treatment of chant, but it was the starting point for every composer and the foundation of every Requiem Mass of the Renaissance period.

Two major studies have established the musical characteristics of the polyphonic in the Renaissance period and it is to these we turn now in attempt to put Esquivel's work in context.

Harold Luce's pioneering 1958 study, 'The Requiem Mass from its Plainsong Beginning to 1600', charted the evolution of the genre from its antecedents in pre-Christian Egypt, Jewish funeral music, through early Christendom and later developments in the Middle Ages, and finally through to the fully developed polyphonic settings of the sixteenth century.[90]

According to Luce, there appear to have been fewer than forty polyphonic Requiems composed in the two centuries between 1400 and 1600. The bulk of his study is concerned with an examination of the thirty-eight works available to him at the time.[91] His close examination of an extensive corpus of works, dating from the sixteenth century and earlier, shows the considerable variation found in the textual content, external format, choice of chant (reflecting local usage) and treatment of chant. He shows that by the end of the century certain basic principles had

---

89 Juan Vázquez, *Agenda defunctorum*, ed. Samuel Rubio (Madrid, 1975). Vázquez was a native of Badajoz where he eventually succeeded to the post of *maestro* in 1545. In 1550 he left to enter a private household.

90 Harold Luce, 'The Requiem Mass from its Plainsong Beginning to 1600' (Ph.D. dissertation, Florida State University, 1958).

91 Ibid., p. 64.

been established: all polyphonic settings of the *Missa pro defunctis* show a restraint based on the use of long note values and an avoidance of exuberant melodic configurations; an avoidance of secular influences; and, above all, a reverence for the appropriate chant – appropriate because of its long historical association with the relevant liturgical text. The chant assumes a position of the highest importance by being placed usually in the highest part of the polyphonic texture to give it prominence; or it may be placed in an upper range at a distance from the lower parts which therefore appear in a supporting role.[92] It sometimes appeared as a *cantus firmus* in long notes supported by other voices; at other times it appeared as one line of a *falsobordone* texture, all parts proceeding simultaneously in similar rhythm; it appeared as a single-line paraphrase, with the given melody assigned to a specific voice, abridged, expanded or otherwise altered; or it permeated the entire texture in a paraphrased form with its characteristic intervals, motives or entire phrases.[93]

Some sections of the text were reserved for special treatment: verses of the Introit, Communion, Sanctus and Agnus Dei were generally set in a *falsobordone* style. Certain devices were used for dramatic effect: textural phrases like 'de poenis inferni', 'de profundo lacu', 'ne absorbeat eas' from the Offertory were often set for low voices; phrases like 'et lux perpetua' in the Communion were set in a high tessitura and given a lighter texture; notation is sometimes used symbolically, as in the occasional use of blackened notation for 'ne cadant in obscurum'.[94]

A very comprehensive picture of the development of the polyphonic Requiem during the fifteenth and sixteenth centuries unfolds in Luce's study. Composers whose works are represented include Ockeghem, Brumel, La Rue, Prioris, Fevin, Richafort, Sermisy, Morales, Clereau, Bonefont, Clemens non Papa, de Monte, Kerle, Vaet, Guerrero, Ruffo, Asola, Porta, Palestrina, Lassus, Victoria, Brudieu, Belli, Tudino, Moro, Anerio, Amon, Maudit and du Caurroy. Several anonymous works may be added to this list and, of course, additional names from the Iberian peninsula.

Luce ended his study at 1600, but added a partial list of Requiems published shortly after this date, which included Esquivel's two settings. Although he included several Italian figures (Anerio, Belloni, Cavaccio, Croce, Vecchi and Viadana), he omitted the names of many Iberian composers whose names are now familiar to us through modern editions and recordings, such as Sebastián de Vivanco, Duarte Lobo, Manuel Cardoso, Felipe de Magalhães, Pedro Ruimonte, and other researchers have added additional names. Eleanor Russell's studies revealed the existence of Morales's long-lost Requiem à4, to which Bermudo makes reference in his *Declaración de instrumentos musicales* (1555), and which is now available in two modern performing editions;[95] there is also a Requiem by one Antonio Gallego (a

92 Ibid., p. 268.

93 Ibid., pp. 267–8.

94 Ibid., pp. 269–70

95 Modern editions: Alicia Muñiz Hernández, *Cristophori de Morales, Pro defunctis missa à4*, in *Música Hispana*, Series B: Polifonía 3. (Barcelona: Consejo Superior de Invetigaciones Cientificas, 1975). This edition is based on the version of the work found in Malaga cathedral (Malaga MS 4). Sister Marie Sagués, *Anonymous, Valladolid codex Missa pro defunctis*, *Música Liturgica* II (Cincinnati,

composer yet to be identified) copied into a manuscript at Valladolid cathedral.[96] More recently, a *Missa pro defunctis* by the Portuguese composer Alfonso Perea Bernal has come to light.[97]

Luce's groundwork has been updated by a lengthy and detailed study of polyphonic settings of both mass and Office for the Dead before 1630 by Grayson Wagstaff.[98] What is now clear is that compositional activity in this field after 1600 was considerably more extensive than Luce thought. In the first twenty years of the new century, in addition to Esquivel – and, of course, Victoria – there are other names to consider: Francisco D'Ávila y Paez (a mass published in a revised form by Lopez de Velasco in his *Libro de missas, motetes* . . . 1629), the Catalan, Juan Brudieu, Estêvão de Brito, Francisco Garro, Pedro Ruimonte, Gonçalo Mendes Saldana, Antonio Palleres (in manuscript ÁvilaA 9), Juan Pujol and Sebastián de Vivanco. In addition, there are anonymous masses in manuscript sources: a choirbook prepared for use at the Escorial (NewH 380/861), a mass (possibly by Gines Peres since it is set alongside various works by him) in Valenc 2 and a mass for two choirs in GranCR 7.[99] Moreover, it is clear from the list of settings published by José López-Calo and Joám Trillo[100] that polyphonic settings of both Office and mass continued to be important genres for future generations in Spain and many works continued to display the characteristic features of the Renaissance polyphonic tradition.[101]

Among the earliest surviving settings of the Mass for the Dead in Spain are the two works by Pedro Escobar and Juan Garcia Basurto; the stylistic language of these suggests that they were completed before 1520.[102] Although polyphonic music

1960), based on VallaP s.s. There has been much scholarly debate about this work. See Eleanor Russell, 'A New Manuscript Source for the Music of Cristóbal de Morales: Morales'"Lost" *Missa pro defunctis* and Early Spanish Requiem Traditions', *Anuario musical* 33–5 (1978–80), pp. 9–49.

96 Valladolid 5, fols. lxvii–lxviii. See Russell, 'A New Manuscript Source', p. 20, n. 34.

97 I am grateful to Dr Owen Rees of Oxford University for providing me with a copy of his transcription and for kindly giving me a copy of his inventory of Coimbra, Biblioteca Geral de Universidade, MM34, in which this work is listed.

98 Grayson Wagstaff, 'Music for the Dead: Polyphonic Settings of the *Officium* and *Missa pro defunctis* by Spanish and Latin American Composers before 1630' (Ph.D. dissertation, University of Texas at Austin, 1995).

99 I am grateful to Grayson Wagstaff for his help in the compilation of this list. A discussion of some of these works may be found in Wagstaff, 'Music for the Dead', pp. 599–605.

100 José López-Calo and Joam Trillo, *Melchior Lopez Misa de requiem: el requiem en la música española* (Santiago de Compostela, 1987), pp. 15–23.

101 Two early-seventeenth-century examples may be cited: the Requiems of Dûarte Lobo (Lisbon, 1621) and Manual Cardoso (Lisbon, 1625). Despite the fact that these two works contain some striking harmonic progressions not found in the works of composers of the orthodox mainstream (Palestrina, for example), in their linear construction and fidelity to chant they follow past convention.

102 Wagstaff, 'Music for the Dead', p. 248. Pedro de Escobar was of Portuguese origin but was active in Spain, where he was *maestro* at Seville in 1507 until his resignation in 1514. For more information, see Robert Stevenson, 'Pedro de Escobar: Earliest Portuguese Composer in the New World Manuscripts', *Inter-American Music Review* 11/1 (Fall–Winter 1990), pp. 3–24. Escobar's *Missa pro defunctis* is preserved at Tarazona cathedral, where it is now split between TaraC 2 and 3, originally one manuscript. Garcia de Basurto was in Tarazona from 1517 until 1521, when he moved on to Saragossa. TaraC 5 contains an Introit, Kyrie and Gradual attributed to Basurto; the Requiem

for the dead was not a new idea on the Iberian peninsula when Escobar wrote his setting, Wagstaff cites the work as the foundation of a later tradition,[103] since 'it shares in a set of assumptions for setting the mass for the dead that remained unchanged for many Spanish and Latin American composers into the seventeenth century'.[104]

Examination of later masses suggests that all composers of the Spanish school approached the composition of a polyphonic Requiem in a similar way. A distinctive Spanish tradition emerged, and all the works that have come down to us have certain common characteristics not shared by works outside the Iberian peninsula.

Firstly, there is the choice of text for the Gradual. Two different plainsong Gradual texts were used in fifteenth- and sixteenth-century polyphonic settings: 'Si ambulem in medio umbrae mortis' was the choice of Franco-Flemish composers; the other text, which replaced the above in the revised Missal, was 'Requiem aeternam dona eis, Domine'. This was the unanimous choice of the Spanish school.[105]

Secondly, the long note treatment of the *cantus firmus* in the soprano is a distinctive feature of the Spanish Requiem tradition. It is present in the works of Morales, Vázquez, Guerrero, Esquivel and Victoria, although, in the case of Victoria's *Missa pro defunctis* of 1605, the chant appears in *cantus II* and not *cantus I*.

Thirdly, another marked feature is the greater length of several plainchant intonations, in particular those of the Introit and Offertory. Whereas non-Spanish composers began their polyphony with the second word 'aeternam' in the case of the Introit and the phrase 'Rex gloriae' in the case of the Offertory, the Spaniards preferred to render the opening phrases of both 'Requiem aeternam' and 'Domine Jesu Christe, Rex gloriae' complete in their chant form.

Fourthly, a common feature found in the Spanish masses for the dead is the frequent omission of the Offertory verse, 'Hostias'. The Portuguese composers, Cardoso and Magalhães, set the whole verse polyphonically, but neither Morales, Victoria nor Esquivel include a polyphonic setting of this verse in their Requiems.[106]

Mass found in the manuscript is a composite work with a Tract composed by Ockeghem and the Communion by Brumel. For further information, see Wagstaff, 'Music for the Dead', pp. 190–229. TaraC 5 and the Basurto Requiem are also discussed by Eleanor Russell in 'The *Missa in agendis mortuorum* of Juan Garcia de Basurto: Johannes Ockeghem, Antoine Brumel, and an Early Spanish Polyphonic Requiem Mass', *Tijdschrift van de Vereniging voor Nederlandse muziekgeschiedenis* 29 (1979), pp. 1–37. Several other scholars have drawn attention to these important manuscripts, most notably Tess Knighton, 'Music and Musicians at the Court of Fernando of Aragon, 1475–1516' (Ph.D. dissertation, University of Cambridge,1983); Jane Morlet Hardie, 'The Motets of Francisco de Peñalosa and their Manuscript Sources' (Ph.D. dissertation, University of Michigan, 1983); Kenneth Kreitner, *The Church Music of Fifteenth-Century Spain* (Woodbridge, 2004), pp. 140–53. As Kreitner has pointed out, Tarazona 2/3 is the largest surviving source of Spanish Church music from the time of Ferdinand and Isabella. Composers whose works are included demonstrate a strong link between the Catholic courts and the cathedral of Seville.

103 Wagstaff, 'Music for the Dead', pp. 197–8.

104 Ibid., p. 208.

105 Luce, 'The Requiem Mass from its Plainsong Beginnings', p. 270.

106 Luce and Snow present conflicting evidence concerning the inclusion of this verse. In the concluding chapter of his study, Luce says 'the verse of the Offertory is rarely omitted in their works' (i.e. the works of the Spanish school); see Luce, 'The Requiem Mass from its Plainsong Beginnings',

Fifthly, the *Dies irae*, which only became an official part of the liturgy in Spain after the reformed Missal was introduced into various Spanish dioceses in 1570, was not a text customarily selected for polyphonic setting by Spanish composers. It seems to have attracted the attention of Italian composers primarily, although it was the Franco-Flemish composer Brumel who first included a setting of this text in a polyphonic Requiem.[107]

The final common – and most significant – trait was the extremely sombre and heavy texture generally in evidence in all movements of a Requiem. The tendency towards homorhythmic texture to support the chant, the relative absence of syncopes, the persistent use of one vocal texture rarely interrupted by rests, the use of long note values in all parts, not just the *cantus firmus*, are all features which contribute to this quality.[108]

When we begin to examine Esquivel's 1608 *Missa pro defunctis* in detail, we can see immediately how his work relates to the Spanish tradition. In his approach to the text he follows the conventions established by his illustrious predecessors, Morales in particular; the slow-moving melodic lines, the use of long note values, the chordal textures – all features of Morales's settings – are to be found in both Esquivel's Requiems.

The fact that Esquivel published the motet *In paradisum* with the mass strongly suggests that his intention was to provide music for an actual funeral service; that is, it was conceived as a Mass for the Dead and not a votive mass. *In paradisum* is sung after Requiem Mass, during the procession to the grave side, a survival from early Christian times. In the case of the second Requiem published only five years later, it is likely that his intention was to provide music for the many votive masses *pro defunctis* that were celebrated at the time of its composition. The *missa pro defunctis* was the most frequently performed votive mass in the Middle Ages, a time when rites of passage figured hugely in the lives of men and women. It is possible, then, that this second mass would have been sung at such a weekly celebration, perhaps on Friday.[109]

Unfortunately, like the *Missa Batalla*, the 1608 Requiem is damaged in the only source available to us. Pages 237 to 244, covering the whole of the Agnus Dei and part of the Communion, are missing entirely and only the Introit, Kyrie, Tract

---

p. 270. On the other hand, Snow specifically says that the 'Hostias' verse is frequently omitted; see Snow, *The 1613 Print*, p. 3. Snow's view appears to be correct. On the evidence of the texts examined for the present study, polyphonic settings of the 'Hostias' verse appear to be few in number. The Catalan composer, Juan Pujol, is one composer who does set the verse polyphonically, beginning at the phrase 'tibi Domine'.

107 See Luce, 'The Requiem Mass from its Plainsong Beginnings', chapter 3, where this question is discussed in some detail.

108 Ibid., p. 270.

109 Snow, *The 1613 Print*, p. 33. One of the reforms of the Council of Trent was to bring a measure of standardisation to the Mass for the Dead. The revised Missal of 1570 retained only five of the many different masses for the dead used previously: mass of the faithful departed (November 2); mass on the day of the death or on the day of burial; mass of the third, seventh and thirtieth days after death; mass on the anniversary day of death; the daily mass for the dead. See Luce, 'The Requiem Mass from its Plainsong Beginnings', for further details.

Morales (harmonisation as in MálaC4)

Certon

Bernal

Esquivel

Ex. 4.35. 'Et tibi redetur votum in Jerusalem' in the Requiem Masses of Morales (1551?), Certon (1558), Bernal (late sixteenth century) and Esquivel (1608)

and Offertorium are undamaged, along with the first part of the Sanctus and the end of the Communion. The following *In paradisum* from the burial service is also damaged, but since Esquivel includes this piece in his 1608 volume of motets it is possible to reconstruct this movement.[110] Since there is no polyphonic setting of the Gradual and Sequence, we may presume that these two movements would have been sung to plainchant.

The Introit begins with the customary Spanish practice of a two-word intonation noted in *superius I*. The chant appears throughout the following polyphony in this part in long note values, although it is not, in fact, the highest sounding part since the second soprano sounds above it. Thus, Esquivel's manner of procedure is similar to Victoria's in his *Officium defunctorum* (Madrid, 1605) where the procedure is reversed: *cantus II* bears the chant and *cantus I* generally rises above.

Following established Spanish practice, Esquivel sets the polyphonic continuation of the psalm verse 'Te decet hymnus' in *falsobordone* style. Harmonically and rhythmically, his setting is similar to that found in the Requiems of other late-sixteenth-century composers, the only difference of any significance being the sharpening of the plainsong final to read G–F$^\sharp$ at the end of the second phrase ('orationem meam') – no other sixteenth- or seventeenth-century Spanish setting appears to do this.[111] These similarities are shown in the extracts in Ex. 4.35, all harmonisations of the phrase 'Et tibi redetur votum in Jerusalem'. For the sake of clarity, the extracts are shown without the accompanying text.[112]

The similarities of chord progressions and choice of note lengths are obvious, but given the limited number of permutations possible within the framework of Renaissance polyphonic style, and the well-recognised convention of treating the text in this way, it would be surprising if no such similarities existed. We cannot be certain that Esquivel had first-hand knowledge of either Certon's or Bernal's setting. But he must have known Morales's four-part Requiem since many passages in that work bear a close resemblance to sections in Esquivel's mass. In addition to the above example, further resemblances appear in the Kyrie and Christe of both works, where the chant is presented in a way similar to that in the Introit (see Ex. 4.36).

A similar comparison with the Kyrie from Vázquez's Requiem of 1556 shows similar characteristics: all these works demonstrate the solemnity of the Spanish idiom. Moreover, when these movements are placed alongside each other and

---

110 Modern edition: Mapa Mundi, Spanish and Portuguese Church Music 89, transcr. and ed. Bruno Turner.

111 Michael O'Connor, 'The 1608 and 1613 Requiem Masses of Juan Esquivel Barahona: A Study of the Tridentine *Missa pro defunctis* in Spain' (MM dissertation, Florida State University School of Music, 1995), p. 43. O'Connor points out that Esquivel discards a noticeable amount of plainsong material from the antiphon – most of it from the melisma on the word 'Domine'; his 1613 setting is not so compressed.

112 Grayson Wagstaff lists known sources of this work of Morales as follows: ÁvilaC 1, pp. 101–21; LedesmaC s.s., fols. 109–20; MálaC 4, fols. 10–23; MontsM 753, fols. 8–22; SegC 3, 13–19; SilosA 21, fols. 63–76; VallaC s.s., fols. 23–47; VallaP s.s., fols. 127–41. With the exception of ÁvilaC 1, which is a late-eighteenth-century source, all date from the last quarter of the sixteenth century or the first quarter of the seventeenth. See discussion of these sources in Wagstaff, 'Music for the Dead', pp. 445–8. The harmonisation in Ex. 4.35 is as in MálaC 4.

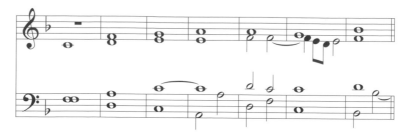

Ex. 4.36a. Morales: Kyrie from *Missa pro defunctis à4*

Ex. 4.36b. Esquivel: Kyrie from *Missa pro defunctis* (1608)

examined in their entirety, it is obvious that their composers draw upon the same chant source.[113] This has been identified by Eleanor Russell.

   In her discovery of, and research into, Morales's 'lost' Requiem, she examined twenty-one Hispanic chant sources, dating from the twelfth to the late sixteenth centuries, and ten non-Hispanic sources from the same period, which led her to conclude that the Kyrie of Morales's four-voice Requiem Mass is based on a special non-Roman chant of long standing, an early source being the *Processionum secundum ordinem fratrum predicatorum* (Seville, 1492).[114] Esquivel's Kyrie must also be

113 See Luce, 'The Requiem Mass from its Plainsong Beginnings', pp. 36–60, where the author gives examples of some of the variant forms of chant in the sources he consulted. As Luce's work shows, there are many minor variants on obviously common models in chant sources, but his statement that 'In spite of minor differences, the known fifteenth and sixteenth-century Requiems are all composed on essentially the same plainsong models' ('The Requiem Mass', p. 116.) is not correct, at least as far as the Ordinary of the Mass was concerned. There was clearly no one accepted set of melodies used by every composer for the Ordinary sections of the *Missa pro defunctis*.

114 Russell, 'A New Manuscript Source', p. 19. Russell gives the present location of this source as the Huntington Library, San Marino, California, where it is listed as Rare Book 95523; the chant appears on fol. 1. Montanos also gives the same Kyrie chant for his *Missa defunctorum*: Francisco de

based on this source since the chant-bearing line is almost identical to Morales's *cantus*.

In the Tract, the next section Esquivel sets polyphonically, the number of parts is reduced from five to four, scored SSAT, and the chant is paraphrased in *superius I*. The text is that of the reformed missal 'Absolve Domine'. As is common in Requiems of this period, a C replaces the ₵ of the Introit and Kyrie, indicating shorter note values and a more lively sense of harmonic movement. The melodic contours of the plainchant are used to shape the initial motives of the accompanying contrapuntal lines. Only the first section of the text is set, leaving the verses 'Et gratias' and 'Et lucis' to be sung to the appropriate chant. Like Guerrero, Esquivel uses the Roman chant melody.

The Offertory was set to polyphony more often than other parts of the Requiem Propers during the Renaissance, perhaps because it was among the earliest parts of the Proper to be generally accepted into the Requiem liturgy.[115] It is similar in style to the Tract: after the opening intonation 'Domine Jesu Christe Rex gloriae' notated in the bass clef (F3), the chant is again paraphrased in *superius I*. Again, C replaces ₵ and there is an emphasis on shorter note values and a more rapid harmonic movement. As was customary in the late sixteenth century, only the antiphon is set polyphonically, leaving the verse 'Hostias et preces' to be sung to chant. Although the general contour of the chant follows the melody as given in the *Liber usualis* (p. 1813), there are significant differences of detail. Again, the chant appears to be that used by Morales in his four-part Requiem, where the melody follows the shapes of chants sung in Spain as early as the fourteenth century.[116] (The same chant source is used again in the 1613 Requiem and it is treated in exactly the same manner.)

The chant of the Sanctus – again identical to Morales's version – is not that used by other Andalusian composers (such as Vázquez, Escobar and Guerrero), but is found in Francisco de Montanos's *Arte de canto llano* (Salamanca, 1610).[117] It can be identified today, with only slight variables, as the Sanctus of Mass XV, *Dominator Deus*, in the *Liber usualis*. The same melody is used by Estêvão de Brito in his Requiem, another composer with Malaga connections; Morales served as chapelmaster there from 1551 to 1553, and Brito from 1613 to 1641. Morales's four-part Requiem was found in the same manuscript source as Brito's work, but why Esquivel should use this same melody, as opposed to that used by the majority of composers, is not clear. His procedure in the Sanctus is very like that demonstrated by Morales in his setting à4 and there are even thematic connections which, again, seem to indicate that he had direct knowledge of Morales's work.

Montanas *Arte de canto llano* (Salamanca, 1610), p. 124. The chant was a favourite with composers of polyphonic Requiems and was used by Basurto, Vázquez and Guerrero (see Russell, 'A New Manuscript Source', p. 19). The chant sources in both Esquivel's Requiems are similar to those found in a *Manuale sacramentorum* printed in Mexico City in 1568. See O'Connor, 'The 1608 and 1613 Requiem Masses', p. 41.

115   O'Connor, 'The 1608 and 1613 Requiem Masses', p. 52.

116   Russell, 'A New Manuscript Source', p. 22. The source consulted by Russell is a fourteenth century Gradual: Madrid, Biblioteca Nacional, ms. 1361, fols. 138–9.

117   Ibid., p. 22.

Ex. 4.37. A comparison between the Sanctus movements in
Morales's Requiem *à4* and Esquivel's Requiem *à5*

If the openings of these Sanctus setting are compared (see Ex. 4.37*a*), it can be seen that each composer presents the plainsong in long note values in the *superius*. There are similarities in the choice of chord progression and the treatment of the same imitative points. Later in the movement, Esquivel's use of the 'Osanna' motive, borrowed from the chant, is again similar to Morales's treatment, as shown in Ex. 4.37*b*.

In contrast to the passages shown above, Brito's opening (see Ex. 4.38) shows a more rapid rate of chord change and more contrapuntal imitation in the lower voices; solemnity is imparted to the whole passage by the adoption of low pitches in the three lower voices. The 'Domine Deus' motive, though still based on the chant melody, has a different rhythmic shape from the motives of Morales and Esquivel.

Unfortunately, only the *superius* and *tenor* parts have survived from Esquivel's Benedictus so that we cannot pursue these parallels further.

Ex. 4.38. Estêvão de Brito: *Missa pro defunctis*, Sanctus, bars 1–12

From the fragments that remain of the Communion, we can see that the chant is paraphrased in the customary way. Again, there is nothing unusual in Esquivel's approach, which appears to be similar to that adopted in the 1613 Requiem, where the shape of the chant line dictates the shape of the other contrapuntal lines. The first word of the verse is not intoned, as it frequently is in Requiems of the period.

The Requiem concludes with the beautiful burial motet *In paradisum* in which the Postcommunion versicle, 'Resquiesca(n)t in pace' – a two-note chant ascending and descending in semitones – is heard six times in all as an ostinato in *superius II*, beginning alternately on a and d at each repetition. The device recalls the procedures of Morales and Guerrero in many of their motets; in this context, it was almost certainly used as a means of making audible the request for the repose of the soul of the deceased.

An atmosphere of serenity prevails in both Esquivel's Requiems: a serenity achieved by the predominantly step-wise motion of the melodic lines, except the bass, the slow harmonic rhythm, the dissonances limited to carefully prepared suspensions, the sparing use of passing notes in the Introit, Kyrie and Sanctus, the preponderance of root position triads in the same three movements, and the predominance of long note values. The result of the combination of all these features is a simplicity and severity of style, typically Spanish, and comparable with that of Morales; the vigorous contrapuntal lines found in the Requiems of Lassus and Palestrina, for example, have no place in either of Esquivel's Requiem settings.

Like all the works in this volume, the Requiem was written at a time of change in European music, when the modal language of the past was slowly being eroded by chromatic inflections of melodic lines, and by innovative chromatic harmonies. There is little sign of these changes in the masses of the *Liber primus*, but there is one instance of chromatic inflection in the Requiem, at the opening of the Tract, which is a characteristic of Esquivel's style (Ex. 4.39).

Ex. 4.39. Esquivel: *Missa pro defunctis* (1608), Tract, bars 1–4

As can be seen, F and C in *superius II* and *tenor* in bar two are chromatically inflected (the result of a suspension in the *tenor* coinciding with a rising passing note in *superius II*), going outside the mode (mode 8) of the *cantus firmus* in *superius I*; moreover, the resulting coincidental movement creates parallel fourths. The same parallel chromatic movement occurs at the same point in the Tract of the 1613 Requiem, no doubt for the same reasons – to underscore the word 'absolve'. We shall encounter more examples of this in later chapters.

But beyond these instances of chromatic inflection, Esquivel does not step outside the boundaries of what we now call the 'High Renaissance' tradition. If the work does sound 'modern' to the ear, it is for different reasons.

The predominance given to the chant-bearing line, supported by a firm independent bass line, perhaps inevitably conveys to twenty-first century ears a sense of tonality – a feature already pointed out in relation to our discussion of *Missa Ut re me fa sol la*. The bass line frequently outlines a IV–V–I chord progression, and persistent use of bass leaps of the fifth give passages a sense of tonal direction: there is a point of arrival, as shown in Ex. 4.40.

Ex. 4.40. Tonal direction in the closing bars of the Introit
from Esquivel's *Missa pro defunctis* (1608)

The same phenomenon can be observed in much of Palestrina's music, and in Victoria's (including the Requiem of 1605), and in many of the newer-style polychoral works becoming fashionable in continental Europe by composers more in the mainstream of musical development than Esquivel. In relation to much pre-Baroque music, the Schenkerian analyst, Saul Novak, has argued that 'the outer voices do become more important than the others by virtue of their double roles of stating thematic design and of projecting tonal prolongation and direction' and 'the bass line is carefully moulded to prolong chords and to reach goals.... there are bass leaps of fifths that repeatedly project harmonic function'[118] and finally 'harmonic

118 Saul Novack, 'The Analysis of Pre-Baroque Music', in David Beach, ed., *Aspects of Schenkerian Theory* (Newhaven, 1983), pp. 128/9. Other studies applying Shenkerian theory to pre-Baroque music include: Saul Novack, 'Fusion of Design and Tonal Order in Mass and Motet: Josquin Desprez and Heinrich Isaac', *The Music Forum* 2 (New York, 1970), pp. 187–263; Felix Salzer and Carl Schachter, *Counterpoint: The Study of Voice Leading* (New York: McGraw-Hill, 1969); David Stern, 'Tonal Organization in Modal Polyphony', *Theory and Practice* 2 (1981), pp. 5–39.

practices and the various expansions of the I–V–I relationship are strengthened and exploited throughout the sixteenth century'.

This view is open to rejection, of course. Some writers have gone even further and trace the origins of later functional harmony as far back as the fifteenth century; others see the application of such analytical tools as a method of analysis more appropriate for music of a later age, as anachronistic and entirely inappropriate.[119] It is only aural evidence that makes this 'modernist' interpretation tenable.

It seems clear that, if Esquivel was aware of new stylistic and technical developments, he had no desire to be innovative in his mass settings. In style and technique, his masses are rooted in an older tradition; they exemplify the spirit of Counter-Reformation orthodoxy – the same spirit that characterised the music of his more illustrious Spanish contemporaries. The upholding of tradition, not innovation, is what interested him, and in this respect his masses are worthy examples of a once powerful tradition.

---

119 For a fuller discussion of this topic, see Miguel A. Roig-Francolí, 'Playing in Consonances', *Early Music* 23 (1995), pp. 461–71. Among studies quoted there are B. Rivera, 'Harmonic Theory in Musical Treatises of the Late Fifteenth and Sixteenth Centuries', *Music Theory Spectrum* 1 (1979), pp. 85–8; Edward Lowinsky, *Tonality and Atonality in Sixteenth-Century Music* (Berkeley, CA, 1961); Don Randel, 'Emerging Triadic Tonality in the Fifteenth Century', *Musical Quarterly* 57 (1971), pp. 73–86; D. Stern, 'Schenkerian Theory and the Analysis of Renaissance Music', in H. Siegel, ed., *Schenker Studies* (Cambridge, 1990), pp. 49–59.

5

THE MOTETS OF 1608

The motets within the context of liturgy

T HE MOTET was the most popular sacred genre of the sixteenth century.[1] It was a medium for the expression of devotion, both private and public: it could be heard, and interpreted by one individual in the privacy of his own private apartments or chapel, or it could find its place in a wider religious community, to be used as a vehicle for corporate devotion in a liturgical context. This may be what Guerrero had in mind when, in dedicating his *Sacrae cantiones* of 1555 to the duke of Arcos, he claims that his motets (or 'certain songs' as he calls them) are suited to divine worship, but also may be found useful in 'alleviating the sadness of any unoccupied hours'. Given the importance of the motet, it is not surprising that Esquivel should wish to make public his own contribution to this highly flexible genre.

A general description of the contents of the 1608 motet volume was given in Chapter 3. There it was noted that Esquivel's ordering of his motets follows the cycle of the liturgical year, a well-established principle by the time the composer published his volume, though not one followed by all composers; Esquivel's Zamoran contemporary, Alonso de Tejeda (*c*.1556–1628), for example, grouped his motets non-liturgically in three separate volumes for four, five, six and eight voices, and he was not alone in this.[2] Although books of motets with an expressed liturgical

---

1 A number of late-twentieth-century studies have re-examined the relationship between the motet and the liturgy in the sixteenth century, and these have been used to inform the following paragraphs. Studies consulted include the following: Jacquelyn Mattfeld, 'Some Relationships between Texts and Cantus Firmi in the Liturgical Motets of Josquin des Pres', *Journal of the American Musicological Society* 14 (1961), pp. 159–83; John Shepherd, 'A Liturgical-Musical Reappraisal: Two Studies', *Current Musicology* 23 (1977), pp. 69–78; Jerome Roche, 'Liturgical Aspects of the Motets of Andrea Gabrieli Published in 1565 and 1576', in *Andrea Gabrieli e il suo tempo: Atti del convegno internazionale* (Florence, 1987), pp. 215–29; Anthony Cummings, 'Towards an Interpretation of the Sixteenth-Century Motet', *Journal of the American Musicological Society* 34 (1981), pp. 43–59; Dolores Pesce, ed., *Hearing the Motet; Essays on the Motet of the Middle Ages and Renaissance* (New York and Oxford, 1997); Todd Michael Borgerding, 'The Motet and Spanish Religiosity ca.1550–1610' (Ph.D dissertation, University of Michigan, 1997).

2 Tejeda's motets existed in manuscript only, but see modern edition, Alonso de Tejeda (*c*.1556–1628), *Obras completas*, ed. Dionisio Preciado (Madrid, 1974–6). In addition to the examples given in Chapter 3 the following may be noted: Palestrina, *Motecta festorum totius anni cum communi sanctorum ... liber primus* (Rome, 1563); Victoria, *Motecta festorum totius anni cum communi sanctorum* (Rome, 1585); Zorita, *Liber primus ... motectarum* (Barcelona, 1584); Pedro Rimonte, *Cantiones sacrae* (Antwerp, 1607).

purpose had begun to appear during the 1530s,[3] their liturgical designation was incomplete; moreover, examples of such collections are by no means numerous. The increased degree of calendrical organisation after the Council of Trent may reflect an increasing sensitivity on behalf of Church composers and a desire to respond to criticisms of Church music made by the council.[4]

Esquivel's *Motecta festorum* shares common ground with the published collections of some of his contemporaries, notably Guerrero, Rimonte, Zorita and Vivanco. One of the distinctive features of all these is the appearance of cycles of works for the penitential seasons: Advent, Septuagesima (the third Sunday before Lent and, in the Tridentine Rite, the beginning of the penitential season) through Lent. Lenten texts received special attention: as Robert Snow has observed, Spanish composers 'produced an unusually large number of motets based on Gospel passages sung at mass on the Sundays from Septuagesima through Passion Sunday';[5] Vivanco went further and provided motets for Wednesdays and Fridays. The Gospel motet – the term used by Snow – can be traced back to an earlier generation of composers; there are Gospel motets by Escobar, Ceballos and Morales among others, so that Esquivel and his generation may be seen as continuing an established Spanish tradition, albeit a tradition in its infancy, rather than breaking new ground. It is a peninsular tradition, however; Spanish composers abroad – Victoria and Infantas, for example – did not include Septuagesima–Lent or Advent cycles in their prints.[6]

An analysis of texts used by Esquivel shows that, with a few exceptions, obviously drawn from local liturgies,[7] all were taken from liturgical sources in accordance with the new Roman rite, although by no means all can be found in modern compilations such as the *Liber usualis*. All except two of the ten motets from Septuagesima to Palm Sunday are based on the Gospel of the day as found in the condensed

---

3 See Borgerding, 'The Motet and Spanish Religiosity', p. 11. The following examples may be cited: Pierre Attaingnant, *Liber septimus . . . modulos dominici adventus nativitatisque ac sanctorum eo tempore occurrentium habet* (Paris, 1534); Nicholas du Chemin, *Moduli undecim festorum solemnium totius anni . . .* (Paris, 1554); J. Montanus and U. Neuber, *Evangelia dominicorum et festorum . . . De Nativitate. De Epiphanÿs. De Resurrectione Jesu Christe.* (Nürnberg, 1554); C. Gerlach, *Sacrae cantiones . . . de festis praecipius totius anni . . .* (Nürnberg, 1585). For full details of the contents of these prints, see Harry B. Lincoln, *The Latin Motet: Indexes to Printed Collections, 1500–1600* (Ottawa, 1993).

4 Borgerding, 'The Motet and Spanish Religiosity', p. 24.

5 Robert J. Snow, *A New-World Collection of Polyphony for Holy Week and the Salve Service: Guatemala City, Cathedral Archive, Music MS 4* (Chicago and London, 1996), p. 65.

6 Victoria's motets, published during his period of residency in Rome, were calendrically organised but without the inclusion of Advent or Septuagesima–Lent cycles. His principal motet publications were *Motecta* (Venice, Antonio Gardano, 1572); *Motecta* (Rome, Alessandro Gardano, 1583) and *Motecta festorum totius anni* (Rome, Dominico Basa, 1585). All three of Infantas's volumes, entitled *Sacrarum varii styli cantionum tituli Spiritus Sancti*, were published in Venice: *Liber primus* (Gardano, 1578); *Liber II* (Scotto, 1578); *Liber III* (Scotto, 1597). See Borgerding, 'The Motet and Spanish Religiosity', pp. 46–7.

7 See Francisco Rodilla León, *El libro de motetes de 1608 de Juan Esquivel de Barahona (c.1560–c.1624): estudio y transcripción* (Ciudad Rodrigo, 2005), p. 113. Rodilla lists the following five motets, all drawn from what he terms 'liturgias particulares': *O beate Iacobe, Salve sancte pater, Ave Maria, O fortissimi milites* and *O Ildephonse*.

version of the Office chants; the exceptions, *Emendemus in melius* and *O vos omnes*, use Office texts which are non-scriptural. The five Advent motets draw on texts from the mass and Office.

The pool of Office texts for the Common of the Saints changed little with the advent of the post-Tridentine liturgy, and in common with other Spaniards, Esquivel favoured texts already set by Guerrero.[8] The *Sanctorale* provided him with a further pool of texts from which to choose when honouring individual saints. Major saints appear in all motet collections, but Esquivel seems to be the only composer to honour St Ildephonse, a specifically Spanish saint of Toledan origin, although the text he sets does not appear in the *Breviarum Romanum* of 1607. Motets to St Lawrence, a saint who found special favour with Philip II,[9] also appear in collections by Vivanco, Infantas and Palestrina. For some reason Esquivel includes two motets for St Francis (4 October) while including one motet for every other feast.

Esquivel's settings broke new ground in two ways: firstly, the composer assigned each motet to a specific feast or Sunday *by rubric*. Although Guerrero's four published collections of motets are evidence of an increasing specificity in this respect, even the *Mottecta* of 1597 do not assign all motets to a specific occasion. Secondly, with one exception – the opening motet *Ave Maria*, which may be considered a special case for reasons to be explained later – the Marian motets in Esquivel's volume are each allotted to a named feast, a procedure that is rare amongst Spanish composers at this time.[10] Leaving aside the opening *Ave Maria*, there are ten motets in honour of the Virgin, reflecting her unique role as intercessor, Mother of God and model of Christian virtue according to contemporary belief, but only one motet (*Ave Maria Domini*) recording her immaculate conception, a widely held belief which was, however, still in dispute in the late sixteenth century.[11]

In selecting his texts, Esquivel draws on a narrower range of text types than does Guerrero, who includes hymn texts in his 1597 collection, but neither composer (nor any other Spanish composer of their generation) uses the Sequence as a basis for motet texts. As Oliver Strunk noted as far back as 1939, by the end of the sixteenth century the Sequence did not have the significance it had had for composers of Josquin's generation.[12] Over thirty of Esquivel's motets (almost half the collection) are based on antiphon texts; other text types include introits, responds and Alleluia verse. Precise classification of the liturgical context is difficult, however,

8 Borgerding, 'The Motet and Spanish Religiosity', p. 52.

9 Stevenson, *Spanish Cathedral Music*, p. 292.

10 Borgerding, 'The Motet and Spanish Religiosity', p. 55.

11 Ibid., p. 161. Borgerding points out that belief in the Immaculate Conception did not finally reach the status of official doctrine until the nineteenth century, although it was strongly supported in Spain during the sixteenth century at all levels of society.

12 See Oliver Strunk's pioneering study of 1939, 'Some Motet-Types of the Sixteenth Century', originally presented as a conference paper to the International Congress of Musicology (New York, 1944) and reprinted in his *Essays on Music in the Western World* (New York, 1974), pp. 108–13. Confining his argument to the works of Palestrina, Strunk notes that, of that composer's 224 motets, only twelve are sequence motets; 'the great bulk of his motet-production falls, almost equally divided, into two main classes – Antiphon and Respond'.

because some texts served more than one function.[13]

A characteristic of Esquivel is his tendency to use only a section of a complete text. This is particularly marked in the case of motets which, according to Strunk's typology, may be described as Respond motets.

Strunk described antiphon-based motets as 'small motet forms' in contrast to Respond motets. The Respond is the typical large form for the Office, occupying a position analogous to that occupied in the mass by the Sequence.[14] In its fully developed form it follows the binary division of the plainsong Respond from which it takes its text in the following manner:

Prima pars – a setting of the Respond proper

Secunda pars – a setting of the Verse; conclusion of line or lines from Respond.

Thus, we have the musical form AB (*Prima pars*): CB (*Secunda pars*). For Palestrina, the Respond in its fully developed form was a composition conceived for a larger group of voices than the smaller-scale Antiphon–Motet, but the four-part Respond motets of Palestrina are on a smaller scale, works for fewer voices without a setting of the Verse or the *repetitio*. Esquivel's Respond motets, *Emendemus in melius* and *O vos omnes*, follow this practice, although their texts are truncated.

In setting *Emendemus in melius* Esquivel used less than half of the full-length text of the plainsong Respond, and his treatment of the words is undramatic when compared with Morales's distinguished setting. Morales also did not include the verse or the repetition in his five-voice setting, but his symbolic use of ostinato technique for the phrase 'Memento, homo, quia pulvis es, et in pulverem reverteris' (the words intoned by the celebrant as he placed the ashes on the foreheads of the faithful) is highly effective as a rhetorical device.[15] Esquivel's setting of *O vos omnes* will later be compared in some detail with Victoria's setting of 1572, with which it shares many similarities; for the moment it is sufficient to observe that Esquivel, like Victoria, set only the opening section of the full text. None of the other remaining text-types listed above calls for any special treatment and it is not therefore possible to enumerate any specific musical characteristics of these works as a class.

13 For example, the text of the motet *Repleti sunt* served as a Vespers antiphon and a Matins responsory. In addition to the thirty-plus antiphons, Borgerding's Inventory classifies ten motet texts as reponds, and six as versicles. See 'The Motet and Spanish Religiosity', pp. 274–5. Francsico Rodilla's clasification is more detailed: after a full discussion of the liturgical context of the motet texts, he sets out his findings in the form of a graph. According to his research, 48 per cent of the motets are based on antiphon texts, 10 per cent on responsories and 3 per cent on versicles; 11 per cent are designated 'textos polivalentes', i.e. texts which appear in different places under different names in the *Breviarium Romanum*, or the Missal; 21 per cent of the motets use 'composite' texts ('textos compuestos'), in the sense that they are derived from more than one liturgical source and 7 per cent draw on local liturgies. See Rodilla León, *El libro de motetes de 1608*, pp. 100–13, for further discussion. Many sixteenth- and seventeenth-century texts have survived and are to be found in the *Liber usualis* (often with some change of wording), but carry different designations. For example, the text of the motet, *Filie Ierusalem venite et videte*, assigned by Esquivel to the feast of St Mark (following its assignment to this feast in the *Breviarium Romanum* of 1588), and classified by Borgerding as a respond, is designated as an antiphon in the *Liber usualis*.

14 Strunk, 'Some Motet-Types of the Sixteenth century', p. III.

15 In the *Harvard Dictionary of Music* (Cambridge, MA, 1966), p. 705, this work is described by Willi Apel as 'one of the greatest works in all music history'.

The fact that Esquivel chose his texts from a pool used by so many other composers enables some interesting comparisons to be made when individual settings are placed side by side, as we shall see later.

Scoring

WE COME NOW to the question of vocal scoring. A survey of over 280 motets in the collections of Esquivel, Guerrero, Rimonte and Vivanco suggests that four- and five-part texture was the prevailing compositional norm for Spanish motet composers at the turn of the sixteenth century. Of this sample, 148 are four-voiced works, 105 are five-voiced and only 34 are written for more than five voices.[16] What does this information tell us about the late-sixteenth-century motet composer, and Esquivel in particular?

Spanish motet collections in the late sixteenth century reflect two strains of religiosity, one devotional and one liturgical.[17] The former is represented in settings of texts addressed to the Virgin and saints: these typically include prayers of intercession, often using the second-person form of address, or dwelling on the attributes of a particular saint, and it has been suggested that composers matched such texts with music rich in texture. In contrast, the liturgical strain, represented by settings of texts with a more didactic intent – narrative events from the Gospels, or Christ's own words – require a thinner texture to present a 'calmer narrative tone'.[18]

There is no doubt that, at times, this is the case. But not all richly scored motets are addressed to the saints: multi-part writing can be used for symbolic reasons. To quote one well-known example, Guerrero's magnificent setting of *Duo seraphim* is scored for twelve voices – a number exceptional for Guerrero – but three choirs (of four voices each) are clearly necessary for a symbolic interpretation of the text.

Though it is true that many didactic works included in this survey are scored *à*4, it is also true that many motets which may be devotional in tone and addressed to the saints are also scored *à*4. By way of example, in Esquivel's work alone the following – all four-part motets – may be quoted: *Benedicta tu in mulieribus, O beate Iacobe, Francescus pauper, O quam gloriosum, O beatum pontificem, Beata Dei genitrix Maria, Virgo Dei genitrix, O Ildephonse.*

The predominance of four- and five-part works found in this sample may be explained pragmatically. In proportion to the total number of motets in a single volume, there are more four-part works in Esquivel's 1608 set than there are, say, in Guerrero's earlier 1570 volume (44 out of 72 and 17 out of 38 respectively), but these statistics may reflect practical circumstances. Guerrero may well have had

---

16 This information is drawn from a survey of works by these composers listed by Borgerding, 'The Motet and Spanish Religiosity', pp. 265–77.

17 Ibid., p. 10.

18 Ibid., p. 59.

a more competent choir available at the time of composition of his motets than Esquivel had. As we saw in Chapter 1, evidence from Coria cathedral suggests that choir sizes there were small over a long period. It may well be, then, that Esquivel, employed throughout his professional life in middle- and lower -status dioceses, less well-off than Seville,[19] may have worked with choirs of similar sizes.

Function and purpose

Before we examine the musical contents of the volume in detail, we need to give more consideration to the performance context and function of this large body of material. Exactly where and when were these motets, and many others like them, performed, and what purpose did they serve? Some answers to these questions have already been given: the ordering of contents clearly implies a liturgical function; but what role did these motets play in the liturgy and to which liturgical 'event' do they belong? Until relatively recently the prevailing view seemed to be that a liturgical text set as a motet functioned within the liturgy associated with it; at least this was the assumption made by Oliver Strunk in his 1939 study of the typology of sixteenth-century polyphonic motets, to which reference has already been made. Strunk argued that by the end of the century there were distinct motet-forms, or types, identifiable and separated from each other by the association of the text with a specific liturgical occasion and the musical treatment the text received.

Strunk's system of classification carried the implication that each distinct motet-form was associated with a specific liturgical 'event', the mass or the Office, and that its performing context was located within that event and that event only. However, later studies questioned this assumption that a motet necessarily functioned within the liturgical context suggested by its text. As far back as 1977, John Shepherd used Josquin's four Matins motets (*Responde mihi, Stetit autem Solomon, Liber generationis Jesu Christe* and *Factum est autem*) to demonstrate the impracticality of performing highly complex polyphonic music at what we today would regard as 'anti-social hours':

> Matins was prescribed for the eighth hour of the night, i.e., 2 a.m.... the practicalities involved in achieving musical coherence from a group of musicians or a group of musical ecclesiastics at 2 a.m. or 6 a.m. would be formidable, especially if confronted with the demands of a motet by Josquin.[20]

The same study concluded:

> it is more likely for motets to have been sung at the Mass than at the Office in view of the time available for meditation. At the Office there was total participation from all present. Everyone could join in throughout. Not so in the Mass. Much time

---

19 See chart in Rawlings, *Church, Religion and Society*, pp. 62–3.
20 Shepherd, 'A Liturgical-Musical Reappraisal', p. 74.

was made available for the laity to proceed with their private devotions, especially throughout the consecration, elevation, and reception of communion by the clergy. It is in these periods of silent adoration that the liturgical motet . . . would have the most meaningful place.[21]

Similar views were expressed by Anthony Cummings in 1981. In an investigation into the relationship between a motet text and its liturgical background Cummings drew upon evidence from the Cappella Sistina diaries for the years 1509 to 1616 to prove his case, setting out the issue as follows:

> while manuscript rubrics and liturgical directives contained in sixteenth-century manuals indicate occasions on which motets may have been sung, namely those occasions for which their texts were liturgically specified, they offer no clear proof that they were in fact performed at all.[22]

Cummings suggested that the locations of the motet were freer than generally supposed. The relevance of the diaries to his argument lies in the fact that they specify the context in which motets were actually performed. For example, the diaries frequently indicate that a motet was sung during mass, either at the Offertory, Elevation or Communion. From these records it becomes obvious that motets were sung outside the liturgical context suggested by the texts. Examples given by Cummings include the following: in 1616 the diaries record the singing on the feast of Epiphany of Palestrina's *Surge illuminare Jerusalem*, a text designated as the 'Lectio ysaye prophete' for the day; at the Offertory on the first Sunday of Lent, Josquin's *Qui habitat*, which takes its text from the Tract for the day and the psalm to the Introit, was performed; the Offertory motet on the third Sunday in Lent was Morales's *Lamentabatur Jacob*, a Responsory text assigned to the Ninth Lesson of Matins.[23] Other examples are given to support Cummings's hypothesis that the mass was the liturgical context in which motets were performed, although their texts may be drawn from the Office.

Cummings concluded that 'freedom in choice of text, the sometimes marginal relevance of texts to the liturgical provisions of the feast that occasioned their performance . . . are features requiring that the motet in the sixteenth century be defined as a para-liturgical compositional type.'[24]

---

21 Ibid., p. 76.
22 Cummings, 'Towards an Interpretation of the Sixteenth-Century Motet', p. 44.
23 Ibid., p. 48.
24 Ibid., p. 59. Cummings mentions several other studies which have investigated the question of the liturgical function of the motet. In addition to Strunk, he cites the following: Mattfeld, 'Some Relationships between Text and Cantus Firmi' – a study which assumes an identification of liturgical association with liturgical function; Brown, *Music in the Renaissance*, p. 133: 'More than half of Josquin's 100-odd motet texts have been found in early liturgical books. Some of them were intended for performance as a part of the mass proper, especially as Gospel lessons or as sequences. But most of them, including those for some twenty-five psalm settings and thirteen Marian antiphons, belong to those shorter, votive services (such as Matins and Lauds) that consist of psalm, antiphons, responsories, lessons and prayers and that comprise the Canonical Hours or Divine Office'; Johannis Lheritier, *Opera omnia*, ed. Leeman Perkins, Corpus mensurabilis musicae 48 (Middleton, WI, 1969), p. 25: 'The balance

There is no reason to suppose that what was standard practice in Rome was not also standard practice in Spain. Firm evidence is available in the case of Alonso Lobo. His *Liber primus missarum* (Madrid, 1602) contains, in addition to six masses, seven motets 'suitable for devout singing during the celebration of mass'. Each of these motet texts has a liturgical association not in the mass, but with the Office. For example, the first motet, *O quam suavis*, is a setting of a Vespers antiphon from the feast of Corpus Christi; the second motet, *Quam pulchri sunt*, sets a text from the Song of Songs; the third, *Ave regina*, is a Compline antiphon for the season from Christmas to the Purification. Three other motets have no similar links with the Office; two are associated with the dead (one, *Versa est in luctum*, specifically written for the funeral of Philip II) and another has a Lenten text of biblical origin: 'As I live, saith the Lord, I desire not the death of the sinner, but that he turn from his ways and live'. Thus, given Lobo's own description of these motets, we may deduce that the singing at mass of motets based on texts drawn from another liturgical source was a practice carried out in Spanish churches at the end of the sixteenth century, at least in Toledo and Seville where Lobo served as chapelmaster; there are no compelling reasons to suggest that the situation would be any different in the churches in which Esquivel served. The liturgical associations embodied in the texts of Spanish motets in the late sixteenth century are clear and it would therefore not seem entirely inappropriate, as Lobo clearly demonstrates, to perform a motet in the context of mass at an appropriate point when a specific feast day or other ritual occasion called for a particular association to be made.[25]

of Lheritier's motets are based upon texts of the kind usually referred to somewhat loosely as devotional, meaning, it would seem, that they have no legitimate place in the standardized liturgical usage of the present day. The purpose served by compositions of the sort is a matter yet to be fully investigated, but in those of Lheritier, textual and musical allusions either point to a close relationship with the liturgy or suggest observances that, while no longer current, were common enough in his time.' Cummings, 'Towards an Interpretation of the Sixteenth-Century Motet', pp. 43–4, n. 2.

25 Lewis Lockwood has also shown that motets were sometimes inserted into the mass in the early part of the sixteenth century: 'A View of the Parody Mass', p. 57: 'We also have a few instances of motets inserted into masses, though not as models: as in Josquin's *Mass D'ung aultre amer* and Pierre de La Rue's *Mass De Sancta Anna*'. In a previous paragraph he raises the question of the relationship between a parody mass and its source: 'it becomes at least ideally possible that a motet and its parody mass are conceived of as belonging together … in the sense that the two works are open to the possibility of being performed on the same liturgical occasion'. He cites as examples Attaingnant, *Liber tertius missarum … cum suis motetis* (1540), which has Claudin's *Missa Domine quis habitabit*, followed by the motet of the same name and Gombert's *Missa sancta Maria* along with its model motet by Verdelot. Lockwood is far from dogmatic about the function of the motet, however, and acknowledges that there is a lack of concrete evidence on which to draw. Edward Lerner goes as far as to suggest that motets with non-liturgical texts were interpolated into the mass in order to gloss or elaborate certain portions of the Ordinary and Proper: Edward R. Lerner, 'Some Motet Interpolations in the Catholic Mass', *Journal of the American Musicological Society* 14 (1961), pp. 24–30. Much of Lerner's evidence, however, is based on a study of Lutheran practice and, therefore, any connection with Spanish practice is very remote. Moreover, like some of the other studies quoted earlier, Lerner's work is based on an examination of pre-Tridentine polyphonic material. For both these reasons it would be dangerous to draw inferences for late-sixteenth-century Spanish practice beyond making the general observation that there is evidence to suggest that throughout Europe during the course of the sixteenth century the liturgical use of a motet was probably wider than the liturgical context suggested by its text.

Moreover, there is further evidence from Seville to suggest that the singing of a motet during the Offertory, at the Elevation, or during Communion was common practice there in the later stages of the sixteenth century. Sebastián de Vicente Villegas, who was a member of the cathedral community and *maestro de ceremonias* after 1619, records in his manuscript ceremonial 'Norma de los Sagrados Ritos' – a document completed for the cathedral in 1630 – that 'it is usual to have some motet or song sung at the Offertory or after the Elevation'.[26] By the sixteenth century, the Elevation had become the central ritual moment in the mass. Since the end of the twelfth century the host had been raised up to such a height that it could be seen and venerated by all present.[27] But the visual and olfactory impact of this sacred moment is obscured for those outside the *coro*. By marking this moment aurally, the motet could become a means of communicating the significance and mystery of the eucharist to all present; as a moment free from any prescribed liturgical text, it offered a means of facilitating private devotion and participation.[28] Moreover, in Seville, the practice of singing a motet seems to have become so well established that motets were performed at the Elevation even during penitential seasons when mass was sung in plainsong without organ or instrumental accompaniment. Villegas records that 'the "et incarnatus est" of the Credo is sung in polyphony as well as a simple motet at the Elevation, with music and texts appropriate to the season, or to the Sunday in question'.[29]

There was a very practical reason for the insertion of a motet at this point: the Elevation follows the Sanctus, and a monophonic Sanctus would not allow sufficient time for the action of the Elevation, a point again noted by Villegas: 'after the Elevation, or at the same time, the choir having finished the final verses and repetition of the Sanctus, the musicians then sing a polyphonic motet proper to each Sunday'.[30]

How widespread was the practice of singing a motet at the Offertory, Elevation and Communion in other centres is difficult to judge, but given the weight of evidence from Italy, and Sevillian practices described by Villegas, there seems to be no compelling evidence why the practice should not have been replicated elsewhere, including those institutions served by Esquivel.

Other Counter-Reformation rituals provided further opportunities for motet performance. In addition to mass and the Office, the independent *Salve* service

26 Villegas, 'Norma de los sagrados ritos', fol. 46 . 'suele aver a la ofrenda o despues de alcar alguna motete o chançoneta', cited in Borgerding, 'The Motet and Spanish Religiosity', p. 102.

27 Ludwig Eisenhofer and Joseph Lechner, *The Liturgy of the Roman Rite*, trans. A. J. and E. F. Peeler, ed. H. E. Winstone (Edinburgh and London, 1961), p. 315.

28 Borgerding, 'The Motet and Spanish Religiosity', p. 105.

29 Villegas, 'Libro de ceremonias II', fols. 35–5. 'la misa toda se ofiçiara a Canto llano: y sin organo ni musica contrapunto . . . enpero Cantarse en el credo el incarnatus est. y un motete aun sençillo al alçar, con musica y letra que sea a proposito con el tiempo, o con el ofiço de la dominica', cited in Borgerding, 'The Motet and Spanish Religiosity', p. 101.

30 Villegas, 'Libro de ceremonias II', fols. 44–4': 'despues de aber alçado o a el mesmo tiempo de el alçar, abiendo y acabado de cantar el choro los ultimos versos y Repetiçion siguientes a los sanctus; los musicos entonçes cantaran a canto de organo un motete de quel dia proprio para cada domingo', cited in Borgerding, 'The Motet and Spanish Religiosity', p. 101.

– which grew out of the practice of honouring the Virgin Mary by singing the *Salve Regina* on Saturdays or Sundays after Vespers or Compline – established its independence some time in the sixteenth century; it included in addition to a *Salve Regina* setting the performance of a motet in honour of the Virgin. Evidence for the musical contents of such is a service is available from Seville cathedral, where a *Salve* service was held daily,[31] but we cannot be certain how widespread this practice was outside this centre, nor how long it continued.[32]

Religious processions too provided a performing context for the motet. Such processions were a feature of religious life in the Counter-Reformation; in addition to providing spectacle they offered opportunities for the public display of devotion, and there is ample evidence to suggest that the performance of motets was an integral part of these. In addition to the large-scale extravagant processions of Holy Week and Corpus Christi, which provided important opportunities for reinforcing Counter-Reformation ideals, more modest processions were a feature of cathedral and monastic worship on Sundays and feast days.[33] At Seville sung polyphony was a feature of processions from at least mid-century,[34] and processions connected with *autos de fe* were accompanied by singers there from at least 1573, although there is no record of what they actually sang.[35] As we saw in Chapter 1, the Inquisition was active in Ciudad Rodrigo, so that Esquivel may have been expected to provide singers for processions connected with *autos de fe* as well, of course, as annual processions like Holy Week and Corpus Christi.

RHETORICAL EXPRESSION

B UT IF THE PERFORMANCE of a motet in the context of mass offered the worshiper an opportunity for devotion, adoration and silent reflection, it may well have been perceived in the eyes of the Church authorities as serving another purpose, that of promoting Church doctrine. The Lenten motets in particular, with their emphasis on Gospel texts, were a useful means of reinforcing Counter-Reformation theology, and a carefully chosen text clothed in an appropriately expressive language offered an additional means of exegesis, of re-presenting or reinforcing ideas expounded in more detail in the sermon;[36] for, as all sixteenth-century educated clergy and Church musicians were aware, both words and music had the power to 'move' the listener.

---

31 See Snow, *A New-World Collection of Polyphony*, pp. 68–73.

32 Robert Snow has drawn attention to MS 6 in Palencia cathedral, which is entitled 'Libro de salves, motetes y pasiones'. This contains a set of six *Salve* settings, each paired with a motet by Joaquin Martínez, suggesting that the practice was continued at Palencia until at least the end of the eighteenth century. See Snow, *A New-World Collection of Polyphony*, p. 73.

33 Borgerding, 'The Motet and Spanish Religiosity', pp. 63–4.

34 Ibid., p. 66.

35 Ibid., p. 67.

36 This point is discussed in great detail, and with many examples, in chapter 3 of Todd Borgerding's doctoral dissertation, 'The Motet and Spanish Religiosity', pp. 107–59.

Before we explore this link in more detail, we need first to examine the preacher's role and his use of the ancient technique of rhetoric to convey his message.

In classical texts, the purposes of rhetoric were commonly declared to be to inform, to persuade or move, and to entertain or delight ('ut docet, moveat, delectat'),[37] and rhetorical techniques formed part of the armoury of the Counter-Reformation preacher. Preaching reached a new height of emphasis in Counter-Reformation Spain; both Catholics and Protestants laid great stress on biblical exegesis, and by the mid-sixteenth century a firm foundation of rhetorical delivery had been laid, an outcome of the better quality of training for the priesthood demanded by the Council of Trent and one encouraged by a number of theologians and writers.

Although a thoroughgoing sacred rhetoric, as opposed to a preacher's handbook, appears not to have been published in Spain during the century,[38] the Spanish rhetorical tradition may be traced back to Antonio de Nebrija (1444–1522), who had an immense influence on Spanish intellectuals through the production in 1492 of his *Gramatica sobre la lengua castellana*[39] and his subsequent writings on language and rhetoric. Another powerful and influential figure was Cardinal Cisneros, archbishop of Toledo, who, as we saw in Chapter 1, established a centre for humanist culture, the University of Alcalá, in 1508. This institution became a training centre for clergy with a curriculum based on the classics, the Bible and the Church Fathers. Nebrija was appointed professor in rhetoric in 1514, and humanistic study soon spread to other centres including Seville and Salamanca. The tradition of rhetorical preaching was further encouraged in the writings of Luís de Granada, in particular his *Retórica eclesiastica* of 1575, which provided generic models for preachers.

Granada's principal intention was the Christianisation of pagan rhetoric – the first time that such a task had been attempted. Granada listed five types of sermon, although other writers chose different numbers, ranging from five – the exclusively Christian *genera* suggested by St Paul (2 Timothy 3: 16 and Romans 15: 4) – to twelve, or numbers in between.[40] The two most distinctive types current in the Spanish Golden Age were the *sermon de un tema* and the *homilía*, or as Granada termed it, the *sermo evangelicus*, in effect a paraphrase or explanation of a Gospel text.[41] It is this form that is most commonly associated with Lenten *sermonarios* of the period.[42] In contrast to the *sermon de un tema*, which was modelled on the

---

37 Judy Tarling, *The Weapons of Rhetoric* (St Albans, 2004), p. 1. This text is described as 'A guide for musicians and audiences' and offers a useful introduction to the subject of rhetoric and its application to the performance of Renaissance and Baroque music. It includes many musical examples drawn mainly, however, from Baroque music.

38 Hilary Dansey Smith, *Preaching in the Spanish Golden Age* (Oxford, 1978), p. 90.

39 Borgerding, 'The Motet and Spanish Religiosity', p. 215.

40 Smith, *Preaching in the Spanish Golden Age*, p. 46. In 2 Timothy 3: 16, St Paul wrote: 'All scripture is inspired by God and is useful for teaching, for reproof, for correction, and for training in righteousness', and in Romans 15: 4, 'For whatever was written in former days was written for our instruction'. St Paul's epistles provided a basis for several writers. See Frederick McGinnes, *Right Thinking and Sacred Oratory in Counter-Reformation Rome* (Princeton, 1995), pp. 58–60, for further discussion on this point.

41 Smith, *Preaching in the Spanish Golden Age*, p. 46.

42 Ibid., p. 53. The *sermonarios* were published collections of a preacher's sermons; they acted as

classical rhetorical oration schematised by Aristotle[43] – *propositio, narratio, confir-matio, peroratio* – Granada advocates a much freer form, and a freer style of speaking; Cicero's three styles (the grand, the intermediate and the lowly) could be mixed according to the purpose of the sermon.

According to Aquinas, the task of preaching belonged to the bishop,[44] but by the mid-sixteenth century all priests were expected to fulfil this task, delivering a short homily at each mass celebrated. A preaching rota, or *tabla*, was drawn up by the *canónigo magistral* in every cathedral and collegiate church.[45] Public sermons, based on scripture and Church doctrine, were preached on Sundays, with a homily (five to ten minutes) delivered either before or after the Creed on Sundays. In Lent, longer sermons were preached on weekdays as well as Sundays. There were regional differences in the timing of these: in Castile, they were given on Mondays, Wednesdays and Fridays;[46] an explanation of the Gospel reading of the day formed the substance of these sermons.

According to Terrones del Caño, an influential writer of the period, a homily should consist of a short salutation, an introduction and the body of the sermon, a clause-by-clause exposition of the prescribed Gospel narrative.[47] Another writer, Fray Diego Murillo declared: 'ordinarily, those who write sermons only expound on the first two clauses of the Gospel, and these are those on which one preaches'.[48]

Sermons were delivered with an agreed system of rhetorical gestures, ranging from finger-wagging to beatific facial expressions of anticipated ecstasy, with the aim of arresting attention, delighting, teaching, moving and effecting a change in attitude of those listening.

The suggestion that the motet may function as a commentary on the sermon, or as an additional means of exegesis – in addition, that is, to its traditional role as a devotional tool – does not appear completely out of the question when we consider that, for composers, the idea of borrowing the techniques of eloquence and oratory as applied to speech to improve communication with an audience was commonplace in the Renaissance.[49] In writing about vocal music, many Renaissance theorists from Gaffurius onwards spoke of the need to express the text, by which they meant making its ideas and affections musically comprehensible. Thus the *avant garde* Italian, Nicola Vicentino could write:

> The movement of the measure should be changed to slower or faster according to the words . . . The experience of the orator teaches us to do this, for in his orations

models for the novice preacher. See ibid., pp. 30 ff., for further details.

43 Ibid., p. 46.
44 Ibid., p. 18.
45 Ibid., p. 20.
46 Ibid., p. 31.
47 Ibid., p. 52. Francisco Terrones del Caño, *Instrucción de predicadores* (posthumous, Madrid, 1914).
48 Smith, *Preaching in the Spanish Golden Age*, p. 53. Fray Diego Murillo, *Discursos predicables* . . . (Saragossa, 1607). ('de ordinario los que escriben sermones sólamente declaran las dos primas cláusulas del Evangelio, y éstas son las que casi siempre se predican').
49 See Tarling, *The Weapons of Rhetoric*, pp. 3–4.

he speaks now loudly, now softly, now slowly, now quickly, and thus greatly moves the listeners: and this manner of changing measures has great effect upon the soul.[50]

His fellow-countryman Zarlino went further in advising how this 'great effect upon the soul' could be achieved in practice:

it is essential that we ... make a choice of harmony [i.e. mode, intervals] or of number [i.e. rhythm] similar to the nature of the subjects that are contained in the text, so that from the composition of these elements [harmony, number] and their proper adjust-ment to each other a melody may result in accordance with the [poetic] intentions.[51]

In Spain, Juan Bermudo states categorically:

The composer who wants to succeed must first understand the text, and make it so that the music serves the text, and not the text the music. If the text is happy, sad, devotional and profound, so should be the music.[52]

And in a similar vein, Thomas Morley writes of the expressive purposes of motet writing:

This kind [ie. the motet] of all others which are made on a ditty requireth most art and moveth and causeth most strange effects in the hearer, being aptly framed for the ditty and well expressed by the singer, for it will draw the auditor (and especially the skilful auditor) into a devout and reverent kind of consideration of Him for whose praise it was made.[53]

Morley goes on to talk about the performance of the motet in church: 'they [ie. the singers] ought to study how to vowel and sing clean, expressing their words with devotion and passion whereby to draw the hearer, as it were, in chains of gold by the ears to the consideration of holy things'. This is a direct reference to the classi-cal rhetorical tradition as sometimes demonstrated visually in the title pages and emblem books of the Renaissance period, and reminds us of the important role of the performer in 'getting the message across' (see Plates 5 and 6).

50 Nicola Vicentino, L'antica musica ridotta alla moderna prattica (1555), trans. Claude V. Palisca, 'Ut oratorio musica', in Palisca's Studies in the History of Italian Music and Music Theory (Oxford, 1994), pp. 305–7.

51 Zarlino, Le istituzioni harmoniche, p. 339, part V, chap. 32 (Venice, 1558; facs. edn New York, 1965). Cited in Don Harrán, In Search of Harmony: Hebrew and Humanistic Elements in Sixteenth-Century Musical Thought (Middleton, WI, 1988), p. 109.

52 Juan Bermudo, Declaración de instrumentos musicales, fol. 125: 'El componedor que acerter quisiere: entienda primero la letra, y haga, que el punto sirva a la letra; y no a letra al punto'. A similar point is made by Francisco de Montanos in his Arte de música theoretica y pratica (Valladolid: Diego Fernández de Córdoba y Oviedo, 1592), p. 27: 'la parte mas essencial [es] hazer lo que la letra pide, alegre, o triste, grave, lexos, o cerca, humilde, o levantada. De suerte que haga el effecto que la letra pretende para levantar a consideración los animos de los oyentes' ('The most essential part is to do as the text requests: happy or sad, grave or light-hearted, complex or simple, humble or elevated, in such a way that the effect which the text asks for can be raised in the souls of the listeners').

53 Thomas Morley, A Plain and Easy Introduction to Practical Music, ed. Alec Harman (London, 1952), pp. 292–3.

Plate 5.   Hercules driving the oxen of Geryon (Achillis Bochii Bonon, *Symbolicarum quaestionum*, 1574). © The Warburg Institute

334   ANDREÆ ALCIATI,

Eloquentia fortitudine præstantior.

EMBLEMA CLXXX.

Arcum læva tenet , rigidâ fert dextera clavam,
    Contegit & Nemees corpora nuda leo.
Herculis hæc igitur facies ? non convenit illud
    Quòd vetus, & senio tempora cana gerit.
Quid quòd lingua illi levibus trajecta catenis,
    Queis fissa facileis allicit aure viros ?
Anne quòd Alciden lingua non robore Galli
    Præstantem populis jura dedisse ferunt ?
Cedunt arma togæ , & quamvis durissima corda
    Eloquio pollens ad sua vota trahit.

EX-

Plate 6. Alciati emblem: 'Eloquentia fortitudine praestantior'
(Andreae Alciati, *Emblemata*, 1621)

Plate 5 shows the ancient God Hercules – recognisable by his attributes, the club and the lion skin – mounted on a cart and driving the oxen of Geryon. The people are driven by the chains of his speech. In Plate 6,[54] Hercules is again shown with his weapons of war; to his club is added the bow of his youth. But these tools are useless in old age; his tongue is now much more powerful than tangible weapons of warfare. This is symbolised by the slackened chains of speech which reach from his mouth to the ears of the crowd behind. The message is clear: eloquence is superior to physical strength.

Joachim Burmeister's codification and application of rhetorical devices to music in his *Musica poetica* (1606) has attracted much attention; he was the first writer to pursue the analogy between the two arts. But, as Claude Palisca has pointed out:

> not every device considered by Burmeister is expressive or has an expressive purpose. Many of them are simply constructive devices, artifices that grew out of the need to knit together the voices of a composition once the cantus firmus was abandoned as the main thread earlier in the century. The words *musica poetica* in Burmeister's title do not signify the art of poetic music or musical poetry, as some have inferred, but the art of 'making' musical compositions (from the Greek *poiein*): . . . *fuga, mimesis, anadiplosis, hypallage,* and *anaphora* are various ways of interrelating the parts of a polyphonic composition. *Climax* and *auxesis* are means of achieving continuity. They are artfully disguised repetitions that permit the total sound to be renewed while details are being reused.[55]

Relating Palisca's comments to Esquivel's works, although we can identify examples of *figurae* in his motets – as in the works of Lassus, from whom Burmeister quotes extensively to illustrate his argument – identification and mere labelling alone do not necessarily enhance our appreciation and understanding of the expressive gestures of his music. Such rhetorical devices as those in Palisca's list were commonplace in sixteenth-century music, even though composers may not have given them conscious recognition, or, indeed, thought of them in terms of classical rhetoric.

To examine this question in more detail, let us focus on the motet *Christus factus est*, paying particular attention to its expressive characteristics, and the relationship between words and music.

Christus factus est appears as the motet for Thursday of Holy Week, marked *In Coena Domini* in Esquivel's rubric. The text is a partial setting of Philippians 2: 8–9, the gradual text found in the *Breviarium Romanum* of 1588; only the first half is set (for the full text, see *Liber usualis*, p. 669): 'Christus factus est pro nobis obediens usque ad mortem, mortem autem crucis' ('Christ was made obedient for us unto death, even to death on the cross'). The whole motet is printed as Ex. 5.1. As we can see, it begins conventionally with paired imitation at the fifth, but with chromatic inflections – F♯ and C♯ – on the word 'est', and an E♭ in bar 4, emphasising that Christ's death was 'for

---

54 Andrea Alciato, *Emblemata* (Augsburg, 1531). The original book went through more than 150 editions in the sixteenth and seventeenth centuries and was highly influential throughout Europe. The last edition appeared in the eighteenth century.

55 Palisca, 'Ut oratorio musica'.

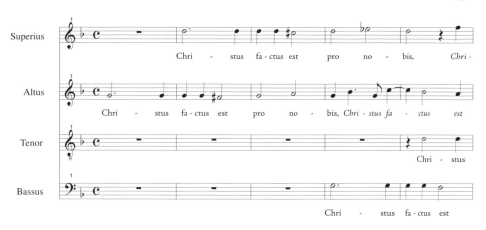

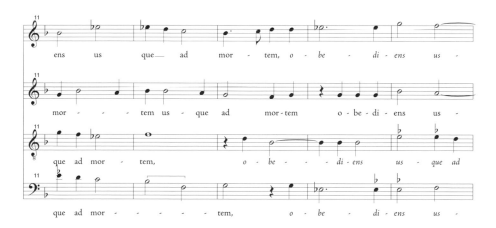

Ex. 5.1.   Motet: *Christus factus est*

Juan Esquivel

que   ad mor - - - tem,   mor - tem au -

que   ad mor - - - tem,   mor - tem au -

mor - - - - - - tem,   mor - tem au -

que ad mor - - - - - tem,   mor - tem au -

tem cru - - - cis, _____   mor - tem au - tem cru - cis.

tem cru - - - cis, mor - tem au - tem cru - cis, au - tem cru - cis, mor -

tem cru - - - - - cis,   au - tem cru - cis,   mor -

tem cru - - - cis, mor - tem au - tem cru - cis, au - tem cru - -

mor - tem au - tem cru - cis,

tem au - tem cru - - - cis, mor - tem au - tem cru - cis,   mor - tem

tem au - tem cru - cis, mor - tem au - tem cru - cis,   mor - tem

cis,   mor - tem au - tem cru - cis, au - tem   cru - cis,

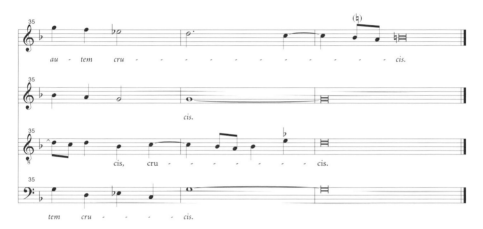

us'. This heightening of emotional tension by chromatic means is labelled *pathopoeia* in Burmeister's classification: '*Pathopoeia* is a figure suited for arousing the affections, which occurs when semitones that belong neither to the mode nor to the genus of the piece are employed'.[56] It is a commonly used device in late Renaissance music.

In bar 19, the text 'mortem autem crucis' ('even to death on the cross') is highlighted in homophonic declamatory style (*noema* in Burmeister's terminology) – a technique that Esquivel uses sparingly, but one frequently used by other Renaissance composers as a means of singling out important phrases. He then emphasises yet again this amazing self-sacrificial death by beginning a section of text repetition at different pitch levels (*gradatio*), which finally reaches its climax with the final soprano entry at the upper reaches of the modal ambitus. Again, the expressive intention is clear: Holy Thursday with its commemoration of the Last Supper and Christ's Passion would be very much in the minds of worshippers, and this repetition is the means by which the significance of Christ's death is brought home to the

56 Joachim Burmeister, *Musical Poetics*, trans. Benito V. Rivera (New Haven and London, 1993), p. 175.

believers gathered together on one of the solemnest occasions of the Church year. The fact that such imitation as this is the stock-in-trade of every Renaissance composer does not diminish its value here, and one cannot deny the rhetorical power of this gesture – an expressive conjunction of words and music which is a practical working out of the advice offered by Zarlino, Bermudo, Morley *et alii*.

In passing, one might add that, from a technical standpoint, some of the intensity of this expressive device is lost in bar 29 of Ex. 5.1, where one might have expected a new entry on Bᵇ in the *altus* on the last beat to create a suspension over the bar, in place of the static minim on beat three in all parts; an adjustment to the underlay, and a minim F in the *bassus* in bar 30 would have maintained the intensity of expression at this point.

As was pointed out earlier, a characteristic of Esquivel is his tendency to use only a section of a complete text, and *Christus factus est* is a good example of this. The high incidence of short texts – very often only a single sentence – results, of course, in works which occupy a short time span in performance. Nearly half of the contents of *Motecta festorum* are single-sentence works and many more motets have only two sentences. But this brevity is not the result of incompetence on the composer's part. If motets were performed at the moment of Elevation, as seems to be the case, the amount of time required for contemplation would not have exceeded two or three minutes. And further, Esquivel's brevity may reflect 'a style of preaching which emerged at the turn of the century which encouraged not so much an explication of the gospel from its context as a meditation upon a single verse, leaving the listener to reflect upon the doctrine contained in the gospel'.[57] This is an important point: as a priest and a musician, Esquivel must have conceived his motets as contributing to the pattern of musically expressive works aiding the preacher's attempt to inform, interpret and instruct and 'move' listeners, as well as providing a means of devotion.

How would his congregation have reacted, one wonders? The performance of a motet may well have met with a very mixed response. One may assume that the singers, and at least some of the clergy seated in the *coro* enclosure – those who had had the benefit of the higher standard of training demanded by the Council of Trent – would understand the Latin text and would appreciate the rhetorical gestures of the setting. But the uneducated lay members of the congregation, excluded from the elite clerical body, perhaps crowded into side isles and transepts,[58] with ears not trained to listen to elaborate polyphony set in Latin, may have had little knowledge on which to draw; sadly, their appreciation of a motet's subtleties may have been minimal, for, as Claude Palisca has pointed out in relation to laymen listening to Lassus's motet *In me transierunt* (Burmeister's famous example of musical rhetoric), 'This music is for an in-group, one that understands Latin, is sensitive to the constructive devices, recognizes the allusions'.[59] What was true for Lassus is probably true for Esquivel and many of his contemporaries. Nevertheless, the case for interpreting the motet as a tool for teaching and as an aid to meditation seems well made and, as we shall see, Esquivel made full use of expressive devices in his motet settings.

57 Borgerding, 'The Motet and Spanish Religiosity', p. 155–6.
58 Smith, *Preaching in the Spanish Golden Age*, pp. 14–15.
59 Palisca, 'Ut oratorio musica', p. 307.

Plate 7. Canon: *Ave Maria*, from the *Libro de facistol*, no. 64, Coria

JUAN ESQUIVEL

Ex. 5.2. Hypothetical transcription of the motet, *Ave Maria*

STYLISTIC AND TECHNICAL FEATURES

WHEN WE COME TO CATEGORISE Esquivel's motets according to their musical characteristics, we may group them under the following headings: 1. Motets employing canon; 2. Chant-related motets; 3. Motets making use of an ostinato; 4. Motets showing contrapuntal equality between all parts. The page references to Esquivel's *Motecta festorum* given in the examples below are those found in the source. Bar numbers refer to unpublished transcriptions made by the author.[60] Bar numbers in works not by Esquivel refer to published editions, details of which may be found in the relevant footnotes. Since there are only two canonic motets these will be discussed first.

The canonic motets

Esquivel opens the volume with the canonic motet *Ave Maria*, a mere thirteen bars in transcription. Because it is so short and raises many questions, it is shown in its entirety as Plate 7, accompanied by a hypothetical transcription (Ex. 5.2).

This piece only survives in the Coria copy of the volume (*Libro de facistol* no. 64), which is unfortunate since the page is heavily mutilated. Top and bottom right-hand corners have been torn off, obliterating the final note of the given *superius* and the rubric for realising the implied canon with *superius II*. Further, it is obvious that the printer has made an error in printing the given *superius* with a C1 clef; the only way that the part can be made to fit with *altus, tenor* and *bassus* is by the adoption of a C2 clef. There may be other errors too: a missing or misplaced *signum congruentiae*; a missing pause over the initial semibreve of the given *superius*, for example. Moreover, the significance of the single bar line is unclear and its use in this context is unusual.

Esquivel's instructions for the resolution of the canons to be derived from *altus* and *bassus* are clear: the *altus* carries the tag 'Trinitas in unitate' indicating a three-in-one canon; *altus secundus* is derived from this, as is the second tenor in conformity with the instruction 'Tenor secundus in subdiatesaron' (canon at the lower fourth). The first tenor is derived from the *bassus* in accordance with the printed instruction 'Tenor primus in secunda supra bassum', indicating a canon at the second.

But a problem arises when the *superius* is considered. The absence of the rubric for the canon's resolution leads to considerable guess-work on behalf of the transcriber. An additional problem is the invisibility of the final note of the printed *superius*, obliterated by the torn page. Both F and A are possible harmonically, but since this incipit is a quotation from Josquin's celebrated motet *Ave Maria . . . Virgo serena* the last note must surely be A.[61] Since there is no evidence of a note stem,

60 See J. C. Walkley, 'Juan Esquivel: An Evaluation and Partial Transcription of his Publications of 1608', vol. II (M.Phil. dissertation, University of Lancaster, 1996).

61 The text of this work is a medieval sequence, found in Perugia Biblioteca Comunale 'Augusta', MS 2789, fol. 272v. The chant was used by Dominicans throughout Europe in the fourteenth century,

the most likely durational value is a breve and not a long as shown in the *altus* and *bassus*.

Now we come to the point of entry and the pitch of the canon's resolution. An entry in bar eight of Ex. 5.2 'ad unisonum', as the *signum congruentiae* suggests, is impossible, however attractive such a solution looks at first glance. It can quickly be seen that this would create parallel octaves with *tenor II* in bar 9 of the transcription, and further harmonic improprieties would be committed if such a course were to be pursued. The most natural point of entry for *superius II* is bar three of Ex. 5.2; and, given the brevity of the piece and the long coda-like passage in the *bassus*, a second entry is likely and possible in bar eight, but in retrograde. Maybe the missing Latin tag read something like: 'Superius secundus vadit et venit, cancrizando', or 'Superius secundus recta et retro canit'. With this in mind, a possible but hypothetical solution is suggested in Ex. 5.2.[62] This solution is slightly irregular, however, in that it breaks an established convention whereby a derived part enters later than the part from which it is derived, and it also makes other assumptions – the misprints and omissions already listed. But it does work!

But apart from the missing information, which gives rise to some uncertainties and a certain amount of guess-work, this piece raises some intriguing questions: why did Esquivel give so much prominence to such an inconsequential piece? Was it perhaps an early work, the product of the young Esquivel who wanted to impress the world with his ingenuity? After all, to write a three-in-one canon and to combine it with even more canons is no mean technical achievement, however contrived the final result may be. Is there some hidden symbolism at work here? Perhaps the canon was not intended for performance at all?

The placing of the canon in such a prominent place at the head of the volume offers a clue: it may be both a symbolic and decorative device, a sign of learning not intended for performance. Such symbolic, decorative canons were common on engraved frontispieces in the sixteenth century. One example is Alonso Lobo's *Liber primus missarum* (Madrid, 1602), to which reference was made earlier in this chapter. There, at the bottom of the elaborately decorated title page, is a small oval vignette showing the composer holding a sheet of music on which is printed a three-in-one canon, while at the centre of the page is an engraving of the Virgin Mary.[63]

The suggestion was made in Chapter 3 that this volume of motets, like the composer's companion 1608 volume, the *Liber primus*, may have been dedicated to the Virgin, and this canon is further evidence of this. Moreover, this explanation is more convincing when we begin to search for hidden meanings. This is a seven-

---

although Josquin's version of the chant melody differs slightly from the medieval version.

62 I am most grateful to Hugh Keyte for his many helpful suggestions in relation to this canon; in particular, his suggestion for the *superius II* entry in bar three.

63 Another example of the symbolic use of three-in-one canon as a feature of an engraving on a title page is that of Vivanco's *Liber magnificarum* of 1607, to which Robert Stevenson first drew attention in 1961. The engraving shows the composer on his knees before a crucifix; the text of the canon reads in translation: 'O come let us adore Christ the King, hanging upon a cross for us'. See Stevenson, *Spanish Cathedral Music*, pp. 277–8.

part piece and the number seven is a Marian number, and in ancient times was considered a 'virginal' number. Michael O'Connor links the canon with the Seven Sorrows of Mary, which in his view may have a connection with the Dominican order (and therefore with Don Pedro Ponce de León) since rosary devotion based on the Sorrows was a strong component of Dominican life.[64] However, given the huge significance attached to the number seven in the ancient world and Christianity, this is not an entirely convincing argument. There are many biblical references to the number seven, and medieval devotion also described the *Joys* of the Virgin.[65]

If the canon has an emblematic function, this would explain why it is given pride of place in the volume.

The second canonic motet, *Ave Maria, Domini mei mater*, for the feast of the Immaculate Conception (pp. 106–9) is a much less complex canon. The text reads as follows:

> Ave Maria, Domini mei mater, alma caelica, plena gratia, tu benedicta in saecula. Orbis Regina. Tu es pulchra Dei sponsa, Domina in caelo et in terra.

> Hail Mary, mother of my Lord, heavenly mother, full of grace; thou art blessed throughout all ages, queen of the universe; thou art the beautiful bride of God, mistress in heaven and on earth.

Superius I and *II* are in canon *ad unisonum* supported by the three lower parts which, after the opening, make very little reference to the melodic material of the upper voices. The motet begins in the *bassus* with a different permutation of the four principal notes of the *superius* opening (Ex. 5.3).

Ex. 5.3. *Bassus* and *Superius* in the canonic motet *Ave Maria, Domini mei mater*

---

64 Michael B. O'Connor, 'The Polyphonic Compositions on Marian Texts by Juan de Esquivel Barahona: A Study of Institutional Marian Devotion in Late Renaissance Spain' (Ph.D dissertation, Florida State University, 2006), p. 130.

65 See Elders, *Symbolic Scores*, p. 156–7. Elders points out that the oldest repertoire of works for seven voices originated in England: the Eton Choirbook contains a seven-part *Salve Regina* by John Sutton and a seven-part Magnificat by John Browne. A full discussion of Marian symbolism relating to the number seven may be found in Elders, pp. 157–8.

Esquivel's procedure in this motet is akin to that of Guerrero in his well-known *Ave Virgo sanctissima* motet and there are many similarities between the two works.[66] In both, the canon is *ad unisonum* between the two upper voices, and both composers treat their highly intimate devotional text in a similar way, with one adjectival phrase separated by rests from the next as one piece of imagery succeeds another. At one point, Esquivel appears to make reference to Guerrero's head motif (Ex. 5.4).

tu es__ pul-chra De - i

A - ve Vir_____ go

Ex. 5.4. Esquivel: *Ave Maria, Domini mei mater. Superius*, bars 12 ff. (above)
Guerrero, *Ave Virgo sanctissima. Superius*, bars 3 ff. (below)

Ave Maria, Domini mei mater runs to a mere thirty-eight bars in transcription. The style is essentially syllabic, with only one prominent melisma reserved to emphasise Mary's role as *Regina*. Typically, Esquivel works in short motives rather than the longer lines of classic Palestrina-style polyphony. Whereas Guerrero plans his piece over a wide canvas, allowing his ideas to unfold at a leisurely rate, Esquivel presents his textual images in rapid succession, wrapped up in short musical phrases which are heard only once before a new idea makes its appearance; only the last phrase of the text is repeated (three times in the *superius*), obviously to stress the important point that Mary is mistress of heaven *and* earth. But considered from a technical point of view, the motet is a well-wrought miniature, its counterpoint conventional but sound.

Chant-related motets

Only one motet in the collection, the Epiphany motet *Tria sunt munera* (pp. 122–3), employs the old-style *cantus firmus* writing where the chant is stated in long notes of equal value throughout. This is a technique much favoured by composers of previous generations; it still appears in the works of composers of Esquivel's generation and stylistically may equate with the demands of an appointment exercise. In *Tria sunt munera* the chant melody is preserved throughout in breves (semibreves in transcription) in *superius II* while the other four parts weave a contrapuntal web around it (Ex. 5.5).

66 Victoria's Marian motet *Gaude, Maria Virgo* (1572) also employs *canon ad unisonum* between *cantus* and *quintus*.

Ex. 5.5. Motet: *Tria sunt munera*, opening

The four accompanying parts preserve their independence and inter-relation-ships throughout. The gifts presented by the Magi to the Lord are three, but Esquivel makes no attempt to convey this symbolically; he does, however, empha-sise the precious quality of the gifts by indulging in long melismas for the key words 'pretiosa' and 'Domino' on each textual repeat.

One other motet, *Ecce ancilla Domini* for the feast of the Annunciation (pp. 140–1), employs a *cantus firmus*. The motet is a contrapuntal setting of the Magnificat antiphon: 'Behold the handmaid of the Lord: be it unto me according to thy word'. Text and melodic line bear an exact correspondence with the antiphon as found today in the *Liber usualis*, p. 1417, apart from the F♯ in bar 18, necessary in a contrapuntal context because the F forms the third of the chord in the cadence at this point. Set out in semibreves and breves in the middle voice (*altus*), the chant-bearing line becomes of equal importance with the other four voices for the last phrase of the text, 'secundum verbum tuum', where the *altus* voice picks up the point of imitation first stated by the *bassus* (Ex. 5.6).

Although not strictly *cantus firmus* compositions, it is convenient to consider at this point a group of motets which quote isolated chant phrases without stating the whole melody.

Taking them in order of appearance, the first work to quote chant overtly is the brief Nativity motet (twenty-seven bars in transcription), *Gloria in excelsis Deo*. The text quotes the first two lines of the Gloria from the tenth-century mass *Cunctipotens genitor Deus* (*Liber usualis*, p. 26) with the seventh note of the chant incipit (F) in the *altus* voice sharpened, and the B of the *superius* in bar 5 likewise

Ex. 5.6. Motet: *Ecce ancilla Domini*

(Ex. 5.7). The contrast between the upper and lower voices is effective and perhaps symbolic, the rising melodic lines of the upper voices suggesting the movement towards heaven, the falling motif in the lower voices suggesting the descent to earth – a reminder of the mass text 'et in terra pax hominibus'.

Beginning on pages 142–3, Esquivel presents us with a cycle of motets for the Commons of apostles, bishops, doctors, etc.: *Istorum est enim regnum*, and *Omnes sancti*, for the feast of Many Martyrs; *Ecce sacerdos* and *Sacerdos et pontifex*, for the feast of a confessor bishop and *Similabo eum* for the Common of a confessor not a bishop. All these four-part motets are chant-based; each gives prominence to fragments of chant in long note values at some point; however, they cannot be classed

Ex. 5.7. Motet: *Gloria in excelsis Deo*, bars 1–7

as *cantus firmus* works since the chant-bearing line contains free material and is not clearly differentiated throughout from the other contrapuntal lines.

Of these four works, *Istorum est enim regnum* comes the nearest to being a *cantus firmus* motet. The complete chant melody – very close in outline to the chant as found in the *Liber usualis* (p. 1154) – is heard in the *superius* throughout, with melismatic elaboration of the final word in each line of the text in a manner which blurs the syllabic outline of the chant. The opening (Ex. 5.8) demonstrates the close relationship that exists between the chant-bearing line and the other three voices, a feature which is maintained throughout the motet.

Ex. 5.8. Motet: *Istorum est enim regnum*, bars 1–8

The other three motets in this group all quote only fragments of the chant melody. *Omnes sancti* begins by quoting the chant incipit (G E F G G, 'Omnes sancti') in the bass, closely followed by its restatement a fifth higher in the *superius* combined with free material in the supporting voices, as Ex. 5.9 demonstrates; thereafter, the melodic contours of the chant pervade all parts but there is much use of original material in which the *superius* assumes equality with the other parts.

Ex. 5.9.   Motet: *Omnes Sancti*, bars 1–5

Ex. 5.10.   Motet: *Ecce Sacerdos*, bars 1–9

In *Ecce sacerdos* we see again a pairing of voices at the opening with *altus* and *superius* setting out the chant incipit (Ex. 5.10). Thereafter, the chant ceases to exist as a *cantus firmus*; its melodic contours shape the contrapuntal texture in which all voices are of equal importance.

The first phrase of *Sacerdos et pontifex* quotes the chant incipit in all four voices; all are equal partners in the unfolding counterpoint, but again the influence of the chant can be seen in Esquivel's melodic contours. A fragment of chant emerges again at the end of the motet. When setting the final line of the text, 'ora pro nobis', the composer floats the chant melody in long note values in the *superius*. Since a third of the motet is devoted to a setting of this one line, we can interpret this as a rhetorical gesture, a means of giving this plea greater prominence.

Similabo eum again makes use of the pairing technique for the opening section: *superius* and *altus* work together, closely followed by *tenor* and *bassus* using the same material (Ex. 5.11); the contrapuntal lines setting subsequent lines of the text are closely modelled on the melodic contours of the chant, but no one voice predominates.

Ex. 5.11. Motet: *Similabo eum*, bars 1–7

Finally, in this discussion of chant-based motets, mention must be made of the five-part Marian motet, *Sub tuum praesidium*, for feasts of the Blessed Virgin Mary on Saturdays – one of the longest motets in the volume (eighty-four bars in transcription). The outline of the initial phrase of the plainsong antiphon associated with this text can be traced in all five parts in the opening bars. Again, the contrapuntal lines are clearly influenced by the melodic contours of the chant but at no stage does any one voice predominate; for this reason we will delay further discussion until later.

The process of chant assimilation can be seen in the motets of Guerrero, where similar quasi-*cantus firmus* writing forms the structural basis of his four settings of the Marian antiphons *Alma Redemptoris mater, Ave Regina coelorum, Regina caeli, Salve Regina.*[67] The *Salve Regina* chant incipit frequently appears in motets not linked to the Blessed Virgin in the Spanish school, for example in motets addressing the saints whose texts begin with the salutation 'Salve'. Thus in Esquivel's case, we find it in *Salve sancte pater* (pp. 88–91) for the feast of St Francis the Confessor, and *Salve crux* (pp. 102–5) for the feast of St Andrew.[68]

Before moving on to a consideration of another of Esquivel's motet-types, it is worth noting in passing that the melodic lines of both *Ecce ancilla Domini* and *Tria sunt munera* contain angular melodic motifs, suggesting that elegance and smoothness of melodic line was not always something the composer valued highly. Angularity and disjunct intervals occur in outer and inner parts, as demonstrated in Ex. 5.12.

Such examples as this, which could easily have been avoided, suggest that the composer was prepared to tolerate melodic angularity, particularly when the lines concerned were submerged in his inner parts. Moreover, the wide-ranging melodic contours of some of his voice parts may be regarded as an individual characteristic of his style and not as a sign of general incompetence. Indeed, as Bruno Turner has pointed out, angular vocal writing was a provincial feature of certain Spanish composers of the time:

> The Roman smoothness and perfection of line that we find in Palestrina and even in Victoria is not characteristic. The style is provincial in the proper sense; just as the style of Byrd, Weelkes and Gibbons was peculiarly English, so the motets of Lobo and his contemporaries, Esquivel and Vivanco, are beginning to be recognised as peculiarly Spanish.[69]

---

67 Modern edition: Francisco Guerrero, *Opera omnia*, III, transcr. José Maria Lloréns Cistero (Barcelona, 1978), pp. 44–71.

68 Esquivel's indebtedness to chant, however, does not match that of his contemporary Infantas, whose motets are saturated with Gregorian chant to such an extent that he frequently heads his works with the inscription 'super excelsus Gregoriano cantu'. Notable examples are his motet *Sancte Spiritus*, from vol. II of his 1578 collection, where, in the first and third sections of the work, the *tenor* presents the old plainsong hymn *Veni Creator Spiritus* in long note values throughout, and *Virgo prudentissima*, which opens with the chant in long note values in the *cantus* before it migrates from part to part.

69 See the introduction to the Mapa Mundi edition of Alonso Lobo's Motet, *O quam suavis est, Domine, spiritus tuus*, ed. Bruno Turner, Spanish Church Music 14 (London, 1978).

se - cun - dum ver - bum tu - um,

Tri - a sunt———— mu - ne - ra.

mi - hi se - cun - dum ver bum tu———————— um.

Ex. 5.12. Melodic angularity in the motets *Ecce ancilla Domini* and *Tria sunt munera*. Above: *Ecce ancilla Domini*. Superius I, bars 20 ff. Centre: *Tria sunt munera*. Superius I, bars 1–2. Below: *Ecce ancilla Domini*. Tenor, bars 13–17.

Ostinato-based motets

Three motets, *Tu es pastor ovium*, *Veni Domine* and *In paradisum* all use the ostinato device as a constructional principle. The melodic ostinato, or *soggetto ostinato*, was used as a structural girder well before the time of Esquivel. Perhaps the best-known example from an earlier generation is Josquin's deeply moving five-part setting of Psalm 150, *Miserere mei*, written at the request of Duke Ercole d'Este and printed by Petrucci in 1519, in which the phrase 'Miserere mei, Deus' is intoned twenty-one times in the tenor voice throughout the work; the ostinato appears in the three parts respectively in descending, ascending and descending form. It is probably not without significance that this device is employed in a work of a commemorative nature; this seems to be the key to its use by later composers. It also seems to be used symbolically as an act of evocation, a prayer offered to the Virgin or to a specific saint. Palestrina uses the device only twice: once in his early *Missa Ecce sacerdos magnus*; and again in the motet *Tribulare, si nescirem*, where he quotes the same ostinato melody as that used by Josquin in his *Miserere* motet.

Although its use was not confined to Spain, Spanish composers seem to have had a particular liking for the *soggetto ostinato* device: there are many examples. From the *Cancionero musical de Palacio* comes a secular example, *A los baños del amor*, where an inner voice repeats a four-note motto-theme in breves incessantly throughout: G A E D = sol la mi re = Sola m'iré ('Alone I shall go').[70] For Morales,

---

70 Stevenson, *Spanish Cathedral Music*, p. 19. The 'Cancionero musical de Palacio', MS 1335 of the library of the Palacio Real, Madrid, was copied between 1505 and 1521, thus spanning the reigns of

it became a recurring structural feature in his music. He may have been influenced by the work of one of his predecessors in the papal choir, the French priest Jean Conseil (Consilium), whose motet *Tempus faciendi Domine* bears a strong likeness in its constructive plan to Morales's *Jubilate Deo omnis terra*, written for the peace celebrations at Nice in 1538.[71]

Morales employs the *soggetto ostinato* in a number of motets: *Veni Domine à6, Tu es Petrus, Andreas Christi famulus, Exaltata est sancta Dei Genitrix, Gaude et laetare, Ferrariensis civitas.* Fellow Spaniards adopting the device include Infantas (several examples, including *Veni Domine*), Vivanco (*Ecce sacerdos magnus*), Alonso de Tejeda (several works including a setting of *Veni Domine*) and Guerrero, who above all made the device his own and used it more extensively than any of his contemporaries. One of his most celebrated examples occurs in the motet *Surge propera amica mea* (Venice, 1570) where the phrase 'Veni sponsa Christe', set in long note values in *superius II*, gradually descends a fifth from its starting point at the beginning of the work throughout the *prima pars*, only to rise again to its initial starting pitch at the end of the *secunda pars*. Guerrero frequently shifts the pitch of his ostinato, separating each appearance by rests, and this is the procedure adopted by Esquivel (and also by Vivanco and Tejeda).

In *Tu es pastor ovium*, commemorating the feast of Ss Peter and Paul (29 June), the ostinato in *superius II* functions as a litany, a prayer of petition to St Peter, and is worked out with mathematical precision. The phrase 'Sancte Petre ora pro nobis' is intoned in semibreves and minims beginning on F (F E F G E E F D E F F). The time interval before its next appearance, commencing on C, is two and a half bars; and on its next appearance on F, it is separated from the previous statement by one and a half bars. This process, two and a half bars followed by one and a half bars, is repeated consistently throughout the piece. The supporting four voice parts all share the same melodic material and are sharply differentiated from the ostinato line.

The same procedure is adopted in *Veni Domine*, a motet of similar proportions to *Tu es pastor*, and of interest for two reasons. Firstly, the *altus* line is shown in the 1608 print with accidentals in the opening phrase, as shown in Ex. 5.13.

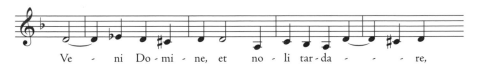

Ve - ni Do - mi - ne, et no - li tar - da - - - re,

Ex. 5.13. Motet: *Veni Domine. Altus*

The C♯ was suppressed in the later Plasencia MS 1 (and in Rubio's *Antología polifónica sacra 1* of 1954). It has been the subject of comment by at least one modern editor.[72] Certainly, it is unusual. There is no compelling reason why it should be

John II, Henry IV and Ferdinand and Isabella.

71 See Stevenson, *Spanish Cathedral Music*, pp. 19–20 for more details. A modern edition of *Jubilate Deo* is published by Mapa Mundi, Spanish Church Music 43, ed. Martyn Imrie (London, 1980).

72 Bruno Turner. See Mapa Mundi, Spanish Church Music 21 (London, 1978), where the editor

there, and good reasons for arguing for its suppression: the ostinato, from which this phrase is taken, does not indicate a semitone at this point, nor does the leading voice; there are no harmonic requirements dictating the need of a C♯ at this point. Its appearance, therefore, is difficult to explain, although there is a similar example of the juxtaposition of C♯ and E♭ in the motet *Christus factus est* (see Ex. 5.1), and it may be that the chromaticism is there for expressive reasons: in the case of *Veni Domine*, to accentuate the emotional intensity of Christ's coming, and in the case of *Christus factus est*, to point up the crucifixion.

The second feature of interest in this work is the close relationship it bears to Guerrero's motet with the same title in his *Sacrae cantiones* of 1555.[73] Both motets are in the same mode; both carry the ostinato in the same melodic line, *superius II*; in both cases, even-numbered statements are pitched a fourth higher than odd-numbered statements; moreover, the melodic and rhythmic contours of the ostinato are strikingly similar, as Ex. 5.14 illustrates.

Ex. 5.14. The melodic ostinato in the *Veni Domine* motets of Esquivel (above, *Superius II*, bars 9–13) and Guerrero.(below, *Superius II*, bars 8–12)

So close is the parallel with Guerrero that it has been suggested that Esquivel's work was perhaps a conscious funerary tribute to the older master.[74] However, it is probable that the likeness of the two works has an even greater significance: when the *Veni Domine* settings of Esquivel and Guerrero are set alongside the settings of Morales, there are strong resemblances, suggesting a chain of emulation linking the three men.

There are two surviving *Veni Domine* motets by Morales: a setting for four voices, and a six-voice setting included in an anthology entitled *Il primo libro de motetti a sei voce da diversi eccellentissimi musici composti* (Venice, 1549); both settings have a bearing on Esquivel's motet. Morales's six-voice setting is built around the *soggetto ostinato* shown in Ex. 5.15.

allows the sub-semitone to stand 'with reservations'. Stevenson comments on the 'daring' of this chromaticism in *Spanish Cathedral Music*, pp. 293–4.

73 Modern edition: in *Francisco Guerrero (1528–1599)*, *Opera omnia* VI, Monumentos de la música española XLV, ed José Maria Llorens Cisteró (Barcelona, 1987), pp. 106–14.

74 Stevenson, *Spanish Cathedral Music*, p. 293.

Ex. 5.15. Morales: Motet, *Veni Domine à6. Quintus*

We can see that the ostinato begins with the same rhythmic pattern, and it has a phrase structure similar to Guerrero's motet, although, melodically, the two phrases are not identical. However, if we look at the melodic motives set to the same textual phrases in Morales's four-voice version, we find a very close connection which cannot be coincidental (see Ex. 5.16).

Ex. 5.16. Morales: Motet, *Veni Domine à4.*
Melodic motives for 'Veni Domine' and 'et noli tardare'

Guerrero's indebtedness to his master in shaping his melodic material seems obvious. Moreover, although Morales's ostinato treatment in his six-voice setting is more elaborate than that of his pupil – he lowers the pitch of the ostinato by one tone on each appearance – the overall constructional principle is the same in both motets, and it is used for the same aesthetic end: the unyielding repetition of a melodic phrase symbolises the hope of deliverance expressed in the words: 'Come, O Lord, and do not delay'. Clearly, Esquivel, in choosing to use the same technique for this text, is once again paying homage to Guerrero. But, more than this, his work becomes part of a historical link in a chain joining three generations of composers; together they bear witness to a living tradition, each generation passing on to the next the skills of the trade.

The chain is extended still further when the motets of Alonso de Tejeda are taken into consideration. Tejada's *Veni Domine* motet also appears to be closely modelled on Guerrero's setting: the work is in the same mode and carries the ostinato in the same voice part. Although the text of his motet varies considerably from

Ex. 5.17. Alonso de Tejeda: Motet, *Veni Domine. Tiple II*, bars 2–10

that used by Guerrero, the musical treatment of the penitential evocation again follows the same ostinato principle and, like Guerrero, he pitches his pattern a fourth higher on even-numbered repetitions; the second phrase of his ostinato also bears a strong melodic resemblance to Guerrero's 'et noli tardare' (Ex. 5.17). Again, the correspondence between two works is too close for coincidence; it seems that Tejeda too must have admired Guerrero's work and wanted to imitate it.

Infantas also included a version of *Veni Domine* in his *Sacrarum varii styli cantionum* (book III). He too states the opening phrase of the motet in the form of an ostinato, giving it to the *sextus* throughout, although without varying the pitch in the manner of his contemporaries.[75]

The only other motet to employ an *soggetto ostinato* in Esquivel's volume is the burial motet *In paradisum*. Here, the composer combines the words of the burial service 'In paradisum deducant eum Angeli . . .' with the words and melody of the post-communion versicle 'Resquiescant in pace', which is assigned to the ostinato in *superius II*. The procedure is the same as in his other two ostinato motets: the phrase is repeated every alternate time a fourth higher, each repetition being separated by rests. Thus, the voice part bearing the ostinato functions in the same way: it has a symbolic significance, in this case invoking divine peace for the deceased in an act of commemoration. Three times during the piece the ostinato floats above the first soprano line and Esquivel shows great sensitivity in response to the text in this setting. Technically, the piece is of a high order; melodic lines are smooth, the harmonic movement is well controlled and the work is well proportioned. All these features combine to create the sense of repose required of a funereal composition.

Motets showing contrapuntal equality between all parts

By far the largest category of Esquivel's motets is that group which demonstrates a measure of contrapuntal equality between the parts; that is to say, no one part dominates the texture by being in the nature of a *cantus firmus*. The rest of this chapter will be devoted to a study of these works, drawing on a representative sample for comment.

At this point we should notice that a significant number of Esquivel's chosen texts were set by his Spanish predecessors and contemporaries, among them Guerrero, Infantas, Tejeda and Victoria; and five were set by Palestrina, as the following list demonstrates:

75 José Maria Lloréns Cisteró lists several settings of *Veni Domine* in *Francisco Guerrero, Opera omnia* VI, p. 23. Alongside the settings already discussed, there are also settings by Penalosa, Ceballos, Rimonte, Zorita and Palestrina. There are textual variations, but in all cases the motets are ascribed to the Advent season, although the same Sunday is not prescribed by all composers; for example, Palestrina attributes the motet to the third Sunday of Advent, Esquivel to the second, while Guerrero writes simply 'in Adventu Domini'. For fuller discussion of this motet and, in particular, Guerrero's emulation of Morales, see Owen Rees, '"Recalling Cristóbal de Morales to Mind": Emulation in Guerrero's *Sacrae cantiones* of 1555', in Crawford and Wagstaff, *Encomium Musicae*, pp. 365–94.

Canite tuba	Guerrero, Palestrina, Vivanco
Christus factus est	Vivanco
Descendit angelus Domini	Victoria
Ductus est Jesus	Guerrero, Tejeda, Vivanco
Duo seraphim	Guerrreo, Tejeda, Victoria
Ecce sacerdos	Palestrina, Tejeda, Vivanco, Victoria
Emendemus in melius	Morales, Infantas
Ego sum panis	Palestrina
Erat Jesus	Tejeda
Exaltata est sancta Dei Genitrix	Morales, Rodrigo Ceballos, Guerrero, Tejeda
Ibant apostoli	Guerrero
In illo tempore	Vivanco
Istorum est enim regnum	Tejeda
O beate Iacobe	Tejeda
O beatum pontificem	Tejeda
O crux benedicta	Guerrero
O quam gloriosum	Victoria
O vos omnes	Palestrina, Victoria
Similabo eum	Guerrero
Simile est regnum	Guerrero, Tejeda
Sub tuum praesidium	Infantas
Tu es pastor ovium	Palestrina
Veni Domine	Morales, Guerrero, Tejeda, Infantas

We shall draw on this list to make further comparisons between Esquivel's settings and those of fellow composers, examining first a number of four-part works.

Robert Stevenson has already drawn attention to some of the technical features of Esquivel's motets; he mentions in particular the composer's liking for imitative points involving two pairs of voices in which the lower pair either proceed in opposite direction to the upper pair, or two different head motives are imitated simultaneously – one in the upper voices and another quite different motive in the lower voices.[76] He cites as examples of these procedures *Gloria in excelsis Deo* (see Ex. 5.8) and *Vox clamantis* (both à4), and *Sancti angeli* (à6) and *Suscipiens Simeon* (à5).

However, too much should not be made of this; the procedure is not unique to Esquivel (compare works by Lobo and Vivanco, for example) and for much of the time he begins with just one point, which is then taken up by each voice part in turn. Typical four-part examples of this procedure, which is of course standard for many hundreds of Renaissance works, can be seen in the motets *Ego sum panis* and *O quam gloriosum*.

Ego sum panis begins with a head motive of a falling fourth (A to E) in the *altus* followed by a tonal answer (E to A) in the *superius*. The motet proceeds in a conventional manner with some vivid word-painting to illustrate the phrase 'qui de

---

76 Stevenson, *Spanish Cathedral Music*, p. 292.

caelo descendit' (descending fifths, octave leaps, falling melodic line) until the joy-ful 'Alleluia' in triple time. Triple time, indicated in this case as 3, is extremely rare in Esquivel's music. His usual mensuration sign is C, and this motet is only one of two to include a section in triple time, the other being the joyful resurrection motet *Surrexit Dominus*. Other examples of triple time in his work occur in the *Osanna* sections of some of the masses.

O quam gloriosum is similarly conventional in layout. Put alongside Victoria's thrilling setting it appears dull; it proceeds in unrelieved polyphony throughout, lacking the dramatic contrasts of texture and rhythmic fluidity found in Victoria. Like Victoria, Esquivel indulges in word-painting for his setting of the word 'gaud-ent', using the same figuration; and the overlapping entries of rising scale passages are undeniably effective. However, Victoria's setting is made even more impressive at this point by the independence of his soprano line, which rides triumphantly over the rising scale passages in long note values. His homophonic treatment of the phrase 'amicti stolis albis', the mid-point in the work, is in welcome contrast to the rhythmic vigour of the previous passage, while the series of suspensions which follow add further contrast in mood and texture. All these features, which serve to make this motet a work of distinction, are lacking in Esquivel's setting. His setting is technically highly competent, but lacks the subtleties of expression found in the older master's work.

It has already been pointed out in this chapter that one of the most notice-able characteristics of Esquivel's motets is their brevity: many of them do not fill more than two pages of the choirbook and often amount to no more than thirty to forty bars in transcription; no motet in the collection runs to a *secunda pars*. One explanation for this has already been given, and, as was shown earlier, the nature of the texts set by the composer – short antiphons – may lead us to expect that a musical setting will display a similar brevity. But the same text in the hands of a different composer can result in a much more expansive setting. For example, if we compare Esquivel's Advent motet *Canite tuba in Sion* (antiphon for Vespers on the fourth Sunday before Advent) with Guerrero's setting, we find two very different approaches to the same text. In Esquivel's hands, this motet covers a mere 34 bars in transcription. The full text reads: 'Canite tuba in Sion, quia prope est dies Domini: ecce veniet ad salvandum nos. Alleluia'. Although Guerrero, and also Vivanco, add additional text from the third Vespers antiphon ('erunt prava in directa, et aspera in vias planas, veni Domine et noli tardare'), their settings of the portion of text set by Esquivel run to much greater length; a comparison with the works of the two latter composers is revealing.

In transcription, Esquivel covers this portion in a mere twenty-five bars before beginning his Alleluia: Guerrero takes thirty-five bars, and Vivanco forty-three bars. Esquivel allows only five complete bars for his opening phrase and overlaps the fourth appearance of his head motive with the second phrase; Guerrero allows fifteen bars for the working out of his head motive with two appearances or more in each voice; Vivanco gives his head motive even more time – twenty bars – arriving at a perfect cadence in four of his five parts before beginning a new point for the next phrase of the text.

Esquivel's motet is built up on a succession of short imitative points; verbal phrases are compressed into a short timescale in a manner typical of many other motets in the volume. However, in spite of this compression, the composer does show a sensitive response to the demands of his text. The opening motive, for example, with its falling arpeggio and octave leap up to the work 'tuba' set to a dotted rhythm, is a real clarion call. Considered rhythmically, and in terms of its verbal stress, it is perhaps more effective than Guerrero's rather four-square opening where the preposition 'in' is emphasised by the leap of a fifth and its long note value.

Ex. 5.18a.   Esquivel: Motet, *Canite tuba in Sion. Superius*, bars 1 ff.

Ex. 5.18b.   Guerrero: Motet, *Canite tuba in Sion. Superius*, bars 1 ff.

Vivanco's opening is more complex: he begins with two imitative points, and then, on the entry of his fourth voice (*tenor II*), in illustration of the text 'sound the trumpet', he introduces a descending arpeggio, a motif which is repeated several times in other voices in diminution. He closes his setting by quoting exactly the first phrase of Morales's head motive from his *Veni Domine* motet – yet another example of the influence of Morales on future generations, and the esteem in which he was held by all his successors.

Another effective and technically well-wrought four-part miniature, not quite as compressed as *Canite tuba*, is the motet for the feast of the Holy Cross, *O crux benedicta*. The composer allows himself more time to unfold his thematic material in this motet; the melodic lines are longer and in the upper parts each textual statement is repeated twice. The piece has two contrasting sections: the first, extolling the virtues of the Holy Cross, takes up thirty-two bars of transcription; the second, twenty-two bars in length, sets the one word 'Alleluia'. The contrast in mood is achieved by the use of shorter note values in section two and the closeness of the imitation. Guerrero set a longer version of this text in honour of the Holy Cross in his two motets *O crux benedicta* (Seville, 1555) and *O crux splendidior* (Venice, 1570, 1597) and Esquivel's 'Alleluia' motive is not unlike Guerrero's in the latter's *O crux splendidior* setting (Ex. 5.19).

Moreover, Esquivel treats his text in a similar way to Guerrero: all three works share the same mode (mode I) and both composers abandon the customary practice of a homophonic opening for works beginning with the 'O' exclamation in favour of a polyphonic treatment of the text, shown by the pairing of voices SA/TB in the case of the four part setting *O crux benedicta*.

Al-le - lu - ia,

Ex. 5.19a.   Esquivel: Motet, *O crux benedicta. Superius*, bars 34–7

Al-le - lu - ia

Ex. 5.19b.   Guerrero: Motet, *O crux splendidior. Superius*, bars 68–9

One of the finest, and certainly one of the most expressive, motets in the volume is *O vos omnes*, one of the motets Stevenson had in mind when he wrote: 'Unlike Vivanco [Esquivel] chose texts already set with outstanding success'.[77] Stevenson was, of course, referring to Victoria's renowned four-part setting of 1572, which Pedrell, in 1894, mistakenly attributing the work to Morales, described as 'one of the most sublime creations in the art of music'.[78] A comparison with Victoria's setting reveals some fundamental differences in approach to composition, although there are certain similarities in the outward appearance of these pieces.

For some reason, Esquivel chose not to set the full text of this Holy Week respond. It is designated for use on Palm Sunday in his publication, but in the *Breviarium Romanum* of 1607 (and in the *Liber usualis*) it appears as a respond from the second Nocturn at Matins on Holy Saturday. Unlike Victoria, who sets the complete text and makes his polyphonic composition correspond to the liturgical form of the chant, Esquivel omits the word 'similis' from line two and does not set the verse 'Attendite universi populi et videte dolorem meum'. But he does allow himself more space to expand his thematic material over a longer period than is usual for him. In fact, each section of the text is given more detailed treatment than the comparable section in Victoria's setting.

Table 17 shows the way the text is distributed throughout each work. (Bar numbers in this and subsequent examples of works by Victoria refer to the *Opera omnia* edition.) The comparison is revealing: we can see that Esquivel is intent on bringing out the anguish of the text by his emphasis on the word 'dolor'; the dolorous passage is as long as the first two sections combined. Victoria, on the other hand, is more concerned with the structural balance of the whole, devising a plan which runs long, short, long, short, long (long). Each of these sections is clearly separated from the next by rests; but Esquivel runs one section into the next with a series of overlapping entries in a continuous flow of counterpoint. Victoria's work is a carefully devised piece of musical architecture with clear points of reference indicated by cadences arrived at simultaneously in all parts. Moreover, the cadence points

77 Ibid., p. 294.
78 Felipe Pedrell, *Hispaniae schola música sacra* (Barcelona, 1894–8, repr. New York, 1971), p. 29.

are emphasised not only by the rests separating out the main sections of the piece but also by clear-cut harmonic progressions. The piece has strong tonal tendencies, moving from one fixed point to another. To a certain extent this is also true of Esquivel's setting, but its modal characteristics are nevertheless strong and marked from the very beginning.

TABLE 17. Distribution of text in
Esquivel's and Victoria's settings of O *vos omnes*

Esquivel

Bar numbers	Total no. of bars	Text
1–12	12	O vos omnes . . . per viam,
12–25	13.5	attendite et videte:
25–48	24	Si est dolor . . . dolor meus

Victoria

Bar numbers	Total no. of bars	Text
1–10	10	O vos omnes . . . per viam,
11–16	6	attendite et videte:
16–32	17	Si est dolor . . . dolor meus
33–8	6	Attendite universi populi,
40–51	12	et videte dolorem meum.
52–68	17	Si est dolor . . . dolor meus.

(Repeat of bars 16–32 with addition of final cadence)

The piece begins firmly in mode III, but G♯s and C♯s soon begin to make an appearance, leading to intermediate cadences on A and D; cadences are also formed on G (bar 24) and C (30–1) before the final plagal cadence, A–E. Victoria's setting is Dorian in conception, but the sense of modality is immediately destroyed by the C♯ in bar 3. Although Victoria does not entirely free himself from the modal world of his time, his tendency to outline chord progressions that suggest a major or minor key is even more marked than Esquivel's in this and other compositions; the frequent accidentals specified in his works blur the edges of modality perhaps further than those of any of his contemporaries.[79] However, in spite of this

79 This point has been argued by Robert Stevenson. On Victoria's *Missa quarti toni* he writes that Victoria 'anticipates the harmonic procedures that a Baroque composer writing in A minor would have followed, a fortiori his other masses prove even more amenable to major–minor analyses'. Stevenson then seeks to prove statistically, by examining the number of E minor – A minor chord progressions that occur in this work that 'Victoria no longer felt himself bound by the old laws of modal usage, and gave allegiance instead to the newer laws of major and minor key'. Stevenson, *Spanish Cathedral Music*, p. 399. Although the description and analysis of Renaissance music in terms of a later period is a controversial issue, the position taken consistently throughout this study (see Chapter 4) is that the tools of description and analysis offered by a later age are simply tools of convenience. This point has been persuasively argued by Don M. Randel: 'We need to be concerned primarily with discovering the best way for us to look at music and not exclusively with discovering

fundamental difference in approach there are, as mentioned above, certain external similarities in these two motets which may be coincidental but which raise the question: was Esquivel familiar with Victoria's setting of this text? Consider, for example, Ex. 5.20.

at - ten - di - te

Ex. 5.20a.   Esquivel: Motet, *O vos omnes. Superius*, bar 14

at - ten - di - te

Ex. 5.20b.   Victoria: Motet, *O vos omnes. Superius*, bar 12

The use of the rising perfect fourth and the dotted rhythm for the phrase 'attendite' is a fitting device in both cases; and when the fourth becomes a fifth in the soprano line in bars 18–19 of Esquivel's version the effect is particularly poignant.

Both composers exploit the expressive potential of the minor second interval as a symbol of grief, although Victoria makes more extensive use of this interval than does Esquivel (Ex. 5.21).

si - cut do - lor me - us

Ex. 5.21a.   Esquivel: *O vos omnes. Bassus*, bars 35–8

si - cut do lor me - us

Ex. 5.21b.   Victoria: *O vos omnes. Superius*, bars 24–6

Another similarity is the use the same figuration to express the idea of journeying 'per viam' (Ex. 5.22).

the way it was looked at by its composer or his contemporaries' ('Emerging Triadic Tonality in the Fifteenth Century', pp. 76–7).

Ex. 5.22*a*.   Esquivel: *O vos omnes. Tenor*, bars 7–10

Ex. 5.22*b*.   Victoria: *O vos omnes. Tenor*, bars 8–10

Finally, both composers make telling use of the 7/6 suspension at this and other points in the work and both adopt the same cadence figure as can be seen in Ex. 5.23.

Ex. 5.23*a*.   Esquivel: *O vos omnes*, bars 7–8

Ex. 5.23*b*.   Victoria: *O vos omnes*, bars 8–10

However, the drop of a fifth in the *Superius* of Victoria's setting, which is such a characteristic of his style, is never found in Esquivel's writing.

Esquivel's setting shows that, given a text with such emotional overtones as *O vos omnes*, he can respond with sensitivity, clothing the words with music of an appropriate dignity to produce a work which closely rivals the technical and

aesthetic powers of the older master. Although other motets in the volume give
him opportunity to reveal his expressive powers when called upon to do so, only
one other four-part work in the volume has the same depth of pathos as this setting
– the motet *Christus factus est*, discussed earlier.

Interestingly, Esquivel's fellow Spaniards, Vivanco and Lopez de Velasco (*c*.1590–
c.1650), a composer of the next generation, reveal two very different approaches to
this text, sung as the final antiphon at Lauds on the last three days of Holy Week.
Both made it an occasion for a large-scale work. All Velasco's known compositions
are in eight or more voice parts. His setting, *à*8, of *Christus factus est* is in two parts:
part one has the text of the antiphon as it was sung on the first night (the same text
as Esquivel); a second section, a repeat of the phrase 'mortem autem crucis', is added
as was the custom on the second night. His style is contrapuntal throughout.

Vivanco's setting is on an even greater scale. Written for twelve voices, it sets the
whole of the Gradual text as performed at evening mass on Maundy Thursday. It
exploits the possibilities of multi-choral writing to the full: contrapuntal passages
for one, two and three choirs are included; antiphonal passages emphasise important phrases such as 'exaltavit illum', 'et dedit illi nomen'.

Comparison with Vivanco reminds us that the buoyant springy rhythms, found

Ex. 5.24. Vivanco: Motet, *Cantate Domino. Superius I*, bars 52 ff.

in other double-choir works of his *Liber motectorum* (Salamanca, 1610), and which
are such a characteristic of this composer, are completely foreign to Esquivel. He
never indulges in the kind of jubilant rhythms of the kind shown in Ex. 5.24, from
Vivanco's motet *Cantate Domino*.[80]

80 Bar numbers refer to the Mapa Mundi edition, Spanish Church Music 61, ed. L. Dean
Nuernberger (London, 1985).

Five-part motets

The addition of a fifth voice allows a composer to make contrasts in voice grouping, two upper voices contrasted with two lower, for example. Surprisingly perhaps, Esquivel takes little opportunity to do this. With the exception of the two five-part works already discussed – where the fifth voice acted in one case as a *cantus firmus*, and in the other as an ostinato – Esquivel sees the addition of a fifth voice mainly as a means of strengthening texture and giving more scope for textual illustration.

The Ascension motet *Ascendo ad Patrem meum* is a good example. This short work, a mere thirty-three bars in transcription, is again in Mode I. Again, the work is in two sections with an 'alleluia' second section. Esquivel indulges in conventional word-painting for his opening motive, fashioning a theme not unlike those of Guerrero and Victoria in their Ascension settings of the text *Ascendens Christus in altum* (Ex. 5.25).

A - scen - do ad Pa-trem me   -   um

Ex. 5.25*a*.   Esquivel: Motet, *Ascendo ad Patrem meum. Superius*, bars 1–6

A - scen   -   dens Chri-stus in   al   -   tum

Ex. 5.25*b*.   Guerrero: *Ascendo ad Patrem meum. Superius*, bars 1–6

A-scen-dens Chri-stus in——— al   -   tum

Ex. 5.25*c*.   Victoria. *Ascendo ad Patrem meum. Cantus*, bars 1–4

A full texture is maintained throughout, and in the final bars the composer again shows his disregard for the conventions of the classic polyphonic style by once more resorting to some very angular melodic writing in his tenor line, an angularity already demonstrated in this chapter (Ex. 5.26).

Al - le - lu   -   ya,   A - le - lu - ya.

Ex. 5.26.   Esquivel: Motet, *Ascendo ad Patrem meum. Tenor*, bars 30–3

The large-scale Marian motet, *Sub tuum praesidium*, calls for comment for a number of reasons. Firstly, it is one of the longest motets in the volume, running to eighty-four bars in transcription (the longest is the motet designated for the first Sunday of Quadragesima, *Ductus est Jesus*, 117 bars in transcription); secondly, because of the agility of the vocal writing: the three lower voices, particularly, cover a wide vocal range with many octave leaps and sudden changes of register; thirdly, the narrow avoidance of consecutive fifths at one point between *tenor1* and *bassus* as in Ex. 5.27.

Ex. 5.27.   Esquivel: Motet, *Sub tuum praesidium*, bars 28–9

It can be seen that parallel fifths are only avoided by the composer's insertion of an additional (quaver) G in *tenor I*. The tenor motif here has in itself no thematic significance and the figure is merely a device fashioned somewhat arbitrarily and clumsily to avoid the parallel fifths that would otherwise ensue. Moreover, it creates difficulties, for the Renaissance singer would need to use his ears to apply the required sharp to the G; in doing so he would, of course, create the interval of the diminished fourth (G♯ – C).

Although Esquivel's use of the interval in this context may appear ungainly, in theory and practice it is by no means uncommon and appears fairly frequently in Victoria's music; moreover, its use is explained and justified by Bermudo in his *Declaración de instrumentos musicales*:

> Some performers use this same interval of a tone and two minor semitones (i.e. the diminished fourth) by leap in one voice only (though in fear and trembling), because it appears to them to be contrary to accepted procedure to use the leap of a fourth other than that of two and a half tones (i.e. the perfect fourth). In order to both reassure them, and to instruct beginners, I say it is possible to use it . . .

Bermudo then gives us his example with an explanation: his bass moves downward by step, as in *Sub tuum praesidium*, and he arrives at an interrupted cadence (*cláusula disimulada*) as Esquivel does:

> As it [the diminished fourth] is used so much in step-wise movement I do not see why it should not be used by leap, especially when it is associated with an interrupted cadence . . . I give as a definite rule, that in polyphony a part can use this progression, conceived in terms of stepwise movement (especially on the organ, where it can certainly be done) as a direct leap, when it is properly prepared.[81]

81 Juan Bermudo, *Declaración de instrumentos musicales*, book V, chapter 32, fol. 138. Translated

Bermudo's reference to 'fear and trembling' and the organ is interesting; perhaps he is not entirely convinced of singers' ability to sing the interval accurately!

The last comment to make regarding this piece concerns the appearance of the interval of the augmented sixth, B♭ to G♯, between *bassus* and *altus*, as in Ex. 5.28.

Ex. 5.28.   Esquivel: Motet, *Sub tuum praesidium*, bars 74–5

What are we to make of this? The fact that Esquivel allows this interval in other motets in the volume suggests that this was his intent, in spite of the fact that stylistically the interval is not usually found in sacred polyphony of the period. However, it is worth noting that Guerrero notates the same interval (B♭ to G♯) in the *tenor* and *bassus* of his four-part setting of *Regina caeli* (first published in Seville in 1555 and later reprinted in his motet collections of 1570, 1597 and his *Liber vesperarum* of 1584). Furthermore, Tomás de Santa María arrives at an imperfect cadence by way of an augmented-sixth triad (E♭, G, C♯) in one of his notated examples of *fabordon* harmonisations.[82]

There are three possible explanations for Esquivel's procedure: 1. This may be the sound he intended. Given the degree of harmonic experimentation, especially in the secular sphere, around the turn of the century when music was in a state of transition, this is possible. There are other traces of stylistic change in Esquivel's music – the presence of more notated accidentals; the leaping bass lines which often function as a harmonic bass, to name but two. 2. It is clear from the writings of contemporary theorists that the standard practice in the sixteenth century, when approaching an octave between two parts by a sixth, was to make the sixth a major interval – what was known as 'the law of closest proximity'.[83]

> Whenever we write an octave (either in the cadence, or in passing) moving from the sixth, we shall use a major sixth (that is to say, perfect) which is nearer to the octave than the minor sixth. If it is written this way no difficulty arises. If not in the written music, adjustment must be made in the upper voice with a black key sharpening it. If for some particular reason it is not possible to make such an adjustment, this must

in Rubio, *Classical Polyphony*, pp. 67–8.

82 Fray Tomás de Santa María, *Arte de tañer fantasia* (Vallladolid, 1565), book II, fol. 43. For a modern edition, see *The Art of Playing the Fantasia by Fray Tomás de Santa María*, ed. Almonte C. Howell, Jr, and Warren E. Hultberg (Pittsburgh, 1991), book II, p. 141.

83 Rubio, *Classical Polyphony*, p. 55.

be made in the lower voice with a black key, flattening it. In this case a fourth mode cadence will be formed concluding in the lower voice with a semitone and in the upper voice with a whole-tone.[84]

In the light of this rule, we could regard the B♭ and G♯ as offering the singers two alternatives: they could sing one or the other, but not both. If this were the case, clearly the singers would have had to come to some arrangement as to which procedure to adopt. 3. It is possible that Esquivel, on correcting proofs, failed to notice that he had already indicated an alteration in one part and added another in error. Such an error, if it is such, could easily arise in choirbook format, where parts are not vertically aligned; the addition of an accidental in one part clashing with that in another is not as immediately obvious to the eye as it is today when we use score format. However, given the presence of the augmented sixth in other motets, this explanation is not entirely convincing.

Considering all these arguments, it seems that 2. is the most likely explanation. However, if Esquivel wanted to offer his singers alternatives, why was he not consistent? There are many instances of the identical progression in other works where the conventional procedure – B♭ or G♯ – is followed.

Six-part motets

There are only three 6-part works in the volume: *Duo seraphim*, *In paradisum* and *Sancti angeles*. The last is thickly scored throughout, it uses high clefs, perhaps because its subject matter is angels, and the texture is fully imitative, without the upper/lower voice groupings that are common in six-part works. The individual melodic lines cover the full extent of the modal ambitus with leaps of fourths and fifths employed to set the central phrases 'Custodes nostri, defendite nos in praelo' ('Custodians, defend us in battle').

The opening of *Duo seraphim* offers an example of overt symbolism. The two upper voices are in counterpoint with each other; the suspensions are telling, and Esquivel's approach to setting the opening words is similar to Victoria's, as Ex. 5.29 demonstrates. All voices enter for the word 'clamabant', emphasising in a very concrete way the message of the text. The device is, of course, an obvious one, but nevertheless effective in establishing a relationship between words and music. A full texture is retained almost throughout, with some sub-grouping of three voices for 'Dominus Deus Sabaoth', as the choir sing 'the whole world is full of your glory'. A pedal point over a sustained G in alto and tenor voices leads to a final plagal

---

84 Juan Bermudo, *Arte tripharia* (Osuna, 1550), chapter 38, fol. 33 ff. Cited in Rubio, *Classical Polyphony*, pp. 56–7. The original text reads as follows: 'Todas las veces que hiciéremos octava (ahora sea en la cláusula o de huida [de paso] viniendo desde la sexta, será hecha con sexta mayor (que es dicha perfecta), la cual está más cercana de la octava que la sexta menor. Si en lo puntado estuviere, no hay dificultad en hacerla. Hágase como está puntada. Si en lo puntado no estuviere, remediarse ha en la voz superior con tecla negra, que es mi [sostenido]. Si desta manera no se pudiese remediar por causa particular, remediarse ha en la voz baxa con una tecla negra, que será fa [bemol]. En tal caso haciendo cláusula será de cuarto modo, concluyendo en la voz con semitono y en la alta con tono.'

cadence on G. Esquivel's approach to this text is in marked contrast to Guerrero's magnificent 12-part setting, where the two seraphs call to each other before alternating groups of four voices cry 'Sanctus' and the whole choir, covering a range of three octaves, declaim 'pleni sunt coeli'.

Ex. 5.29*a*.   Esquivel: Motet, *Duo seraphim*. *Superius* 1 and 2, bars 1–4

Ex. 5.29*b*.   Victoria: *Duo seraphim*. *Cantus I* and *altus II*, bars 1–4

Before concluding this chapter, there are some further characteristics of Esquivel's contrapuntal technique which require comment: one is his use of homophonic passage work in the motet genre.

As was pointed out earlier in relation to the motet, *Christus factus est*, Esquivel uses this technique sparingly; indeed, the sparsity of examples is certainly one striking difference between the composer and many of his contemporaries (particularly Victoria, for example). Passages in which the rhythm is uniform in all voices are extremely rare, but Esquivel does make dramatic use of homophony in the following works: *Ductus est Jesus* (à4), *In illo tempore loquente Jesu* (à5), *Suscipiens Simon* (à5). In all these cases, the technique is used for reported speech: in the first case, Jesus's words on being tempted by the devil, 'scripture says'; in the second case, the words of the woman in the crowd who says to Jesus, 'blessed is the womb that bore thee' (Luke 11: 27–8); in the third case, Simeon's joyous response on being told that the child in his arms is the Messiah. In other examples, the technique is used to highlight important ideas, as in the following: the motet *Assumpsit Jesus* (à4), commemorating the transfiguration, in which Christ's face is described as shining like the sun ('sicut sol'); *O fortissimi milites* (à5), a motet in honour of Ss Fabian and Sebastian, where Sebastian's status ('Martyr Sebastianus') is singled out for homophonic treatment (in contrast to the contrapuntal opening commemorating his fellow saint, Fabian); *Salve sancte pater* (à4), where the phrase 'virtutis speculum' ('mirror of virtue') is singled out for emphasis; *Pater misercordiae* (à4), where all voices come together after a rest in a prayer of supplication, 'te supplicantes exoramus' ('we suppliants entreat thee'); *De quinque panibus* (à4), where a chordal texture is used to single out mention of the two fishes ('duobus piscibus') in contrast to the five loaves ('quinque panibus', the text of the opening of the motet set in polyphony) which Christ gave to the crowd of five thousand – the subject of this motet for the fourth Sunday in Quadragesima.

Whenever the composer uses homophony in this way, the passage is always brief, and sometimes given more emphasis by the introduction of a short rest; as we observed earlier, the technique is employed as a rhetorical device.

Chordal writing also appears in the eight-part motet, *Sancta Maria*. This is a two-choir work, as the choirbook makes clear: a *Primus chorus* with *superius, altus, tenor* and *bassus* (clefs, C1, C3, C4 and F4), and a *Secundus chorus* with *superius I, superius II, altus* and *tenor* (clefs, C1, C1, C3, C4). It is not a *cori spezzati* work in the Italian manner, however; the true bass line is in the lower choir, which, for the last phrase of the text, functions as a harmonic bass moving up and down in fourths and fifths, supporting the imitative contrapuntal lines moving above it. Sometimes the two choirs work antiphonally; sometimes they work as an eight-voice unit sharing the same thematic material. The texture throughout the piece is predominantly contrapuntal, but brief passages, vertically conceived, do appear. Absolute rhythmic uniformity occurs only once, however – four chords in choir two when prayers are asked *pro clero* ('for the clergy'). Thus, the vertical sonorities that appear in this work provide an additional means of creating textural contrast and are probably introduced for this reason alone, although, of course, the singling out of the clergy for this special treatment may have symbolic significance.

In his treatment of dissonance, Esquivel follows the conventions of the period; in 4/3 and 7/6 suspensions, for example, the suspended note is heard first as a concord. However, there are several instances in his motets where he departs from this practice, and where, in a 4/3 suspension, the fourth appears as a dissonant note in the preparatory chord, as happens, for example, in bars 21–2 of the motet *Christus factus est* (Ex. 5.1). There, on the last crotchet of bar 22, the tenor E♭ is heard against an F in the *altus*. In every case where this happens, the suspended note forms a consonant fourth with the bass and is approached by step in the conventional manner, thus lessening the impact of the dissonance.

Thirdly, there are cases where Esquivel appears to breach the rule forbidding the appearance of parallel fifths. By way of example, let us consider a passage from the four-part motet, *Istorum est enim* (Ex. 5.30).

Ex. 5.30. Esquivel: Motet, *Istorum est enim*, bars 9–10

Here, the anticipated resolution of the suspended discord in the *superius* in bar 10 coincides with the passing note (C) in the *altus*, creating parallel fifths. H. K. Andrews states categorically: 'Direct consecutive perfect fifths ... between any two voices were rigidly prohibited in sixteenth-century polyphony. It does not matter on what pulses or fractions of pulses of the measure they occur.'[85] However, he does give some examples from the works of Palestrina, including that in Ex. 5.31,[86] where the Italian master's procedure is remarkably similar to that of Esquivel's.

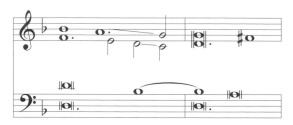

Ex. 5.31.   Palestrina: *Missa primi toni*. Sanctus

This is an example of what Andrews calls a 'Portamento' note, an unaccented note introduced by step from above and anticipating the next consonant. As Andrews rightly points out, it is one of the most commonly used ornamental resolutions of a suspended discord. Perhaps, then, both composers in the above examples were willing to tolerate the parallel fifths for the sake of this decoration. If this is the case, we need not chide Esquivel for a seeming lapse in technique; we must also remember that hidden consecutives, where the actual fifths are separated by notes less in value than a minim (i.e. crotchet where note values are reduced in transcription), or by a short rest, are common in Renaissance polyphony. Esquivel was fully aware of this as his motet *Gloria in excelsis Deo* demonstrates (Ex. 5.32).

Ex. 5.32.   Esquivel: Motet, *Gloria in excelsis Deo*, bar 24

He was also not averse to allowing parallel fourths to arise in order to create an interesting vocal line, as Ex. 5.33 shows. There is nothing contrary to sixteenth-century practice in this extract, however, and many others examples can be found in Renaissance polyphony: the G of the *superius* in bar 55 forms a consonant fourth with the *bassus* and is approached and quitted by step in the normal way; the A of the tenor is an accented passing note and the parallel fourths are created when the movement of the tenor coincides with the movement of the *altus*, the quaver D being followed by the lower auxiliary. Parallel fourths occur frequently between

85 H. K. Andrews, *An Introduction to the Technique of Palestrina* (London, 1958), p. 63.
86 Ibid., p. 102.

upper parts,[87] and given the careful training that Esquivel must have had over a period of many years, it would be surprising to see examples of serious flaws in his contrapuntal technique; indeed, it is unlikely that he would have been given permission to publish if his works had not met the demands for 'correctness' expected of a Church composer in Spain in his time. As we saw in Chapter 3, Esquivel's *Tomus secundus* of 1613 was praised not only for the way in which the publication met liturgical requirements, but also because it was considered 'music of good quality, sound in theory and in practice'.

Ex. 5.33.   Esquivel: Motet, *Istorum est enim*, bars 55–6

Finally, we cannot leave this study of the motets without making some observations on the appearance of diminished and augmented fourth and fifth intervals.

As a melodic interval, the diminished fourth – an interval used with some frequency by Victoria – occurs only occasionally in Esquivel's motets; the diminished fifth occurs only once, and as a dead interval,[88] in the motet *Ductus est Jesus*; there are no instances of augmented fourths or fifths, but there is one instance of an augmented second, in the motet, *In illo tempore loquente*.

But when we look at the vertical alignment of the parts within the texture, we find that the practice of sharpening a note in a voice-part to produce the interval of augmented fourth or its inversion, the diminished fifth, with another voice, occurs with some frequency throughout the volume. This produces in effect a diminished triad, but – to use modern nomenclature – always in its first inversion; that is to say, the interval is produced between the top voice and an inner voice, or between two inner voices, but never between an inner voice and bass. This is common procedure in Renaissance music and Esquivel demonstrates full knowledge of this procedure.

---

87 Some Renaissance theorists strongly disapproved of this practice. See, for example, Johannes Lippius, *Synopsis musicae novae*, trans. Benito V. Rivera (Colorado Spring, 1977), and Zarlino, *Le istituzioni armoniche* (1558, reprinted 1562 and 1573). In book 3 of this work Zarlino writes: 'we ought also not to take two fourths in any composition whatever, as some do in certain short sections of their *canzoni* which they call *falso bordone*, for the fourth is without doubt a perfect consonance'; translation from Strunk, *Source Readings*, p. 238.

88 Samuel Rubio defines a 'dead interval' as an interval whose notes have no melodic connection owing to the fact the first is the conclusion of one phrase or period while the second is the beginning of another. See Rubio *Classical Polyphony*, p. 157, n.6.

Instances of augmented triads arising via the interval of the augmented sixth have already been given, but we now need to examine some instances of the vertical combination of pitches producing the interval of the diminished fourth or its inversion, the augmented fifth. Consider Ex. 5.34.

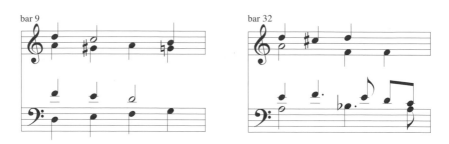

Ex. 5.34a. Esquivel: Motet, *Omnes Sancti*, bar 9 and bar 32

Ex. 5.34b. *Istorum est enim*, bar 31   Ex. 5.34c. *O crux benedicta*, bars 51–2

In each of these examples, the part-writing results in what, in later terminology, is in effect an augmented triad in its first inversion, a consequence of the interval of the diminished fourth in the first case, and an augmented fifth in the other two. As in the case of the diminished triad, the root of the augmented triad never appears in the bass.

Esquivel seems to make part-writing which produces an augmented triad a feature of his personal style, although of course he was not the only Renaissance composer, and certainly not the only Spanish composer, to produce this vertical sonority. One well-known secular example is the appearance of the augmented triad in Orlando Gibbons's madrigal, *The Silver Swan*. For another example, in Spanish Church music of the period, we need look no further than Victoria's motet *O vos omnes* (1572), where the chord appears twice.

Esquivel's part-writing is logical and the dissonances that occur can be explained by the conventions in force at the time he was writing. Thus, in the example of *Omnes sancti* above, the G♯ in bar 9 appears as a result of the rule of closest proximity stated above, in this case applied to the interval of the fifth:

Whenever an imperfect third (i.e. a lesser third) is followed immediately by a fifth or any other perfect interval, with ascending stepwise movements, that imperfect third should be made perfect with a sharp, being changed into a major third.[89]

This rule explains the G♯ in *Omnes sancti* (bar 9) and *Istorum est enim regnum* (bar 31); and the C♯ in *O crux benedicta*. The C♯ in bar 32 of *Omnes sancti* appears as the *superius* cadences at the end of a phrase, and this coincides logically with the *tenor* voice as it moves to an F to avoid the movement of parallel fifths with the bass. In permitting these dissonances Esquivel is being more daring than many of his contemporaries but is not in any way breaking the established conventions in force at the end of the sixteenth century. The apparent chromaticisms that appear in his music are the result of a type of accidentalism or degree-inflection, a point made some years ago by Charles Jacobs:[90]

> In sixteenth-century Spain, a remarkable development took place in connection with the application of musica ficta. Contemporary writings seem to suggest an almost licentious delight, by the musicians, in applying the accidentals and in the exotic sound such accidentals often produced. Yet there is no intimation that chromaticism – as an integral part of the original conception of the music – ... was in use; rather a type of accidentalism or degree-inflection that – in accordance with certain *modus operandi* common in Spain during the sixteenth century – was applied ex tempore by performers and perhaps was regarded by them as a nuance of performance.

The point is well made, and Jacobs argues his case with reference to contemporary theoretical writings by Bermudo and other writers of the period. Esquivel, then, is merely demonstrating the 'licentious delight' to which Jacobs refers; but, rather than leave the addition of accidentals to the whim of performers, he makes his intentions clear in print.

The motets of the *Motecta festorum* make an interesting comparison with Palestrina's *Motecta festorum totius anni quaternis vocibus . . . Liber primus* (Rome, 1563). Esquivel's collection of motets, however, is more comprehensive and contains a larger number of works. At a time when few liturgical collections reached the printing press in Spain, there can be no doubt that the compilation and publication of the *Motecta festorum* represented a considerable achievement for the composer; for us in the twenty-first century, it is a precious document affording valuable insight into the liturgical and musical requirements of Spanish cathedral life at the turn of the century.

---

89 Ibid., p. 148. Rubio quotes from Johannes de Muris, *Ars discantus*, vol. III, in E. Coussemaker, *Scriptorum de musica medii aevi nova series* (Paris, 1864–76), 68 ff.

90 Charles Jacobs, 'Spanish Renaissance Discussion of Musica Ficta', *Proceedings of the American Philosophical Society* 112 (August, 1968), pp. 277–98.

6

THE *TOMUS SECUNDUS* OF 1613

HAVING PROVIDED HIS CHURCH with two collections of music for the mass, it seems logical that Esquivel should now turn his attention to music for the Office. The first five sections of the *Tomus secundus*, then, are given over entirely to polyphonic settings of the three liturgical items – psalms, hymns and Magnificats – which form the choral basis of the service of Vespers.

PSALM SETTINGS

PENINSULAR COMPOSERS of the first half of the sixteenth century, men such as Francisco de Peñalosa, Juan Escribano, Juan de Anchieta, Bartolomé Escobedo and also Morales, were not drawn to the composition of psalm settings. The second half of the century, however, saw a huge increase in this activity when a number of significant figures sought to provide polyphonic material to enhance the liturgy of the Hours, Vespers in particular. Esquivel took his place in a line of distinguished musicians, who, in addition to familiar names like Guerrero and Victoria, and his teacher Juan Navarro, included among others Andrés de Torrentes (three times *maestro* at Toledo), Rodrigo de Ceballos, Fernando de las Infantas, Ginés de Boluda (*maestro* at the cathedrals of Cuenca and Toledo), Melchor Robledo and Diego Ortiz.[1]

A description of the psalm settings was given in Chapter 3. There it was noted that the seven psalms given polyphonic treatment are those which were sung at First Vespers at different times of the year. *Dixit Dominus* appears twice, one setting being in psalm tone 1 and a second setting in tone 6.

The psalm tones, with their basic structure of intonation, reciting note and termination, elucidated the structure of the text, and polyphonic settings were designed to fulfil the same practical function: to get through the text quickly and efficiently, without the elaborate polyphonic treatment accorded for example to motet texts.

In his psalm settings, Esquivel follows the conventional procedures of his time: unison verses, sung to the psalm tone, alternate with polyphonic settings in which

---

1 José Ma. Llorens Cisteró, *Francisco Guerrero, Opera Omnia XI, Salmos de Visperas – Pasionarios* (Barcelona, 2001), p. 20 ff.

the chant is paraphrased – sometimes very freely – in either the *superius* or an inner voice, or occasionally in the *bassus*, as in verse 8 of *Dixit Dominus* (first setting).

It is not clear from Esquivel's polyphony which version of the psalm tones he used as his source for these settings. Generally, his psalm tones bear more resemblance in their melodic outline to the chant formulas as shown in the *Intonarium Toletanum* (1515). This is certainly the case with the setting of *In exitu Israel*; on the other hand, the chant formula in the second setting of *Dixit Dominus* shows a melodic outline closer to that found in the *Liber usualis*. The degree to which the psalm tone original is subject to variation varies from verse to verse, as can be seen in Ex. 6.1, the second and sixth verses of *Dixit Dominus* (first setting in psalm tone 1).

In verse 2, the psalm tone (marked with x in Ex. 6.1) appears in the *altus* and then migrates to the *tenor*, where it is transposed; in verse 6, it again appears in the *altus* but with less elaboration; in verse 10, the doxological verse, it appears transposed, and with its first line much disguised, in the *superius*.

This *primus tonus* version of *Dixit Dominus* contrasts with the second setting, which presents the psalm tone in the *superius* in verses two, four and six, in the *tenor* in verse 8, and in the *superius* in verse 10.[2] The transformation of the chant formula is even more elaborate in verse 4, in line with the principle of giving the psalm tone individualised treatment in each verse. This free treatment is one means of creating variety from verse to verse. Another is to vary the voice groupings in the contrapuntal verses. The standard grouping is SATB, but *Dixit Dominus* (first setting) has verse 8 scored SSAB, while in the second setting, this verse is scored SAT,[3] with the number of voices in the Gloria (verse 10) increased to five (SSATB). Other voice groupings are SSAT in the Gloria of *Lauda Jerusalem*, and SSAB for the second half of the Gloria. The harmonisations of the chant-bearing line are largely homophonic, with contrapuntal elaboration kept to a minimum.

Such procedures as those just described appear conservative when we consider that well before 1613 more progressive composers in Italy were already immersed in Baroque techniques. One has only to think of Monteverdi's celebrated *Vespers of 1610* to realise just how traditional were the procedures adopted by Esquivel, Guerrero and other Spanish composers of their generation, who maintained an *alternatim* practice of psalm singing dating back to earlier times, when psalm-tone harmonisations were in simple *falsobordone* style – a technique of simple chordal harmonisation related to the even earlier practice of *fauxbourdon*.[4]

The final psalm, *In exitu Israel*, is treated rather differently from the other settings. Because of its subject matter – the flight from Egypt of the captive Israelites – this

2 A complete transcription of this second setting of *Dixit Dominus* may be found in Snow, *The 1613 Print*, pp. 39–42.

3 Interestingly, both Navarro, Esquivel's teacher, and Guerrero score this verse *à3* in their settings of this psalm verse.

4 This practice is discussed at some length by Leeman L. Perkins in *Music in the Age of the Renaissance* (New York, 1999): see pp. 341–5 and 561–4 for further details. Monteverdi, of course, does not shun *falsobordone* completely in his psalm settings; in the *Vespers of 1610* there are echoes of the former practice in his setting of *Dixit Dominus* and *Nisi Dominus*.

Ex. 6.1. *Dixit Dominus*, verses 2 and 6

6. Do - minus a de - xtris_____ tu - is, con fre - git in

6. Do - minus a de-xtris tu - is, con fre - git in

6. Do - minus a de - xtris tu - is, con fre - git in

6. Do - minus a de - xtris tu - is, con fre - git in

di - e i - rae su - ae re - ges.

di - e i - rae su - ae re - ges.

di - e i - rae su - ae re - ges.

di - e i - rae su - ae re - ges.

psalm was traditionally associated with what is now called the *Tonus peregrinus*,[5] the tone which has two reciting notes, the one for the second half of the chant being a tone lower than that in the first half. Set alongside Guerrero's expansive setting, where all twenty-nine odd-numbered verses receive varied contrapuntal treatment, creating a setting of great beauty and producing in effect a series of mini-motets,[6] Esquivel's setting of only verse 1 and the Gloria is perfunctory. However, considering contemporary performance practice, it may be that variety was achieved by the employment of the *ministriles*, with different instrumental groupings being used for alternate verses; or, given the training afforded to singers of the time, further harmonised verses may have been improvised in the *falsobordone* style of verse 1. This simple declamatory style remained popular into the eighteenth century, perhaps because it was seen as an ideal way to satisfy the concerns of the Council of Trent for text intelligibility.[7] But given the dramatic text of this psalm – rich in imagery – and considering the instrumental forces that by 1613 were available, it is inconceivable that a performance in the early seventeenth century would have been as entirely monochrome as the two-verse harmonisations printed suggest, unless, of course, Esquivel was erring on the cautious side, deliberately including this simple setting to accommodate churches where musical resources were indeed limited.

HYMNS

A S WAS NOTED IN CHAPTER 3, adherence to Spanish tradition is a feature of Esquivel's hymn settings,[8] but before we examine these in detail it is necessary to sketch out the development of this tradition, which in several ways was markedly different from that of other European countries.

The singing of hymns as part of the liturgy has a long history in Spain; along with the Church of Milan and the Church of Ireland, the Spanish Church was among the first to encourage this communal activity.[9] A few hymns with music survive from the ancient Visigothic-Mozarabic rite but the Spanish Church gradually replaced the old hymns with a new repertory, very different from the original Spanish sources and the Roman repertory.[10]

5 Perkins, *Music in the Age of the Renaissance*, p. 563.

6 For an accessible modern edition, see Mapa Mundi, Spanish Church Music 108, ed. Bruno Turner (2000).

7 Perkins, *Music in the Age of the Renaissance*, p. 563.

8 Only four of Esquivel's hymns are available in a modern edition. See Mapa Mundi, Spanish Church Music 222, ed. Bruno Turner and Clive Walkley (2004), which contains the following hymns: *Christe Redemptor omnium*; *Hostis Herodes impie*; *Vexilla Regis prodeunt* and *Pange lingua*.

9 Higini Anglés, 'Early Spanish Musical Culture and Cardinal Cisneros's Hymnal of 1515', in J. la Rue, ed., *Aspects of Medieval and Renaissance Music. A Birthday Offering to Gustave Reese* (New York, 1666), p. 3. This article was republished in *Scripta musicologica*, ed. José López-Calo (Rome, 1975), pp. 261–78.

10 The ancient Mozarabic liturgy evolved during the sixth and seventh centuries; it was abolished in the eleventh century and later restored by Cardinal Cisneros at Toledo in the fifteenth century. See Anglés, 'Early Spanish Musical Culture', p. 7.

The *Intonarium Toletanum*, published by Cardinal Cisneros in 1515, and one of a series of liturgical books he published when he was archbishop of Toledo (1495–1517), is one of the significant surviving monuments to the Spanish tradition of hymn writing. The volume, 119 folios in total, includes over three hundred hymns with music; although some of these use the same melody, a total of ninety-three different melodies can be found in the collection. Some of these melodies are of universal origin, familiar Gregorian melodies known across Europe; others are unique to Spain.[11]

What is striking about this collection is the musical notation: some hymns are printed in square notation, others (the majority) in mensural notation, and some with a mixture of square and mensural notation. Although the notational characteristics found in the *Intonarium Toletanum* are not unique to this collection, they do serve to remind us that the hymn melodies which formed the basis of polyphonic settings by Esquivel and other composers of his generation and earlier were not all *cantus planus* or 'plainchant'. Alongside this tradition, there grew up, especially in Spain, an alternative tradition of notating hymns in notes of unequal value – in effect, *musica mensurabilis*, 'measured music'; hymn melodies in their monophonic form are found notated in both duple and triple metre.

The interpretation of plainchant is – and always was, it seems – a complex and controversial subject. Prior to the late fifteenth century, few Spanish treatises dealt with chant notation and its rhythmic interpretation, but from this time onwards the number of writers dealing with these matters increased quite dramatically. Two schools of interpretation emerged: the 'equalists' – those who advocated the performance of plainchant with notes of equal duration, and the 'non-equalists', who advocated performance in notes of varied duration.[12]

Juan Bermudo deals with the topic of performance in a very practical manner. In chapter 18 of book 1 of his *Declaración de instrumentos musicales* (1555), he gives a clear, detailed account of the three different styles of rhythmic performance practice used in chant:

> There are three time measures [*compases*] in the plainsong. One serves for the psalmody, another for particular hymns, and the third for all the rest that is noted.... The time measure of some hymns is in proportion of *sesquialtera*, where three semibreves enter in a measure. Such hymns are well noted in few parts, as they have all the notes squared. The hymns which are sung in ternary metre, or in *sesquialtera* are

11 See Márius Bernadó 'The Hymns of the *Intonarium Toletanum* (1515): Some Peculiarities', in *Cantus Planus, Papers Read at the 6th Meeting of the International Musicological Society Study Group* (Budapest, 1995), pp. 367–96. This paper (presented in 1993) gives a full description of this important document.

12 See Kathleen E. Nelson, *Medieval Liturgical Music of Zamora* (Ottawa, 1996), pp. 41–75, where this subject is discussed in some depth. Other modern sources covering the topics of mensural aspects of chant notation include Jane Morlet Hardie, 'Proto-Mensural Notation in Pre-Pius Spanish Liturgical Sources', *Studia musicologica Academiae scientiarum Hungaricae* 39/2–4 (Budapest, 1998), pp. 195–200; Richard Sherr, 'The Performance of Chant in the Renaissance and its Interactions with Polyphony', in Thomas Forrest Kelly, ed., *Plainsong in the Age of Polyphony* (Cambridge, 1992), pp. 178–208.

the following: that of Advent, which says *Conditor alme*, that of the Resurrection, *Ad cenam agni*, *Rex eterne* and *Aurora lucis*: that of the Sacrament, *Pange lingua gloriosi* and *Sacris solemniis* and other similar ones. Other hymns are sung in *por medio* metre, where one note is said in one measure, then two, then three, these being *Aures ad nostras* of Lent, *Pange lingua* and *Lustris* of the passion, of the Holy Spirit *Veni creator*, *Iam Christus* and *Beata nobis*, of the Trinity *In magestatis solio*, of the Sacrament *Verbum supernum*, the three of John the Baptist, the two of St Michael, of the Martyrs *Sanctorum meritis*, of the Confessors *Iste confessor* and two of the dedication of the church, which is understood in Spain, and in the Roman. All the other hymns take the measure of the other chant, where in each of the notes a measure is used.[13]

Luís de Villafranca makes reference to ternary measures used in some hymns in his *Breve instrucción de canto llano* (1565), using the term *compás de proporción* in place of Bermudo's *proporción de sesquialtera*:

> Proportion measure is when there are three to the measure as in the above-mentioned hymn, *Te lucis ante terminum*.[14]

And in his *El melopeo y maestro*, written in 1613 and therefore contemporary with Esquivel's *Tomus secundus*, Pietro Cerone makes a distinction between plainchant (*canto llano*) and mensural music (*canto de órgano*). He refers to ternary measures as *proporción ternaria*.[15] Thus, all three writers explain what the written sources themselves demonstrate – notes of unequal note value are to be treated unequally in performance.

The practice of producing liturgically ordered cycles of polyphonic hymns for Vespers dates back to the late fourteenth century. From the fifteenth century onwards, such cycles become more common; the best-known example is Dufay's collection, written for the papal choir around 1430, in which two of the hymns appear in quasi-mensural notation, *Conditor alme siderum* and *Vexilla Regis prodeunt*. The practice increased in the sixteenth century with cycles by composers as diverse as Costanzo Festa, Jacquet of Mantua, Willaert, Victoria, Lassus, Guerrero and Palestrina. A principle was established of alternating monophonic chant with one or more strophes sung in polyphony. The chant was embedded in the surrounding polyphony, sometimes in *cantus firmus* manner, at other times in the manner of paraphrase; each strophe was given individual treatment by varying the texture and the number of voices, changing the locus of the chant melody within the contrapuntal fabric and by tempo changes. In effect, hymn settings became a set of variations on a theme.

A distinctive Spanish voice is heard in the polyphonic hymn settings of Escobar, Dalva (de Alba), Peñalosa and Urreda in that these composers based their

---

13 Juan Bermudo, *Declaración de instrumentos musicales*, book I, chapter 18, fol. xviiv. Translation from Bernadó, 'The Hymns of the *Intonarium Toletanum*', pp. 375–6.

14 Luís de Villafranca, *Breve introducción de canto llano* (Sevilla, S. Trugillo, 1565, fols. vii and ixv), quoted in Bernadó 'The Hymns of the *Intonarium Toletanum*', pp. 376–7: 'Compás de proporción es quando van tres semibreves al compás como en el hymno sobredicho, *Te lucis ante terminum*.'

15 Cerone, *El melopeo y maestro*, I, book IV, chapter XII, fols. 413–15.

polyphonic settings on Spanish hymn melodies, or local variants of tunes known elsewhere.[16] Thus, when Esquivel came to compile his polyphonic hymn collection, following in the footsteps of Victoria (whose hymns appeared in 1581), Guerrero (*Liber vesperarum*, 1584) and of course his illustrious teacher, Navarro, he had an established tradition to follow, fine models to emulate and a rich source of melodic material on which to draw: melodies notated rhythmically in notes of equal value, and those mensurally notated, in long and short note values and sometimes in *tripla* mensuration.

Unlike Victoria, who preceded his polyphonic elaborations with the chant melody, Esquivel does not. This creates problems for the modern-day performer seeking to match a chant melody with its polyphonic elaboration and thus revive a lost tradition; he is left to guess the source of Esquivel's chant. Although there are close resemblances to the melodies of the *Intonarium Toletanum* in some of his hymn settings, in others it is obvious that he used a different, perhaps local, source. This should not surprise us, however, since even after the revised Breviary of 1568, when all texts were expected to conform to Roman usage, there was nothing to prevent composers from drawing on local chant traditions when it came to setting the texts; local variants of widely known hymn melodies are common, but since there are no chant books from the sixteenth century remaining in Ciudad Rodrigo the question of Esquivel's sources must, in some cases, be left open.

However, two points may be made here. Firstly, all the hymn tunes set by Esquivel – with two exceptions – are to be found in the *Intonarium Toletanum*, but some hymn texts are set to tunes different from those with which they are associated in that source.

One example is the first hymn in the cycle, the Advent hymn, *Conditor alme siderum*, which is not based on the melody notated in *tripla* mensuration found in the *Intonarium Toletanum* (the one used by Guerrero for that hymn in his *Liber vesperarum* of 1584) but an entirely different tune, which in the *Intonarium Toletanum* is set to the hymn *Verbum supernum prodiens*. Clearly, local custom played a part in Esquivel's use of this tune; the composer provided a polyphonic elaboration of a chant melody that was well known and, by tradition, in current use in his diocese at the time he was writing – common practice in his day.

Secondly, several tunes are used more than once by the composer. A good example is the *Intonarium Toletanum* tune associated with the Christmas hymn *Veni redemptor gentium*, sung at Matins in most dioceses in Spain until the 1570s. Esquivel uses this twice: firstly, for his setting of the Christmas hymn *Christe*

16 For discussion of the polyphonic hymn settings by these composers in TaraC 2/3, see Juan Ruiz Jiménez, *'Infunde amorem cordibus*: An Early Sixteenth-Century Polyphonic Hymn Cycle from Seville', *Early Music* 33 (2005), pp. 619–38. The study establishes a Sevillian origin for this most important manuscript from the time of the Catholic Monarchs, Ferdinand and Isabella. Chant melodies for the settings are identified, and these are compared with those found in other Iberian chant sources listed in an Appendix. Earlier studies of the Tarazona hymn cycle include: Tom R. Ward, *The Polyphonic Office Hymn 1400–1520: A Descriptive Catalogue* (Neuhausen-Stuttgart, 1980); Carmen J. Gutiérrez, 'Himno', in *Diccionario de la música española e hispanoamericana*, VI (Madrid, 2000), pp. 304–6.

Redemptor omnium – now, post 1568, ordained for use at Vespers and Matins – and then for the hymn for Holy Innocents, *Salvete flores martyrum*, immediately following. Several other tunes are used twice in this way – again not an uncommon practice.[17]

Juan Navarro's *Psalmi, hymni, ac Magnificat totius anni* appeared in 1590, a decade after the composer's death, containing polyphonic settings of twenty-seven hymns – twenty-four different melodies with the *Intonarium Toletanum* as their obvious source. Consciously, or unconsciously, Esquivel follows his master's procedures closely in his own cycle, providing polyphony for one or two even-numbered verses, except in two instances: *Vexilla Regis*, where verses 1 and 6 are set polyphonically, and *Pange lingua*, where verse 5 ('Tantum ergo') receives the same treatment. In doing this, Esquivel was following Spanish custom, which traditionally emphasised these verses by setting them polyphonically.[18]

The compositional techniques displayed are those found in similar collections of the period; apart from Navarro's settings, Guerrero's *Liber vesperarum* is an obvious model. The traditional chant melody is embedded in one or another vocal part in its entirety – frequently the upper voice part but sometimes in an inner part (and once in the bass, as in *Aurea luce*, the hymn for the feast of Ss Peter and Paul). Sometimes the melodic line is left plain, stated in long note values in the manner of a *cantus firmus*; at other times it is more decorated. Sometimes it is divided between voices; sometimes it appears transposed. Sometimes it may be treated imitatively; at other times the accompanying lines are completely independent. The modality of the original melody shapes the harmonic constructs and determines the cadence structure; often the entry of the chant-bearing line is delayed so that it can make a full impact and the text can be heard; sometimes Esquivel resorts to homophony when setting individual phrases to underscore the text – as in the sixth verse of *Vexilla Regis*, where the text refers to 'this Passiontide' ('hoc passionis tempore') and harmonic colouring is used to great effect (see Ex. 6.2).

In all bar three cases, the hymns are set for the usual SATB combination of voices. Unlike Navarro's cycle, none of the hymns displays canonic devices. Navarro demonstrates his ability to construct elaborate canons in his setting of *Ut queant laxis*, the hymn to John the Baptist, where enigma canons appear in the first and second verses. The fact that the hexachord syllables derive from the words of this hymn may be the reason Navarro chose this particular text as a demonstration of his learning.

Local tradition plays its part in the ordering of material in the cycle in one instance. The hymn, *Custodes hominum*, for the feast of guardian angels – a feast long celebrated throughout Spain – appears between the Epiphany hymn, *Hostis Herodes impie*, and *Vexilla Regis*, the Vespers hymn from Passion Sunday and beyond. Pope Paul V mandated this new Office in 1605 and prescribed that it was to be celebrated on the first free day after the feast of St Michael, 29 September. However, it seems that the church for which Esquivel composed his cycle – presumably

---

17 I am grateful for the helpful comments made by Bruno Turner on this topic, and for his willingness to share his vast store of knowledge of the Spanish hymn repertory with me.

18 Snow, *The 1613 Print*, p. 19.

Ciudad Rodrigo – and churches elsewhere continued to celebrate the feast on one
of the traditional Spanish dates in February or March.[19]

Ex. 6.2. *Vexilla Regis*, strophe 6: 'hoc passionis'

TRIPLE-TIME HYMNS

FOUR OF ESQUIVEL'S HYMNS are in triple metre. One of these is the Corpus
Christe hymn *Pange lingua*, based not on the familiar melody associated with
this hymn and found in the *Liber usualis* (pp. 950–2), but the uniquely Spanish tune,
known since the fourteenth century and popular in Spain for centuries afterwards.
In its triple-time version, the hymn is found in hundreds of chant books, including
the *Intonarium Toletanum*, where it is notated in black breves and semibreves. It is
the version of the tune used by Guerrero in his *Liber vesperarum*, and by Navarro as
well as Esquivel. In addition to its association with the Corpus Christe hymn text,
the melody is used again for the Michaelmas hymn *Tibi Christe splendor Patris*. In
both cases Esquivel uses the mensuration O, setting the tune in long note values
in the *superius* for the second verse of *Pange lingua*, and in the *tenor* of *Tibi Christe*;
'Tantum ergo' (verse 5 of *Pange lingua*) is in duple time with C mensuration, the
sign he employs consistently for all duple time hymns, although it may not indicate
a real tempo difference between ₵ and C as it would have done to composers of an
earlier generation.

19 Robert J. Snow, 'Liturgical Reform and Musical Revisions: Reworkings of their Vespers
Hymns by Guerrero, Navarro and Durán de la Cueva', in M. F. Cidrais Rodrigues, M. Morais and R.
V. Nery, eds., *Livro de homenagem a Macario Santiago Kastner* (Lisbon, 1992), pp. 463–99, at p. 483.

The other two triple-time hymns, *Pater superni luminis* for the feast of St Mary Magdalen and *Fortem virili pectore* for Holy Women, are more vigorous in style and show O3 and O3½ respectively. Both hymns were written for Clement VIII's new revised Breviary of 1602 (and also the hymn for the feast of St Jacob, *Defensor alme Hispaniae*, which formed part of the new Office for the feast of St James).[20] *Fortem virili* is set to a tune which may have been composed locally; it was obviously written for this hymn and is not found elsewhere. That it was still being sung in the eighteenth century is clear from the fact that the jaunty tune is found in one of the eighteenth-century chant books remaining in Ciudad Rodrigo cathedral, notated as shown in Ex. 6.3. As Ex. 6.4 demonstrates, this was clearly the tune used by Esquivel; it is heard in the *tenor* in verse 2 and in the *superius* in verse 4.

PERFORMANCE ISSUES

ESQUIVEL'S HYMN CYCLE stands midway between the practice that was common in Spain in the sixteenth century, when each alternate strophe was provided with its own setting, and that which prevailed from about the middle of the seventeenth century onwards, when sources usually give polyphony for a single strophe.[21] Because Esquivel never provided polyphony for more than two strophes of each hymn even when the total number of strophes exceeded five, the question arises, how were the hymns performed?

Assuming the pattern of alternating chant with polyphony, the same setting may have served for more than one verse, perhaps in different arrangements; as with the psalms, wind instruments or organ may have substituted for some of the voice parts, for example. And it is likely that the last verse would have been performed polyphonically since this Roman practice was mandated in 1600 by the *Caeremoniale episcoporum* of Clement VIII.[22]

A question arises in connection with the four hymns in triple mensuration: what is the tempo relationship between verses sung in chant and those in polyphony? A detailed study of this subject is beyond the confines of this study; a full discussion can be found elsewhere.[23] However, there is sufficient evidence to suggest that the black breve and semibreve, the note- values used to notate the chant in sources available to the composer, are the equivalents of the corresponding white semibreve and minim of the polyphony. While there may be other ways of performing these particular hymns, this provides a workable solution to the problem of establishing a 'correct' tempo relationship.

---

20 Snow, 'Liturgical Reform and Musical Revisions', p. 483.
21 Snow, *The 1613 Print*, p. 19.
22 Snow, 'Liturgical Reform and Musical Revisions', p. 473.
23 Bruno Turner, 'Spanish Liturgical Hymns: A Matter of Time', *Early Music* 33 (1995), pp. 473–82.

Ex. 6.3. *Fortem virili pectore* in chant

Ex. 6.4. *Fortem virili pectore* in polyphony

Juan Esquivel

res - cit, hor - res - cit,_____ ad cae-le-sti-

res-cit,_____ ad cae-le-sti - a I - ter per -

Hor - res - cit, ad cae - le-sti -

ad cae - le-sti - a I - ter per - e - git

a I - ter per - e - git ar - du - um.

e - git ar - du - um.

a I - ter per - e - git ar - du - um.

ar - du - um, ar - du - um.

4. Rex Chri - ste, vir - tus for - ti - um,

4. Rex Chri - ste, vir - tus for - ti - um,

4. Rex Chri - ste, vir - tus for - ti - um,

4. Rex Chri-ste, vir - tus for - ti - um, Qui

MAGNIFICATS

AFTER THE ORDINARY OF THE MASS, no other liturgical text was set polyphonically with such frequency during the sixteenth century as the Magnificat. Well over four hundred different composers between 1436 and 1620 left
settings.[24] There are Magnificats by Dunstable and Dufay; among Spanish composers, a mini-cycle by Peñalosa and others can be found in TaraC 2/3 and other
well-known manuscripts of the period. In Spain, the pattern of writing Magnificat
cycles in sets of eight, based on all eight plainsong recitation tones, seems to have
been initiated by Morales, and the practice was continued by Guerrero, Navarro,
Vivanco, Victoria and Esquivel.

Esquivel's settings – again, typical of their time – follow the Spanish procedure
of alternating verses in chant with verses in polyphony. As we saw in Chapter 3, in
conformity with widespread custom, Esquivel's works are grouped in two cycles of
eight, cycle one consisting of settings of odd-numbered verses, intended for First
Vespers; cycle two, settings of even-numbered verses for Second Vespers. The provision of a cycle based on all eight tones enabled a match to be made with the mode
of the framing antiphon.

The Magnificat, being the climax of Vespers, had a greater liturgical significance
than the psalms, and so it is not surprising that Esquivel lavished greater attention on these works than on his psalm settings. This is particularly true of the
first cycle, since the service of First Vespers had a slightly higher rank than Second
Vespers.[25] The contrapuntal technique here demonstrated is considerably more
elaborate than in the psalm settings: canon is used frequently, the recitation tone is
often cleverly disguised, and scoring is varied from four to eight parts and used as a
means of highlighting the text.

Esquivel's odd-numbered settings invite comparison with those of his teacher,
Navarro: there are some similarities but some significant differences in their respective approaches. Like Navarro, Esquivel begins with the incipit 'Magnificat' printed
in chant notation in a version which differs only slightly from that found in the
Liber usualis. In the following polyphony, the chant formula dominates the texture,
being present sometimes in the manner of a *cantus firmus*, at other times heavily
ornamented or paraphrased; or it suggests points of imitation for the accompanying polyphony. It can appear in any part, including the bass in Esquivel's case,
although there are some verses which make little or no reference to it, being based
on original material.

The basic scoring of both composers is SATB with the number of voices
increased for the doxological verse 11; with one exception in Esquivel's case (tone 3
Magnificat), both composers use canonic techniques in this verse, following common practice.

In five of his odd-numbered settings, Esquivel follows Navarro's procedure
of reducing the number of voices to three for verse 5 ('et misericordia') as if to

24 Stevenson, *Spanish Cathedral Music*, p. 81.
25 Snow, *The 1613 Print*, p. 21.

emphasise God's mercy. This procedure is reversed for verse 7 ('deposuit') where the full texture is restored, except for tone 2 where the scoring is ATB and where the image of 'putting down the mighty' is suggested by a falling melodic motif. Word-painting is restrained in the work of both composers, since more extremes of word illustration would have been totally out of place in the context of Vespers in a Spanish cathedral at the time Esquivel was writing.

But there are significant differences in each composer's use of canonic techniques. Navarro's approach is highly systematic, with the interval of the canon corresponding to the number of the mode: thus, verse 11 in tone 1 is canon at the unison; in tone 2, canon at the second; in tone 3 at the third, and so on to tone 8 – canon at the octave. Esquivel's approach is less systematic, in the sense that there is no discernible over-arching plan determining the interval for the canon.

TABLE 18. Voice designations of first Magnificat cycle

Tone	No. of voices	Verse 1	Verse 3	Verse 5	Verse 7	Verse 9	Verse 11
1	5	SSATB	SSATB	SSAT	SSATB	SSATB	SSAATB
2	4	SATB	SATB	SATB	ATB	SATB	SSAATTBB
3	4	SATB	SATB	AAB	SATB	SATB	SSAT
4	4	SATB	SSATB	SAT	SSAATB	SATB	SSATB
5	6	SSAATB	SSAATB	SAT	SSAATB	SSAATB	SSAATTB
6	4	SATB	SATB	SSA	SATB	SATB	SSATTB
7	4	SATB	SATB	SSATB	SSAB	SATB	SATTB
8	4	SATB	SATB	SAB	SSATB	SSAATB	SSAATTB / SSAATTBB

TABLE 19. Canonic rubrics for Magnificats of first cycle

Tone	Verse		
1	11	Altus I:	*Altus secundus in secunda*
2	11	Superius I:	*Altus secundus in sub Diatessaron retro canit.*
		Altus I:	*Tenor secundus in sub Diatessaron.*
3	No canons		
4	7	Altus I:	*Superius secundus in Diatessaron.*
	11	Bassus:	*Tenor in Diatessaron.*
5	11	Altus II:	*Tenor primus in Diapason.*
6	11	Superius I:	*Trinitas in unitate.*
		Superius II:	*quod ascendit descendit in sexta.*
7	11	Altus:	*Tenor secundus in sub Diatessaron, semibrevia tantum.*
8	9	Superius I:	*Superius secundus in Diatessaron.*
	11	Superius II:	*Altus primus in sub Diapente.*
	11 (2nd setting)	Superius II:	*Altus primus in secunda.*
		Altus II:	*Superius primus in Diatessaron.*
		Tenor I:	*Bassus secundus in sub Diapente.*
		Bassus I:	*Tenor secundus in Diapason, semibrevia, et eorum pausas tantum.*

Although his contrapuntal mastery cannot quite equal the dexterity of his contemporary, Vivanco – whose *Magnificat quarti toni* Gloria from his *Liber magnificarum* of 1607 combines three plainsong melodies associated with the Virgin, plus the psalm tone, plus the plainsong formula for the words 'anima mea Dominum' in all eight tones set out in numerical order[26] – his canonic achievements are equally comparable to those of Navarro. Navarro never goes beyond five parts; Esquivel goes up to seven and eight, expanding his four voices by means of adroitly devised canons, as shown in Table 18, showing the voice designations for each of the verses of the first Magnificat cycle, and Table 19, showing the canonic rubric given by the composer for each canon.

In his tone 5 setting, the composer is perhaps trying to emulate Vivanco's achievement outlined above. Printed on page 216 of the print (the beginning of the Gloria) we find the phrase, 'Super octo tonos'. On investigation, we find that the *Euouae* formulas for the eight tones (the melodic pattern setting the final two words 'saeculorum. Amen' of the Gloria) with text are used as the first eight of the ten phrases of *altus I* (see Ex. 6.5).

As we see from Table 19, Esquivel provided two versions of the doxological verse for the *Magnificat octavi toni*. The second setting is shorter and requires an additional bass voice; it was, perhaps, intended as an alternative to the first setting, to be sung on a feast day of a greater ranking when an extra voice could be bought in for the occasion (see Ex. 6.6).

The fact that Esquivel left it to his singers to work out their part from the instructions provided is further proof of the skills required of a cathedral singer at this time. In the case of Ex. 6.6, for example, the second tenor is required to invent his part from that of the first bass according to the instruction 'Tenor secundus in Diapason semibrevia, et eorum pausas tantum' ('Second tenor at the octave above the bass, using only semibreves and their rests'). This is no mean feat – unless, of course, he had worked it out in rehearsal and then sang this section from a manuscript copy in performance.

The Magnificats of the second cycle do not show the same degree of polyphonic elaboration. Only verse 13, 'Sicut erat', of tones 2, 5, 6 and 7 is set for more than four voices and canon is utilised only in the tone 5 setting. This is, perhaps, surprising since, even before the sixteenth century, the last verse had often been seen as the climax of the composition, similar to the Agnus Dei of the mass ordinary.[27] However, the fact that Second Vespers occupied a lower rank than First Vespers may be the reason for this.

Although the compositions of Costanzo Festa and Sebastián de Vivanco

26 Further details of Vivanco's astonishing contrapuntal achievements in his Magnificat settings may be found in Stevenson, *Spanish Cathedral Music*, pp. 279–81. Stevenson reproduces in open score the Gloria from Vivanco's *Magnificat quarti toni* (*Liber Magnificarum*, pp. 112–13) on pp. 282–5.

27 Stefan Gasch , '"Sursum deorsum aguntur res mortalium": Canons in Magnificat Settings of the Fifteenth and Sixteenth Centuries and the Case of Mattheus Le Maistre's Magnificat Sexti Toni', in Katelijne Schiltz and Bonnie J. Blackburn, eds., *Canons and Canonic Techniques, 14th–16th Centuries: Theory, Practice, and Reception History. Proceedings of the International Conference, Leuven, 4–6 October 2005* (Leuven, 2007), p. 254

may represent the climax of the application of canonic technique in Magnificat settings,[28] Esquivel, in his settings, demonstrates his ability to maintain a long-standing tradition of providing richly textured music for this Marian canticle, one of the most important genres in the liturgy.

This section of the print concludes with a short, concise four-part setting of *Benedicamus Domine*, notated under the mensuration sign O3 and paraphrasing the chant in the *superius*.

28 Ibid., p. 257. Gasch's conference paper includes a comprehensive, although by no means complete, list of composers who employed canonic technique in their Magnificat settings. Esquivel's works are not listed, but those of Festa and Vivanco appear alongside the works of thirty-five other composers; ten anonymous settings are also listed. This is a useful list, not least because it shows the range, diversity and complexity of canonic usage in the Magnificat.

Ex. 6.5. *Magnificat quinti toni* (first cycle), verse 11

JUAN ESQUIVEL

JUAN ESQUIVEL

Ex. 6.6. The second Gloria of *Magnificat Octavi toni*, First Vespers

THE FOUR MARIAN ANTIPHONS

IN KEEPING WITH ESQUIVEL'S OBVIOUS INTENTION of providing music for the Office throughout the liturgical year, it is logical that the next items to appear should be the four seasonal Marian antiphons. In the Roman Breviary of 1568, these are assigned as follows: *Alma Redemptoris mater* from Vespers of Saturday before the first Sunday of Advent to the Second Vespers of the Purification (2 February); *Ave Regina caelorum* from Compline of the Purification to Compline of Wednesday in Holy Week; *Regina caeli* from Compline of Holy Saturday to None of the Saturday after Pentecost; and *Salve Regina* from the First Vespers of the feast of the Holy Trinity to None on the Saturday before the first Sunday of Advent. Esquivel provides most of this information in his rubric: 'Alma Redemptoris mater. In Adventu Domini usque Purificationem' (from Advent to Purification); 'Ave Regina caelorum. Post Purificationem usque ad feriam quintam in Coena Domini' (from Purification to Thursday in Holy Week); 'Regina caeli. Tempore Paschali' (at Paschal time).

No rubric is given for the *Salve Regina*, however. This may be because the anti-phon was often sung polyphonically in Spain during Lent.[29] The sentiments of the text, with its emphasis on 'mourning and weeping in this vale of tears', accord well with the traditional Spanish focus on the suffering and death of Christ during this penitential season. As we saw in Chapter 4, belief in the power of polyphony to enhance the Church's teachings was widespread during the sixteenth century, and Spanish composers produced large numbers of motets on Gospel readings throughout the Lenten period for this reason. The composition of polyphonic set-tings of the *Salve Regina* in this season was, then, a natural extension of the Spanish use of polyphony at this time: a means of increasing devotion to the Virgin in her role as protector, mediator and advocate.[30]

All four antiphon settings paraphrase, primarily in the *superius*, the chant mel-ody to which they were sung monophonically. However, we should note again that the version of the chant melody used by Esquivel in both *Ave Regina* and *Regina caeli* is not the same as that found in modern chant books such as the *Liber usualis*; many variants are found in local chant books in Spain.

Esquivel clearly lavished great care on the composition of these Marian anti-phons, and this is particularly noticeable in the case of the *Salve Regina*. This antiphon had enjoyed continuing popularity since the eleventh century; it served as the basis for polyphonic settings by forty-four known composers in the period

---

29 Snow, *A New-World Collection of Polyphony*, p. 65.

30 The date and authorship of this antiphon is still in dispute but it probably dates from the end of the eleventh century or the beginning of the twelfth. It was introduced into the liturgical services of Cluny about 1135. The *Statutes of the Congregation of Cluny* order the *Salve Regina* to be chanted on feasts of the Assumption during the procession. The antiphon was taken over by the Cistercians and later by the Dominicans. See Hilda Graef, *Mary: A History of Doctrine and Devotion* (London, 1985; orig. 2 vols., New York, 1963), p. 229 and pp. 241/2. Graef's book provides much useful coverage on the subject of Marian devotion.

1425–1550 alone; in addition, there are over sixty-two anonymous settings.[31]

The first three antiphons are through-composed in polyphony, but *Salve Regina*, as was Spanish practice, alternates polyphony with chant, or perhaps instrumental paraphrase. In the polyphonic verses, 'Vita dulcedo', 'Ad te suspiramus', 'Et Jesum', Esquivel makes expressive use of melismas for key words like 'salve', 'suspiramus', 'flentes', 'vale'; in the last verse, after setting the phrases 'O clemens: O pia' in polyphonic imitation, he emphasises the sweetness of the Virgin ('O dulcis virgo Maria') in homophonic declamatory style – the rhetorical figure of *noema* in Burmeister's classification (see Chapter 5) – and a style commonly used by Victoria, for example, to express thoughts of admiration, adoration and supplication.

The five miscellaneous items which make up the fifth section of the book have already been discussed briefly in Chapter 3 and require no further comment. We pass on, therefore, to a discussion of the mass ordinaries and the *Missa pro defunctis*, which make up the last section of the volume.

THE MASS ORDINARIES

THE GENERAL STYLISTIC FEATURES of this second book of masses are not dissimilar to those of the first book. For this reason, the following discussion of the masses in the *Tomus secundus* will be less extensive than the coverage of the masses of 1608. Readers requiring more extensive information should consult Robert Snow's excellent monograph, to which reference has been made many times in this and in previous chapters.

One of the essential differences between the two sets of works is the nature of the source material. Parody masses featured heavily in the 1608 collection; here, in 1613, only two masses are based on pre-existing polyphonic works while four are based on chant material, as was pointed out in Chapter 3. Of the four chant-based masses, *Tu es Petrus* is the first printed.

This mass, scored for five voices – SSATB – is based on the Office antiphon *Tu es Petrus*, which is sung on the feasts of Ss Peter and Paul (29 June). Only the first part of the chant antiphon is used, however; it provides the main structural girder for the mass, appearing frequently throughout. It is given most prominence in the Kyrie, Sanctus and the two Agnus Dei movements, sometimes appearing as an ostinato, at other times as a motif to be developed, or used as a point of imitation.

The reason for the prominence of the antiphon incipit is not far to seek when we remember that the *Tomus secundus* is dedicated to Pedro Ponce de León. Standing as the work does, at the head of this section of the volume, it is clear that Esquivel intends this mass as an act of homage to his patron.

Seen as such, the work bears comparison with the 'homage' mass *Gloriose confessor Domini* in the *Liber primus*, which was discussed in Chapter 4. There it was argued that *Missa Gloriose* may be interpreted as a tribute to Don Pedro in his

31 Sonja S. Ingram, 'The Polyphonic *Salve Regina*, 1425–1550' (Ph.D. dissertation, University of North Carolina, 1973), p. 90.

role as a Dominican and a man of learning, an interpretation arrived at because of the learned techniques on display in the Osanna, and the repeated use of the head motif from Guerrero's source motet on which the mass is based. This motif is given particular emphasis through the ostinato treatment it receives in the Sanctus and Osanna.

In *Tu es Petrus*, the symbolism is even more overt, and similar erudition is on display in the Agnus Dei. In the first Agnus, the antiphon motif is quoted with its original text six times in all as an ostinato on two alternate pitches – G and D. In the second Agnus, where the number of voices is now increased to six with the addition of a second *altus*, the ostinato moves to *superius I* (again with original text) with the *tenor* in canon *sub diapente*; meanwhile, *superius II* pursues its own course with a part derived from *altus I* as a canon *in diatessaron*.

Thus, we have another display of learning in honour of the composer's patron: his very name is proclaimed while the master exercises his contrapuntal skills in his honour. But another interesting feature of this work is the fact that it may have been modelled on Morales's *Missa Tu es vas electionis*. As Robert Snow has pointed out, Morales's mass, which opens his *Missarum liber secundus* (Rome, 1544), was also dedicatory in intent, being dedicated to Pope Paul III. The pre-existing material in this case consists of a single phrase sung to a text containing the name of the dedicatee, 'Tu es vas electionis, sanctissime Paule'. This is utilised in the same manner as the opening phrase of Esquivel's *Missa Tu es Petrus*: in both cases, the dedicatory motif appears as a *cantus firmus* or as an ostinato sung with its original text, while at other times it provides source material for points of imitation.[32]

This is an important observation. Not only is it another example of the kind of compositional continuity that was typical of the Renaissance age – the passing on of certain techniques of construction from one generation to another – it is also a double tributary gesture: Esquivel, the servant, honours both the patron, and a master composer, Morales.

The *Missa quarti toni*, scored for the same forces as *Missa Tu es Petrus*, has a number of features setting it apart from other late Renaissance mass ordinaries.[33] In the first place, only the Gloria and Credo paraphrase chant melodies; the other three movements are based on original material. Secondly, the Credo paraphrases a chant in the first mode and not in mode 4 as implied by the work's title. Thirdly, the movements are of disproportionate length: the Kyrie extends to forty-three bars in transcription and is the longest of the mass ordinaries in the volume; the Sanctus is short, consisting of only the first section of the text – a mere eighteen bars in transcription; the Agnus Dei sets only the first invocation, yet is longer than average.

Taken together, these features suggest that perhaps the work is a compilation of separate movements written over a period of time rather than having been conceived as whole; or, perhaps under the pressure of other commitments, these disparate elements were hastily assembled when Esquivel required another mass to add to his collection. But the omission of part of the Sanctus can be explained by

32 Snow, *The 1613 Print*, p. 27, n. 22.
33 Ibid., p. 27.

the seventeenth-century tendency to shorten this choral section, perhaps to make way for the singing of a motet at this point,[34] and the second and third sections of the Agnus could have been sung to a familiar chant, or the first section repeated (with some textual adaptation). But why should a work given the title *quarti toni* contain a movement in mode 1? Or why should movements paraphrasing chant be combined with other movements which are not chant-based? There is no clear answer to these questions.

The contours of the melodic lines of the Kyrie are typical of mode 4 and the cadences on E and A are those associated with this mode, although the material does not appear to be chant-related. On the other hand, the Gloria most definitely is. The very simple chant formula which forms part of Mass XV in the *Liber usualis* appears in a slightly modified form, first in *superius I* and then, from *Qui tollis*, in *superius II*. (There is a printer's error on page 422 where the *superius I* reads *bassus* in the score.) The movement contains little contrapuntal movement, being best described as a simple harmonisation of the all-pervading chant, as Robert Snow observed when he first described this mass.[35] The Credo paraphrases a pre-existent chant in *superius I*; this time the source is a chant which appears as Credo IV in the *Graduale Romanum*. As in the Gloria, there is little contrapuntal movement: the parts move together in simultaneous declamation of the text. There is clearly a concern for textual clarity, and the absence of melismas is a characteristic of both movements.

Simplicity of style is the chief characteristic of both the Sanctus and Agnus Dei. There is no added voice in the Agnus, nor any attempt to write elaborate canons. These and other features lead to the opinion that the *Missa quarti toni* is perhaps the least interesting of Esquivel's mass settings: it is technically competent but displays little in the way of contrapuntal brilliance. It might be interpreted as a typical example of what was expected of any competent *maestro de capilla*. And yet, it does reveal one individual typical stylistic trait, one that we encountered in earlier chapters – a liking for parallel fourths, as at the beginning of the Gloria (Ex. 6.7).

In spite of Gioseffe Zarlino's strictures 'we ought also not to take two fourths in any composition whatever ... for the fourth is without a doubt a perfect consonance', examples of parallel fourths abound in Renaissance music.[36] But the really interesting feature here is the sharpening of both the F and the C in *altus* and *tenor* in bar two of Ex. 6.7. One might have expected only the F to be sharpened: instead a mild chromaticism is created by the presence of a C♯ and F♯. The chromatic alteration in these two parts is surprising in the context of a mode 4 mass since the composer clearly seeks to preserve the modal purity of the chant on which the movement is based by not inserting a sharp before the G in bar two of *superius I*.

This, and other examples of chromatic alteration in parallel-fourth movement, has caused one writer to say that this feature is 'a characteristic of the composer's

34 Ibid., p. 24.
35 Ibid., p. 28.
36 Zarlino, *Le istituzioni armoniche*, book 3, trans. in Strunk, *Source Readings*, p. 238.

Ex. 6.7. Gloria: *Missa quarti toni*, bars 1–3

mature style'.[37] It is certainly true to say that the progression occurs with some frequency throughout Esquivel's music (other examples include the hymn *Ave maris stella*, the Marian antiphons *Regina caeli* and *Salve Regina*, the Tract in both Requiems, and the motet *O vos omnes*), leading to the conclusion that the composer developed a preference for the sound – in effect a double leading note. However, there is a theoretical explanation for this procedure: 'what the theorists called "the law of the closest proximity"; any perfect consonance (unison, fifth or octave) should be preceded by the imperfect consonance nearest to it'.[38]

In each case, where Esquivel uses this progression, he is simply following these rules, which were no doubt instilled into him by his teacher. In the above case, the interval of the perfect fifth between *tenor* and *bassus* in bar three is preceded by a major third (the imperfect consonance nearest to it); the octave between *altus* and *bassus* is preceded by a major sixth (the imperfect consonance nearest to it). Put in another way: the bass moves down by a whole tone step; and the two upper parts move up by semitone steps to form a perfect consonance.

As the title indicates, the *Missa de Beata Virgine in Sabbato* was intended for use at the Marian votive mass usually celebrated every Saturday.

37 O'Connor, 'The Polyphonic Compositions on Marian Texts', p. 60.
38 See Rubio, *Classical Polyphony*, pp. 54–6, for a full discussion of this matter.

The idea of Saturday as a day of Marian devotion dates back to the Middle Ages. The theological principle is based on the notion that Jesus appeared to Mary on Saturday, the day after his death, as a reward for her steadfast faith in his divinity. Inherent in the principle there is also another tradition of devotional thought which suggests that the divine wisdom 'rested' on Mary as on a bed. Thus, Saturday, the Jewish Sabbath day, a day of rest, was considered a suitable day to honour the Blessed Virgin in the mass and Office; Saturday was Mary's Day, just as Sunday was the Lord's Day.[39]

The Saturday Marian liturgy was the work of many medieval theologians, among them the Benedictine monk, Alcuin (735–804). One of the principal architects of liturgical reform, he composed six formularies for votive masses, one for each day of the week. Later in the twelfth century, on the advice of Cardinal Peter Damien (1007–72), Hugh of Cluny (1024–1109) introduced a Saturday votive mass in honour of the Virgin,[40] while during the time of the first crusade Pope Urban II (c.1042–99) admonished the faithful to pray the Hours of the liturgy in honour of the most holy Virgin.[41]

The growth of devotion to Mary, and the custom of dedicating a Saturday mass to her, spread rapidly beyond the monastic cloisters throughout the whole of Western Christendom, resulting in numerous feasts and the institution of two additional offices: the *Officium parvum Sanctae Mariae*, and the *Officium Sanctae Mariae in Sabbato*. The *Missa de Beata Virgine* became a major genre in the sixteenth century; there are at least a hundred extant examples, among them works by Morales, Guerrero (two masses, 1566 and 1582), Victoria, Ruimonte, Vivanco and Esquivel.[42]

Esquivel's *Missa de Beata Virgine in Sabbato* is the shortest of his masses (Kyrie II is only seven bars in transcription) and has no Credo because this was not sung at a votive mass. As was customary throughout the sixteenth century when composing a Missa de Beata Virgine, Esquivel took his compositional material to a large extent from the chant of the mass ordinaries associated with the Virgin. Thus, the Kyrie and Gloria draw on material from Mass IX in the *Graduale* (*Cum jubilo*), while the Sanctus and Agnus Dei quote material from Mass XVII. Morales, Guerrero, Victoria, Ruimonte and Vivanco all used the same chant material in their polyphonic settings, so again Esquivel is continuing a well-established tradition.

References to the chant original are confined in the Kyrie to two motifs only; freely invented counterpoint works in harness with these in the accompanying parts. In the Gloria, on the other hand, the chant melody is predominantly in the *superius*, although it is also discernible in one or another part throughout. As in the *Missa quarti toni*, the Sanctus appears in a truncated form – 'Sanctus, Dominus

39 Jean Frisk, The Marian Library/International Marian Research Institute, Dayton, Ohio. This website offers useful information on the development of the cult of the Virgin Mary. See http://www.udayton.edu/mary/resources/firstsaturday.html

40 Ingram, 'The Polyphonic *Salve Regina*', p. 10.

41 Frisk, The Marian Library/International Marian Research Institute, Dayton, Ohio.

42 See Nors Josephson, 'The *Missa de Beata Virgine* of the Sixteenth Century' (Ph.D dissertation, University of California at Berkeley, 1970).

Deus Sabaoth' – twenty bars in transcription. Fragmentary motifs from the chant melody appear, but most of the movement is based on original material. It is interesting to note that, although perhaps entirely coincidental, the opening tenor motif bears a melodic resemblance to the opening of the tenor line in *Missa Gloriose confessor Domini*.

Motifs from the Agnus Dei chant of Mass XVII appear in both Esquivel's invocations, again in fragmentary form. For the second invocation Esquivel adds a fifth voice part, *superius secundus*: a *bassus* is to be derived canonically from this part according to the rubric 'Qui se humiliat exaltabitur. Duodecim'. This is a quotation from Luke 14: 11: 'Quia omnis qui se exaltat humiliabitur et qui se humiliat exaltabitur' ('Whoever exalteth himself shall be humbled; whoever humbles himself shall be exalted'). This may or may not have had some hidden symbolic significance, known only to Esquivel's singers, but the musical meaning is clear: the motion of falling and rising implicit in the imagery is symbolised in a mirror canon as the *bassus* inverts the *superius secundus*, as Ex. 6.8 demonstrates.

Ex. 6.8. *Missa de Beata Virgine in Sabbato*.
Beginning of the mirror canon, Agnus Dei II, bars 4–11

Perhaps a link with the Magnificat is intended here, this being a mass in honour of the Virgin. As we have seen, canons frequently had symbolic significance in the sixteenth century, and Jesus's words in Luke 14: 11 echo the words of Mary in Luke 1: 52: 'He hath put down the mighty from their seats, and exalted them of low degree'.

This example invites further comparison with similar instances of canonic writing in the works of Vivanco. As sophisticated as Esquivel's canonic device may seem, in effect it is a simple demonstration of a mirror canon, and is not as elaborate as Vivanco's canon in his *Missa de Beata Virgine*, just to take one example. There, at the head of the movement, there are instructions for an alternative Osanna for eight voices: 'Verte foliam et alteram videbis' ('Turn the leaf and you will see another'). In this alternative movement, obviously for expert singers, four parts are derived canonically from the part marked *bassus*. The fact that Vivanco's mass was published in the same year, and by the same printer as Esquivel's *Liber primus*, may have prompted the composer to show that he too was capable of continuing the Franco-Flemish puzzle canon tradition within the context of a mass; as he showed us in the canons of his first Magnificat cycle, he was certainly capable of constructing elaborate canons.

A three-voiced Marian motet, *Surge, propera, amica mea*, setting the text of Song of Songs 2: 13–14, follows the Agnus Dei on pages 466–9 of the print. The erotic verses, so rich in imagery, have long had Marian associations. and it is perhaps surprising that the composer does not feel the need to use a richer texture to express the sentiments of the text. The setting – the only known three-voiced motet he composed – is remarkably restrained; its scoring, SSB, is untypical of a Renaissance motet and may have been intended for the composer to sing with his boys. The absence of more colourful means of expressing this text may be indicative of a conservatism that prevailed in the cathedral of Ciudad Rodrigo, assuming the work was written during his time there; or it may be an early work introduced into this volume for more pragmatic reasons. Page 468 has the inscription at the top of the page, 'MOTETUM: Beatae Mariae cantandum in organo', perhaps suggesting that it could be sung on any Marian occasion, and the added instruction 'cantandum in organo' could indicate that Esquivel envisaged a vocal performance with organ.

The motet's presence in the print at this point suggests that it was probably intended to be sung after the Sanctus as an elevation motet. Although the modes of the two pieces do not match (the Sanctus is in a major mode, with a B♭ signature cadencing on C – *ambita* of *superius* and *tenor*, F–F; the motet is in mode 1 transposed, with a B♭ signature cadencing on G), the presence of a G in the *altus* of the Sanctus final chord would make a transition possible.[43]

The *Missa Hoc est praeceptum meum*, scored for SATB, has features in common with *Missa Tu es Petrus*: both masses are based on Office antiphons – in this case the first antiphon sung at Vespers on feasts of Apostles and Evangelists out of paschal time; both derive their motivic material from phrases from their respective antiphons; both make use of *cantus firmus* technique to give the chant prominence in places, but for different reasons.

In *Missa Hoc est praeceptum meum*, Esquivel draws on the entire chant for motivic material, not just the first line as in the *Missa Tu es Petrus*. Indeed, this

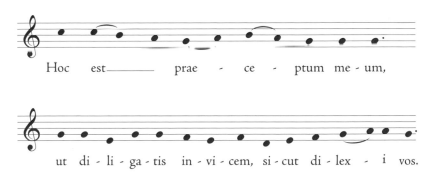

Ex. 6.9. The antiphon, *Hoc est praeceptum meum*

43 For a modern edition of this motet, transposed up a tone, see Mapa Mundi, Spanish Church Music 216, ed. Martyn Imrie.

use of the whole chant is the most significant feature of this mass, which in its construction follows conventional principles and is in no other way particularly out of the ordinary. It is short in length (there is no Hosanna) and concise in structure, with the minimum of text repetition and few long melismas. The antiphon is presented in Ex. 6.9.

The first phrase of the antiphon provides much of the motivic material for the Kyrie I and II; it appears in *cantus firmus* form a fourth higher in the *superius* of the Christe, and again in the *altus* of Kyrie II, this time a fifth higher but without the necessary sharp needed to produce an exact transposition. The Gloria, however, utilises the full chant with its original text at the opening of both sections. At 'Et in terra', Esquivel notates it in the *altus* under the mensuration sign Ø, the only time that he uses this sign in a mass; at 'Qui tollis', the antiphon appears in the *tenor*, again a fifth higher (without F$^\sharp$). *Cantus firmus* appears again in the Sanctus (tenor voice on G) and finally in the second Agnus Dei, where a *superius II*, floating above *superius I*, becomes the chant-bearing voice as the four voices are expanded to the customary five with the tenor derived from alto *in subdiatessaron*.

The prominence given to the chant in its entirety in every movement except the Credo is more than a clever technical device; its presence is symbolic. Like the Office chant, the mass, too, may have been intended for use on feast days commemorating apostles and evangelists. The antiphon text is taken from John 13: 34: 'A new commandment I give unto you, That ye love one another; as I have loved you'. The concept of divine love enshrined in these words, spoken by Jesus after the washing of the disciples' feet at the Last Supper and just before his conversation with Peter concerning the disciple's denial of the Lord, is at the heart of the Christian gospel. The disciples of Jesus were the first saints of the Christian Church so the prominence given to this text in this mass is a further reminder of the Last Supper – celebrated, of course, in the mass itself – and also calls to mind the first representatives in the long line of apostles and evangelists whose lives are celebrated on this feast day. Moreover, it emphasises an essential precept to be followed by all worshipping communities, including the canons of Ciudad Rodrigo; it could even be read as a gentle reprimand, given their petty quarrels reported in the chapter acts! The quotation of this particular chant in the context of mass of commemoration, then, seems highly appropriate and serves to underscore an important principle of Christianity as well providing Esquivel with a useful structural device.

It is not necessary to describe the two remaining mass ordinaries in great detail: they are both parody masses, and enough has already been said on this subject to indicate Esquivel's compositional procedures when reworking borrowed material. Both works have certain features in common: both are scored for four voices, with an expansion to five for the second Agnus Dei with a fifth part created by canonic procedure; both are relatively taut in construction, allowing little time for text repetition beyond the minimum; both employ conventional techniques in reworking borrowed material from a motet – in the first case a motet by Guerrero, and in the second by Rodrigo de Ceballos; both are in the same mode, mode I transposed by the B$^\flat$ signature.

Guerrero's bi-partite motet *Quasi cedrus*, from his *Sacrae cantiones* of 1555, has a text for the feast of the Assumption (15 August): Ecclesiasticus 24: 17–20 and Songs of Songs 4: 7–8. The motet provides Esquivel with a rich source of material, enabling him to draw motifs from both sections.

As we have previously observed, Esquivel does not follow the classic convention of beginning each movement of a parody mass with the same motivic material; he works in borrowed motifs rather than vertical structures. So, for example, the opening material of the motet, sung to the words 'Quasi cedrus exaltata sum' serves as the source for the first section of the Kyrie and Gloria; material from the beginning of the *secunda pars*, sung to the words 'Tota pulchra es, amica mea', is reworked for the beginning of the Credo and Sanctus; the phrases 'veni sponsa mea' and 'veni coronaberis', sung towards the end of the *secunda pars*, provide material for the beginning of the first Agnus Dei, while the second Agnus borrows the motif set to the word 'exaltata'. It is easy to see why Esquivel chose this motet as a source to quarry. Apart from its obvious richness of thematic material, it reflects yet again his admiration for Guerrero and his devotion to the Virgin Mary.

But if Guerrero was the composer Esquivel most admired – as seems to be the case, considering the number of times he borrowed techniques and materials from the older master – he must also have known and respected the works of Rodrigo de Ceballos, for it is to this master that he now turns for material for his final mass ordinary. Perhaps it was the seemingly widespread popularity of the motet *Hortus conclusus* which attracted him;[44] or maybe the musical quality of the work, or its Marian associations.

The one essential difference between this work and *Missa Quasi cedrus* is the fact that Esquivel – unusually for him – did observe the common convention of beginning all five movements with motivic material drawn from the opening of the motet. Finally, it is interesting to note a feature shared by both works; that is to say, the final cadence of Agnus Dei II in both *Hortus conclusus* and *Quasi cedrus* is identical – a *nota cambiata* figure appearing in the *superius* over a dominant in the *bassus*.

A brief polyphonic setting à4 (seven bars in transcription) of *Deo gratias*, and the response to the versicle *Ite missa est* concludes this section of the volume. Then follows music for the Office of the Dead in the following order: a four-part setting of a lesson from Matins, *Responde mihi*; the four-part *Missa pro defunctis* together with the final three versicles of the *Dies irae*; a setting, à5, of the Matins responsory, *Ne recorderis*, and finally the versicle *Requiescant in pace* and the *Amen* response.

---

44 The motet appears in at least four extant sources: Granada, Capilla Real, 'Archivo capitular', MS 3, 39*v*–44*r*; Seville, Catedral, 'Archivo capitular', MS 1, 87*v*–91*r*; Toledo, Catedral, 'Biblioteca capitular', MS 7, 9*v*–13*r*; Valladolid, Parroquia de Santiago, 'Archivo', MS s.n. (=Diego Sánchez codex), 4*r*–56*r*. See Snow, *The 1613 Print*, p. 32.

MUSIC FOR THE OFFICE FOR THE DEAD
AND THE *MISSA PRO DEFUNCTIS*

THE OFFICE FOR THE DEAD is primarily a prayer for the departed. It is clearly modelled on the liturgy for the last three days of Holy Week, the *triduum sacrum*, in that it omits anything that would be considered a sign of joy. It developed in a monastic context over a period of many years, and in its established form consisted of two parts: Vespers, commonly known as *Placebo*, from the words of the opening antiphon, *Placebo Domino in regione vivorum*; and Matins and Lauds, usually treated as a continuous Office.[45]

Matins for the Dead in the Roman Office is a much longer service than the night Office of Matins. It begins with the Invitatory antiphon *Regem cui omnia vivunt* and Psalm 94, *Venite exsultemus Domino*. Following this, the Office is divided into three identical sections called nocturns; each nocturn consists of a psalm with its antiphon, three lessons from the book of Job with their responsories,[46] and a versicle and response.[47]

Although the structure of these services was fixed well before the end of the sixteenth century, there was considerable variation throughout Spain in the texts used for individual items, which varied from diocese to diocese, especially in relation to the responsories and sometimes also in the lessons.[48] Most of these were replaced with a uniform liturgy conforming to the Roman Rite as mandated by the Council of Trent and as set out in Pope Pius V's *Breviarum Romanum*. Only churches which could prove that their liturgies were more than two hundred years old were allowed to maintain their traditions.[49]

In providing music for Matins for the Dead, Esquivel had to conform to the set texts. He chose texts from the second nocturn of the Office, the nocturn in the breviary of Clement VIII (1602) prescribed for votive celebrations on Tuesday and Friday.[50] As mentioned in Chapter 4, this suggests that his intention was to provide

45 Rowell, *The Liturgy of Christian Burial*, p. 66.

46 In an age when suffering and death were an everyday reality for many people, it is not surprising that the Book of Job was a familiar text. Job was venerated as a patron of those suffering various diseases, as well as the patron of musicians. See Wagstaff, 'Music for the Dead', pp. 14–15.

47 See the *Liber usualis*, pp. 1779–99, for texts of the various components of the service. As Rowell records, the final reform of the Roman funeral rite was carried out in the Ritual promulgated by Paul V in 1614, a ritual that was used until very recently in the Roman Church. See Rowell, *The Liturgy of Christian Burial*, pp. 71–2.

48 See Wagstaff, 'Music for the Dead', p. 16, where this issue is discussed in detail.

49 Richard Rutherford writes that, although Pope Paul V allowed greater freedom in his promulgation of the Roman Ritual of 1614, the Roman liturgical books ordered by the Council of Trent were considered normative practice. Certain consequences followed from this. As the liturgy became more a matter of correctly executing appropriate rites, funeral liturgy became more and more divorced from the harsh experience of death and from the pastoral care for the dying and the bereaved. In the minds of the faithful, 'pious practices like visits to the Blessed Sacrament and the rosary, as well as indulgences "for the poor souls" meant more than the funeral liturgy'. This 'became more a reliquary of faith, expressed in a very one-sided late medieval way'. See Rutherford, *The Death of a Christian: The Rite of Funerals*, pp. 87–9.

50 The rubrics from this breviary prescribe that on the day of burial either all three nocturns of

music to be sung at a weekly votive celebration of the liturgy for the dead that probably took place every Friday.

In setting these texts, Esquivel again followed well-established Spanish procedures. The four-part *Responde mihi* (Job 13: 22–8) – the first lesson of the second
nocturn – is sung simply in quasi-chordal manner, reflecting the essential features
of a lesson tone so that the words are clearly audible in accordance with the wishes
of the Council of Trent. The responsory *Ne recorderis* – which follows the third
and final lesson of the second nocturn – incorporates the chant into the *superius*.
In conformity with Spanish practice, only the initial words of each section of the
text are set polyphonically, leaving the remaining portions to be sung to chant.[51] The
setting concludes with the customary three versicles – *Kyrie eleison, Christe eleison,
Kyrie eleison.*

Finally, we come to the *Missa pro defunctis.* The general musical characteristics
of the Spanish Requiem Mass were pointed out in Chapter 4: the prominence of
chant; the use of long note values; the sombre, heavy textures. These are all features
which appear in the 1613 Requiem, which, unlike its predecessor, is complete in the
source.

In each of the three ordinary items, and also in the Tract, Esquivel locates the
specific chant melody in the *superius*, obviously using the same chant source as in
1608. Chant provides thematic material for the Offertory and Communion, shaping the melodic lines of all four parts. These more contrapuntal movements are
notated under C, as opposed to ₵, a customary distinction reflecting the fact that
movements under C move in long note values, tend to be less contrapuntal and
have a slower rate of harmonic change.

In commenting on this mass, Grayson Wagstaff has drawn attention to the conservative presentation of liturgical melodies, the representation of the contrasts
between the different portions of the chant, and the absence, except at the beginnings of items, of imitative treatment. Of the Introit and Kyrie he says 'the presentation of the chant melodies supported by very traditional contrapuntal lines
and consonant harmonic sonorities suggest that it could have been written by a
composer several generations earlier'.[52] This is undoubtedly true, as even a casual
glance at Morales's Requiem *à4*, representing the work of an earlier generation, and
Esquivel's work will confirm.

The most interesting feature of the 1613 Requiem is the inclusion of music setting the final section of the *Dies irae*: 'Lacrimosa dies illa, / Qua resurget ex favilla
/ Judicandus homo reus. / Huic ergo parce Deus. / Pie Jesu Domine / Dona eis
requiem. Amen.' Since there was no Spanish tradition of setting this text, which
only became an official part of the liturgy in Spain after 1570, Esquivel was breaking

---

Matins were to be said, or only the first. For votive celebrations, individual nocturns were assigned
to different days. The first nocturn was prescribed for Sunday, Monday and Thursday, the second
for Tuesday and Friday, and the third for Wednesday and Saturday. See Snow, *The 1613 Print*, p. 33.

51 See Snow, *The 1613 Print*, p. 34. The author sets out in detail the difference between Spanish
custom and that found elsewhere.

52 Wagstaff, 'Music for the Dead', p. 598.

new ground by including a polyphonic working.[53] The characteristic mood of serenity traditionally associated with the Spanish Requiem – achieved by the mainly stepwise melodic lines, limited uses of dissonance and slow rate of harmonic movement – is shattered by this brief but graphic reference to the Day of Judgement as the composer responds to the dramatic imagery of the text. By way of example, see Ex. 6.10, where the rising minor sixths in the lower voices of the opening section's paired entries are so effective in expressing the weeping that will occur on this terrible day; the same figure may also be interpreted as a rising again from the ashes to which the text goes on to refer.

Ex. 6.10. *Missa pro defunctis à4. Dies irae*, bars 1–5

The technique of paired entries is used again for 'Huic ergo parce Deus': beginning with the two lower voices moving in parallel thirds, the plea for mercy is heard several times before the movement comes to a gentle close.

Robert Snow has remarked that Esquivel may have included a polyphonic setting of this *Dies irae* in his volume possibly as an afterthought.[54] This may well be the case, given the lack of a Spanish tradition for setting this text; but we must also

53 There is, however, an anonymous Requiem located in a manuscript source in Valencia cathedral (ValenC 2), and possibly by the sixteenth-century choirmaster Gines Peres, which does contain a setting of the sequence. This is listed in Wagstaff, 'Music for the Dead', p. 603. Peres served at Valencia 1581–94, but as Wagstaff is careful to point out, traditions in Valencia may have been different from elsewhere – particularly those in Andalusia and Castile, where so many of the settings discussed in his dissertation were composed.

54 Snow, *The 1613 Print*, p. 35.

note the fact that it is notated in high clefs ('clavas altas transportados'), the only movement to be notated in this way.

It is also the only movement not chant-based, and therefore its pitch is not determined by any chant incipit. Using the freedom this gave him, Esquivel may have deliberately chosen to notate the music in high clefs for expressive reasons, as a means of drawing attention to the dramatic text. A performance based on pitch theories working on the principle of a downward transposition by the interval of a fourth obliterates much of the distinction, of course; but it is possible that performance at the high pitch indicated in the source was the composer's intention, for these reasons. However, even if transposition theories are accepted, the use of a C signature marks the movement out as being different. A faster rate of harmonic movement enables the composer to convey the sense of desperation implied by the text.

There are additional performance issues to be addressed in relation to this movement: at what point should it be included in the liturgy? Should it follow the Tract, with the missing preceding versicles of the *Dies irae* sung in plainchant?[55] Or should it be included as a para-liturgical addition?

We do not know what the practice was in Ciudad Rodrigo and so any answers to these questions are mere guesswork. A full performance of the *Dies irae*, with the addition of an appropriate chant for the missing versicles of the sequence, would be one answer; alternatively, the setting could stand on its own and be given a performance at some appropriate point in a service on some special memorial occasion.

If any proof were needed as to how well Esquivel could respond to the demands of text setting, it can be found in these final three verses of the *Dies irae*. Using the conventional techniques at his disposal, he sets the desperate plea for forgiveness, 'spare this one, O God', succinctly and with emotional restraint. There is no denying the dramatic power of this music. Together with the other works that make up the *Tomus secundus*, this mass marks the composer as a worthy representative of the Spanish cathedral tradition in the Golden Age.

55 See my edition of this work, Mapa Mundi, Spanish Church Music 87 (1996), where the Lacrimosa, transposed down a fourth, appears between Tract and Offertory.

7

CONCLUSIONS

THIS STUDY has attempted to outline the facts of Esquivel's life as far as they can be ascertained, and has examined in some depth the characteristics of the master's compositional technique as demonstrated in his three known publications. What conclusions can be drawn concerning his place in the history of Spanish Church music and his standing as a composer within that tradition?

If quantity of works alone were to be regarded as a measure of a composer's skill, then Esquivel would score highly: eleven mass ordinaries, two Requiem masses, seventy-two motets, eight psalms, thirty hymns, sixteen Magnificat settings, four Marian antiphons and further additional items for use in Matins, Lauds and Compline and in Masses for the Dead. This is a substantial body of material – a rich legacy. But there are still questions that remain: how good a composer was Esquivel, and where does he stand in the hierarchy of composers of his time? In order to find an answer to these questions, we look first at the writings of contemporary Renaissance theorists.

Regrettably, they are remarkably silent when it comes to offering criteria for critical appraisal of the music of their time. They recognise the achievements of composers we admire greatly today – Josquin, Morales, Palestrina, Lassus, and many more – but their vocabulary tends to lack precise meaning, as does that used by fellow-writers when offering a critique of the visual art of the period. In the latter case, for example, we find paintings described as having a 'virile air' (*aria virile*), or a 'good air' (*bona aria*); as being 'very sweet' (*molto dolce*); or they are done with the 'best method' (*optima regione*) and 'complete proportion' (*integra proportione*).[1] These descriptors are useful as a means of recording personal impressions, but they are subjective and say nothing of the technique employed to create the paintings viewed.

Similar terminology pervades writings on music, and offers little help when we are seeking to establish contemporary criteria for assessment. However, one Italian theorist, Lodovico Zacconi, does offer descriptors which are more helpful in making judgements.[2]

---

1 These are all terms used by an agent of the duke of Milan around 1470 when seeking to report back to his master on the qualities of paintings by Botticelli, Filippino Lippi, Perugino, and Ghirlandaio. See Michael Baxandall, *Painting and Experience in Fifteenth-Century Italy* (Oxford, 1972), pp. 26–7.

2 Lodovico Zacconi was born in Pesaro in 1555 and died in 1627. He was ordained priest at Pesaro in 1575 and later studied with Andrea Gabrieli in Venice. As a theorist, his most important

In the second part of his *Prattica di musica*, published in 1622, he records topics of a conversation held in 1584 with, among others, the composer and theorist Gioseffo Zarlino. Through the words of Zarlino he touches on certain characteristics of musical compositions which, although not intended to be read as criteria for assessing quality, do go further than the vague qualitative comments sometimes found in contemporary descriptions of musical works. The distinguished American scholar, James Haar, has examined Zarlino's conversational record in some detail and has suggested that 'Zacconi's criteria . . . represent a genuine effort at combining technical analysis with aesthetic judgment'.[3]

Zacconi set out seven characteristics of what he termed *musica armoniale*, and gave examples of Renaissance composers known to him whose music possessed one or other of these. Here is the relevant passage:

> I say that *musica armoniale* [polyphonic music] is distinguished by seven particular aspects: that is, by *arte, modulatione, diletto, tessitura, contraponto, inventione*, and *buona dispositione*. Each of these things is necessary to the composer; and to however small or great a degree one finds them in one composer, a single quality will stand out more than another, and from this a composer will make his name and become famous.[4]

There are echoes of Quintilian in his classification, as Haar points out, and the orator's standard five divisions of oratory may have suggested the idea of classification in music to Zacconi; moreover, the terms *arte, diletto* and *modulatione* are found in Quintilian's work.

Although we may debate what precisely each of these terms means, Haar attempts to interpret Zarlino's terminology in a way which is both insightful and helpful when offering criteria by which to judge Esquivel's music.

Arte may be understood as skill in planning; the skilful manipulation of the materials of music.

Modulatione to the sixteenth-century theorist meant measured, or mensurally organised, melody. It would seem, therefore, that beauty of melodic line was a feature to be judged and admired.

Diletto implies that music, like oratory, should give pleasure.

Tessitura is a puzzling term. Given Zacconi's use of the verb *tessere* (to weave), Haar suggests it implies the interweaving of materials; the practical art of contrapuntal writing. It does not refer to vocal range, the way we use the term today.

Contraponto has a specific meaning: it is the writing of a counterpoint over a *cantus firmus*.

---

work was the *Prattica di musica*, published in two parts (Venice, 1592, 1622).

3 James Haar, 'A Sixteenth-Century Attempt at Music Criticism', in Paul Corneilson, ed., *The Science and Art of Renaissance Music* (New Jersey, 1998), pp. 3–19.

4 *Prattica di Musica Seconda Parte. Divisa, e distinta in Quattro Libri. Ne quali primieramente si tratta de gl'Elementi Musicali; cioè de primi principij come necessarij alla tessitura e formatione delle Compositioni armoniali* . . . (Venice, 1622; repr. Bologna, 1967), pp. 49–50. This is the translation printed in Haar, 'A Sixteenth-Century Attempt at Music Criticism', p. 4. Haar gives the Italian text of the whole of this famous passage on pp. 14–15, n. 6.

Inventione means either the product of imaginative creation in general, or some single idea. It is a term which overlaps with Zacconi's final category, *buona dispositione*. This seems to be an umbrella term which covers the good ordering of a range of musical materials, among them melody, rhythm, mode, texture, cadence formation and counterpoint.

In summary, then, we have a set of criteria for the evaluation of a Renaissance musical work, even if that may not have been Zacconi's original intention.

If it is to be regarded as good music, a piece will be artfully planned with fine melodies, and will give pleasure to singers and listeners; its contrapuntal lines should be well meshed, and where appropriate be based on a *cantus firmus*; its materials should be fresh and imaginative, and ordered melodically and contrapuntally in such a way as to create satisfying sonorities.[5]

If we read Zacconi correctly, not all Renaissance composers exhibited in their music all the above qualities in equal measure. Zacconi singles out Willaert for his *arte* and *dispositione*; Lassus for his *arte* and *bonissima inventione*; Palestrina for his *arte*, *contraponto*, *ottima dispositione* and *una sequente modulatione* – the much praised smoothly sculpted melodic lines that have been admired for centuries, but are not universally present in all sixteenth-century music. Morales, the only Spanish composer mentioned by Zacconi, combines *arte* with *contraponto* in his layout of chant *cantus firmi* and also writes good tunes. His Magnificats are singled out for praise for these reasons.[6]

Zacconi's examples, of course, are drawn from works by composers known to him, those whose music was admired beyond their native country. It is highly unlikely that he would have known any of Esquivel's works since there is no evidence that they reached Italy. Nevertheless, since Esquivel was his contemporary and wrote in what we now refer to as the 'High Renaissance' style, there is no reason why Zacconi's criteria should not be applied to the composer's music.

As we saw in Chapter 3, the only contemporary appraisal we have of Esquivel's music is that of Vicente Espinel, whose approbation of the *Tomus secundus* praises the music in terms which translate as its qualities of 'gentle harmony' (*apacible consonancia*) and its 'elegant craftsmanship' (*gentil artificio*), and it is music which, he says, is 'well cast' (*buena casta*).

Some of these attributes can be matched with some from Zacconi's list. Thus, for Espinel's *gentil artificio*, we might read Zacconi's *arte*; in place of *música buena casta*, we might read *buena dispositione*, or possibly *tessitura*. An Italian parallel might be Vincenzo Galilei's accolade in praise of Alessandro Striggio, whose compositions he described as *ben tessute*.[7]

These, then, are some of the qualities of Esquivel's music which his contemporaries may well have admired. We may wish to use different and more precise

5 This is a summary of Haar's discussion and interpretation of Zacconi's work. See Haar, 'A Sixteenth-Century Attempt at Music Criticism', pp. 8–13, for a full discussion.

6 Ibid., pp. 12–13. Haar points to the popularity of Morales's Magnificats ; a dozen editions appeared between 1542 and 1614.

7 Ibid., p. 18 n. 81.

terminology today, and we may wish to add additional criteria; for example, we may wish to comment on the composer's sensitivity to his text, since a concern for text expression was such a key issue in the Renaissance. But before we make our own critical judgements, it is essential for us in our day to be aware of the historic criteria used when we evaluate music of an earlier time; we must take care to avoid using certain critical instruments from a later period, some of which may be invalid when it comes to offering a critique of sixteenth-century music.

Prior to recent studies, the only reliable twentieth-century appraisals of Esquivel's music, based on knowledge of all three volumes of his work, were those of Robert Snow[8] and Robert Stevenson.[9] Previous attempts at critical appraisal, by Higinio Anglés and Howard Mayer Brown, were unreliable because they were not based on first-hand knowledge of all three volumes of printed music; Esquivel was seen as a second-rate composer.[10] Transcriptions of Esquivel's music only began to appear in the 1950s, when Samuel Rubio included seven of Esquivel's motets in his *Antología polifónica sacra*.[11] To these seven, we can now add a relatively small, but growing, number of publications (see Appendix); moreover, transcriptions of seventy-one of Esquivel's seventy-two motets can been seen in part two of Francisco Rodilla León's *El libro de motetes de 1608 de Juan Esquivel de Barahona*.[12]

Robert Stevenson describes Esquivel as 'one of the most prolific, and also one of the finest Spanish composers of his time'. He argues that 'his motets stand comparison with those of Victoria on the same texts'.[13]

Snow acknowledges that the composer's technical skills were considerable, citing as evidence the great variety of canonic devices found in the final verses of his Magnificat odd-numbered verse settings, and his reworking of borrowed material in his parody masses. Snow is lukewarm, however, on the subject of Esquivel's sensitivity to the Latin of his texts. He suggests that the composer could write highly distinctive melodic lines for the beginnings of text phrases, but was less successful in extending these lines into accompanying 'countersubjects'; occasionally, these 'are somewhat less felicitous in their relationship to the text'.[14] Unfortunately, he gives no examples to support his claim.

In Snow's opinion, not all Esquivel's work was consistently of the highest quality, a view which is endorsed by the present study. Nevertheless, he was, undoubtedly, a fine craftsman. Some of his motets take economy to extremes, giving them an

---

8 Snow, *The 1613 Print*.

9 Robert Stevenson, 'Esquivel Barahona, Juan (de)', in *The New Grove Dictionary of Music and Musicians*, 2nd edn, VIII, pp. 325–6.

10 In 1968, Higinio Anglés placed Esquivel after Victoria, describing him as 'a lesser worthy'; in 1976, Howard Mayer Brown used the phrase 'a lesser composer' to describe Esquivel. See Higinio Anglés, 'Latin Church Music on the Continent – 3', in Gerald Abraham, ed., *The New Oxford History of Music*, IV (London, 1968), pp. 405–6; Brown, *Music in the Renaissance*, p. 314,

11 *Antología polifónica sacra*, 2 vols., ed. Samuel Rubio (Madrid, 1954–6). These volumes contained the motets (1608): *Veni Domine, Gloria in excelsis, Emendemus in melius, O vos omnes, Ego sum panis, Exaltata sum* and *O quam gloriosum*.

12 Rodilla León's *El libro de motetes de 1608*, pp. 253–548.

13 Robert Stevenson, in *The New Grove Dictionary*, VIII, pp. 325–6.

14 Snow, *The 1613 Print*, p. 36.

almost perfunctory quality; but, as we saw in Chapter 5, external influences may account for this tendency to some extent. Some of his settings lack the brilliance of those of his contemporaries. For example, Anthony Petti has commented on Esquivel's setting of *Duo seraphim*, which, though 'expressive and delicate', as he describes it, cannot rival the brilliance of Victoria's four-part equal-voice setting.[15] It is, however, like so many other motets, a soundly crafted work. What is lacking in some of his motets is the surety of design which we find in the works of Guerrero, for example, where finely balanced proportions, and a series of well-placed intermediate cadences, appear to lead in a seamless and almost inevitable manner to a natural close. In comparison, some of Esquivel's motets are modally ambiguous and lose their sense of direction through the addition of accidentals foreign to the mode. Occasionally, his part-writing, too, can be clumsy.

But for whatever reason historians have placed Esquivel in a lower rank, there can be no doubt as to his position as a major provider of new musical material for the post-Tridentine Church. His music fully embodies the spirit of the Counter-Reformation and is carefully organised to reflect this. His motets, for example, form a near-complete cycle for the Church year and are clearly designated and calendrically ordered – a characteristic common to many motet collections after Trent;[16] modest in scope, they are realistic in the demands they make on singers and may have been deliberately written with the limited musical resources of smaller institutions in mind. His masses are a major contribution to the genre in the way in which they match Trent's requirements for textual clarity and freedom from impurities (i.e. the absence of secular melodies). The one exception to this is, of course, the composer's use of thematic material from Janequin's chanson *La guerre* in the *Missa Batalla* of 1608; but in using material from this work he is, as we have seen, in good company since Guerrero and Victoria followed the same course.

Interestingly, Janequin's well-known chanson was almost certainly one of the works which the committee appointed to gather examples of 'abuses of the mass', to be presented to the twenty-second session of the Council in 1562, had in mind. A note on music was presented to the papal legates on 8 August and cited, as examples of 'lascivious' works which had found their way into the mass, those *della caccia* and *la battaglia*.[17]

The huge volume of 1613 certainly had the Council's requirements in view and,

15 Anthony G. Petti, *The Fourteenth Chester Book of Motets*, VI (London, 1982), p. 43.

16 Todd Borgerding cites two Italian examples: Luca Marenzio, *Motectorum pro festis totius anni* (Venice,1585); Guglielmo Gonzaga, *Sacrae cantiones quinque vocum in festis duplicibus maioribus ecclesiae sanctae Barbarae* (Venice, 1583). See Borgerding, 'The Motet and Spanish Religiosity', p. 26.

17 See Monson. 'The Council of Trent Revisited', p. 8. Monson compares this comment with a reference to *La battaglia* in Vincentino's *L'antica musica ridotta alla moderna prattica* published in 1555. Vicentino was complaining about this secular profanity, as he saw it, as the following quotation shows: 'Some compose a Mass upon a madrigal or upon a French chanson, or upon *La battaglia*, and when such pieces are heard in church they cause everyone to laugh, for it almost seems as if the temple of the Lord had become a place for the utterance of bawdy and ridiculous texts – as if it had become a theater, in which it is permissible to perform all sorts of music of buffoons, however ridiculous and lascivious' (Lewis Lockwood, ed., *Palestrina: Pope Marcellus Mass* (New York, 1975), p. 17).

as we saw in Chapter 3, met the requirements of the newly reformed breviary issued in 1602. It is a model of pragmatism, and the large number of hymns for the Tridentine rite, the psalm settings, Magnificats and other miscellaneous items, all meet the liturgical needs of the Counter-Reformation Church in Spain, and the Church in the New World, where the adopted model was plainsong and liturgical polyphony from central Europe.

Given this fact, it is perhaps surprising that there is no direct evidence to suggest that his music was sung in Mexico or Guatemala, in marked contrast to music by his contemporaries and forebears. Perhaps the presence today of a copy of the *Motecta festorum* in the Hispanic Society of New York City is evidence of its use in the Spanish colonies in an earlier time; its worn state certainly shows evidence of heavy use at some time.[18]

Esquivel's contribution to music of the Golden Age, then, if not unique, was significant, and may be more so than was once realised, for his music reveals a number of personal stylistic traits not found in the music of all composers working around the turn of the century. This is a point which is insightfully touched on once again by Robert Snow. In the final paragraph of his 1978 monograph, he writes as follows:

> Perhaps the most interesting aspect of Esquivel's music from the standpoint of the historian is the conflict often to be found in it between its technical vocabulary and that which it seems to wish to express. The technical vocabulary is, of course, that of the late Renaissance but the expressive intent frequently seems to be that of an incipient Baroque spirit, particularly in a number of the motets. Esquivel's effort to solve this problem was limited to the introduction of a mild chromaticism similar to that to be found in the music of a number of Italian composers active some three or four decades earlier. The spirit of the place and age in which he worked made nothing else possible. It is equally to Esquivel's credit, however, that he seems to have sensed this new spirit, which was not to come to full fruition in Spanish music, more strongly than did most of his contemporaries.[19]

Several examples of what Snow calls 'mild chromaticisms' have been given throughout this book, and now that more of his music is available for study, we can see the full extent of these. They do indeed lend to his music a touch of individuality. Although they do not saturate his works, and are a great deal less daring than the chromaticisms of many Italian composers to whom Snow refers, they nevertheless occur with some frequency.

---

18 The music of Spanish musicians figured prominently in the newly established Church in Guatemala. For example, the Lilly Library of Indiana University houses a manuscript of Guatemalan provenance containing works by, among others, Peñalosa, Escobedo, Anchieta, Basurto, Escobar and Morales. Of composers of a later generation, works by Guerrero feature prominently in manuscripts in the archives of Guatemala cathedral. See Robert J. Snow, 'Music by Francisco Guerrero in Guatemala', *Nasarre* 3 (1987), pp. 153–202, for further details. See also Stevenson, *Renaissance and Baroque Musical Sources*, for further discussion of the Guatemalan archival material and other sources.

19 Snow, *The 1613 Print*, p. 36.

Esquivel has been described as a 'mannerist',[20] a term borrowed from visual art, and a term used by Ivan Moody in connection with the harmonic 'eccentricities' of the early-seventeenth-century composers Cardoso, Magalhães and Lôbo.[21]

'Mannerism' has been a term much debated by art historians; it can be used as a derogatory term, of course, and in this sense is best avoided. But in a positive sense, construed as 'an extension of the ideals of the High Renaissance',[22] it can be useful. Moody argues that the technical basis of Cardoso's harmonic language is indisputably that of the late Renaissance period (the 'High Renaissance') and that any 'eccentricities' are merely extensions in the same spirit.

This is what Snow implies with reference to Esquivel in the paragraph quoted above. Although Cardoso's music leans even more strongly towards the new emerging trends of the seventeenth century, some of his harmonic colourings are not dissimilar to those found in Esquivel's music. By way of illustration, note the augmented triad resulting from the part-writing in bar two of Ex. 7.1.[23]

Many examples of Esquivel's chromaticisms have been given throughout the preceding chapters. Esquivel goes further than the raising of the leading-note at cadences, which, as is well-known, was common practice at the end of the sixteenth

Ex. 7.1. Cardoso: Introit, *Missa pro defunctis*, opening

20 O'Connor, 'The Polyphonic Compositions on Marian Texts', p. 96.

21 Ivan Moody, 'Portuguese "Mannerism": A Case for an Aesthetic Inquisition', *Early Music* 23 (1995), pp. 451–8.

22 H. Honour and J. Fleming, *A World History of Art* (London, 1982), p. 379, cited in Moody, 'Portuguese "Mannerism"', p. 452.

23 A modern edition of Cardoso's *Missa pro defunctis* is to be found in Mapa Mundi, Spanish and Portuguese Church Music 77, transcr. and ed. Ivan Moody.

century; like Victoria, he adds an increasing number of accidentals – accidentals not required by the rules of *musica ficta* – as a colouristic nuance. He has a particular liking for parallel fourths with their double leading-note effect as they approach a perfect consonance; harmonically, he occasionally indicates an augmented sixth by signing a flat in the bass and a sharp in an upper voice (for example, B♭ and G♯ in the motet *In illo tempore*). If these are examples of 'mannerism' in the true sense, then Esquivel is indeed a mannerist.[24]

But, in spite of these tendencies, his roots are firmly in the past: his technique is fashioned out of the techniques of Franco-Flemish polyphony as it developed in Spain; he has respect for the modes and, of course, a deep reverence for plainchant. His working methods are those common to all Spanish Church composers in the generation after Trent – they could not be otherwise if his music was to be accepted by the Church – and he successfully combined the roles of pragmatist and craftsman.

Although Esquivel's music may be seen today to be variable in quality, at its best it is worthy to stand alongside the work of those masters of the Golden Age whose music is now accepted as part of the Western canon. Without a knowledge of his contribution to the field, our understanding of late-sixteenth-century sacred polyphony in that part of Spain where he worked would be considerably impoverished and our total view of the Spanish school greatly diminished. Musically and historically, his contribution to his art is significant, and his music, much admired in his own time for its 'gentle harmonies' and solid craftsmanship, is worthy of greater consideration in the twenty-first century. If we fail to recognise his achievements, and those of other composers like him whose works have yet to be transcribed and made available to a wider public, we fail to do justice to men who faithfully preserved their musical and spiritual inheritance, who sought through music to communicate their faith and the faith of their Church to a wider world. In an age of doubt and turmoil, we can find some security in the timeless nature of the liturgy and an affirmation of faith through music. We cannot afford to ignore the music of men like Esquivel if we are to understand and preserve our spiritual and musical inheritance.

---

24 Not all scholars recognise this term as applied to Spanish Golden Age music. For example, no less a figure than José López-Calo states categorically that he cannot see how the term, borrowed from the visual arts, can be applied to music. See López-Calo, *Historia de la música española 3. Siglo XVII*, p. 10. Louise Stein, echoing the thoughts of López-Calo, is no less categorical when she states that 'Spanish music did not go through a Mannerist phase, nor did a particular musical publication, a specific controversy or the work of any composer around the turn of the century represent a challenge to the late Renaissance aesthetic'. Price, *The Early Baroque Era from the Late Sixteenth Century to the 1660s*, p. 327.

APPENDIX

MODERN EDITIONS OF MUSIC BY ESQUIVEL

Antología polifónica sacra, 2 vols., ed. Samuel Rubio (Madrid, 1954–6). Contains the following motets (1608); *Veni Domine, Gloria in excelsis, Emendemus in melius, O vos omnes, Ego sum panis vivus, Exaltata sum, O quam gloriosum.*

Mapa Mundi Renaissance Performing Scores. Series A: Spanish Sacred Music (London and Marvig, Isle of Lewis).

Publications to date include the following:

Motets: *Sancta Maria, Veni Domine, Vox clamantis in deserto, In paradisum, Ego sum panis vivus, O vos omnes, O Crux benedicta, Surge propera.*

Missa pro defunctis, ed. Clive Walkley (1996).

Missa Ave Virgo sanctissima, ed. Clive Walkley (2003).

Four Hymns (*Christe Redemptor omnium, Hostis Herodes impie, Vexilla Regis prodeunt, Pange lingua*), ed. Clive Walkley and Bruno Turner (2004).

Missa Gloriose confessor Domini, ed. Clive Walkley (forthcoming).

The Chester Books of Motets. 16 vols., ed. Anthony G. Petti (London, 1977–82): *Duo seraphim* (vol. XVI), *Ego sum panis vivus* (vol. III), *Repleti sunt omnes* (vol. X).

BIBLIOGRAPHY

Aguirre Ricón, Soterraña, 'The Formation of an Exceptional Library: Early Printed Music Books at Valladolid Cathedral', *Early Music* 37 (2009), pp. 379–99.

Aldea, Quintín, *et al.*, eds., *Diccionario de historia eclesiástica de España*, 4 vols (Madrid, 1972–5).

Aldrich, Putnam, 'An Approach to the Analysis of Renaissance Music', *The Music Review* 30 (1969), pp. 10–21.

Andrews, H. K., *An Introduction to the Technique of Palestrina* (London, 1958).

Anglés, Higinio, *La música española desde la edad media hasta nuestros dias* (Barcelona, 1941).

Anglés, Higinio, *Diccionario de la música labor* (Barcelona, 1954).

Anglés, Higinio, 'Latin Church Music on the Continent – 3', in Gerald Abraham, ed., *The New Oxford History of Music* IV (London, 1968), pp. 372–418.

Anglés, Higinio, 'Esquivel', in *Die Musik in Geschichte und Gegenwart* (Kassell und Basel, 1954), pp. 1538–42.

Anglés, Higinio, 'Early Spanish Musical Culture and Cardinal Cisneros's Hymnal of 1515', in Jan LaRue, ed., *Aspects of Medieval and Renaissance Music. A Birthday Offering to Gustave Reese* (New York, 1966), pp. 8–16.

Apel, Willi, *Gregorian Chant* (London, 1958).

Apel, Willi, *Harvard Dictionary of Music* (Cambridge, MA, 1966).

Araiz, Martinez, *Historia de la música religiosa en España* (Barcelona, 1942).

Arias, Enrique, 'Canonic Usage in the Masses of Sebastián de Vivanco', *Anuario musical* 41 (Barcelona, 1986), pp. 135–45.

Arias, Enrique, 'The Masses of Sebastián de Vivanco (*c.*1550–1622): A Study of Polyphonic Settings of the Ordinary in Late Renaissance Spain' (Ph.D dissertation, North Western University, 1971).

Arias dell Valle, Raul, 'El magisterio de capilla de la catedral de Oviedo en el siglo XVI (1508–1597)', *Studium Ovetense* 6–7 (1978–80), pp. 128–32.

Atlas, Allan W., *Renaissance Music: Music in Western Europe, 1400–1600* (New York and London, 1998).

Attwater, Donald, *The Penguin Dictionary of Saints* (London, 1965; repr. 1983).

Barrios Manzano, Maria del Pilar, 'La música en la catedral de Coria (Cáceres) (1590–1755)' (Ph.D dissertation, University of Extremadura, 1993).

Bécares, Vicente, *Aspectos de la producción y distribución del nuevo rezado*, in Ian Fenlon and Tess Knighton, eds., *Early Music Printing and Publishing in the Iberian World* (Kassel, 2006), pp. 1–22.

Bermudo, Juan, *Declaración de instrumentos músicales* (Osuna, 1555). Facs. edn, ed. Marcario Santiago Kastner (Kassel, 1957).

Bernadó, Márius, 'The Hymns of the *Intonarium Toletanum* (1515): Some Peculiarities', *Cantus Planus, Papers Read at the 6th Meeting of the International Musicological Society Study Group* (Budapest, 1995), pp. 367–96.

Bilinkoff, Jodi, *The Avila of Saint Teresa. Religious Reform in a Sixteenth-Century City* (Ithaca and London, 1989).

Bombi, Andrea, Juan José Carreras and Miguel Ángel Marín, eds., *Música y cultura urbana en la edad moderna* (Valencia, 2005).

Borgerding, Todd Michael, 'The Motet and Spanish Religiosity ca. 1550–1610' (Ph.D. dissertation, University of Michigan, 1997).

Boyd, Malcolm, 'Structural Cadences in the Sixteenth-Century Mass', *The Music Review* 33 (1972), pp. 1–13.

Brothers, Lester C., 'Avery Burton and his Hexachord Mass', *Musica disciplina* 28 (1974), pp. 153–76.

Brothers, Lester C., 'New Light on an Early Tudor Mass: Avery Burton's *Missa ut re me fa sol la*', *Musica disciplina* 32 (1978), pp. 111–26.

Brown, Howard M., 'Emulation, Competition and Homage: Imitation and Theories of Imitation in the Renaissance', *Journal of the American Musicological Society* 25 (1982), pp. 1–48.

Brown, Howard M., *Music in the Renaissance* (Englewood Cliffs, 1976; 2nd edn, with Louise K. Stein, Upper Saddle River, 1999).

Brown, Jonathan, *The Golden Age of Painting in Spain* (New Haven and London, 1991).

Bruner, G. Edward, 'Editions and Analysis of Five *Missa Beata Virginis Maria* by the Spanish composers Morales, Guerrero, Victoria, Vivanco and Esquivel' (Ph.D. dissertation, University of Illinois Urbana, 1980).

Burmeister, Joachim, *Musical Poetics*, trans. Benito V. Rivera, ed. Claude V. Palisca (New Haven and London, 1993).

Call, Jerry, 'Spanish and Portuguese Cathedral Manuscripts', in Stanley Sadie, ed., *The New Grove Dictionary of Music and Musicians* (London, 2001), XXIII, pp. 927–9.

Cantor, Montague, 'The Liber magnificarum of Sebastián de Vivanco' (Ph.D. dissertation, New York University, 1967).

Casares Rodicio, Emilio, *La música en la catedral de Oviedo* (Oviedo, 1980).

Casares Rodicio, Emilio, ed., *Diccionario de la música española e hispanoamericana* (Madrid, 1999).

Casares, E., and C. Villanueva, eds., *De musica hispana et aliis, miscellánea en honor al Profesor José Lopez-Calo, S.J., en su 65 cumpleaños* (Santiago de Compostela, 1990)

Census-Catalogue of Manuscript Sources of Polyphonic Music, 1400–1550. Renaissance Manuscript Studies (Neuhausen and Stuttgart, 1979–88).

Cerone, Pietro, *El melopeo y maestro* (Naples, 1613). Book xii trans. in Oliver Strunk, *Source Readings in Musical History* (New York, 1950), pp. 262–73.

Chase, Gilbert, *The Music of Spain* (New York, 1941; repr. 1959).

Christian Jr, William A., *Local Religion in Sixteenth-Century Spain* (Princeton, 1981).

Christoforidis, M., and J. Ruiz Jiménez, 'Manuscrito 975 de la Biblioteca de Manuel de Falla: una nueva fuente polifónica de siglo XVI', *Revista de musicología* 17 (1994), pp. 499–504.

Cifre, E. (ed.), *Antología coral* (Madrid, 1979). Contains *Gloria in excelsis* taken from *Antología polifónica sacra*, ed. Samuel Rubio.

Coates, Henry, *Palestrina* (London, 1938).

Cornides, A., 'Liturgy of Requiem Mass', in *New Catholic Encyclopedia* (New York, 1967), XII, p. 384.

Crawford, David, and G. Grayson Wagstaff, eds., *Encomium Musicae: Essays in Memory of Robert J. Snow* (Hillsdale, NY, 2002).

Cruz, Anne J., and Mary E. Perry, eds., *Culture and Control in Counter-Reformation Spain* (Minneapolis, 1992).

Cummings, Anthony M., 'Toward an Interpretation of the Sixteenth-Century Motet', *Journal of the American Musicological Society* 34 (1981), pp. 43–59.

Daniel-Rops, H., *The Catholic Reformation*, trans. John Warrington (New York and London, 1962).

Dean, Jeffrey, 'Listening to Sacred Music c.1500', *Early Music* 25 (1997), pp. 611–36.

Dedieu, Jean P., '"Christianization" in New Castile: Catechism, Communion, Mass, and Confirmation in the Toledo Archbishopric, 1540–1650', in Anne J. Cruz and Mary E. Perry, eds., *Culture and Control in Counter-Reformation Spain* (Minneapolis, 1992), pp. 1–25.

Delumeau, Jean, *Catholicism between Luther and Voltaire: A New View of the Counter-Reformation* (London, 1977).

Dickinson, Edward, *Music in the History of the Western Church* (New York, 1902; repr. 1969).

Eire, Carlos M. N., *From Madrid to Purgatory: The Art and Craft of Dying in Sixteenth-Century Spain* (Cambridge, 1995).

Eisenhofer, Ludwig, and Joseph Lechner, *The Liturgy of the Roman Rite*, trans. A. J. and E. F. Peeler, ed. H.E. Winstone (Edinburgh and London, 1961).

Elders, Willem, *Studien zur Symbolik in der Musik der alten Niederlander*. Utrechtse bijdragen tot de muziekwetenschap (Utrecht, 1968).

Elders, Willem, *Symbolic Scores: Studies in the Music of the Renaissance* (Leiden, 1994).

Elustiza, Juan B. de, and D. Gonzalo Castrillo Hernández, *Antología musical: siglo de oro de la música liturgica de España* (Barcelona, 1933).

Erasmus, Desiderius, *Praise of Folly*, trans. Betty Radice, introduction and notes by A. H. T. Levi (Harmondsworth, 1971).

Evennett, H. Outram, 'Counter-Reformation Spirituality', in John Bossy, ed., *The Spirit of the Counter-Reformation* (Notre Dame, 1970), pp. 32–42.

Expert, Henry, ed., *Les maîtres musiciens de la renaissance française, Clement Janequin: Chanson (Attaignant, 1529)* (Paris, 1897).

Ezquerro Esteban, Antonio, 'Memoria de actividades de RISM-España/1995', *Anuario musical* 51 (1996), pp. 247–69.

Fenlon, Ian, and Tess Knighton, eds., *Early Music Printing and Publishing in the Iberian World* (Kassel, 2006).

Fortescue, Adrian, and J. B. O'Connell, *The Ceremonies of the Roman Rite Described* (London, 1962).

Franke, Veronica M., 'Palestrina's Fifteen Five-Part Imitation Masses Modelled upon Motets: A Study of Compositional Procedure' (D.Phil. dissertation, University of Oxford, 1990).

Friske, Jean, The Marian Library/International Marian Research Institute, Dayton, Ohio. http://www.udayton.edu/mary/resources/firstsaturday.html

Gasch, Stefan, '"Sursum deorsum aguntur res mortalium": Canons in Magnificat Settings of the Fifteenth and Sixteenth Centuries and the Case of Mattheus le Maistre's Magnificat Sexti Toni', in Katelijne Schiltz and Bonnie J. Blackburn, eds., *Canons and Canonic Techniques, 14th–16th Centuries: Theory, Practice, and Reception History. Proceedings of the International Conference, Leuven, 4–6 October 2005* (Leuven, 2007), pp. 253–82.

Geiger, Albert, 'Juan Esquivel: Ein unbekannter spanischer Meister des 16 Jahrhunderts', *Fetschrift zum 50. Geburstag Adolf Sandberger* (Munich, 1918), pp. 138–69.

Gembero Ustárroz, María, 'Circulación de libros de música entre España y América (1492–1650): notas para su estudio', in Ian Fenlon and Tess Knighton, eds., *Early Music Printing and Publishing in the Iberian World* (Kassel, 2006), pp. 147–77.

Gerber, Rudolf, ed., *Spanisches Hymnar um 1500*. Das Chorwerk LX (Wolfenbüttel, 1957).

González Dávila, Gil, *Teatro eclesiástico de las iglesias metropolitanas y catedrales de los reynos de las dos Castillas, vivad de sus arzobispos y obispos y cosas memorables de sus sedes*, 4 vols. (Madrid, 1645–1700).

Graff, Hilda, *Mary: A History of Doctrine and Devotion* (London, 1994).

Griffiths, John, and Javier Suárez-Pajeres, eds., *Políticas y prácticas musicales en el mundo de Felipe II: estudios sobre la música en Espana, sus instituciones y sus territorios en la segunda mitad del siglo XVI*. Coleccion Música Hispana. Textos. Estudios 8 (Madrid, 2004).

Gudmundson, Harry Edwin, 'Parody and Symbolism in Three Battle Masses of the Sixteenth Century' (Ph.D. dissertation, University of Michigan, 1976).

Gutiérrez, Carmen J., 'Himno', in *Diccionario de la música española e hispanoamericana*, VI (Madrid, 2000), pp. 304–8.

Haar, James, 'A Sixteenth-Century Attempt at Musical Criticism', in Paul Corneilson, ed., *The Science and Art of Music* (Princeton, 1998), pp. 3–19.

Hardie, Jane Morlet, '"Wanted, One Maestro de capilla": A Sixteenth-Century Job Description', in David G. Crawford and Grayson Wagstaff, eds., *Encomium Musicae: Essays in Memory of Robert Snow* (Hillsdale, NY, 2002).

Harper, John, *The Forms and Orders of Western Liturgy* (London, 1991).

Harran, Don, *In Search of Harmony: Hebrew and Humanistic Elements in Sixteenth-Century Musical Thought* (Neuhausen and Stuttgart, 1988).

Hernández Vegas, Mateo, *Ciudad Rodrigo: la catedral y la ciudád*, 2 vols. (2nd edn, Salamanca, 1982).

Hiley, David, *Western Plainchant* (Oxford, 1993).

Hirschl, W. H., 'The Styles of Victoria and Palestrina: A Comparative Study with Special Reference to Dissonance Treatment' (MA dissertation, University of California, 1931).

Ingram, Sonja S., 'The Polyphonic "Salve Regina", 1425–1550' (Ph.D. dissertation, University of North Carolina, 1973).

Jacobs, Charles, 'Spanish Renaissance Discussion of Musica Ficta', *Proceedings of the American Philosophical Society* 112 (August, 1968), pp. 277–98.

Janequin, Clément, *Chansons polyphoniques 1. Chansons maistre Clement Janequin*, ed. A. Tillman Merritt and François Lesure (Monaco, 1965).

Jedin, Hubert, 'Catholic Reformation or Counter-Reformation?', in David M. Luebke, ed., *The Counter-Reformation* (Oxford, 1999), pp. 21–45.

Jeppesen, Knud, *The Style of Palestrina and the Dissonance*, trans. Margaret Hamerik (London, 1946; repr. New York, 1970).

Josephson, Nors S., 'The *Missa de Beata Virgine* of the Sixteenth Century' (Ph.D. dissertation, University of California at Berkeley, 1970).

Judd, Cristle Collins, ed., *Tonal Structures in Early Music* (New York, 1998).

Jungman, Joseph A., *The Mass of the Roman Rite*, trans. Francis A. Brunner (New York, 1959).

Kamen, Henry, *The Phoenix and the Flame: Catalonia and the Counter Reformation* (New Haven and London, 1993).

Kamen, Henry, *Spain 1469–1714* (Harlow, 2005).

Kelly, Thomas Forrest, *Plainsong in the Age of Polyphony* (Cambridge, 1992).

Kerman, Joseph, *The Masses and Motets of William Byrd* (London, 1981).

Kirk, Douglas Karl, 'Churching the Shawms in Renaissance Spain: Lerma, Archivo de San Pedro, MS. Mus. 1' (Ph.D. dissertation, McGill University, 1993).

Kirk, Douglas, 'Instrumental Music in Lerma, c.1608', *Early Music* 23 (1995), pp. 393–408.

Knighton, Tess,' La circulación de la polifonía europea en el medio urbano: libros impresos de música en la Zaragoza de mediados del siglo XVI', in Andrea Bombi, Juan José Carreras and Miguel Ángel Marín, eds., *Musica y cultura urbana en la edad moderna* (Valencia, 2005), pp. 337–249.

Knighton, Tess, *Libros de canto*: The Ownership of Music Books in Zaragoza', in Ian Fenlon and Tess Knighton, eds., *Early Music Printing and Publishing in the Iberian World* (Kassel, 2006), pp. 215–39.

Knighton, Tess, and Álvaro Torrente, eds., *Devotional Music in the Iberian World, 1450–1800: The Villancico and Related Genres* (Aldershot, 2007).

Koenigsberger, H. G., George L. Mosse and G. Q. Bowler, *Europe in the Sixteenth Century* (2nd edn, London, 1989).

Kreitner, Kenneth, 'Minstrels in Spanish Churches, 1400–1600', *Early Music* 20 (1992), pp. 533–46.

Lang, Paul Henry, *Music in Western Civilization* (London, 1941).

Lenaerts, Rene B., 'The Sixteenth-Century Parody Mass in the Netherlands', *The Musical Quarterly* 36 (1950), pp. 410–21.

Lerner, Edward R., 'Some Motet Interpolations in the Catholic Mass', *Journal of the American Musicological Society* 14 (1961), pp. 24–30.

Lewkovitch, Bernard (ed.), *Twelve Motets of the Spanish Golden Age* (London, 1961). Contains *Gloria in excelsis* and *Ego sum panis vivus* taken from *Antología polifónica sacra*, ed. Samuel Rubio.

Liber usualis, edn no. 801 (Tournai, 1956).

Lincoln, Harry B., *The Latin Motet: Indexes to Printed Collections, 1500–1600* (Ottawa, 1993).

Lockwood, Lewis, 'A View of the Early Sixteenth-Century Parody Mass', in Albert Mell, ed., *The Department of Music, Queens College of the City of New York Twenty-fifth Anniversary Festschrift (1937–1962)* (New York, 1964), pp. 53–77.

Lockwood, Lewis, 'On "Parody" as a Term and Concept in Sixteenth-Century Music', in Jan LaRue, ed., *Aspects of Medieval and Renaissance Music: A Birthday Offering to Gustave Reese* (New York, 1964), pp. 560–75.

Lockwood, Lewis, *The Counter-Reformation and the Masses of Vincenzo Ruffo* (Venice, 1970).

López-Calo, José, *Historia de la música española 3. Siglo XVII* (Madrid, 1983).

López-Calo, José, *La música en la catedral de Burgos, IV: Documentario musical, Actas capitulares*, II (1601–28) (Burgos, 1996).

Luebke, David M., ed. *The Counter-Reformation: The Essential Readings* (Oxford, 1999).

Luce, Harold T.,'The Requiem Mass from its Plainsong Beginnings to 1600' (Ph.D. dissertation, Florida State University, 1958).

MacCulloch, Diarmaid, *Reformation: Europe's House Divided 1490–1700* (London, 2004).

McGinnes, Frederick, *Right Thinking and Sacred Oratory in Counter-Reformation Rome* (Princeton, 1995).

Mattfeld, Jacquelyn,'Some Relationships between Texts and Cantus Firmi in the Liturgical Motets of Josquin des Pres', *Journal of the American Musicological Society* 14 (1961), pp.159–83.

Meier, Bernhard, *The Modes of Classical Vocal Polyphony*, trans. Ellen Beebe (New York, 1986).

Meier, Bernhard, 'Rhetorical Aspects of the Renaissance Modes', trans. Geoffrey Chew, *Journal of the Royal Music Association* 115 (1981), pp. 182–90.

Merino, Luis Felix, 'The Masses of Francisco Guerrero (1528–1599)' (Ph.D. dissertation, University of California, 1972).

Moffitt, John F., *The Arts in Spain* (London, 1999).

Monson, Craig A., 'The Council of Trent Revisited', *Journal of the American Musicological Society*, 55 no. 1 (2002), pp. 1–37.

Monumentos de la música española 24, 34. Cristóbal Morales, *Opera omnia*, ed. Higinio Anglés (Barcelona, 1964–71), vols. VII–VIII.

Monumentos de la música española 36, 38, 43, 45, 48. Francisco Guerrero, *Opera omnia*, ed. Jose M. Lloréns Cistero (Barcelona, 1978–91), vols. III–VII.

Monumentos de la música española 26. Tomás Luis de Victoria, *Opera omnia*, ed. Higinio Anglés (Barcelona, 1965), vol. II.

Monumentos de la música española 31. Tomás Luis de Victoria, *Opera omnia*, ed. Higinio Anglés (Barcelona, 1968), vol. IV.

Moody, Ivan, 'Portuguese "Mannerism": A Case for an Aesthetic Inquisition', *Early Music* 23 (1995), pp. 451–8.

Morales, Cristóbal de, *Missa pro defunctis à4*, transcr. Miguel Querol Galvadá and Alicia Muniz Hernandez (Barcelona, 1975).

Morley, Thomas, *A Plain and Easy Introduction to Practical Music*, ed. R. Alec Harman (London, 1952).

Morris, R. O. *Contrapuntal Technique in the Sixteenth Century* (London, 1922; repr. 1958).

Nalle, Sara T., *God in La Mancha: Religious Reform and the People of Cuenca, 1500–1650* (Baltimore and London, 1992).

Nelson, Kathleen E., *Medieval Liturgical Music of Zamora*. Musicological Studies 67 (Ottawa, 1996).

Noone, Michael, 'Printed Polyphony acquired by Toledo Cathedral, 1532–1669', in Ian Fenlon and Tess Knighton, eds., *Early Music Printing and Publishing in the Iberian World* (Kassel, 2006), pp. 241–74.

Novack, Saul, 'The Analysis of Pre-Baroque Music', in David Beach, ed., *Aspects of Schenkerian Theory* (Newhaven, 1983), pp. 113–33.

O'Connor, Michael B., 'The 1608 and 1613 Requiem Masses of Juan Esquivel Barahona: A Study of the Tridentine *Missa pro defunctis* in Spain' (MM dissertation, Florida State University, 1995).

O'Connor, Michael B., 'The Polyphonic Compositions on Marian Texts by Juan de Esquivel Barahona: A Study of Institutional Marian Devotion in Late Renaissance Spain' (Ph.D. dissertation, Florida State University, 2006).

O'Malley, John W., SJ, 'Was Ignatius Loyola a Church Reformer? How to Look at Early Modern Catholicism', *Catholic Historical Review* 77 (1991), pp. 177–93.

Palacios Sanz Ignacio, Jose, 'Música y tradición en la fiesta del Corpus en la catedral de El Burgo de Osma (Soria)', *Anuario musical* 49 (1994), pp. 179–210.

Palestrina, Giovanni Pierluigi da, *Opera omnia*, ed. Franz Xavier Haberl *et al.* 33 vols. (Leipzig, 1862–1907).

Palestrina, Giovanni Pierluigi da, *Le opere complete di Giovanni Pierluigi da Palestrina* ed. Rafaelle Casimiri (Rome, 1939).

Palisca, Claude V., *Studies in the History of Italian Music and Music Theory* (Oxford, 1994).

Pedrell, Felipe, *Diccionario biográfico y bibliográfico de músicos y escritos de música españoles* (Barcelona, 1894–7).

Perkins, Leeman L., *Music in the Age of the Renaissance* (New York, 1999).

Peers, E. Allison, *A Handbook to the Life and Times of Saint Teresa and Saint John of the Cross* (London, 1954).

Pesce, Dolores, ed., *Hearing the Motet: Essays on the Motet of the Middle Ages and Renaissance* (New York and Oxford, 1997).

Petti, Anthony G., ed. *The Chester Books of Motets* (London, 1977–82), vols. III, X, XII, XIV.

Powers, Harold S., 'The Modality of Vestiva i colli', in Robert L. Marshall, ed., *Studies in Renaissance and Baroque Music in Honour of Arthur Mendel* (Kassel, 1974), pp. 30–46.

Powers, Harold S., 'Tonal Types and Modal Categories in Renaissance Polyphony', *Journal of the American Musicological Society* 34 (1981), pp. 428–70.

Price, Curtis, ed., *The Early Baroque Era from the Late Sixteenth Century to the 1660s* (Basingstoke and London, 1993).

Quereau, Quentin W., 'Sixteenth-Century Parody: An Approach to Analysis', *Journal of the American Musicological Society* 31 (1978), pp. 407–41.

Randall, Don M., 'Emerging Triadic Tonality in the Fifteenth Century', *Musical Quarterly* 57 (1971), pp. 73–86.

Randell, Keith, *The Catholic and Counter Reformation* (London, 1990).

Rawlings, Helen, *Church, Religion and Society in Early Modern Spain* (Basingstoke and New York, 2002).

Rees, Owen, '"Recalling Cristóbal de Morales to Mind": Emulation in Guerrero's *Sacrae cantiones* of 1555', in David Crawford and G. Grayson Wagstaff, eds., *Encomium Musicae: Essays in Memory of Robert J. Snow* (Hillsdale, NY, 2002), pp. 365–94.

Reese, Gustave, *Music in the Renaissance* (London, 1954).

Reif, Jo-Ann, ' Music and Grammar: Imitation and Analogy in Morales and the Spanish Humanists', *Early Music History* 6 (Cambridge, 1986), pp. 227–43.

Roberts, Alyson E., 'Parody Masses based on Janequin's *La guerre*: A Critical Edition and Study' (MA dissertation, Queen's University, Belfast, 1977).

Rodilla León, Francisco, 'La música en la catedral de Ciudad Rodrigo. Estado de la cuestión y líneas generales de investigación', in E. Azofra, ed., *La catedral de Ciudad Rodrigo a través de los siglos. Visiones y revisiones* (Ciudad Rodrigo, 2005), pp. 281–320.

Rodilla León, Francisco, *El libro de motetes de 1608 de Juan Esquivel de Barahona (c.1560–c.1624): estudio y transcripción* (Ciudad Rodrigo, 2005).

Rodilla León, Francisco, 'Nuevos datos sobre la capilla musical de la catedral de Calahorra a finales del siglo XVI: el magisterio de Juan Esquivel de Barahona (1585-1891)', *Revista aragonesa de musicología* 20/1 (2004), pp. 403–30.

Rodriguez, Solis, 'El archivo musical de la catedral de Badajoz', in *El patrimonio musical de Extramadura: cuaderno de trabajo no. 1*, ed. García Alonso María (Trujillo, Caceres, 1991), pp. 15–38.

Roig-Francolí, Miguel A., 'Playing in Consonances', *Early Music* 23 (1995), pp. 461–71.

Rowell, Geoffrey, *The Liturgy of Christian Burial: An Introductory Survey of the Historical Development of Christian Burial Rites* (London, 1977).

Rubio, Samuel, 'El archivo de música de la catedral de Plascenia', *Anuario musical* 5 (1950), pp. 147–51.

Rubio, Samuel, *Antología polifónica sacra*, 2 vols. (Madrid, 1954, 1956).

Rubio, Samuel, *Classical Polyphony*, trans. Thomas Rive (Oxford, 1972).

Rubio, Samuel, ed., *Juan Vázquez, Agenda defunctorum* (Madrid, 1975).

Rubio, Samuel, *Historia de la música española 2. Desde el 'ars nova' hasta 1600* (Madrid, 1983).

Rubsamen, Walter, H., 'Some First Elaborations of Masses from Motets', *Bulletin of the American Musicological Society* 4 (1940).

Ruiz Jiménez, Juan, 'Ministriles y extravagantes en la celebración religiosa', in John Griffiths and Javier Suárez-Pajeres, eds., *Políticas y prácticas musicales en el mundo de Felipe II: estudios sobre la música en España, sus instituciones y sus territorios en la segunda mitad del siglo XVI*. Coleccion Música Hispana. Textos. Estudios 8 (Madrid, 2004), pp. 199–239.

Ruiz Jiménez, Juan, '*Infunde amorem cordibus*: An Early Sixteenth-Century Polyphonic Hymn Cycle from Seville', *Early Music* 33 (2005), pp. 619–38.

Ruiz Jiménez, Juan, *La librería de canto de órgano: creación y pervivencia del repertorio del renacimiento en la actividad musical de la catedral de Sevilla* (Seville, 2007).

Rumery, Leonard R., 'Music at Seville under a Renaissance Master', *American Choral Review* (April, 1981), pp. 11–17.

Russell, Eleanor, 'A New Manuscript Source for the Music of Cristóbal de Morales: Morales' "Lost" *Missa pro defunctis* and Early Spanish Requiem Traditions', *Anuario musical* 33–5 (1978–80), pp. 9–49.

Russell, P. E., ed., *A Companion to Spanish Studies* (London, 1973).

Rutherford, Richard, *The Death of a Christian: The Rite of Funerals* (New York, 1980).

Sadie, Stanley, ed., *The New Grove Dictionary of Music and Musicians* (London, 1980); 2nd edn with John Tyrell (London, 2001).

Salazar, Adolfo, *La música de España* (Buenos Aires, 1953).

Sánchez Sánchez, A., 'La música en la catedral de Ávila hasta finales del siglo XVI', *De música hispana et aliis: miscelánea en honour al Prof. Dr. José López-Calo, S.J., en su 65° cumpleaños*, I (Santiago: Universidad de Santiago de Compostela, 1990).

Sanchez Cabañas, Antonio Don, *Historia Civitatense. Estudio introductorio y edición*, ed. Ángel Barrios García and Iñaki Martín Viso (Ciudad Rodrigo, Salamanca, 2001).

Sanchez Cabañas, Antonio Don, *Historia de Ciudad Rodrigo*, ed. Jose Benito Polo (Salamanca, 1967).

Santa María, Tomás de, *Arte de tañer fantasia* (Valadolid, 1565), ed. Almonte C. Howell and Warren Hultberg (Pittsburgh, 1991).

Schiltz, Katelijne, and Bonnie J. Blackburn, eds., *Canons and Canonic Techniques, 14th–16th Centuries: Theory, Practice and Reception History. Proceedings of the International Conference, Leuven, 4–6 October 2005* (Leuven, 2007).

Schroeder, H. J., *Canons and Decrees of the Council of Trent* (Rockford, Illinois, 1978).

Shepherd, John, 'A Liturgico-Musical Reappraisal: Two Studies', *Current Musicology* 33 (1977), pp. 69–78.

Sherr, Richard, 'The Performance of Chant in the Renaissance and its Interactions with Polyphony', in Thomas Forrest Kelly, ed., *Plainsong in the Age of Polyphony* (Cambridge, 1992), pp. 178–208.

Sibley, David J., 'The Sixteenth-Century Parody Mass' (Ph.D. dissertation, University of Nottingham, 1989).

Sierro Malmierca, Feliciono, *Judios, moriscos e inquisición en Ciudad Rodrigo* (Salamanca, 1990).

Smith, Hilary Dansey, *Preaching in the Spanish Golden Age* (Oxford, 1978).

Snow, Robert J., *The 1613 Print of Juan Esquivel Barahona*. Detroit Monographs in Musicology 7 (Detroit, 1978).

Snow, Robert J., 'Music of the Requiem Mass', in *New Catholic Encyclopedia* (New York, 1967), XII, pp. 386–7.

Snow, Robert J., 'Liturgical Reform and Musical Revisions: Reworkings of their Vesper Hymns by Guerrero, Navarro, and Durán de la Cueva', in M. F. Cidrais Rodrigues, M. Morais and R. V. Nery, eds., *Livro de homenagem a Macario Santiago Kastner* (Lisbon, 1992), pp. 463–99.

Snow, Robert J., *A New-World Collection of Polyphony for Holy Week and the Salve Service: Guatemala City, Cathedral Archive, Music MS 4* (Chicago and London, 1996).

The Spanish School for Four Voices, Kalmus Edition (New York, 1968). Contains *Veni Domine* taken from *Antología polifónica sacra*, ed. Samuel Rubio.

Stein, Louise K., 'Spain', in Curtis Price, ed., *The Early Baroque Era from the Late Sixteenth Century to the 1660s* (Basingstoke and London, 1993), pp. 327–48.

Stevenson, Robert, *Spanish Music in the Age of Columbus* (The Hague, 1960).

Stevenson, Robert, *Spanish Cathedral Music in the Golden Age* (Berkeley, 1961).

Stevenson, Robert, *Renaissance and Baroque Musical Sources in the Americas* (Washington, DC, 1970).

Stevenson, Robert, 'Esquivel Barahona', in Stanley Sadie, ed., *The New Grove Dictionary of Music and Musicians* (London, 2001), VIII, pp. 325–6.

Strunk, Oliver, *Source Readings in Musical History* (New York, 1950).

Strunk, Oliver, 'Some Motet-Types of the Sixteenth Century', in his *Essays on Music in the Western World* (New York, 1974), pp. 108–13.

Tarling, Judy, *The Weapons of Rhetoric* (St Albans, 2004).

Taylor, Thomas F., 'The Spanish High Baroque Motet and Villancico', *Early Music* 20 (1984), pp. 64–73.

Tejeda, Alonso de, *Obras completas*, ed. Dionisio Preciado, 2 vols. (Madrid, 1974, 1977).

Tilmouth, Michael, 'Parody', in *The New Grove Dictionary of Music and Musicians*, ed. Stanley Sadie (London, 2001), XIX, pp. 145–7.

Tinctoris, Johannes, *The Art of Counterpoint (Liber de arte contrapuncti)*, trans. and ed. Albert Seay. Musicological Studies and Documents 5 (Rome, 1961).

Trend, J. B., *The Music of Spanish History to 1600* (Oxford, 1926).

Turner, Bruno, 'Spanish Liturgical Hymn: A Matter of Time', *Early Music* 23 (1995), pp. 473–82.

Turner, Bruno, *Five Spanish Liturgical Hymns* (Marvig, Isle of Lewis, 1996).

van den Borren, Charles, 'De quelques aspects de la parodie musicale', *Academie royale de Belgique. Bulletin de la classes des beaux-arts* 20 (1938), 146–63.

Vicentino, Nicola, *L'antica musica ridotta alla moderna prattica* (1555), trans. Claude V. Palisca, 'Ut oratorio musica', in Palisca, *Studies in the History of Italian Music and Music Theory* (Oxford, 1994), pp. 305–6.

Victoria, Tomás Luis de, *Opera omnia*, ed. F. Pedrell, 8 vols. (Leipzig, 1902–13).

Villafranca, Luís de Villafranca, *Breve introducción de canto llano* (Sevilla, 1565).

Wagstaff, George Grayson, 'Music for the Dead: Polyphonic Settings of the *Officium* and *Missa pro defunctis* by Spanish and Latin American Composers before 1630' (Ph.D. dissertation, University of Texas, 1995).

Walkley, J. C., 'Juan Esquivel: An Evaluation and Partial Transcription of his Publications of 1608' (M.Phil. dissertation, University of Lancaster, 1996).

Walkley, J. C., 'Juan Esquivel: An Unknown Spanish Master Revisited', *Early Music* 29 (2001), pp. 76–90.

Ward, Tom R., *The Polyphonic Office Hymn 1400–1520: A Descriptive Catalogue*. Renaissance Music Studies 3 (Middleton, WI, 1980).

Wegman, Rob C., 'Another "Imitation" of Busnoy's Missa L'homme armé – and Some Observations on *Imitatio* in Renaissance Music', *Journal of the Royal Music Association* 114 (1989), pp. 189–202.

Wienpahl, Robert W., 'Modality, Modality and Tonality in the Sixteenth and Seventeeth Centuries', *Music and Letters* 52 (1971), pp. 407–17; 53 (1972), pp. 59–73.

Wilder, Robert D., 'The Masses of Orlando di Lasso with Emphasis on his Parody Technique' (Ph.D. dissertation, Harvard University, 1952).

Wright, A. D., *Catholicism and Spanish Society under the Reign of Philip II, 1555–1598, and Philip III, 1598–1621* (New York, Ontario and Lampeter, 1991).

Zarlino, Gioseffo, *Le istituzioni armoniche* (Venice, 1558; facs. edn, New York, 1965).

INDEX